# AFRICA CIRCA 1880

TUNISIA

Mediterranean Sea

ALGERIA

TRIPOLI

EGYPT

Red Sea

SENEGAL

Niger

GAMBIA

PORTUGUESE GUINEA

SIERRA
LEONE

GOLD
COAST

LAGOS

LIBERIA

Grand Bassam (French)
Assini (French)
Cotonou (French)
Porto Novo (Spanish)

FERNANDO PO
(Spanish)

GABON

Congo

Assab (Italian)
Obock (French)

Nile

ETHIOPIA

Lake
Victoria

Lake
Tanganyika

INDIAN
OCEAN

ANGOLA

Lake
Nyasa

ATLANTIC
OCEAN

Zambezi

MOZAMBIQUE

SOUTH
AFRICA

British

French

Portuguese

Turkish

0          1000 Mi.

0      1000 Km

E. McC. '95

# Africa in 1914

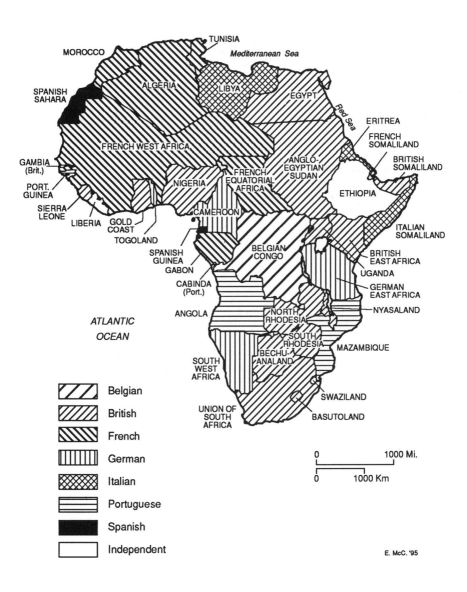

MOROCCO
TUNISIA
*Mediterranean Sea*
ALGERIA
LIBYA
EGYPT
SPANISH
SAHARA
*Red Sea*
ERITREA
FRENCH
SOMALILAND
FRENCH WEST AFRICA
ANGLO-
EGYPTIAN
SUDAN
BRITISH
SOMALILAND
GAMBIA
(Brit.)
PORT.
GUINEA
NIGERIA
FRENCH
EQUATORIAL
AFRICA
ETHIOPIA
SIERRA
LEONE
GOLD
COAST
CAMEROON
LIBERIA
TOGOLAND
ITALIAN
SOMALILAND
SPANISH
GUINEA
BELGIAN
CONGO
BRITISH
EAST AFRICA
GABON
UGANDA
CABINDA
(Port.)
GERMAN
EAST AFRICA
*ATLANTIC*
ANGOLA
NORTH
RHODESIA
NYASALAND
*OCEAN*
SOUTH
RHODESIA
MAZAMBIQUE
BECHU-
ANALAND
SOUTH
WEST
AFRICA
SWAZILAND
UNION OF
SOUTH
AFRICA
BASUTOLAND

Belgian

British

French

German

Italian

Portuguese

Spanish

Independent

0          1000 Mi.

0          1000 Km

E. McC. '95

# *Divide and Rule*

# Divide and Rule

## The Partition of Africa, 1880–1914

### H. L. WESSELING

### TRANSLATED BY ARNOLD J. POMERANS

Westport, Connecticut
London

Library of Congress Cataloging-in-Publication Data

Wesseling, H. L.
    [Verdeel en heers. English]
    Divide and rule : the partition of Africa, 1880–1914 / H. L.
    Wesseling ; translated by Arnold J. Pomerans.
        p.    cm.
    Includes bibliographical references and index.
    ISBN 0–275–95137–5 (alk. paper). — ISBN 0–275–95138–3 (pb : alk.
paper)
    1. Africa—History—To 1884.  2. Africa—History—1884–1918.
    3. Africa—Colonization—History—19th century.  4. Africa—
    Colonization—History—20th century.  5. Europe—Colonies—Africa—
    History—19th century.  6. Europe—Colonies—Africa—History—20th
    century.  I. Title.
DT28.W4713  1996
960.3'12—dc20          95–38253

British Library Cataloguing in Publication Data is available.

Library of Congress Catalog Card Number: 95-38253
ISBN: 0–275–95137–5
       0–275–95138–3 (pbk.)

First published in 1996

Praeger Publishers, 88 Post Road West, Westport, CT 06881
An imprint of Greenwood Publishing Group, Inc.

Printed in the United States of America

The paper used in this book complies with the
Permanent Paper Standard issued by the National
Information Standards Organization (Z39.48–1984).

10  9  8  7  6  5  4  3  2  1

Originally published in Dutch, H. L. Wesseling, *Verdeel en Heers: De Deling van Afrika,
1880–1914*, Uitgeverij Bert Bakker (1991). © 1991 by H. L. Wesseling.

I would annex the planets if I could.
*Cecil Rhodes*

# CONTENTS

# III
## "Cool and Courageous": Germany and Great Britain in East Africa, 1885–1890

# IV
## Soldiers and Traders: France and Great Britain in West Africa, 1890–1898

# VII
## Epilogue:
## The Partition of Morocco, 1905–1912

# ILLUSTRATIONS

MAPS

# PREFACE

The Romans used to say that books have a destiny of their own: *habent sua fata libelli.* That saying certainly applies to this book. When it came out in Dutch, in April 1991, it was the first comprehensive work on the subject to have appeared for nearly a century. The last and indeed the only other relevant text I knew of when writing my own book was Scott Keltie's *History of the Partition of Africa.* That had been published in 1903, while the partition was still proceeding. It must surely be one of the minor ironies of history that there should have been close on ninety years of silence, and that then, just six months after my book came out, another and even longer work on the partition should have been published, namely, Thomas Pakenham's *The Scramble for Africa.* It is not for me to comment on the differences between the two, but perhaps I may be allowed to say that there are enough dissimilarities to warrant the publication of two books on the same subject.

Of a book such as this it can indeed be said that it is a dwarf standing on a giant's shoulders. Without the work done over the decades by African, American, and European historians, this general survey could never have been written. The bibliography gives eloquent proof of their impressive contribution. However, we do not learn from books alone, but also from discussion and debate, and these cannot be recorded in a bibliography. That is why I should like to make special mention, not only of the late Henri Brunschwig—who was the first to teach me something about the history of Africa—but also of my friends and colleagues John Hargreaves (Aberdeen), Jean-Louis Miège (Aix-en-Provence), Wolfgang Mommsen (Düsseldorf), Ronald Robinson (Cambridge), and Jean Stengers (Brussels). The notes show how much I owe to their work. Their names are also here because I have learned so much from them in other ways.

I owe special thanks to Dr. Leo van Maris, Dr. Carla Musterd, and Dr. Robert Ross. All three have read and corrected the manuscript, have commented on it, each in his or her own way, and have thus helped to obviate many mistakes. It is unnecessary—but nevertheless customary—to add that the responsibility for the opinions and interpretations put forward here, as well as for what errors have persisted, is entirely my own.

Finally, I would like to thank Professor Pierre Vinken for his help in finding an American publisher, and the Netherlands Organization for Scientific Research (NWO) for its financial support.

*H. L. Wesseling*

# INTRODUCTION

*Nehmt hin die Welt! rief Zeus von seinen Höhen*
*Den Menschen zu. Nehmt, sie soll euer sein.*
*Euch schenk ich sie zum Erb und ewgen Lehen—*
*Doch teilt euch brüderlich darein!*

Take ye the world! called Zeus down from his height
To all mankind. Yours it shall be eternally.
Your promised heritage and right—
But share it out fraternally!

Schiller, *Die Teilung der Erde*

Does Africa have a history? Not so long ago this question received a negative answer. In a now famous passage written in 1965, the well-known English historian Hugh Trevor-Roper, comparing European with African history, concluded that the latter did not really exist. The African past, he wrote, has little more to offer than "the unrewarding gyrations of barbarous tribes in picturesque but irrelevant quarters of the globe."[1] Trevor-Roper may be called a conservative, but the Hungarian Marxist Endre Sik expressed more or less the same view in 1966: "Prior to their encounter with Europeans the majority of African people still lived a primitive, barbaric life, many of them even on the lowest level of barbarism. . . . Therefore it is unrealistic to speak of their 'history'—in the scientific sense of the word—before the appearance of the European invaders."[2]

These are unusually strong views, which, however, were shared to a greater or lesser extent by most historians at the time. It is in any case a fact that African historiography then barely existed. Almost no one took an interest in the subject. Today the picture has completely changed. The rise of African history is one of the most impressive chapters in modern historical studies. Begun by British historians, and to a lesser extent by French historians, and quickly taken up and developed by American scholars, African historiography has developed apace and is nowadays pursued for the most part by Africans. Dozens of journals, monographs and compilations bear impressive witness to their achievements. Africans have mounted the stage of history.

In this book, however, Africa is presented in a different, as it were old-fashioned, way. It appears mainly as an object, an object of European interest, love of conquest and diplomacy, and ultimately as an object of political partition. This does not mean that the role of Africans was purely passive. Far from it. Such Africans as the khedive of Egypt, the sultan of Morocco, the Zulu king Cetshwayo, King Lobengula of the Matabele, the almami Samori, and the makoko of the Bateke exerted a marked influence on the course of events. Their actions have accordingly been taken into account in this book. The reason why I have paid particular attention to these African leaders is not that I have a predilection for men in high positions, but is linked to the very nature of this study. What contacts Europeans made during the partition of Africa were necessarily with the political leaders of that continent. Yet the influence of these leaders was small. The important decisions were ultimately taken by European politicians, although a great deal often happened before that. Many people were involved in the process; not a few were able to take initiatives or exert some influence, but in the end Africa was carved up in Europe. To this phase of African history, too, there applies what the leading Africanist Andrew Roberts wrote about the following period, that from 1905 to 1940: "Between these dates, the history of Africa was more obviously being made by Europeans than by Africans."[3] That is why the decisions and thoughts of Europeans have a central place in this book.

What exactly did the partition of Africa entail? The answer is not simple. One can, of course, always point to the two maps that may be found in practically all textbooks and that also appear at the front of this volume: "Africa circa 1880" and "Africa in 1914." On the first we see a very small number of European possessions in Africa; on the second, virtually the whole of the black continent is divided into European colonies. The problem starts when we ask what these maps really show. When an area on the map of the British Empire was colored red and given a particular date, it was not necessarily an indication that the British flag had been hoisted there, that British taxes were first levied, or that English law was introduced in that year. It simply meant that the European Powers had recognized these territories as British possessions, colonies, protectorates, spheres of influence, or the like. With few exceptions, therefore, the colors do not so much represent genuine conquests or administrative changes as a European political consensus. The map of Africa is, to cite the title of the great standard work on the subject, *The Map of Africa by Treaty*, no more but also no less. That has to be said with some emphasis, for although the maps did not or did not yet express the African reality, their importance was anything but slight.

The treaties did, in fact, fix the borders of the European possessions, and these borders, with all their consequences, have remained the borders of the African states to this day. In a sense these treaties can be said to have been the most permanent feature of European imperialism in Africa. Some may find the actual conquest of Africa or the colonial epoch itself more important than the political partition of Africa. They have a point. However, we must remember that the conquest of Africa is a thing of the past and that the colonial system no longer exists. The consequences of the partition, however, persist. Contemporary Africa, with all its territorial problems and the crises they bring in their wake, emerged during the period under review and on the basis of those treaties. The colonial age in Africa was of short duration, in general less than a century, sometimes barely half that. Morocco has now been independent for almost as long as it existed under colonial rule. But the consequences of the partition are still there. The Africa of today was, in a political sense, created by the Europeans of that time.

This book describes the history of that partition, a history that was as brief as it was spectacular. When it began, in about 1880, European expansion into other parts of the world had been proceeding for centuries. However, it had all but passed Africa by, being directed in the main at the New World and at trade in, and the exploitation of, Asia. Africa was marginal to these activities. There had been a European settlement in the Cape since 1652, and in 1830 a second had been added in Algeria, but these were exceptions. From 1830 on, however, relations between Europe and Africa began to grow closer, and Africa became increasingly drawn into the expanding network of European trade. Penetration at an informal level had started, although in the political field little changed. The great turning point came just half a century later, in about 1880, when the process of dividing up the continent was adopted by the Europeans at breakneck speed. Twenty years later the partition was all but complete. What remained was no more than a postscript. Almost the whole of Africa, over 11 million square miles, had been placed under European rule. On average, an area of nearly 400,000 square miles (twice the size of France) was added to the European possessions every year. By the end of the century, Europeans ruled over virtually the entire continent, an area nearly ten times as large as India.

The history presented here is only a part of a much bigger story, that of the subjection and exploitation of Africa. It is a story full of cruel and shocking episodes. Not all of them are recorded here, not because of a wish to gloss over them but simply because many of them took place either before the period under review (the slave trade, for instance) or after it (the Congo atrocities). But even without these, there is enough that is disturbing. Europeans have waged greater wars on one another than they have waged in Africa, and committed graver outrages on one another than on Africans. But they seem also to have taken these outrages more seriously. The most shocking thing about the carve-up of Africa is perhaps not what was done, but the casual way in which it was done.

The partition of Africa has been written about and discussed at extraordinary length, usually with great passion, often with great discernment. The debate has focused in particular on the question of why it took place. There are hundreds of articles and studies in which new theories about the causes of the partition have been advanced. Even while the partition was still proceeding, the debate about the respective importance of economic and political factors began: arguments about the role of capitalists, soldiers, politicians, missionaries, ideologists and others. So it has remained to this day. Nowadays the discussion is carried on with fresh fervor as the Africans themselves have turned avidly to this part of their history. The most important aspects of that discussion will be examined here too, but the emphasis in this book will be on the historical account. It has not, of course, been written in the naive belief that one can present the past "as it really was." That is an illusion historians have long since abandoned. They realize that narrating and describing are themselves forms of interpretation, a selection from the many millions of happenings that could have been related, a choice of those deemed fit to be raised from simple fact to historical event. This has been widely accepted for a long time. All historians can hope to do is to present the course of history in as balanced and complete a way as they are able to. They can do no more.

The partition of Africa, like everything else, can be presented in many ways. We can dwell on imperialism and capitalism, on causes and effects, on structures and processes, and so on. This book is concerned mainly with people and their motives. The emphasis is on individuals rather than on groups, on concrete rather than on abstract factors. Those who object to this approach may be reminded of the words of the great historian Marc Bloch: "The basic principles of our profession consist of avoiding the great abstract concepts and seeking the concrete realities behind them: human beings."[4]

# I

# "THE EASTERN QUESTION": THE OCCUPATION OF TUNISIA AND EGYPT, 1881–1882

> . . . the 1870s, that
> golden age of Islamic insolvency . . .
>
> R. Robinson and J. Gallagher

$T$he partition of Africa began in the north. The establishment of a French protectorate over Tunisia in 1881 and the British occupation of Egypt a year later were the first steps on a long road that ended in 1912 with the subjection of Morocco. That at least is the generally accepted view. It is, in fact, a tempting one, not only because of its appealing symmetry—the partition of Africa ending where it began, in North Africa—but also because these two events were indeed of great importance and rich in consequences. The French occupation of Tunisia was the first unmistakable sign that France was once more the great power it had been before its defeat by Germany in 1870. The British occupation of Egypt and the resulting Anglo-French tensions largely set the pattern of subsequent European actions in Africa. Some historians even go so far as to consider all subsequent steps in the partition of Africa a direct result of the Egyptian question.[1]

That view is not, however, fully in keeping with the facts. The first beginnings of an active French colonial policy after 1870 lie not in Tunisia but in West Africa. There, in the hinterland of Senegal, France had been busily at work even during the Second Empire of Napoleon III, and it was there also that after the defeat of 1870 the renaissance of French colonial expansion began. In 1879, when Charles de Freycinet became prime minister of France and Admiral Jauréguiberry his minister of the navy, a new French colonial policy was launched: the French government proceeded to lend more active support to military expansion in the "Western Sudan" or the "Upper Niger," as the region was called. These events can rightly be called the true beginnings of the new French imperialism, and the first steps on the road to the partition of Africa.

Yet there is much to be said in favor of adhering, at least for the time being, to the traditional scheme, and of beginning with Tunisia and Egypt. That is because there was a significant difference between these two types of expansion. What happened in West Africa did not cause much of a stir in Europe. The French were left to go their own way. The Western Sudan was no more than a sideshow of European politics. In France, and also in

England, it is true that there were groups who insisted loudly on the future importance of West African markets, but it was to be a long time yet before such clamor was to sway the decisions of European cabinets. Things were quite different with North Africa. What happened there was caught in the spotlight of world politics. Every action affected the complicated European balance of power. That balance had been radically altered by the events of 1870.

The Franco-Prussian War of 1870 had ended in French defeat. After it, the political map of Europe was radically altered: Germany had become the most important country on the European continent. Its international ambitions and activities were henceforth to determine the fate of the European political system. The order established in 1870 proved to be lasting, not least because it was not based on just one military success, but on Germany's enduring demographic, economic and military strength. As a result, the star player on the diplomatic stage was no longer the French emperor—who had in fact abdicated—but the German chancellor. That role might have been written specially for the first man to hold that office: Otto von Bismarck.

Bismarck was to shape German, and hence European, policy for twenty years, from 1870 to 1890. His political objective was essentially simple: the preservation of the established order, at home as well as abroad. Consolidation and conservatism were its foundations. On the international plane, that meant shoring up Germany's position. To that end, Bismarck needed not only a strong army but also an active and creative diplomatic policy. He became a past master of the diplomatic game, forever engaged in the creation, re-creation and reform of alliances, treaties and special relationships. According to Caprivi, his successor, Bismarck was the only statesman able to juggle with five balls while keeping three in the air at the same time.[2] The main purpose of this intricate game was to lead Germany into, and maintain it in, a position that would shield it from any external threat. Since its southern flank was protected by a firm alliance with Austria, Germany's sister nation, that threat could only come from the west and the east, that is, from France and from Russia.

Bismarck would have been happy to see France resign itself to the defeat of 1870, to have it forgive Sedan as it had previously forgiven Waterloo.[3] But that was not to be. The peace treaty signed at Frankfurt after the French defeat laid down that France had to cede Alsace-Lorraine to the German Reich. That was the original sin of the new European order, a sin not expunged until the signing of the Versailles Peace Treaty half a century and a whole world war later. No French statesman could afford to ignore the lost provinces and to become "Bismarck's friend." Bismarck was fully aware of this and hence directed his chief diplomatic attentions toward Russia. He tried to win the czar over to his plans, but that proved a difficult task. The difficulty did not reside in Russia's relations with Germany, but in its relations with Germany's foremost ally, Austria. Russia and Austria were both involved in the Balkans, a region once dominated by the Ottoman Empire, which had been trying to extricate itself from that dominance for several decades. The Balkan question was part of the big problem besetting European diplomacy at the time, namely, the eastern question. The problem, framed in contemporary terms, was "how to manage the decline of the Ottoman Empire." It kept cropping up at regular intervals and also formed the background to the Congress of Berlin held in 1878, at which the ground was laid for the French occupation of Tunisia. Tunisia was handed to France by Germany and Britain on a plate, yet it was to be several years before France accepted the offer. That it took France so long was the result of political circumstances at home.

# 1
# FRANCE AND IMPERIALISM

### FRANCE AFTER 1870

While Germany underwent a period of economic growth and social change after 1870, French society was in the grip of stagnation. The most striking, and in the eyes of most French leaders the most worrying, expression of this phenomenon was its demographic aspect. When France and Germany had clashed on the battlefield in 1870, the population of both countries had been roughly the same, that is, about 40 million people. In 1914, when they clashed again, Germany had about one and a half times the population of France. This stagnation also made itself felt in other spheres. While other countries were fast industrializing, few signs of that could be seen in France. Industry, if present at all, was dominated by the traditional small family concern. Concentration and cartels did not occur. Foreign trade played no part of any importance. All this imposed an attitude of caution and thrift. France was a rich country, and the frugality of its inhabitants was legendary. French savers had a predilection for foreign government loans because these combined relatively high rates of interest with maximum security. There was no such thing as a modern and expansive type of capitalism. France had little need of a colonial empire, of foreign outlets for capital and industrial products, and of industrial raw materials. There was thus no economic call for imperialism.

In its foreign policy France lacked a clear political objective. Not surprisingly, in a country without emigrants and with very few exports, overseas affairs were not uppermost in people's minds. There was just one foreign problem, namely, the German question. Even so, French politics was not dominated by foreign affairs, but by domestic concerns, which were a kind of national sport. The French political scene was highly particularist. There was a permanent struggle between sectional interests, led by the *députés*, who were themselves deeply immersed in a permanent struggle hinging on their reelection. Political parties did not exist; at best there were factions and clubs, combined under more or less common denominators such as "right," "left," "extreme left," and so on. Personal rivalries and factions crossed the political divisions. The opposition was divided, though united against the government. French cabinets were particularly unstable; their average life was no more than half a year.

Foreign policy debates were dominated by a hankering for the territories lost in 1870. The amputation of French soil by the excision of Alsace-Lorraine was a wound that refused to heal, a blow that continued to smart. No French government could afford to give the impression of ignoring this problem. Open collaboration with Germany was therefore out of the question. But unanimous though it was in its anti-German stand, France was divided when it came to the way in which the problem was best tackled. The thought of *revanche*, pure and simple, was continually kept alive by certain groups and persons. Any relaxation, the slightest approach to Germany, was anathema to them. Collaboration with England was the logical consequence. Overseas adventures were taboo. Anything that diverted attention from revenge and reconquest of the lost territories was flawed. However, there were others who thought *revanche* out of the question, at least for the present, and who advocated a different course to regain lost prestige and to restore France's international status. To them, overseas expansion seemed to be a form of compensation, a path to national recovery.

From 1870 to 1914 French foreign policy was dominated by this dilemma: was France to play a continental or an overseas role? Ultimately, the continental questions were always the most important. Nevertheless, during this brief period, France acquired a gigantic colonial empire—the second-largest in the world—and played a leading role in the partition of Africa. No one would have foreseen that in 1870.

### FRANCE AND THE COLONIES

The colonial possessions with which the Third Republic began its life were scant and scattered. Of the old colonial empire not much more had been left after the Napoleonic era than a few islands and a handful of trading posts along the African and Indian coasts. In 1830 something new was added: Algeria. The French occupation of Algeria had come about on the spur of the moment. France owed the dey of Algeria a sum of money borrowed during the Napoleonic wars. The French delayed somewhat over the reimbursement, too long in any case to the dey's mind. He expressed his displeasure by striking the French consul in the face with a fly whisk during an audience, which presented the French with a ready excuse to repay the insult. The insult took place in 1827, but the intervention did not arrive until 1830, and was mainly intended to bolster the prestige of the reactionary king of France, Charles X. The French expedition was successful, but Charles X was swept away ten months later all the same by the July revolution. The French occupation of Algeria, on the other hand, continued. Any withdrawal would have been unpopular.

Soon afterwards, French writers began to extol the promise of the area. Tocqueville compared the new colony with British India,[4] a comparison nearly every French colonialist was to repeat with every new conquest he felt enthusiastic about. For all that, Algeria, unlike India for the British, was never to become a pearl in the French crown. After 1870, indeed, there was to be no more French crown at all. Even so, Algeria was to become the most important part of a colonial empire. It took a considerable time, however, to establish a French colony there, and the process was not concluded until about 1870. In a sense it was never concluded at all, because Algeria stretched away into the Sahara, where there were hardly any frontiers and penetration was slow and possible on a small scale only. In Algeria, France thus not only had a colony but also a "frontier."

The colony itself had a sizable European population; in 1872 more than 10 percent of the estimated total number of close to 2.5 million inhabitants were Europeans.[5] By a decree of the Provisional Government, Algerian Jews were declared French citizens in 1872 and granted equal rights and obligations. After the defeat of 1870 and the loss of the two provinces, about 250,000 acres of Algerian territory were set aside for those citizens of Alsace-Lorraine who had opted for French nationality. The *colons* did not consider Algeria a colony but an integral part of France and wanted to have it governed in the same way. In 1881 they had their way: henceforth the three Algerian departments were treated like their French counterparts. Ministers in Paris were directly responsible for their ministries in Algeria. Algeria became a colony treated as an interior province.

### Colonial Ideas

French kings had often attempted to court popularity and to boost their prestige by enhancing France's colonial renown, but this had never made much of an impression on the populace. Napoleon III excelled in overseas adventures, from Mexico to Indochina, but his regime was held in no greater esteem for it. France had no colonial vocation. Nor did it have a colonial ideology. It had in any case few reasons to gloat about its colonial aspirations in 1870. The Mexican adventure of Napoleon III had ended in fiasco, and in Algeria the colonial administration was faced with a major uprising.

However, two pressure groups, the French navy and the geographers, were bent on trying to change public opinion. While the navy, hotbed of patriotism and guardian of anti-British tradition, extolled France's overseas mission, the geographers advanced a new colonial doctrine. Geography, or "la philosophie de la Terre," as MacMahon, president of the French Republic, called it,[6] had become the queen of the sciences in the late nineteenth century, the age of expeditions and explorations. The navy and the geographers jointly proclaimed the message that France had perforce to join in the great overseas adventure. Sailors and intellectuals thus led the colonial movement. Commercial circles were less interested. Yet it was precisely at them that Paul Leroy-Beaulieu, the great theorist of French colonialism, aimed his message.

Paul Leroy-Beaulieu (1843–1916) was a leading economist. He was also, and above all, France's leading colonial propagandist. His best-known work in the field was *De la Colonisation chez les peuples modernes*, published in 1874. It had been written as an entry for a competition by the Académie des Sciences Morales et Politiques, and was the work of a young man anxious to display his knowledge to the learned members of that society. It also presented an original idea: that the difference between the new form of colonization and the old was the emigration of capital in place of people. Leroy-Beaulieu championed this "new colonization" not only in that academic work but also, and above all, in the press. The *Journal des Débats* and the *Economiste Français*, both of them influential, opened their pages to him for this very purpose. He admonished the government and parliament to be vigilant and more active in their defense of French interests, for instance in Tonkin and Tunis. France, he asserted in 1881 when the tension concerning Tunis was mounting, must not dither but proceed to a total and speedy annexation. It must not be afraid of international reaction, for that would mean relegation to the rank of Belgium.[7] A nation keen to preserve its vitality had to expand and disperse. England, Germany, Russia, America, and even China were doing just that. For France, the future lay in Africa: "Africa lies open to us." The colonial calling was the only true calling for France, its continental policy a "great historical mistake."[8] Daydreams about revenge in Alsace-Lorraine were so much nonsense in the face of a Germany with 60 or perhaps as many as 80 million inhabitants. France's future lay overseas.

Plainly, Leroy-Beaulieu's message was patriotic rather than economic. Small wonder, then, that it was not understood by the people to whom it was primarily addressed. French capitalists had always been notoriously reluctant to invest their cash in Africa. They preferred the security of government stocks and bonds. In 1914, by which time French colonial expansion was over, French investments in sub-Saharan Africa amounted to approximately 4 percent of overall French foreign investments. Of this small percentage, moreover, three-quarters came from public funds and only one-quarter from "capitalists." French private investment in black Africa thus amounted to just 1 percent of all foreign investments. In other words, the capitalists had failed to follow the clarion call of the famous economist.[9] Even so, a colonial policy emerged.

## Colonial Policy

At the beginning of the Third Republic the most important colonial politicians were Jules Ferry and Léon Gambetta. Both are to be counted among the great figures of the Third Republic. Léon Gambetta (1838–1882) was the son of an Italian grocer who had settled in Cahors but had never taken out French nationality. Together with those of Zola, Brazza and Gallieni, Léon Gambetta's was among the greatest contributions Italy had made to the young French Republic. His origins also made him a typical example of the greater political influence of the "new social strata," which he advocated. The law and journalism were for him, as for so many French politicians, springboards to a political career. He became a naturalized Frenchman in 1859. Ten years later, in 1869, he was elected a member of parliament. During the havoc caused by the Franco-Prussian War he was invited to join the Government of National Defense and held the important post of minister of war. His escape from Paris in a balloon was to be as legendary as his patriotism. Gambetta became the symbol of *revanche*, on which subject he coined a phrase later simplified into a famous saying: "*N'en parlons jamais, pensons-y toujours*" [Never speak of it, but think of it always].[10]

Gambetta's finest hour thus came very early, too early perhaps. True, he remained an influential political leader after the Franco-Prussian War, and a famous speaker and parliamentarian. He even became president of the Chamber of Deputies, but he only once rose to prime minister and then for less than a hundred days. Gambetta's *grand ministère* (1881–1882), as his cabinet was scoffingly called, fell within three months. He died that same year on New Year's Eve, as the result of a bullet wound sustained under somewhat mysterious circumstances but probably due to clumsiness on his own part. The French people showed him greater honor after his death than they had in his lifetime. His heart went to the Panthéon, his brains to the laboratory of the Ecole de l'Anthropologie, his right eye to the museum in Cahors (in a bottle), and the rest was buried in Nice: a laborious but meticulous interment.

Gambetta was a radical of the old school, more interested in politics than in economics or social reform, a republican, a democrat and a secularist ("clericalism—there is the real enemy"). He was also a great patriot, though his approach to foreign affairs was judicious. Thus he was obsessed with *revanche*, but he was also a convinced colonialist. He thought—and he was not the only one to do so—that France might be able to regain Alsace-Lorraine in exchange for a number of colonies. In fact, as he himself explained, he was obsessed with that idea.[11] However, that was just one aspect of his colonialism. Gambetta and the Gambettists believed above all that colonial expansion might help to solve the social problem. To them, the colonies were a reservoir for society's outcasts, an arena where they could vent their martial instincts, a means of preserving the status quo and of stemming the rise of socialism. Those who did not colonize, wrote Ernest Renan, were condemned to class warfare, or, as he put it, to "the war between rich and poor."[12] Such ideas and fears were neither new nor original, but after the Commune of 1871 they seemed to be of particular topical interest in France.

Gambetta's influence bore no relation to the importance of the offices he held. He was above all a tribune of the people, an orator and an agitator. His political power rested on his presidency of the Chamber, on his leadership of the republicans, and on his popularity in the country. His influence on colonial policy was decisive. He bore responsibility for the Tunisian expedition, and he planned further expeditions to Tonkin, Madagascar, and black Africa.[13] In addition, through such disciples as Delcassé, Hanotaux and Etienne, he was to have a considerable effect on later French colonial and foreign policy. He also had a great deal of influence on his contemporaries and, last but not least, played a large part in the conversion of Jules Ferry to the colonial idea.

Of all colonial politicians in the Third Republic, Jules Ferry (1832–1893) is the best known. It was he who inaugurated and propagated France's new colonial policy, so much so that he became identified with it and gained the nickname "Le Tonkinois." That role was rather surprising, for there was nothing about him to suggest an innate colonial calling. He came from a solid Lorraine family, went to the lycée in Strasbourg, studied law in Paris, and embarked upon a legal career at an early age. He was a promising young advocate in Paris, but also a scholar who wrote on philosophy and history, and an artist who took painting lessons in Venice. He was a typical eighteenth-century rationalist, but living as he did in the nineteenth century he could not help turning into a positivist. He stood for liberalism and free trade. As a positivist he believed in the power of education, and as a free-thinker he abhorred the influence of the church in this field. Like so many French intellectuals, he became a journalist and, like so many French journalists, a politician. He entered the parliament buildings for the first time in 1869, just before the fall of the Second Empire.

The emperor's surrender at Sedan marked the beginning of Ferry's political career. He became a member of the Provisional Government and was responsible for food supplies in Paris during the siege in the winter of 1870–1871. He did his best to alleviate hunger in the capital, but nevertheless owed his first nickname—"Ferry Famine"—to it. The war, with the loss of part of his own *pays*, Lorraine, and the 1871 Commune were for Ferry, as for so many others, a shocking experience. His career would henceforth be in politics. A parliamentarian since 1873, he became the leader of the right-wing liberals, men who called themselves the "Republican Left." The republican victory of 1879 signaled Ferry's entry into government. For the next few years he was to remain there almost constantly, once as minister of foreign affairs, but his preference was for minister of education or prime minister, sometimes holding both offices at the same time.

As a politician Ferry was respected but not loved. His looks told against him. The Goncourt brothers called his nose "a phallus stuck above his mouth," and his general appearance that of a "manager of some pornographic display cabinet in a restaurant."[14] That was a bit exaggerated, but compared with the hot-blooded Clemenceau and the exuberant Gambetta, Ferry was a fairly unattractive personality. He was often in the right, but that is usually begrudged him as well. He was so interested in education that in the end he came to look like a schoolmaster. Educational policy was his great passion, and he was to be remembered for it. It was in tune with his general outlook and his social principles. There was nothing about him to suggest the least interest in colonial matters. Yet he was to become not only the architect of French colonial expansion, but also one of the theorists of modern imperialism.

Jules Ferry's colonial doctrine can be found in various addresses and writings. It is not particularly original and constitutes a synthesis of ideas that were taking root at that time in liberal circles.[15]

In his famous address to the Chamber of 1885, Ferry distinguished three objectives of colonial policy: an economic, a humanitarian and a political aim. In the economic field, he was a follower of Leroy-Beaulieu. He was an advocate of modern colonization, that is, the export of capital and goods instead of people. The most important economic function of a colony was to serve as a market for the industrial products of the metropolis.[16] Next came a humanitarian objective: the higher races had a duty to civilize the lower.

The most important objective for Ferry was, however, the political one. The colonies could never make up for the loss of Alsace-Lorraine. This wound could not be healed. But that did not mean that, grieving for the loss, one had to sit idly by. That would have led straight to France's decay. "To reason without acting, without involvement in the affairs of the world . . . means descending from the first rank to the third or the fourth."[17] The reader will note that the second rank was omitted.

In view of the world-historical sweep of his writings, it is not surprising that Ferry should have been considered the great prophet and apologist of French imperialism, the more so as he was, in fact, its founder. These writings were not, however, published until after the event. His practical actions cannot really be considered the implementation of a preconceived plan. It was only after much hesitation and under pressure, especially from Gambetta, that Ferry launched the Third Republic on the colonial track with the Tunisian expedition of 1881.

# 2
# TUNISIA

### THE CONGRESS OF BERLIN

The history of the French expedition to Tunis in 1881 began with the Congress of Berlin in 1878. That congress was one of the most spectacular diplomatic gatherings held in the nineteenth century. In splendor and importance it was excelled only by the Congress of Vienna in 1814–1815. The star of the second congress, needless to say, was Bismarck, much as Metternich had played the leading role at the first. In addition there was a cast of other luminaries, including Disraeli and Salisbury from Britain, Gorchakov from Russia, and Waddington, the French minister of foreign affairs. The Sublime Porte was represented by a delegate who had been born in Germany, but was educated by Turks in Istanbul and had become a Muslim. This German in disguise appeared as Mohammed Ali Pasha, which was too much of a good thing for Bismarck.

It was obvious that Turkey must be present at a congress that revolved around the "eastern question." Now, the eastern question was a strange one because it was not strictly speaking a question, or rather, because it begat its own solution. The question was the dissolution of the Ottoman Empire. The solution was the partition of its remains. These two matters were so closely linked that it was sometimes unclear whether the dissolution came before the partition, or vice versa. The only problem was how the partition should be effected, but that too was no real problem because there was more than enough to deal with. If Austria wanted Bosnia, then Russia could have Walachia, Britain could be made happy with Cyprus and France compensated with Tunisia. If necessary, other arrangements were also possible. This merry game could be played for a long time, because the Ottoman Empire was so large. Its two tentacles had once stretched around the Mediterranean, on the lower side through the Near East and Egypt as far as Morocco, and on the upper into the Balkans as far as Bosnia and Herzegovina. But in the course of time a great deal had crumbled away. Czar Nicholas I had said as early as 1853 that Turkey was the sick man of Europe and that it was time to think about sharing out his estate. The Turkish Empire had been decaying for so long that it is hard to understand how it could have rotted away for such a long time without disappearing altogether. Ottoman decay was not a process but a structure.

The eastern question linked the partition of Africa to international political concerns. The strategic interests of Great Britain and Russia in the Dardanelles, the rivalry between Russia and Austria in the Balkans, the rivalry between France and Great Britain in Egypt, the tensions between France and Italy in Tunisia—all involved territories in the Ottoman Empire. It was the job of diplomats to regulate the resulting tensions in such a way as to avoid conflicts between the great powers. Since the Crimean War they had been very successful at it. In a sense the eastern question was a triumph of European diplomacy.

The Congress of Berlin was a new success in this series. It had been called in order to sort out affairs in the Balkans. Russia had declared war on Turkey in 1877, and trounced it decisively in 1878. With the Treaty of San Stefano Russia had collected its dues for this short but costly war, increasing its territory appreciably at the expense of the Turks. In addition, it had set up a kind of satellite state in the form of a Greater Bulgaria that was to stretch as far as the Aegean. This was going too far for Great Britain and Austria-Hungary. Britain did not want to see Russia on this side of the Straits, not even by proxy. Austria-Hungary frowned at the creation of a Greater Bulgarian empire that might appeal to its many Slav subjects. An international congress would have to find the solution. France played no part in this conflict, but was invited all the same, as was Italy. Bismarck was to turn up in the role of "honest broker."

The congress met on 13 June 1878 in Berlin and ended on 13 July. It proved a success for British diplomacy. Disraeli was the first British prime minister to return from Germany with the news that he had attained "peace with honor," and was able to make that claim with more justification than Neville Chamberlain could sixty years later. The Disraeli-Salisbury tandem seemed invincible, not least perhaps thanks to Bismarck's support. Bismarck was in fact as honest as, in the nature of the concept, any broker could be, but he had a great deal of sympathy for Disraeli. "That old Jew, now there's a man for you," he said admiringly.[18]

Russia was thus the loser. Not much was left of the Greater Bulgarian empire. The Straits were kept firmly closed, and Anglo-Turkish relations were consolidated. There was something else: Great Britain occupied Cyprus. It had forced the sultan to accept this step and had made it clear to Russia that it was demanding this as compensation for Russian expansion in and around the Caucasus. Germany raised no objections, and Austria was reliant on British support. But Britain could of course expect protests from France, the leading Mediterranean power. France would have to be compensated, needless to say at the expense of Turkey. The solution seemed obvious: France could have Tunisia. Salisbury called on Waddington and said, "You cannot leave Carthage in the hands of the barbarians."[19] Bismarck, who was only too keen to deflect French attention from the lure of the Vosges, also thought this a brilliant idea. "Why don't you go to Carthage?" he is said to have told Waddington with no less erudition. The minister was willing, but Parisian suspicions of Bismarck were formidable, and so nothing was done for a time. These suspicions were not hard to understand in the light of the recent past. Nor were they unjustified. While Bismarck was urging Tunisia upon the French, the German diplomat Bülow was offering it to the Italians. As Count Corti, the Italian minister of foreign affairs, put it, "Everybody was telling everybody else to take something which belonged to somebody else."[20]

Corti's criticism was fair but of little account. Italy did not join in. It returned from Berlin with clean but empty hands.[21] While Britain and Germany had made their attitude to French intervention in Tunisia more or less clear, the British even failed to inform Italy of the Cyprus coup. The Italians had to read about it in the newspapers, and were later told by the British that there was room enough for everyone in North Africa. Italy's anti-Austrian attitude had, moreover, not gone down very well with Bismarck. Like most statesmen he despised Italy. "Why on earth should Italy demand an increase of territory?" asked a Russian diplomat. "Has she lost another battle?"[22] Bismarck took much the same view. "The Italians," he told the French ambassador, "have a big appetite but poor teeth."[23] Above all, he was appalled by Italian irredentism, embodied in the person of the Italian prime minister, Cairoli, who had lost four sons in wars with Austria. Italy was thus diplomatically isolated during the years following the Congress of Berlin. France, for its part, enjoyed the support of Germany and of Britain. This accounts for the fact that Tunisia, packed though it was with Italian colonists, and lying a mere stone's throw from Italy, went to France instead.

### TUNISIA BEFORE THE OCCUPATION

In geographical terms, Tunisia does not really exist. The country is no more than an extension of Algeria, from which it is not divided by any natural frontiers. Its political identity goes back to 1574, when after the expulsion of the Spaniards it became a province of the Ottoman Empire. In the nineteenth century, too, Tunisia was still a Turkish province, though only in theory. The Turkish ruler had placed a governor, a pasha, in charge of the Tunisian province. However, this pasha quickly lost control to the military commander, the dey. And the dey, in his turn, had been ousted by a civil administrator, the bey. To simplify matters, the sultan subsequently elevated the bey to the rank of dey and pasha, so that decorum was satisfied all round. In 1705 the office fell into the hands of Hussein ibn-Ali, the bey-dey-pasha, who founded a dynasty that was to reign over Tunisia for two and a half centuries. When European influence continued to grow during the second half of the nineteenth century, Tunisia became a de facto independent state. The bey had his own army and navy, struck his own coins, declared war and peace, maintained separate diplomatic relations and signed treaties. Tunisia even had its own flag. Nevertheless, the bey was officially a Turkish governor, invoked the sultan in his prayers, and on first taking office had to apply for a *firman*, that is, for official recognition by the sultan. For the European Powers, this state of affairs, however complicated, was not without practical benefit, because they could treat the bey, at will, either as an independent ruler or as a vassal of the Porte.

The ruler of Tunisia reigned in fact over what was a modest territory, whose southern borders were vague and inconsequential, losing themselves in the Sahara. To the east lay Tripoli, another of the Porte's regencies, which had also made itself independent until the sultan had restored his authority by force in 1835. The bey of Tunisia had observed that event with some fear and trepidation, and was therefore not too unhappy in 1830 that another country, France, had settled on his western borders. The bey considered the reconquest of his country by the Porte a much greater threat than a possible conquest by France. In that he was mistaken.

At the time Tunisia had just over a million inhabitants. Half of these were sedentary farmers who lived mainly in the northeast; the other half were nomadic shepherds who roamed the interior. There were several towns, including Tunis with nearly 100,000 inhabitants, and Kairouan with 15,000, where traders and artisans were active, despite being severely affected by foreign competition. The traditional Tunisian textile industry was no match for European imports. The financial world was dominated by Tunisian Jews, while a growing number of Europeans, almost exclusively Italians and Maltese, settled in Tunisia. In 1870 there were 15,000 of them.[24] The economic situation of Tunisian townsmen may accordingly have been under pressure, but it was flourishing in comparison with that of the *fellahin*, the peasants who labored under a whole series of taxes and requisitions. In the disastrous years of 1867 and 1868 famines were added to these, the result of crop failure, as well as epidemics—first cholera, then typhus—which carried many thousands to their graves. During this period some 20 percent of the population perished.[25]

In these circumstances it was not surprising that the government should have been unable, despite all levies and demands, to squeeze what money it deemed essential out of the population. The government was, in fact, the bey, Mohammed al-Sadok, who ruled from 1859 to 1882, and the powerful prime minister, Mustapha Khaznadar, who had been pulling the strings ever since 1837. Khaznadar was minister of finance and foreign affairs and was assisted by the interior, defense, and naval ministers. In 1864 Tunisia was granted a constitution with a clear division of ministerial powers and responsibilities, but in practice Khaznadar was the absolute sovereign. He followed a policy of reforms, that is, of economic development, aimed at improving the infrastructure as well as the means of communication, the armed forces, and so on. The Tunisian economy did not, however, provide enough money to pay for it all, at least not after deduction of government expenses. In 1864 the director of finance left the country with 20 million piasters in his pocket, slightly more than the annual tax revenue. His nephew and successor was to play the same trick a few years later. And these events took place under the leadership of Khaznadar, the greatest profiteer of them all. Guizot's well-known slogan "Enrich yourselves" might well have been the motto of Tunisia. Another way had to be found to raise funds, and loans were decided upon. In 1863 the first great loan was floated. Various others were to follow.

These loans at first seemed to be miracle cures. The conditions were draconian, but there was always a plentiful supply of money. The stock exchange where the Tunisian loans were quoted was of course the Paris Bourse, the specialist in "turban" loans. The thrift of small French citizens and peasants—and their avarice—fed the prodigality and rapacity of several of the Tunisian great. In 1863 the Bourse provided the required 35 million francs; no more than 5 million of these reached the bey. The rest went on commissions and bribes, particularly to the bey's own treasurer. While that solved few problems, it raised the appetite for further loans. In 1865, 25 million francs were subscribed. This time, the bey received the money not in cash but in kind, that is, in the form of guns and a ship, the price of which was fixed unilaterally. It was with good reason that the British historians J. Gallagher and R. Robinson spoke of "that golden age of Islamic insolvency."[26] Tunisian customs duties were used to cover this new "loan," and hence ceased to be a source of income for the Tunisian state. For that reason the other source of revenue—taxes—had to be driven up. Poverty and hunger increased, and with them social tensions. In 1867 yet another loan was floated. This time the sum involved was no less than a hundred million francs. But the Paris stock exchange had lost confidence in the bey's regime and ignored the flotation. The Tunisian state was bankrupt, and European financial control was inevitable.

When it came it took the form of a financial commission. At its head was a Tunisian, General Khayr al-Din, son-in-law of Khaznadar. The vice-chairman was a Frenchman, the *inspecteur des finances*, Victor Villet, soon nicknamed "Bey Villet." The commission admittedly had an international makeup and introduced a kind of tripartite control (French, British, Italian) over Tunisia, but the real leaders were Khayr al-Din and Villet. This tandem governed Tunisia for a number of years, not without success, as government finances were put into some kind of order. The opposition of the prime minister, however, caused considerable problems. Khaznadar would have to be got rid of, and that required the bey's cooperation.

Mohammed al-Sadok was a weak ruler. A contemporary described him as "a man without intelligence and addicted to the most shameful vices. His harem consists exclusively of small boys . . . something of which he is not in the least ashamed. He is not at all interested in matters of state. . . . His life is nothing but one long orgy."[27] The bey had developed a special passion for a boy of exceptional beauty, picked up in the street by a Maltese barkeeper. The boy had been brought to Mohammed al-Sadok's harem by Khaznadar, always ready to direct his master's attention to matters other than affairs of state.[28] This boy, Mustapha ibn-Ismail, was to gain increasing influence over the ever more senile bey. Eventually he turned against his former patron, Khaznadar, whom he had come to see as a rival. In 1877 he would rise to prime minister. Khayr al-Din and Villet used the influence Mustapha wielded over the bey as "his instrument of pleasure" to topple Khaznadar. In 1873 the coup was mounted. Khaznadar disappeared from the scene, his goods confiscated but his life spared.

### Khayr al-Din

The man who now came to power, Khayr al-Din, or Khérédine as he is called in the French literature, was a genuine reformer. He was born in the Caucasus in 1822 or 1823 and arrived in Tunisia in 1839. There he rose quickly to the rank of general and naval minister. He married the daughter of the mighty Khaznadar. In 1862 he retired from office because he objected to the government's fiscal policy. In his book, *The Surest Way of Becoming Acquainted with the State of the Nations*, written in 1868, he pointed to bad administration as the cause of the decline of the Muslim world, and spoke out strongly in favor of the Turkish reforms. That put a stop to a relatively calm period in his life. In 1869 he took charge of the Financial Commission, and in October 1873 he became prime minister. He would now try to implement his reforming ideas.

Khayr al-Din certainly deserved his title of "Father of the Tunisian renaissance." As prime minister he was full of good intentions. He reformed the administration, improved the system of education, and waged determined war on corruption. However, he was in a difficult position. The demands of the Financial Commission were high. A request for a remission of the debt burden was turned down. Politically, too, his position was precarious. He did not have the ear of the bey, always had to be on guard against his father-in-law's retribution, and could not count on the support of the bey's favorite, who was out for power himself. In July 1887, Khayr al-Din was ousted by Mohamad Khaznadar, who was succeeded in August 1878 by Mustapha ibn-Ismail.

These changes in fortune did not fail to have repercussions on European relations with Tunisia. At first French influence had been preponderant. That influence was based on two factors, the proximity of Algeria and financial involvement. French occupation of Algeria gave France a fresh interest in Tunisia, linked to the safety of its colony. Britain had greater commercial interests in Tunisia than France. It was, however, mainly concerned with the strategic importance of that country: together with Malta and Sicily, Tunisia controlled access to the eastern Mediterranean. Unlike

Khayr al-Din

the French, the British did not support the bey, but as ever played the
Porte's game, which they regarded as the best way of preventing any foreign
occupation of Tunisia. Their influence rested on British investments in Tunisia and on the proximity of Malta. Malta, after all, was a British colony.
The Italians, finally, were more directly involved than all the other Powers.
Carthage had once been a Roman possession, a fact European statesmen
in that age of classical education showed only too often that they appreciated. Italy was a poor country with little potential for expansion. Even
so, it had great ambitions, and its irredentism was unbounded. Tunisia lay,
as it were, in Italy's backyard, just across the sea from Sicily. The second
Italian trump card was a very sizable number of settlers in Tunisia, almost
a hundred times as many as there were French.

All these foreign influences kept one another more or less in check, or
rather, took turns in the Tunisian game. French influence had been considerable after the establishment of the Financial Commission of 1867. It had
waned markedly after the French defeat of 1870. It had waxed again during
Khayr al-Din's administration, which had, incidentally, striven to reconcile
French influence with Tunisian loyalty to the Ottoman Empire. In diplomatic terms, the situation was complicated: because of Turkish suzerainty
there was no way of accrediting foreign diplomats in Tunisia. As a result,
the European Powers were represented not by ambassadors but by consuls.
The three men personifying European influences in the years before the
occupation were accordingly three consuls: Wood, Roustan and Maccio.

Anglo-French and Franco-Italian rivalry in the three crucial years between the Congress of Berlin of 1878 and French intervention in 1881 thus took the form of a number of "consular wars."

TOWARD EUROPEAN INTERVENTION

The Congress of Berlin brought the Tunisian question out from the twilight of vying and intriguing consuls into the glare of power politics. Waddington, like his Italian counterpart, returned from Berlin in 1878 empty-handed, but unlike Count Corti, not with empty pockets. On the contrary, he patted his pockets with satisfaction and declared, "I am bringing Tunis back home."[29] However, his country turned down the exotic present he had brought with him, at least for the time being. There were many reasons for this. To begin with, public opinion was not ready for a new military adventure far from home. The Mexican adventure was still fresh in their memories. There was also the political division: France had a republican Chamber with a monarchist president. Finally, the international situation was still confused. Suspicion of Bismarck was great, and faith in his generous offer of Tunisia correspondingly slight. Pro-Italian circles around Gambetta were not anxious to snub the Italian government. When pressed, Lord Salisbury seemed disinclined to give France carte blanche in writing. It was one thing to promise something concerning a hypothetical course of events in a conversation, and quite another to put it all down in an official document. "We must avoid giving away other people's property without their consent," he wrote in a letter to Lord Lyons, the British ambassador in Paris.[30] That was true enough, but it was precisely what had been done in Berlin. However, it was the tone that mattered. "Waddington," he said, "makes me talk of Tunis and Carthago as if they had been my own personal property and I was making him a liberal wedding present."[31] It described the tone used in Berlin to a nicety.

The Tunisian question was thus to remain a question of local rivalries and conflicts for several years. The first diplomatic repercussions of these local vicissitudes made themselves felt in the British attitude toward Sir Richard Wood. Sir Richard was a Syrian Jew, born in Constantinople, who had converted to Catholicism and had changed his name, Rhattab, to the more English-sounding Wood. He played some part in Turkish politics, but served British interests first and foremost. He was appointed British consul in Damascus and later, in 1855, in Tunisia, where a leading role lay waiting for him. He was the permanent foil to Roustan, the French consul. After the Congress of Berlin he was put under pressure by the Foreign Office, which in turn was being pressed by the Quai d'Orsay, to abandon his fight against his French rival, in keeping with the Berlin agreements. But Wood was too much a slave to his old game to want to listen to the London know-it-alls. Moreover, he had earned too much in defense of the British cause to be brushed aside lightly. The Foreign Office accordingly thought up a ruse: it introduced an age limit of seventy to the consular office. Wood, who was seventy-three and no fool, then declared that he was sixty-seven. London, not to be outwitted, "reorganized" the consular service. On 31 March 1879 Wood retired to Nice. The first fruit of Berlin had been picked. The coast was now clear. Britain reduced its consulate in Tunis to a minimum and appointed a nonentity in Wood's place. Britain's half-century of interest in Tunisia became a thing of the past.[32]

Bismarck, too, made his position clear once again. In a talk with the French ambassador in January 1879, he declared in his picturesque way, "I think the Tunisian pear is now ripe and the time has come for you to pick it; the insolence of the Bey has acted like the August sun on this African fruit, which may well rot or be stolen by another if you leave it on the tree too long."[33] Yet Bismarck's generosity rendered the French even more suspicious, and for the time being they did nothing about it. But all the more was happening in the local arena. Roustan's next opponent was Maccio, the Italian consul. The weapons they used were rather unusual. Roustan, according to Cambon, was "a convinced bachelor," one for whom a welcoming house with a beautiful hostess was "a shelter from the spleen."[34] Such a house and such a hostess were provided by Elias Mussali, the Tunisian director of foreign affairs, originally of Greek nationality. Madame Mussali, Italian born and as beautiful as she was influential, became the mistress of Roustan, the French consul. Even in public she appeared as the first lady of the French consulate. Maccio's riposte was to acquire a mistress of his own, albeit a secret one: the wife of Madame Mussali's brother.

All these goings-on reflected the political will of both countries to consolidate their interests in Tunisia pending more fundamental decisions. The Italians signaled their political ambitions most clearly. Their economic achievements were so small and the price they paid for them so high that they obviously had ulterior political motives. The Rubattino company, for instance, bought a bankrupt railroad line for roughly four times its real value. The Italian government, as it appeared soon afterwards, had guaranteed a return of 6 percent from this acquisition, together with all the costs of running the line. These increasingly transparent Italian activities were probably the decisive factor in the slow and laborious French process culminating in the decision to intervene.[35]

France had a number of financial interests in Tunisia. Financiers with Tunisian investments were fairly closely involved with circles around the government. Jules Ferry's brother, for example, was director of a bank with Tunisian interests. It seems unlikely that these men should have failed to gain the ear of the prime minister, though it is equally unlikely that their influence should have been at the root of the occupation. What these speculators wanted was a French license for fishing in the troubled waters of

Tunisian finance, not the limelight of a French occupation. Moreover, in the second case, their timing would have been less awkward. The year 1881 was an election year, and it would probably have been hard to find a worse time for starting something as unpopular as a military expedition. Inevitably the opposition could be expected to raise a hue and cry at the decision to risk French lives and to weaken the French defenses for the sake of private interests. And that is precisely what happened. The Tunisian expedition was branded from the outset as "a business war." In fact, however, it was not so much a *guerre pour les affaires* as a *guerre pour la grandeur*.

### THE FRENCH OCCUPATION

The intellectual father of the occupation of Tunisia was not Jules Ferry, although he was responsible for it, nor was it Gambetta, although his voice was crucial, but Alphonse de Courcel, director of political affairs—the most powerful civil servant—at the Quai d'Orsay. Courcel was a baron and hence not part of the "new social strata" that were to pull the strings of the Third Republic. He was a man of considerable financial means and not in the least interested in speculation or shady business deals. He was a professional diplomat, and like most of his colleagues he had a thorough contempt for commerce. Last but not least, he was a civil servant and, unlike his minister, did not have to trouble himself about public opinion or the elections.

The way of thinking of men like Courcel, schooled in the doctrines of the balance of power and the national interest, was quite different from that of the professional or amateur politicians of the Third Republic. He had not the slightest interest in such remote areas as Central Africa or Indochina. These were faceless and unimportant parts of the world. Tunisia was a different matter. There one came face to face with the Ottoman Empire, the eastern question, the balance of power in the Mediterranean, and the strategic interests of France in Algeria. In short, the Tunisian question was bound up with Great Power politics. That explains why Courcel was able to gain the ear of his fellow diplomats far more quickly than that of his minister.

Waddington had brought the "Tunisian pear" home with him in 1878, but since then hardly anything had happened. Freycinet had come and gone, and Barthélemy Saint-Hilaire, his successor at the Quai d'Orsay, also seemed unable or unprepared to act. Courcel organized an ambassadors' lobby. These men felt in many respects the equals, and in some respects the betters, of their minister and did not hesitate to lecture him. Thus the French ambassador in Berlin wrote to Saint-Hilaire: "Ah, mon cher ministre, You want to wait for the elections. What thoughtlessness, what blindness. By then it will be too late and France will have suffered a fresh humiliation. One act of courage and resolution and we shall resume our place amongst the nations; a fresh proof of weakness and we shall drop to the rank of Spain."[36] Such pressure did not miss its mark, at least not on the minister of foreign affairs, though it left the rest of the cabinet unruffled. Grévy, the president, thought that Tunisia was not worth a two-cent cigar. Ferry, the prime minister, reacted differently, but no less coolly. "An expedition to Tunis in an election year, my dear Saint-Hilaire, don't even think of it." Gambetta, the president of the Chamber of Deputies and the leader of the Republicans, thought that Tunisia should be put on ice for a few years, or, as he phrased it, "under chloroform."[37]

Gambetta, himself of Italian descent, did not want to snub Italy over Tunisia. In 1881, however, he decided that matters could not be put off any longer. Bismarck had intimated that he was beginning to doubt French intentions. If France did nothing, he would have to support Italy's claim. Gambetta then changed his mind, and his colleagues followed, Ferry last of all. That was not surprising because his cabinet would have to bear political (and electoral) responsibility for the intervention.

Once the political will was there, it was not hard to find a cause for intervention. There were problems enough with the bey, but the best thing, of course, would be a border incident. These happened all the time. In the event, a frontier violation by the Kroumirs provided the pretext for helping the bey to restore order. On 7 April 1881 Saint-Hilaire told the bey how much France valued his friendship. For that very reason, French soldiers would march in as "allies and a relief force under the sovereign authority of the bey."[38] That was an unusual way of proclaiming the abolition of the bey's sovereignty—if he had ever enjoyed it. For that matter, there was some confusion in France itself about what was happening. On 4 April 1881 the Chamber was merely asked to vote the credits—which were granted without dissent—for a military expedition meant to guard against further border incidents. One week later, the expedition was no longer described as therapeutic but as deterrent. The French Chamber then took its Easter recess.[39] Bismarck again conveyed his support. The British were held to their earlier agreement by the expedient of leaking it to the *Times*. The Italians were told coolly that France reserved the right to do whatever the national interest demanded.

The political and diplomatic obstacles having been cleared, the military aspect alone remained to be settled. The expedition proved to be a walkover. On 24 April 1881, 35,000 French soldiers crossed the Tunisian border. On 1 May they arrived at the Bardo, the bey's palace, and gave him two hours to mull over a treaty of ten articles abolishing Tunisia's independence. The bey signed. The Treaty of the Bardo did not formally promulgate a French protectorate, but it did lay the foundations for one. French domination was clearly spelled out. France took charge of Tunisia's diplomatic, military, and financial affairs and stationed troops in Tunisia.

Signing the Treaty of the Bardo

A French minister-resident was appointed. Gambetta was immediately told by Ferry, and replied a day later, on Friday, 13 May: "My dear friend, I do thank you for your communication and congratulate you from the bottom of my heart. . . . France has resumed the status of a great power."[40] In the Chamber, the debate was hardly heated. On 24 May 1881 the Treaty of the Bardo was ratified with 431 votes for and 1 against.

It was only then that the difficulties began. Revolts broke out, and more and more French troops had to be dispatched to "pacify" Tunisia, to use a term that was to be employed quite a few times more during that period. In France they held elections that turned out to be a triumph for Gambetta, but not for Ferry. Attacks on Ferry were widespread; he was accused of having acted for financial motives by, among others, Clemenceau speaking in the Chamber. Guy de Maupassant wrote his famous *Bel Ami*, in which he pilloried the mixture of political and private motives behind an "expedition to Morocco." What he meant, of course, was Tunisia—Morocco's turn was not to come until thirty years later. When parliament returned, the fall of Ferry's cabinet was a foregone conclusion. Criticisms of his Tunisian policy, and particularly of his deception of the Chamber, were bitter, but the occupation itself was not voted down. Gambetta declared that France would meet its obligations loyally. His motion was carried by a large majority. Ferry's motion to pass on to the order of the day, by contrast, was turned down, again by a large majority. Ferry resigned, and Gambetta succeeded him. The occupation of Tunisia continued.

A few years later Tunisia was officially declared a French protectorate, the term being used in the first article of the La Marsa Convention of 8 June 1883. Paradoxically, Tunisia then ceased to be a protectorate in the proper sense of the word and became a colony.[41] That article, in fact, gave France the right to introduce "administrative, judiciary and financial reforms." There was no longer any mention of "internal autonomy"—the essential feature of a protectorate. The protectorate idea was, in any case, alien to the French administrative tradition. It was simply used to pay lip service to the republican ideology, which involved the right of national self-determination by all people, and to pretend that there was a difference between developments in Tunisia and the unpopular direct French rule over Algeria. In the beginning it proved to be cheaper, too, at least to the French taxpayer. French nature, however, proved stronger than the ideology, and in the long run this difference between colonies and protectorates proved to be a fiction, in practice if not on paper.

# 3
# GREAT BRITAIN AND IMPERIALISM

France swallowed up Tunisia, and in due course would become the master of the entire Maghreb. Great Britain, for its part, established itself in Egypt and was eventually to rule over the entire Nile valley. And yet Egypt was a country with which France was more closely involved, much more so than with Tunisia or Morocco. It was also the country in which French influence was the oldest—it went back to Napoleon—and the strongest—the Suez Canal was a French creation. Britain, by contrast, did not seem destined to play a leading role in Egypt. Its interests were traditionally in Constantinople and not in Cairo. Gladstone, the British prime minister during the decisive years of the Egyptian crisis, was moreover a convinced anti-imperialist. The explanation of this paradoxical course of events can be found partly in Egypt, partly in French politics, and partly in British politics and British imperialism.

## GREAT BRITAIN IN THE NINETEENTH CENTURY

The British Empire originated in the New World, during the seventeenth century, but lost its American colonies again quite quickly, beginning with the United States in the eighteenth century. Shortly before, however, the Seven Years' War with France (1756–1763) had helped to consolidate British rule over Canada and India. British commercial, colonial and maritime supremacy was confirmed and established during the wars of the French

Revolution and of Napoleon. Trafalgar and Aboukir threw French expansion back into the European continent.

Britain's early nineteenth-century colonial empire was impressive. It comprised Canada and a number of important West Indian possessions; trading posts in West and East Africa, and the great white colony in the Cape; British India, the pearl in the British Crown, in Asia, together with Malaysia and Singapore; in Oceania, the white colonies of Australia and New Zealand; and finally a number of naval bases along the various sea routes. In the further course of the nineteenth century British expansion continued apace, if possible by informal means, that is, commercially and economically, but if necessary formally as well, that is, politically. From 1840 to 1880 Great Britain annexed the Gold Coast, Lagos, Sierra Leone, Natal, Basutoland, Griqualand West and the Transvaal. In other parts of the world, too, the Empire continued to grow. In 1877 Disraeli, created Lord Beaconsfield by Queen Victoria, elevated her to Empress of India in her turn. It was a title the British considered un-British—it reminded them of Napoleon—but one Victoria herself greatly prized, not least because her children were no longer forced to give humiliating precedence to the imperial families of Germany, Russia and Austria at the dinner tables of the European great.

All that was impressive enough, but there was more. The power and dynamism of nineteenth-century Britain were reflected in its growing prosperity, the vigor of its people, and the expansion of its economy. From 1812 to 1883, that is, within seventy years, the national income had grown fivefold, and from 1883 to 1913 it more than doubled again, from £953 million to £2,013 million. Between 1815 and 1890 more than 12 million Britons left their island home to conquer and populate new worlds. In about 1880 Britain had earned and saved enough money to have invested the total sum of almost £2 billion abroad. Most of that money went to the United States, to the colonies settled by Europeans (Canada, Australia and New Zealand) and to Latin America. Asia and Africa offered fewer prospects, with the sole exception of India, not as a place to emigrate to, but for trade and investments. For that very reason India occupied a special place in the British Empire. It even had its own minister, the secretary of state for India. India was the center of British power in Asia and the Far East. The British-Indian army was an eastern war machine, available on demand for colonial expeditions, paid out of the Indian budget, and hence independent of the British Parliament, an invaluable asset as far as the British government was concerned.

British expansion was based on steady population growth, on a dynamic economy, on social harmony and a stable political system. There was of course a reverse to that coin, as many envious nineteenth-century writers observed. In their view, British stability was, in fact, based on the possession of a colonial empire. After the Paris Commune this "British model" served as a spur to colonial expansion in many European countries. British society was stable. The social and political elite underpinned its continued existence with the gradual incorporation of new social groups and by broadening the political spectrum through the step-by-step extension of the suffrage. Britain was therefore held up as a model of gradual evolution, of continuous change under the leadership of an enlightened elite which wore its privileges in none too blatant a manner. For the rest, political power remained largely in the hands of the propertied classes, and of the landed gentry in particular. True, Gladstone was the son of a businessman, and Chamberlain a self-made millionaire, but in every cabinet, be it Liberal or Conservative, ample room was reserved for the land-owning aristocracy, for such men as Lord Rosebery and Lord Salisbury.

British policy conveyed the simple and attractive picture of two political parties holding office in turn: Tories and Whigs. They would later be called Conservatives and Liberals, although the reality was slightly more complicated than these labels suggested. The differences between them were most clearly reflected in the struggle of the giants, Disraeli and Gladstone, who dominated British politics in the years 1870 to 1880. In those days without radio, television or competitive sports, theirs was the match of the century. Together with the pulpit and horse racing, politics was the chief form of public entertainment. This well-ordered system was, however, about to collapse under the pressure of the great question that was increasingly to dominate British politics, namely, Ireland.

The Irish question was the colonial question, albeit at home. It divided political life more than most things. It touched the very heart of the British state. It dominated politics and tore the Liberal party apart. Gladstone's decision in 1886 in favor of Home Rule for Ireland led to the breakup of the Liberal party and the creation of a new group, the Unionists, ex-Liberals ready to collaborate with the Conservatives. Even earlier, the Liberal party had been a party divided into conservative Whigs and progressive Radicals. What we call Liberal cabinets were thus in a sense coalition cabinets of conservative and progressive Liberals and were hence less stable than they seemed to be. Gladstone's dependence on such conservative cabinet members as Hartington, the later Duke of Devonshire, explains much of his inability to take a consistent line in foreign politics. In particular, it had considerable repercussions on British diplomacy in the Egyptian question.

Britain's position among the European Powers was unique in several respects. It was unlike other European countries, and its influence on the vicissitudes of European history was limited. True, when challenged, as in the Napoleonic Wars or in the Crimea, it did not hesitate to throw its armed might into the international struggle. It had also used its considerable political clout at the great Congresses of Vienna, Paris and Berlin. But it greatly preferred its "splendid isolation." By the end of the century, however, people were increasingly doubting the splendor of that isolation. In a Europe dominated by Bismarck, France was forced to look overseas if it wanted to expand, and particularly at the Mediterranean, thus posing a threat to the position Britain had been building up ever since Trafalgar. Russia preferred to expand in Asia, which brought it into regular conflict with British interests in Persia, Afghanistan, India and China. For a long time any alliance of these two Powers seemed unlikely, and was further thwarted by Bismarck's diplomatic acrobatics in 1890, but it was not unthinkable, nor was it something Great Britain could afford to ignore.

Britain boasted that it ruled the waves, but its navy was not as superior as it seemed. The Royal Commission that looked into the imperial defenses in 1879 discovered a host of problems, and in 1884 the press started a campaign to highlight the threat to British naval power. In 1890 the champions of the navy found their theories proclaimed and corroborated in *The Influence of Sea Power upon History*, the famous book by the U.S. naval officer and historian Alfred Thayer Mahan. One year earlier, in 1889, this approach had already found its first practical expression in the Naval Defence Act, which introduced the so-called two-power standard: the British navy must be superior to the combined navies of any two European Powers. The resulting naval supremacy was to give Britain a decisive strategic superiority over France in the 1890s, as a result of which it was able to turn the Fashoda crisis to its advantage in 1898. Its naval superiority was not, however, great enough to obviate the need for "an agonizing reappraisal," after 1900 and the Boer War, of the splendor of British isolation, a reappraisal that would lead to its alliance with Japan in 1902 and to its entente with France in 1904.

### BRITISH IMPERIALISM

Britain's overseas expansion was thus a special case. It was not purely political, like that of France, nor purely economic, like that of Germany, but one that involved society at large. That explains why there was at first no need for political expansion. Those who hold the whip have little need to crack it. All this rendered the British Empire and British imperialism unique, and was the cause of much confusion. Anyone studying imperialism will naturally study the most successful example first, and that example was Britain. But precisely because Britain was so exemplary a case, it was atypical. Other countries such as France, Germany or Italy followed Britain along the colonial path, but being successors their imperialism was bound to be different: inspired by the British model, but applied in a different national and international context. And because British imperialism had successors, that is, competitors, its own character changed as well. Imperialism amid other imperialisms is necessarily different from imperialism as a lone adventure. That is why we can distinguish two phases in what was otherwise a continuous process of British expansion: the lone mid-Victorian imperialist phase and the phase of rival imperialisms characteristic of the late nineteenth century.

The British historians Gallagher and Robinson have defined the early phase as the "imperialism of free trade."[42] Before them, the mid-Victorian period had been viewed differently, as an anti-imperialist age. The great merit of Gallagher and Robinson is that they corrected this false label and—more important—this false interpretation of British imperialism. In fact, nineteenth-century Britain did not go through an essentially anti-imperialist period. The whole century was one of expansion, an "imperial century." British society was the most dynamic of all in the nineteenth century, or at least until the last quarter of the century. Overseas expansion was one logical consequence. That expansion assumed a variety of forms: emigration and colonization, trade and overseas investments, the transfer of culture and religion, the establishment of naval bases. Imperialism in the form of political authority over foreign people was only one, and not even the most important or lasting, aspect of this process. The reason why that form was chosen more frequently in the late nineteenth century than before was not a change in British policy. It was an effect of the changed international situation.

The traditional division into an early anticolonial and a late-Victorian imperialist phase is therefore not tenable. But this does not mean that there were no changes in method or attitude. As late as 1852 Disraeli still referred to "these wretched colonies," to that "millstone round our necks."[43] Twenty years later, in his famous Crystal Palace speech, he extolled the Conservatives as the party of national greatness, firmly determined "to maintain, if they can, their empire."[44] Lord Salisbury noted a complete change in outlook in foreign affairs. When he left the Foreign Office in 1880 no one had given a thought to Africa. "When I returned to it in 1885, the nations of Europe were almost quarrelling with each other as to the various portions of Africa which they could obtain."[45]

In Britain, too, a colonial movement and an imperial ideology were forging ahead. In 1868 Sir Charles Dilke, that great progressive liberal whose brilliant political career was ended prematurely by a typically Victorian scandal, a citation as co-respondent in a divorce suit, had been the first colonial propagandist in his *Greater Britain*, a paean of praise to the Anglo-Saxon race. The book proved a great success in England. In 1884 Sir John Seeley, professor of modern history at Cambridge, published his collected lectures on the subject as *The Expansion of England*, in a volume that was a plea for greater British imperial unity. That, according to Seeley, was needed at a time of ever-larger empires. James Froude, another historian, published his *Oceana* in 1886, a travel book about Australia that was at the same time an impassioned plea for a British commonwealth of nations. The book was an enormous success. And later, of course, there came the greatest imperialist writer of all, Rudyard Kipling, whose work is one great glorification of white expansion, and of British expansion in particular. The 1880s thus brought great changes even to Britain, and a new approach to imperial affairs.[46] British intervention in Egypt was a telling case in point.

Egypt, like Tunisia, had been part of the Ottoman Empire. Its fate, too, was therefore bound up with the eastern question. Egypt was the first prize in the African lottery. Ever since Napoleon had fought a battle beside the pyramids in 1798, France had felt a special call to spread civilization in the pharaohs' ancient empire. For Britain, Egypt had been one of the most important links in the imperial chain ever since the opening of the Suez Canal in 1869. France may have taken the most important steps in the Egyptian affair, but it was Britain that ultimately took possession of Egypt. British imperialism proved stronger than the French variety.

# 4
# EGYPT

Egypt is a present from the Nile, so the ancient Greeks taught. Without the life-giving waters of that river Egypt would never have produced one of the oldest advanced civilizations. Dependence on the waters of the Nile, however, also brought many dramatic twists to Egyptian history and rendered the country and its inhabitants extremely vulnerable. Some presents should be feared, as the Ancients also taught us.

The history of Egypt is thus in the first place the history of a river, the Nile. In the second place it is the history of a sea, the Mediterranean. Egypt may lie in Africa and its history constitute part of the history of that continent, but equally it constitutes a part of Mediterranean history and is hence inseparably bound up with the history of Europe and the Near East. Egypt's place in the history of Africa is exceptional. On the one hand, it has always been linked to its black hinterland, and its history during the age of modern imperialism resembles that of most other parts of that continent. On the other hand, Egypt is different from the rest of Africa. Its population is not black, but white. Economically, it is a part of the Mediterranean trade system. Culturally, it is linked to Greece, Rome, Christianity, and of course, and above all, to Islam. Politically, it was part of the Ottoman Empire so that its history is bound up with the great problem of nineteenth-century European diplomacy, the eastern question.

Egypt, moreover, borders not just on one sea but on two, the Mediterranean and the Red Sea. The distance between them is about one hundred miles. For that reason, Egypt has been a link between Europe and the East since time immemorial. The idea of rendering that link even more negotiable by means of a canal also goes back to the distant past, but was not to

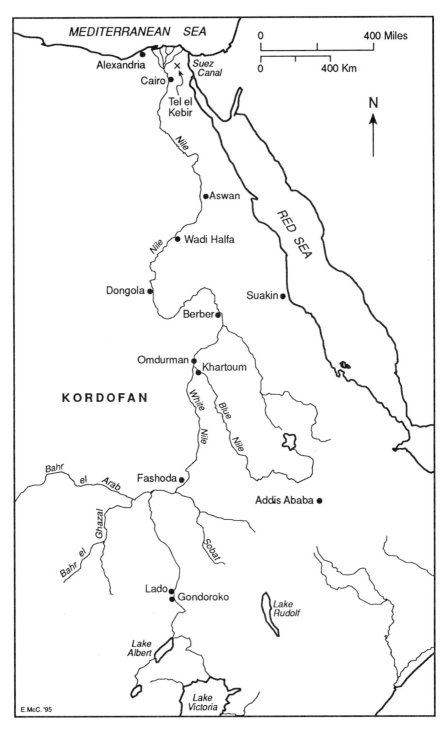

Egypt and the Sudan

Mohammed Ali

be put into practice until the opening in 1869 of the Suez Canal, which was to influence the history of modern Egypt almost as much as the river from which Egypt is a present. Much, however, was to happen before then.

### MOHAMMED ALI

The history of modern Egypt starts with Mohammed Ali. Mohammed Ali (1769–1849) was a tobacco trader from Kavala in Macedonia and arrived in Egypt in 1801 at the head of an Albanian regiment in the service of the Turkish sultan. After a complicated power struggle he managed to have the official Turkish governor removed from Egypt and to have the Porte appoint him instead. That was in 1805. By 1811 his power had been consolidated, and the reign of this first viceroy of Egypt began. It lasted until 1848 and thus spanned the whole of the first half of the nineteenth century, laying the foundations of modern Egypt. Mohammed Ali modernized the administration, built up the army and the navy, and extended the Egyptian sphere of influence. The Sudan was conquered; Egyptian troops helped the sultan in his fight against the Greek rebels, later fought the sultan himself, and conquered parts of Syria and territory around the Persian Gulf. Mohammed Ali became so powerful that the European Powers eventually intervened and forced him to surrender his conquests. He did, however, keep hereditary rule (pashalik) over Egypt, and although under Ottoman suzerainty and obliged to pay tribute, Egypt after Mohammed Ali was to all

intents and purposes an independent power. That special status was reflected in the title "khedive"—roughly equivalent to king—borne by Egyptian viceroys and recognized officially by the sultan in 1867. Political
independence from the Ottoman Empire did, however, go hand in hand
with increasing integration into the international economic system dominated by Europe. Modernization and internationalization were accordingly
the result of the thirst for independence from Turkey. In the event, they led
to increasing dependence on Europe.

Following the French example, Mohammed Ali divided Egypt into pre-
fectures. Egypt's heart lay between Alexandria and Wadi Halfa, a distance
of about 600 miles. The area under cultivation, however, came to less than
15,000 square miles. Villages were the nuclei of the agrarian society that
Egypt largely was. But there were also such metropolises as Alexandria and
Cairo, cities in the nineteenth-century European mold: provided with electricity and sewers, and planned on Haussmannian lines. The great majority
of the population consisted of *fellahin*, casual agricultural laborers and
small peasants. Their lives were dominated by the seasons and the fluctu-
ating level of the Nile. The population had grown quickly, from 2.5 million
at the beginning of the century to 4.5 million in the middle and nearly 10
million by the end of the century. The land was often held in common,
though it was state property in theory and the peasants had no more than
usufructuary rights to it.[47] These rights were fixed annually and were linked
to the level of the Nile.[48] Mohammed Ali not only improved the irrigation
system but also introduced private property. He and his successors aimed
at a stronger and more efficient administration, which to most peasants
meant, above all, compulsory labor and higher taxes. That led in turn to
the sale of land by the smaller peasantry and the emergence of a group of
large to very large landowners, first of all the khedive himself and his family, and then the village notables and the local landowners.

Mohammed Ali's other innovation was the cultivation of cotton. In the
1860s Egyptian cotton boomed following the paralysis of American competition during the American Civil War (1861–1865). For the Egyptian
export economy the American slogan "Cotton is King" held from then on.
Cotton represented 75 percent of all Egyptian exports. For the larger landowners that export held the promise of lucrative trade; for the smaller ones,
by contrast, it was a source of insecurity, debt and, ultimately, bankruptcy.

Egypt had long been a Turkish province, and its upper class was made
up of Turko-Egyptians, descendants of the old overlords. They dominated
the army and the administration.[49] Europeans, by contrast, increasingly
took charge of the economy. On the eve of the British occupation of Egypt,
they numbered about a hundred thousand. They lived mainly in the big
cities, in Alexandria and Cairo, and helped to turn Egypt, after Algeria and
South Africa, into the most European country in Africa. They paid no taxes
and were not answerable to Egyptian courts. These privileges were based

on old Ottoman treaties signed in the sixteenth century. Since this situation created serious problems, new regulations were introduced in 1875. Jurisdiction was henceforth placed in the hand of so-called *tribunaux mixtes*, mixed European and Egyptian courts of law, which took due account of European interests. That explains the enthusiasm for being a European in Egypt and why so many Europeans were Europeans in name only. That was true, for instance, of the close to 40,000 "Greeks" who made up almost 40 percent of the European colony but had generally been born or brought up in Egypt. The "English" were in fact almost all Maltese, therefore British subjects, although that was practically the only English thing about them. The "French" and "Italians" were mainly Levantines, orientalized Europeans. The surprisingly large contingent of 7,000 "Austrians" was made up of people who had either purchased or obtained in some way a passport from the Austrian ambassador.

But there were others as well. There were many native Christians, Copts, Jews, Armenians, Lebanese, and more. Egypt was a multiracial society. For that reason alone, it was natural that so many countries should have been interested in Egyptian affairs, but for the Europeans, and for France and Britain in particular, there were other reasons too. They had large financial commitments in Egypt, especially through Egyptian government bonds, and they were also closely involved in the canal, which made Egypt an object of growing diplomatic interest.

### THE SUEZ CANAL

Plans for joining the Red Sea to the Mediterranean, though not as old as Egypt itself, were in all truth old enough. As early as the reign of Necho, a pharaoh who lived in the seventh century B.C., a beginning was made on a canal between the Nile and the Red Sea. Not much came of that attempt. The modern history of the project starts with Napoleon. His engineers concluded that cutting straight through the Suez isthmus was impossible because of the difference in level between the two seas. This (incidentally mistaken) conclusion was to hold sway for a long time. Maritime traffic between Europe and Asia thus continued to use the Cape route. With the advent of steamships, however, new possibilities emerged. It became possible to navigate the Red Sea in a northerly direction, something that had been a great problem for sailing ships because of the prevailing wind. That rendered the overland route an attractive alternative for passengers and mail.

In 1830 the first journey by steamer was made from Bombay to Suez. In 1834 a regular land connection between Alexandria and Suez was set up. In 1836 the London-Alexandria service was inaugurated, and the time it took to travel from England to India was reduced from five months to forty days as a result. The British were pleased with this outcome, and as proof occupied Socotra in 1835 and Aden in 1839, two strategic points along the new route. They did not, however, favor a canal. That would bring Marseilles and Genoa closer to the Far East than London and Liverpool, and French troops closer to India than British. It would, moreover, increase French influence in Egypt and weaken the ties between Egypt and the Ottoman Empire—Britain's protégé. As a result, the canal project remained for a long time, in fact to the very end, an exclusively French passion.

The original plans had been drawn up by Saint-Simon, the French count who is remembered principally as one of the Utopian socialists. He certainly was a Utopian and an enthusiast as well, and believed that mankind's future lay in industry and trade. He accordingly asked Rouget de l'Isle to write a new, industrial *Marseillaise* in which the famous phrase "enfants de la patrie" was replaced with "enfants de l'industrie."[50] A canal through the isthmus of Suez was also part of his program for the social improvement of mankind. Led by Prosper Enfantin, some of his disciples went to Egypt in 1833, their heads filled with plans for reform, education and canal excavation. Mohammed Ali was sufficiently pro-French to bid them welcome, but also afraid enough of Britain to oppose their canal plan. Enfantin therefore returned to France empty-handed, but did not abandon the project. The creation of an international Société d'Etudes, with a leading place for British representatives, was his next step, in 1846. It concluded that a canal was feasible. The British, for their part, considered a railroad link more practical. From that moment, the Suez question was to be overshadowed by Anglo-French rivalry. Rail or canal, that was the question. British and French influences alternated with changing Egyptian administrations. At first the British were the more influential, and a concession for a railroad line was issued accordingly, but in 1854 a new viceroy came to power. He was Said Pasha, and he was pro-French. More important, he was friendly with a French diplomat, Ferdinand de Lesseps. Their association gave the Egyptian question a new twist.

### De Lesseps

Ferdinand de Lesseps (1805–1894) came from a family of consuls. He was born in 1805 in Versailles, where his father had returned on leave from Alexandria in 1804. Ferdinand followed a similar career, which brought him to Alexandria as vice-consul in 1832. There he became acquainted with Said while the latter was still a child, and gave him riding lessons. In 1849, following some difficulties, de Lesseps left the diplomatic service and devoted himself to his canal plans. In 1852 he sent a note to S. W. Ruyssenaars, the Dutch consul general in Egypt, asking him to enquire if the plan might be acceptable to Said, who had meanwhile become khedive. Ruyssenaars did not think so, but de Lesseps relied on his personal influence. In 1854 he went to Egypt himself and called on Said. His horse-riding skills

Ferdinand de Lesseps

proved useful once more, since they made a great impression on the khedive and his entourage. The day of decision was 15 November 1854. In the morning a rainbow appeared in the sky, which de Lesseps considered a token of the covenant spoken of in the Bible: "the right moment for the true union of east and west."[51] He unfolded his plan to an attentive Said, who gave his consent. On 30 November 1854 de Lesseps was issued with a very broad authorization to form an international company under his own direction, the Compagnie Universelle du Canal Maritime de Suez. This company would be granted a concession, framed in very general terms, to exploit the proposed canal for ninety-nine years following its completion. Thereafter the canal would be handed over to the Egyptian government, which would have received 15 percent of the annual profits during the first ninety-nine years.

De Lesseps was therefore in a position to go ahead, as far as Egypt was concerned, but such a scheme was not of course a matter for private individuals alone. There were political repercussions as well. For one thing the Ottoman emperor, as sovereign of Egypt, also had to give his consent, and he was strongly influenced by Great Britain. Britain, as we have seen, was against the canal. In March 1854, moreover, the Crimean War had begun, a war in which Britain and France took sides with the sultan against Russia. Britain in particular acted as Turkey's protector, while France, having to take care not to offend its ally, kept a low profile. In the end, therefore, the sultan withheld his consent.

The work nevertheless progressed, though for the time being by way of studies and explorations. In 1856, however, these had advanced so far that de Lesseps was granted a new and more detailed concession. This laid down where the canal was to run, how wide and deep it would be, and how the finances were to be raised. The Compagnie de Suez was given its statutes. These specified that the registered office would be in Paris and the head offices in Alexandria. The capital was set at 200 million francs in the form of four hundred thousand shares at 500 francs each. Twenty-five shares entitled the holder to a vote at the shareholders' meeting, but no shareholder could cast more than ten votes. The company was to be run by a board of directors and an executive committee. It was not until 1858, however, that the shares were offered for sale, de Lesseps guaranteeing an interim rate of interest of 5 percent. This was a bold, indeed provocative, step in view of British opposition and French coolness. The flotation turned out to be a success for all that, especially in France, where patriotic feelings were running high. Thus one applicant for shares, confusing Suez with Suède, wrote that he was happy to be helping to build a "railroad in Sweden." When he was told that the shares were not for a railroad but for a canal, and not in Sweden but in Suez, he replied that it did not matter so long as it was against the English.[52]

The canal diggers could now have set to work, but this time it was the khedive who hesitated and began to back-pedal for fear of the sultan. Accordingly he first refused to allow Egyptian workers to be employed, and later, when an attempt was made to use Europeans, he ordered these out of the country. Then de Lesseps raised the matter to the diplomatic level where it belonged. Napoleon III came out in support of the canal, and with his official backing the project was finally completed, albeit in the teeth of British opposition. Said's death and his succession by the dynamic Ismail in 1863 also proved helpful. "No one is more *canaliste* than I am," Ismail declared, and with reason, since he had bought a block of more than 177,000 shares—almost half the total number—and had thus become the largest shareholder.[53] The more than 200,000 French shares were in the hands of over 21,000 private French individuals.[54]

In 1866 the sultan himself finally came round, and, ten years after the event, bestowed his official seal of approval upon the concession. In August 1869 the canal was completed, and on 17 September of that year the official inauguration took place. Many illustrious personages traveled to Egypt for the occasion: the Empress Eugénie of France, Prince Franz-Josef of Austria, Prince Frederick William of Prussia and Prince Henry of the Netherlands. The Empress Eugénie was the first to be conveyed up the canal with de Lesseps in the imperial yacht. The link between the two seas had become a fact. As early as 1832 the Saint-Simonian economist Michel Chevalier had predicted in his *Système de la Méditerranée* that this project would reform Asia and foster world peace.[55] The first may be true, but the canal, far from becoming an instrument of peace, was to be the cause of many disputes and conflicts.

## THE KHEDIVE ISMAIL

The canal was just one of the great works of the khedive Ismail. With him, a new period in Egyptian history began in 1863. The years between Ali's death and Ismail's accession had been peaceful ones. Egypt had been governed by leaders who did not modernize, waged no wars and did not increase the tax burden—conservative rulers, in short. Things were to change under Ismail. He was a man of great vision whose aim was to turn Egypt into a European state, speeding its course in the progress of nations. He offered Napoleon III a battalion to join the French expedition to Mexico. He also took part in the Paris World Exhibition of 1867. That same year, the sultan recognized Ismail's title as khedive. The title was made hereditary, so that in the eyes of the world he was virtually sovereign. At home he ruled like an absolute monarch in any case.

Ismail's influence on the Egyptian infrastructure was enormous. During his reign thousands of miles of railroad tracks were built, 8,000 miles of canal excavated, and 5,000 miles of telegraph cable laid. Arable land was increased by more than 30 percent through improved irrigation. Alexandria was given a modern harbor. Thousands of schools were opened. Sugar refineries were built, forming the basis of a second export commodity alongside cotton. Exports rose from £4 million to £14 million per annum. Ismail did not overlook himself in all this: about one-fifth of the arable land ended up in his hands or in those of his family.[56]

Many people looked upon this progressive system of government with admiration. Countless Europeans profited from it. The European population of Egypt grew by leaps and bounds. The Turkish-Mameluke ruling class also saw new, honorable and lucrative careers on the horizon. The little man, the *fellah*, took a different view. For him, modernization and national grandeur meant more forced labor, higher taxes, more debt and higher interest payments. Everything was taxed. There was, as Lady Duff-Gordon wrote, "a tax on every crop, on every annual fruit . . . on every man, on charcoal, on salt, on the dancing girls."[57] First came the administrator and then the usurer; to quote Lady Duff-Gordon again, "the Greek usurer follows the Coptic tax-gatherer like a vulture after the cow."[58]

And still the taxes were not enough to cover the costs of the ambitious modernization program. Ismail therefore chose another solution: foreign loans. At the beginning of his reign, the Egyptian state debt was £4 million. Under his regime it mounted within a few years to £68 million. In addition there was a floating debt of some £20 million. All in all, the debt came to nearly £90 million, in a country that had an annual taxation yield of £8 million. In this increasing financial dependence lay the whole history of

Ismail, the more so as a large part of the debt sprang from the building of the Suez Canal.

The Suez Canal was the most important link in the new, short bridge between Europe and Asia. It mattered more to Great Britain than it did to any other country. Egypt and South Africa were the two cornerstones of Africa, certainly in terms of imperial strategy. Thanks to the Suez Canal the Egyptian question had been turned from a primarily financial one into a mainly strategic one, and hence from a purely French into an Anglo-French concern. In the nineteenth century France and Britain determined the fate of Egypt. At first, while it was still mainly a matter of financial and cultural influences, France held the upper hand. But once strategic and political factors came into play, Britain took over the main role in the developing venture of Egyptian modernization.

The Suez Canal was one of the projects that drove Ismail's regime to the edge of the financial precipice. For the canal could in no way be financed with the money raised by the sale of the shares. The Egyptian government had spent in all about £8 million on the construction, and in exchange it received 15 percent of the annual profits. The shareholders, who had contributed roughly the same total, received 75 percent. Moreover, the financial exploitation of the canal was at first not a very profitable business. In 1871, two years after the opening, the value of a share had dropped from 500 francs to 208 francs.[59] That was a bad blow in particular for the khedive, who was, after all, the major shareholder. There were many other aspects, however, to the great financial debacle now befalling the ambitious ruler.

Ismail had numerous financial problems and knew of only two solutions: raising taxes and, if that did not work, taking out foreign loans. He had begun to apply these solutions the moment he came to power. The conditions under which the loans had been taken up were disgraceful from the outset; eventually they became draconic, and in the end, crippling. At a time when the normal rate of interest was 6 to 7 percent, these loans paid at least 12 or 13 percent, and sometimes as much as 25 to 27 percent. In addition there were the "commissions," with which Tunisia, too, was familiar. In 1873 Ismail obtained a loan, on paper, of £32 million. In fact, after everyone had been paid, he was left with just £19 million.[60] The Franco-Prussian War of 1870–1871 had jolted the money markets badly and had rekindled the public mistrust of "turban loans."[61] All in all, money did not come cheap for Ismail.

The war had also upset the European balance of power. The position of France, Egypt's traditional protector, had been weakened, and Britain now had a chance of gaining control over a canal to which it had at first objected strongly. Palmerston had called it a "bubble scheme" of "gullible capitalists,"[62] but his successor, Disraeli, thought differently. Now that the canal was there, it was best to have control over it. The khedive's perilous finances provided the key. The hard-pressed ruler first offered his shares for sale to the French Société Générale. However, the French government opposed the transaction for political reasons—France was afraid of British and German reactions so soon after 1870. It was Britain's turn. Parliament was in recess. The cabinet was divided, but came round in the end and agreed unanimously. Disraeli struck. The transaction was completed within three days, the Rothschilds having advanced the required sum. On 14 November 1875 Disraeli wrote to Queen Victoria, "The entire interest of the Khedive is now yours, Madam."[63] The queen was delighted. The khedive received the £4 million he so badly needed, but which were not to solve his financial problems. Edward Stanton, the British consul general in Egypt, received seven gigantic chests containing 177,642 shares. The British government, while not having a majority interest, had become the largest shareholder in the canal company. A majority interest, incidentally, would not have meant a great deal because of the statutory limitation of voting rights. What was only too clear, however, was that Britain had moved into Egypt and meant to stay there. In Cairo, British imperial strategists had established a second line of defense in the Mediterranean alongside Constantinople. For a time Britain continued there in the company of France; in the end it remained alone.

### THE ANGLO-FRENCH CONDOMINIUM, 1876–1882

On 8 April 1876 Egypt went bankrupt. The khedive stopped paying the treasury bills. In May Ismail made two proposals to his creditors: first, the establishment of an international Caisse de la Dette Publique, with a member each from Britain, France, Italy and Austria to settle the debt; second, the consolidation of the entire debt to be fixed at £99 million bearing 7 percent interest. The creditors rejected both proposals. They dispatched a financial mission to Egypt led by Goschen and Joubert, representing British and French interests, respectively, with alternative proposals. The result was the "Goschen-Joubert Decree" of 18 November 1876. A Caisse de la Dette was set up with two French and two British members, together with one Austrian and one Hungarian. France and Britain thus had the upper hand. Next, two European financial controllers-general were appointed, one to superintend the national revenue and the other the national expenditure. These measures marked the beginning of European receivership and of Anglo-French dual control, which was to continue until 1882. The choice for Britain was simple enough. In Salisbury's words: "You may renounce—or monopolize —or share. Renouncing would have been to place the French across our road to India. Monopolizing would have been very near the risk of war. So we resolved to share."[64]

The Caisse de la Dette failed to do the job for which it had been set up. The share of Egyptian revenue needed to pay off the debts was so large that even after a drastic turn of the financial screws not enough could be raised to keep the Egyptian state machinery in operation. A new commission was accordingly appointed, followed by a new report and, in August 1878, by a new system. The khedive was required to introduce a scheme of ministerial responsibility, though for the time being his ministers were responsible to the foreign creditors and not to the Egyptians. European ministers of finance and public works were appointed and tried to keep expenditure down by lowering the pay of Egyptian officials and officers. The upshot was a military revolt in February 1879. The khedive reacted by dismissing the European ministers, forming a new government, setting up a Chamber of Notables, and coming up with a new plan for liquidating the debt which was more advantageous for Egypt. Indignation in Europe was great, especially in France, where most of the creditors were. But the time for direct intervention had not yet arrived. Ismail first had to go. Then it would be possible to revert to the old method, to the familiar model of "moral influence." Salisbury described the latter as "a combination of nonsense, objurgation and worry."[65] It came down to Egyptian control in name and to European control in practice. The Ottoman emperor was asked to arrange the dismissal of Ismail and did so laconically by sending him a telegram on 26 June 1879 addressed to "the ex-Khedive Ismail Pasha."[66]

Ismail was succeeded by his son, Tewfik, who was what Marxists used to call a lackey of European imperialism. Anglo-French financial control was institutionalized by the appointment of two controllers. Both had the right to attend cabinet meetings, to appoint inspectors at the various ministries and to report to their respective governments. The steps taken in 1879 consolidated Anglo-French rule over Egypt. The two controllers were a Frenchman and a Briton. The latter, Evelyn Baring, then still no more than a major, would later become the new ruler of Egypt, first as Sir Evelyn Baring and later as Lord Cromer.

A new international debt committee and a new report were also inaugurated. The report came to a conclusion underwritten by the European Powers. This, the decree of 17 July 1880, known as the Law of Liquidation, settled Egypt's financial position. The financial viability of Egypt was less severely taxed than it had been by earlier arrangements, and the rate of interest lowered, but the payment of the "coupon" was now more or less guaranteed, and the Egyptian government received no more than a modest, fixed sum for its most essential expenses. Any surplus went into the fund for the liquidation of the public debt. The controllers were to keep a tight rein on Egyptian finances in accordance with these terms. The Caisse de la Dette was kept on to administer repayment of the debt and to fix interest rates. The Law of Liquidation became Egypt's financial statute. Changes could only be made with the consent of the Powers. Later, having intervened in Egypt by force, Britain was to gain more direct experience of the problems involved, for it then had to take over the obligations of the Egyptian state and was continuously brought up against the harsh fact that the costs had to be met by the British taxpayer or by Egypt's European creditors.

Its armed intervention in Egypt thus not only earned Britain the enmity of France, but also made it dependent upon the other Powers. That Britain decided to intervene in 1882 despite these obstacles was therefore not so much due to its particular keenness to do so as to the fact that conditions in Egypt had moved completely out of control after the ex-khedive's departure. With him the last semblance of an independent Egypt had gone. On the one hand, this had underlined the formal dependence of Egypt on the sultan, another pawn of the European Powers; on the other hand, it had demonstrated the informal, but only too obvious, dependence of Egypt on these Powers. Tewfik was a puppet and Egypt a satellite, and that had become clear just as something like a nationalist or anti-imperialist movement was making its presence felt in Egypt. This movement reflected ideas of an Islamic renaissance and was spurred by the modernization and disintegration processes in traditional Egyptian society. Its ideals were summed up in the slogan devised by the eccentric and Egyptophile Englishman Wilfred Blunt, a slogan that was as inaccurate as it was explosive: "Egypt for the Egyptians."

### THE EGYPTIAN REVOLUTION

The protest movement of 1881 had several contexts, several factions, and several leaders. The growing influence of Europe and European superiority had in fact led to two different reactions, on the one hand a leaning toward the West, where salvation was expected to come from, and on the other hand a return to Islam. As a result, Egypt witnessed a westernization process and the nationalism that went with it, and at the same time a drift toward a pro-Islamic revival. The great leader of that renaissance was Jamal al-Din. He was born in 1837, probably in Persia, but had lived in Afghanistan for a time and was therefore called al-Afghani. This philosopher and teacher had arrived in Cairo via Constantinople in 1871, and had quickly made his presence felt there.[67] He was very deeply impressed by Western technical superiority. "Science," he wrote, "endows one man with the strength of ten." Even so, spiritual renewal came first. He accordingly called for an Islamic renaissance and a restoration of Muslim unity. The incompetent rulers, those who played the game of the Europeans, had to be deposed.

His movement led to the rise of an Egyptian press and of a political party that voiced a variety of political, social and religious objectives. It lacked social cohesion, containing conservative Islamists and Western constitutionalists, rich landowners and hard-pressed officers. The unifying force was revulsion from foreign influence over Egypt in every form. That influ-

Arabi Pasha

ence, incidentally, was not only, and not even predominantly, Western. Even the Egyptian elite was more or less alien, made up as it was of the descendants of Turkish and Circassian families. That was particularly true of the army, where Egyptian officers were in the minority and felt discriminated against. The Egyptian officers' movement had begun, as we have seen, as early as February 1879 with a demonstration against the dismissal of 2,500 officers. The army had been in a sullen mood ever since, and the same complaints remained: discrimination against Egyptian officers. Their spokesman was Colonel Ahmed Arabi, who was later to become renowned as Arabi Pasha.

This leader of the Egyptian revolution had a modest background. He was born in 1840, the son of a village elder and small landowner. He had embarked upon his military career at the age of fourteen. At seventeen he had been promoted to lieutenant, and at eighteen to captain; he became a major at nineteen and a lieutenant-colonel at twenty. Arabi owed his lightning career to the policy of the khedive Said, who was keen to strengthen the native Egyptian element in the army. Said's successor, Ismail, had different ideas on that subject, however, and was responsible for pushing Arabi into the camp of the dissatisfied and politically conscious Egyptians. Ismail's fall and his succession by Tewfik were therefore welcomed by Arabi but gave him little cause to rejoice. The new minister of war, Arabi's chief, pursued a policy favoring Circassian officers at the expense of the natives.

Arabi himself, known for his contacts with the reform party, was threatened with dismissal. The minister went one step further still. He had Arabi and some other leaders arrested. However, their fellow officers had them released and gave them a triumphant reception. The minister was dismissed and the troubles with the army started in earnest.

The resistance was aimed at the cause of all these problems, the khedive and the European overlords behind him. In 1881 the officers seized power in Egypt. First, they forced Tewfik to dismiss the minister of war and to appoint one of their number in his place. On 9 September 1881, after Tewfik, in a last-ditch attempt to cling to power, had dismissed him again, they marched on the palace and put an ultimatum to the khedive, demanding the dismissal of his cabinet, the convening of the Chamber, and the expansion of the army. The khedive gave in. The army had thus taken power in Egypt, and the foreign overlords were faced with yet another problem. Their policy, which amounted to influencing events through their two controllers but preserving the façade of an independent Egyptian state and of Turkish suzerainty, had plainly failed. Britain and France had come to a turning point. Decisions had to be taken about what steps were needed to protect their financial interests and the canal. In 1881 Britain and France were tantamount to Gladstone and Gambetta.

### TOWARD INTERVENTION

The man responsible for British policy during this crucial phase, William Ewart Gladstone (1809–1898), is considered by some as Britain's greatest nineteenth-century statesman. In the eyes of others he was a hypocritical coward who failed to protect Britain's best interests. Queen Victoria was known to dislike him. She called him "an old, wild and incomprehensible man."[68] Bismarck considered him a worthless politician good for nothing but chopping wood and giving speeches.[69] Gladstone's reputation might therefore be open to question, but not his influence. His life more or less coincided with the duration of the nineteenth century. His political career spanned virtually the entire Victorian period. He entered politics in Metternich's days and became prime minister for the last time when Bismarck had already stepped down.

Gladstone was born in Liverpool, the son of a wealthy merchant. He said of himself that he had not one drop of English blood in his veins, and that was the truth, for he was of pure Scottish descent. His father had, however, settled in Liverpool and made his fortune there, his many possessions including plantations in the West Indies. Gladstone senior was thus a slave-owner, and fortune decreed that his son, the great moralist and humanist, should begin his parliamentary career with an eloquent maiden speech in defense of the institution of slavery. Young Gladstone entered politics at an early age. After Eton and Christ Church, Oxford, he was elected to the House of Commons in 1832 when not yet twenty-three years old. Gladstone was a man of wide intellectual interests, naming Aristotle, St. Augustine, Dante and Butler as his four great teachers. He remained attached to the classics all his life, publishing five books on Homer, including the three-volume *Homer and the Homeric Age*, which ran to 1,700 pages, and translating Horace's *Odes*. His social concerns extended in particular to those known as fallen women, and his nocturnal wanderings through London's less salubrious streets provoked much talk and speculation.[70] Gladstone thus had enough to occupy him, yet politics was his true calling. As early as 1835 he was appointed under-secretary of state for war and the colonies. Many other ministerial posts followed. The crucial step came in 1859 when he was made chancellor of the exchequer in Palmerston's last cabinet. Gladstone, who had been brought up with conservative convictions, now sided with the Liberals and was to become their foremost leader, indeed the leader of their radical wing, so radical that he split the party over Home Rule for Ireland.

His adoption of the radical, moral and progressive line did not, however, come until his famous election campaign of 1879 to 1880, when he stood for the Scottish constituency of Midlothian. He used that occasion to castigate Disraeli's imperialist and militaristic policy, and made fun of the imperial Indian title which the latter had bestowed upon Queen Victoria. His entire rhetoric was a long plea for standards and values, for self-determination and respect for other nations. "Midlothian" proved a great success, not only for Gladstone himself but also for the Liberal party, whom Gladstone led to a resounding victory. Queen Victoria, who had sworn never again to make Gladstone prime minister, had to swallow her words. In 1880 Gladstone presented his second cabinet.

In his election campaign, Gladstone had fulminated against British involvement in Afghanistan, in the Transvaal and in Egypt. Now that he was prime minister, he had to put his words into practice. And he did indeed extricate Britain from Afghanistan, and, after the Majuba disaster, from its involvement in the Transvaal as well. However, he was unable to get out of the Egyptian trap. His cabinet was divided between Radicals such as Dilke and Harcourt on the one hand, and the Whigs led by Hartington on the other, and he needed Whig support to solve his main problem, the Irish question. Gladstone was thus forced to do what he had fought against, to deny that he was doing what he actually did, and to pursue a policy he himself had pilloried so eloquently and in such noble tones: an imperialist one. The result was that in 1882 the Gladstone cabinet foisted British authority upon Egypt, albeit reluctantly.

In France, things were different. France attached a great deal of importance to Egypt, where it wielded considerable influence and had many vested interests. It even took an initiative that was to lead to armed intervention, namely, Gambetta's note of 8 January 1882. The French navy joined the British in a show of strength off the coast of Alexandria, but at the crucial moment, because of the complicated political situation at home, France pulled out. During the decisive phase of the Egyptian crisis, roughly from September 1881 to September 1882, France had had no fewer than four different cabinets: first, the Ferry administration, with Saint-Hilaire at foreign affairs, which fell in 1881 in the wake of another African adventure, Tunisia; second, that of the "grand ministère Gambetta," with the great man himself as prime minister and minister of foreign affairs until 26 February 1882; third, the second Freycinet cabinet, in which the prime minister also ran the Quai d'Orsay, from late January to 31 July 1882; and fourth, the tenth Duclerc administration, in which the prime minister's office was once again combined with the job of running foreign affairs. French politicians were so divided that at the crucial moment they proved powerless.

### THE BRITISH OCCUPATION

The events of 9 September 1881 had demonstrated that there was a power vacuum in Egypt. The suzerainty of the Ottoman sultan was increasingly turning into a fiction. The khedive's government had disintegrated. The soldiers led by Arabi had been able to challenge the existing regime but could not provide an alternative administration. The informal French and British controllers were not (yet) ready to proceed to a formal takeover of the Egyptian state. Hence there was an impasse, and the way out had to be shown by the two countries with real power, Britain and France.

The best solution on paper was to invite intervention by the Sublime Porte. The good thing about the Ottoman Empire was that one could call on it whenever it was convenient to do so and forget all about it on other occasions. This time it proved useful once again, at least for Gladstone, who was trying desperately to satisfy his need for legitimacy. The French were, however, set against the idea. Every attempt to restore Turkish authority in Egypt ran counter to the traditional French policy for dealing with Egypt. Reactivating Turkish suzerainty in North Africa, moreover, posed a threat to French interests in Tunisia, where France had just established a protectorate.[71] As Britain was anxious not to fall out with France, nothing could be done for the time being.

A new phase was ushered in with the advent of the Gambetta administration in November 1881. In 1875 Gambetta had vainly insisted that France buy the khedive's shares in the Suez Canal. Gambetta had always retained his interest in Egypt. Moreover, he was keen to preserve Anglo-French cooperation and to give France a leading role in it. He accordingly drafted a note, countersigned by Britain, and had it read out to the khedive on 8 January 1882. In this so-called Joint Note, Britain and France declared that they considered the continued presence of the khedive on the Egyptian throne a prerequisite of the maintenance of order and material progress in

Egypt, and that they hoped this public assurance might help to avert the dangers with which the khedive was threatened and which Britain and France would jointly help to ward off. The note was intended to intimidate the Egyptian Chamber of Notables. However, because Britain was known to be reluctant to intervene, the note had a provocative rather than an intimidating effect. It galvanized the nationalist groups. In the words of Blunt, it was "a most mischievous document," and would be received as "a declaration of war."[72] It brought the nationalists and the military together for the first time and, as Cromer had predicted, the explosion followed directly.[73] A few weeks later, the Gambetta cabinet fell following a reform of the electoral system. Freycinet, his successor, would try to act more closely in accord with the Chamber of Deputies.

In Egypt, meanwhile, the crisis continued. The following month Arabi Pasha was brought into the government. He gradually broke with the khedive and formed a revolutionary government of sorts. On 29 May the khedive took stock of the new state of affairs and handed Arabi dictatorial powers. That step altered the situation even as far as Gladstone was concerned. Arabi had ceased to be a sympathetic nationalist leader and had become a military dictator. Moreover, the Whigs in Gladstone's cabinet were clamoring for action. Arabi was meanwhile busy building up his army and fortifying Alexandria against a possible invasion. France and Britain responded with a naval show of strength: on 17 May a joint Anglo-French squadron of four ships arrived off Alexandria. That was to be the last act of Anglo-French dual control over Egypt.

The Egyptian crisis had meanwhile reached a climax. The riots in Alexandria had persuaded many Europeans to leave the city. The British admiral, Sir Frederick Seymour, cruised offshore and viewed the Egyptian fortifications with disfavor but was not allowed to intervene. He then forced the hand of the British government. He described the fortifications as a great threat to the safety of his ships and asked for permission to bombard the shore. Freycinet let it be known that a bombardment would be an act of war which he could not countenance. The French naval contingent was withdrawn. Britain was left on its own. Seymour was given the go-ahead, and on 11 July 1882 began to shell the shore. A few days later troops were landed to restore order. The rest followed. The canal would of course have to be protected, and that meant more warships and more troops. France was again asked to join in, and this time Freycinet was prepared to do so, provided it was a small expedition and sent purely for the protection of the canal, but the Chamber demurred, refusing to vote the necessary credits on 29 July 1882. Freycinet resigned.

Once more, Britain went ahead on its own. It took it some time to muster enough troops. On 13 September 1882 the decisive battle was fought at Tel el-Kebir. The British force under Wolseley gained an easy victory over Arabi's men, and Arabi himself was captured. Wolseley wanted to have him shot, Queen Victoria favored hanging, and Gladstone, too, wanted him executed but only after a fair trial.[74] None of this happened. Arabi was banished, taken to Ceylon in a specially chartered ship, and in 1901 he was allowed to return to Egypt.

Britain, having established its presence in Egypt by force, wanted to leave again as soon as the situation allowed, but the situation did not allow because the Egyptian state, weakened by foreign interventions and burdened with foreign debts, was no longer able to recover unaided. Britain stayed on. And from Egypt, it inevitably made its way to the Egyptian colony: the Sudan.

# 5
# THE SUDAN AND THE NILE

The word "Sudan" comes from the Arabic and was first used by Muslim geographers in the Middle Ages when describing the "land of the blacks," the Bilad al-Sudan, by which they meant the area between the Sahara and the tropical rainforest stretching from the Atlantic to the Red Sea and dividing Arabia from Africa. This was the region with which the Arabs came into contact first and where the influence of Islam is great. The area is divided into three parts: the western Sudan, that is, the hinterland of the Senegal and Upper Niger rivers; central Sudan, to the east of the latter; and Egyptian Sudan, immediately south of Egypt. This last part had been conquered by Egypt in the nineteenth century, before being split off again and finally being recaptured as "Anglo-Egyptian Sudan." It is at present the largest African state, the republic of Sudan. It is with this part of the Sudan that we shall be concerned below.

The present frontier between Egypt and the Sudan used not to exist. Southern Egypt and the northern part of the Sudan were jointly known as Nubia, an amalgam of small principalities. The unity of the Sudan—if there ever was such a thing—stemmed from political developments. There is no such thing as a natural Sudanese entity; there is instead a sharp contrast between the north and the rest. The north speaks Arabic in the main, has been converted to Islam, and has ties with Egypt and the Arab world. The remainder is mainly animistic and has links with the African world. In the northern Sudan, which stretches from the Egyptian border near Wadi Halfa to Khartoum, the capital, the annual rainfall is so small that cultivation is confined to the immediate vicinity of the Nile. Here the inhabited region is a narrow strip of land between the Libyan and Nubian deserts. Between Khartoum, at the confluence of the Blue and the White Niles, and Fashoda, just above the confluence of the White Nile—or, to give it its Arabic name, the Bahr el-Jezel (Mountain River)—and the Sobat, lies central Sudan. Here the rainfall supports agriculture and animal husbandry. This explains why the Gezira, a "peninsula" between the Blue Nile and the White Nile, was the center of a great kingdom as early as the sixteenth century, one that would continue until the invasion by Mohammed Ali, Egypt's expansionist viceroy. Below Fashoda begins the southern Sudan, which differs widely, with respect to language, ethnic background, culture and religion, from northern and central Sudan. It is set off from them by a natural barrier constituted by the arms of the Nile running from west to east or from east to west, respectively. In the west, these arms are known as the Bahr el-Arab (the Arabian River) and its continuation, the Bahr el-Ghazal (the Gazelle River). It is from the latter that the entire western Sudan derives its name of Bahr el-Ghazal. In the east, the upper boundary is formed by the Sobat, which runs from east to west.

The Bahr el-Ghazal is dominated by an enormous network of rivers and streams, all of which discharge into it. During the rainy season they flood, rendering transport by land very difficult. The White Nile, for its part, has ceased to be navigable here because it no longer has a definite bed. The Bahr el-Ghazal is choked with floating vegetation, sometimes thick enough for elephants to walk on. This vegetation is known as *sudd*, from the Arabic *sadd*, meaning obstacle.[75] The land here sometimes disappears to make way for water, and the water to make way for land. In short, the *sudd* creates an impenetrable marshland, which for that very reason was almost completely spared the Egyptian invasion. All these elements go into the Egyptian Sudan, a gigantic area covering nearly 1 million square miles, more than ten times the size of Great Britain and not much smaller than India.

### THE ANTECEDENTS, 1820–1881

Mohammed Ali, the founder of modern Egypt, was a progressive. He was also an expansionist, an Egyptian imperialist. What with deserts to the west and the east and the ocean to the north, it was not surprising that his expansive energy should have been directed toward the south.[76] In July 1820 an army set out from Cairo for the Sudan, led by his youngest son. The armies of such emirates as Kordofan and the like were no match for the khedive's troops. Within a year all the land right up to southern Sudan had been conquered, to become an appendage of Egypt which, officially, was still a province of the Turkish empire. This period in the history of the Sudan is accordingly known as the Turkiyya. Khartoum became the headquarters of the Egyptian (or Turkish) army of occupation and the most important town in the whole of Sudan. The conquest of southern Sudan began later, from 1839 to 1842.

The regime Mohammed Ali established in the Sudan was no model of enlightened or disinterested rule. High taxes collected remorselessly—to-

gether with corruption—were its chief characteristics. In view of the declared objectives of the Egyptian expansionist drive, this was not in the
least surprising. "The aim of all our efforts is to acquire slaves," Mohammed Ali himself had declared.[77] Gold was another incentive. Sudanese gold
had been a lure for a host of avaricious people over the centuries. Sudanese
resentment, later to become the basis of popular support for the mahdist
movement, was born during these years. It was reinforced in 1850 when it
became customary to appoint European, that is, Christian, officials, and
attempts were made to suppress the slave trade. Actually, Egypt had little
say over the administration, which increasingly fell into the hands of independent governors-general. The khedive Said (1845–1863) thought so
little of this arrangement that he considered getting rid of the Sudan.[78]

The slave trade was given a fresh boost when a new Egyptian drive into
the Sudan was launched during the reign of the khedive Ismail. Ismail, like
his grandfather, Mohammed Ali, was a man in favor of renewal and reform. He was also, again like his grandfather, an expansionist. Under his
reign, the Sudan was brought up sharply against the superiority of guns
and organizational skills imported from Europe. Darfur fell and southern
Sudan was brought under Egyptian control and divided into two provinces,
Bahr el-Ghazal and Equatoria. Nor was that the end of the khedive's ambitions. His authority spread as far as the Red Sea and Ethiopia, and in
the south nearly as far as Lake Victoria. But Ismail was known as someone
who liked to run before he could walk. The cash for his ambitious policies,
in Egypt as well as in the Sudan, had to come from Europe. The price he
paid for it was taking on European creditors and European ideas. The most
important European idea was the abolition of the slave trade. Ismail was
consistently insincere in his support of this. His endeavors in that direction
were not very successful, nor did they make him popular with his subjects.
In one part of southern Sudan, the Bahr el-Ghazal, his policy failed completely, so much so that the leading slave trader, al-Zubayr, was more or
less able to seize power and to do as he liked. Ismail was forced to put a
good face on this and, as early as 1873, recognized al-Zubayr as governor
of that province. In the other province, Equatoria, his British governor, Sir
Samuel Baker, proved to be more successful.

In Sir Samuel, Ismail found an inspired instrument for realizing his
dreams of an equatorial empire. He had first met him during the opening
of the Suez Canal. Sir Samuel had been asked to accompany the Prince of
Wales there, and more particularly to familiarize the prince with the secrets
of the crocodile hunt. He was a famed big-game hunter, "fearless and an
outstanding shot."[79] In general, he was no stranger to the use of force, and
had stated—euphemistically—that he was no "nigger-worshipper." However, this first European administrator in the African interior also had several more enlightened ideas and believed in the development of Africa's
economic potential. Although lack of finance prevented him from imple-

menting many of his economic plans, his governorship was nevertheless a success story. In particular, Ismail asked him to lead an expedition into southern Sudan to restore Egyptian authority there. Baker and his wife left in 1869, and the British public followed his adventures with rapt attention. Baker advanced so far into the interior that the news service could not keep up with him. People feared for his life. In June 1873, however, a telegram signed by Baker reached England and was read out in both houses of Parliament. It went: "The country as far as the Equator annexed to Egyptian dominion; all rebellious intrigues and slave trade completely put down; country orderly; government perfectly organized; and road open as far as Zanzibar."[80] Baker had not only penetrated the region but brought it under control. These achievements gave Ismail a taste for more, and it was small wonder that after Baker's successes in 1873 he should have chosen another Briton as his successor. This man was such a romantic figure and his death was to prove so heroic that the whole British epic in the Sudan is still evoked by his name: Gordon.

### Gordon

Charles George "Chinese" Gordon (1833–1885) is the most perfect example of the out-and-out Victorian hero, an "eminent Victorian" in the fullest sense of the word. His life was one of heroic deeds in the service of the Empire and of good works for his country. He lived a chaste and Christian life, feared God and always listened to his older sister. He threw himself with unbounded energy into a host of desperate missions, and devoted his free time to the care of what we should nowadays call underprivileged youth. Apart from his alleged addiction to drink, his only weakness—at least in modern eyes—was chain-smoking.

Gordon came from a military family. After attending the Royal Military Academy in Woolwich he obtained a commission in the Royal Engineers. He fought in the Crimean War and was present at the British capture of Peking. He then took service with the Chinese government and helped it to win thirty-three battles against the T'ai P'ing rebels. His troops gained the nickname of the "ever-victorious army" and he himself that of "Chinese" Gordon. In 1874 he became governor of Equatoria, and in 1877 governor-general of the entire Sudan. The khedive offered him a salary of £10,000, but Gordon would accept no more than £2,000. He insisted on this, as he told his sister, to show the khedive and his men "that gold and silver idols are not worshipped by all the world."[81]

As governor, Gordon surrounded himself with European and American assistants and later appointed two Austrians, Schnitzer and Slatin, as provincial governors. That caused a great deal of resentment, as did his struggle against slavery, a struggle with which he was obsessed. Ismail had declared that it would be outlawed by 1880, and Gordon worked like a demon to have this promise implemented. He traveled the country, covering nearly 10,000 miles by camel, raiding the slave markets and arresting the traders. In him and his aides, the spirit of the Crusades seemed to have been reborn. That spirit was not greatly appreciated, not least because the humanitarian crusade had a deleterious effect on the economy. Gordon extended Egyptian authority some fifty miles or more from Lake Victoria, which severely stretched lines of communication. According to him, the southern Sudan could only be developed if a link were opened to the Indian Ocean. For that reason, the khedive, at Gordon's request, equipped an expedition to be sent to Mombasa on the east coast of Africa. Nothing came of this, however, because the British government supported the sultan of Zanzibar against these khedival claims. That the khedive took a very broad view may be gathered from the fact that the distance from Cairo to Mombasa is greater than that from Cairo to the North Cape.

Gordon's administration was not an undivided success. The slave traders were naturally resentful, but ordinary people, too, suffered from the economic consequences of his policies. Moreover, they considered the invasion by Christians a threat to Islam.[82] Gordon was a powerful man and a forceful governor. The same was not true of his master, the khedive, who was deposed and banished in June 1879 after his financial collapse. Gordon resigned in protest in July 1879 and left Khartoum in the hands of his weak Egyptian successor. He had ostensibly kept the area in good order. Uprisings in Kordofan and Darfur had been put down with a strong hand. However, there was a wildfire raging under the relatively calm surface. Resentment at the exploitation by the old "Turkish" governors was reinforced by a hatred of the European invaders that was encouraged by the khedive Ismail. The country was in a turmoil and the people bitterly resentful. Egyptian authority was weak and lacking in self-confidence.[83] That is how things in the Sudan continued until 29 June 1881, when Mohammed Ahmed rose to his feet on the island of Aba and declared that he was the Deliverer.

### THE MAHDI IN THE SUDAN

European history books mention just one mahdi, namely the Sudanese. The Sudanese mahdi was not, however, a unique phenomenon. The idea of the return of a deliverer, a mahdi, can be found in both main branches of Islam, the Shiite as well as the Sunnite.[84] The Sudanese belonged to the second branch. Here, faith in a mahdi may have been challenged by theologians, but not by the common people. They had believed for centuries in the coming of a redeemer sent by God and due to appear toward the end of time when he would be confronting the forces of evil and bringing justice to the earth. In other words, faith in the mahdi is an Islamic form of messianism or millenarianism.[85]

The Sudanese mahdi, Mohammed Ahmed, was born in 1844 on a small island in the Nile in the northern Sudan. In his youth his family moved to a village near Khartoum. They were craftsmen, but this particular descendant felt a strong urge to immerse himself in religious studies. He became a follower of a local religious teacher, and at the age of seventeen joined a mystical order. After seven years he was ready to lead a new religious community. Mohammed Ahmed was famed for his piety, humility and asceticism. He returned to his family, which had again settled on an island, this time little Aba in the White Nile south of Khartoum. This family passion for islands was linked to their occupation as boat builders. The timber they needed was there and, of course, the water. Their young religious son did a great deal of traveling in the Sudan, where he spread his message of world renunciation and religious revival. "Prepare for redemption, pray for God's forgiveness and renounce the world" was his message. But it also had a political side, for the mahdi taught love of the poor at the same time and castigated the rulers for their pride and arrogance.[86]

During this period the future mahdi broke with his teacher. Shortly afterwards he found a disciple, Abdullahi, who would one day be the mahdi's successor, the khalifa. This was something to which he was truly entitled, for it was he who, having fainted twice after beholding his master, first revealed to him that he was the mahdi.[87] The deliverer himself needed time to come to terms with this news, but before long made it known, first to his disciples, and later to a wider circle, though always in secret, that he was indeed the mahdi. It was not until 29 June 1881 that he publicly proclaimed himself as such, not least in letters to various notables in which he made known his new role.[88]

Mahdi Mohammed presented some of the external characteristics a mahdi was supposed to have according to the tradition: a birthmark on his right cheek and a gap between his two front teeth. He also had the right name: Mohammed. His family claimed to be descendants of the prophet. For the rest, the facts could be adapted to the tradition with some imagination. Thus, tradition having it that the mahdi would come from Mount Masa, he accordingly changed the name of the mountain on which he was living from Quadir to Masa.[89]

All this, however, does not fully explain his success. There was a sounder basis. Mahdist expectations in the Sudan were running high. The mahdi was to appear toward the end of the century, and on the Islamic calendar it was then the year 1298, that is, the end of the thirteenth century. There was also much resentment of, and opposition to, the "Turkish" administration, and protests against the low morals of the Egyptian governors.[90] The mahdi therefore found adherents in many different strata of the population: among the religiously inspired, among the slave traders threatened by Ismail's abolitionism, and among the peasants who groaned under Egyptian taxes. The ambitious attempts by the Egyptian administration not only

The Sudanese mahdi

to govern the Sudan but also to reform it, coupled with the internal weakness of that administration, explained a great deal about the phenomenal rise of mahdism. Just like the movement led by Arabi Pasha, the success of the mahdists was due in part to the breakdown of authority after the abdication of Ismail and Gordon's departure that followed.[91]

The weakness of the Egyptian administration was quickly revealed when it tried to suppress the mahdist movement. Two expeditions by the Egyptian army equipped with modern arms ended in crushing defeat following a confrontation with the spears, swords and sticks of the deliverer's adherents. His movement thereafter grew quickly in power and prestige. The message was simple enough: "I am the mahdi, the successor of God's prophet. Stop paying your taxes to the infidel Turks, and let any who come upon a Turk kill him for the Turks are infidels."[92] The mahdi's words were heeded, and the dervishes, as his followers were known, won on all fronts. Their greatest triumph came on 19 January 1883 with the capture of El Obeid, the capital of Kordofan province. It was here that the mahdi set up his headquarters and began to consolidate his new empire.

### THE CRISIS

While the mahdi's impassioned followers had swarmed across the Sudan in 1882, driving off the Egyptian army, the British had occupied Egypt. As a result they had also become involved in the problems of the Egyptian "colony," the Sudan. Gladstone was not unsympathetic to the mahdists. He was in favor of liberation movements and considered the fight of the dervishes in that light. He called them "a people struggling to be free, and rightly struggling to be free."[93] That was not the view of the Egyptian government. Its prestige had been struck an enormous blow by the events of September and was further undermined by what was happening in the Sudan. If Britain were to leave Egypt to its own devices and to withdraw again—and Britain wanted nothing more—then the khedive's authority would have to be restored first, and in the Sudan as well. Nevertheless, there could be no question of Britain, in addition to the burden of the occupation of Egypt, also taking on the job of restoring the khedive's authority over the rebellious dervishes in an area stretching over many thousands of miles. The British government therefore found itself in a dilemma, the consequences of which were to prove anything but negligible.

At first, Britain reacted with indifference. It allowed Egypt to go its own way, looking upon the Sudanese affair as a purely Egyptian matter. The khedive Tewfik was anxious to restore Egyptian prestige by a military success in the Sudan. The British government, not yet used to its new role in Egypt, felt that this was none of its business. On the other hand, it raised no objection to having the expedition commanded by a retired Indian army officer, Colonel William Hicks. The force looked impressive enough on the parade ground: some 10,000 men and 5,000 camels. But Hicks had no experience of the Sudan, and the tension between the few Europeans and the Egyptian officers was great. On 27 September 1883 the advance on El Obeid, the mahdist heartland, began. The deliverer's troops were meanwhile no longer armed with faith alone, but also with guns. On 1 November they poured out of El Obeid to meet the expedition. On 3 November came the first skirmishes, and on 5 November the decisive battle was fought: not so much a battle as a slaughter. The Egyptian troops were mowed down, a mere 250 of them surviving the bloodbath. These included a single European, although not Hicks, who was killed. The Sudan was now in the hands of the mahdi and his "fuzzy-wuzzies," as his soldiers were insultingly called.

The consequences of the defeat were clear. The Sudan would have to be abandoned and the remnants of the Egyptian administration evacuated. The British drew these conclusions more quickly and easily than the Egyptians. The Egyptian prime minister, Sherif Pasha, refused to knuckle under. His successor, Nubar Pasha, on returning to Egypt from exile, did just that. The Sudan was to be evacuated as far as Wadi Halfa. Another British soldier was charged with this operation: General Gordon.

## GORDON'S LAST MISSION

The idea that Gordon would have to go to the Sudan to do "something" about the confused and bleak situation seemed only too obvious. Gordon was the traditional savior in times of need. He was admired in Britain for his heroic struggle against the slave traders, and as far as the press and public opinion were concerned, Gordon was the only man for the job. The government and the top civil servants thought differently, however. Their opinion of Gordon ranged from "impossible" and "eccentric" to "half cracked." They knew that his intellect was as fertile as it was erratic, and that he had an absolute need to be in sole charge. Gordon was not the kind of emissary that ministers and officials care to appoint, but he was the inevitable choice. Gordon could work miracles. If, as it was said, one Englishman was worth twenty "fuzzy-wuzzies," then Gordon was worth a whole army. That at least was the expectation. Gordon was available. True, he had just been asked by King Leopold, at Stanley's suggestion, to go and help Stanley in the Congo, and he had accepted the offer enthusiastically, but his country came first.[94]

Gordon's last mission proved a history of confusion and misunderstandings. The original British plan had been to ask Gordon simply to report on the military situation in the Sudan. However, the British plenipotentiary in Egypt, Sir Evelyn Baring, insisted that Gordon also be put in charge of the evacuation. The instructions with which Gordon left London were ambiguous. He was charged with submitting a report, but was also authorized to carry out such duties as the Egyptian government might delegate to him through Baring.[95] Gordon was not keen on either. What he wanted instead was to save the Sudan, come what may.

On 18 January 1884 Gordon went to Charing Cross station in London to take the boat train to Calais, the first stage on his journey to Cairo and Khartoum. The British government made the occasion a show of respect as well as of great haste. The foreign secretary, Lord Granville, bought Gordon's ticket; Wolseley, Britain's most famous general, carried his luggage; and the Duke of Cambridge, commander-in-chief of the British army and a cousin of Queen Victoria, held the carriage door open for him. When the train was about to leave, Gordon discovered that he had forgotten his money as well as his timepiece. Wolseley emptied his pockets and handed over the contents as well as his gold watch to the traveler. The train then left.

Once on the way, Gordon began to reflect upon his position and the objectives of his mission. He let it be known that he wanted to be made governor-general and that he considered it his task to liberate the Sudanese people. The British government raised no objections, and the khedive did in fact appoint him governor-general after his arrival.[96] Gordon, incidentally, considered that job no more than a stopgap. He thought that the

khedive ought to appoint al-Zubayr to this post in due course. That was
quite a volte-face on Gordon's part, in view of the fact that al-Zubayr had
been the largest slave trader in the Sudan. But Gordon now declared that
he had a "mystic feeling" that al-Zubayr could be trusted.[97] There were,
moreover, rational grounds for the appointment. Gordon felt that al-
Zubayr was the only man who could stand up to the mahdi. He believed
that, notwithstanding his past, al-Zubayr was a better choice for Britain,
for Egypt and for the Sudan than the mahdi.

Gordon left Cairo on 26 January and started to apply his policy, a mixture of evacuation, restoration and reconciliation. He wanted to replace the
Egyptian with a Sudanese administration. To that end, old Sudanese rulers
had to be tracked down and reinstated. He even offered to recognize the
mahdi as governor of Kordofan, and meanwhile sent him a red cloak and
head covering. The mahdi's reply was as dignified as it was haughty:
"Know that I am the Expected Mahdi, the Successor of the Apostle of God.
Thus I have no need of the sultanate, nor of the kingdom of Kordofan or
elsewhere, nor of the wealth of this world and its vanity. I am but the slave
of God. . . . As for the gift which you have sent Us, may God reward you
well for your good-will and guide you to the right. It is returned to you
herewith."[98] That did not bode well. Gordon now changed his policy of
reconciliation for one of confrontation: the mahdi would have to be
crushed.

Responsibility for developments in the Sudan had thus come to rest entirely with Gordon and not with the government in London. Gordon now
interpreted his evacuation task as demanding his presence in Khartoum
until everyone who wanted to leave the Sudan had been given a chance to
do so. On 13 March 1884 the native population north of Khartoum chose
the mahdi's side. Communications with Egypt were cut off, and in particular the telegraph line was brought down. Gordon was isolated. The siege
of Khartoum had begun. The British government's hand had been forced.
Prayers were said for Gordon in churches throughout Britain, and there
were demonstrations in the streets. The British public clamored for a relief
expedition. On 5 August 1884 Parliament voted the necessary credits, but
the expedition, led by Gordon's friend Wolseley, did not leave until 8 January 1885. That was too late. On 26 January the mahdists launched their
decisive attack, a defector from Khartoum having shown them a weak spot
in the defenses. Within a few hours the town had fallen and Gordon was
dead. The mahdists dipped their spears in his blood, severed his head, and
carried it to Slatin in Omdurman for identification. On 30 January the
mahdi entered the sacked capital, but his stay was not prolonged. Khartoum became a dead city. The mahdi state was to have its capital a few
miles away, in Omdurman (City of Pearls), where the mahdi established
his seat, although he himself was not to reign there for long. On 22 June

View of Khartoum

Gordon's death

Gordon's head being shown to Slatin for identification

1885, shortly after his triumph, he died of mysterious causes (typhus, small-pox or poisoning) at the age of forty.

On 5 February 1885 the news reached London that Khartoum had fallen and that Gordon had been killed. The queen was deeply shocked, as was the whole nation. Gladstone was given the blame. He was compared to Pontius Pilate and to Judas Iscariot, and his nickname of the GOM—the Grand Old Man—was changed to the MOG—the Murderer of Gordon.[99] Gordon windows were installed in churches and cathedrals, Gordon clubs for boys were founded, a Gordon statue was erected in Trafalgar Square, and a Gordon monument put up in St. Paul's cathedral. Gordon's family was awarded a handsome pension. There matters rested. In an impulsive reaction, the cabinet gave Wolseley orders to challenge the mahdi and if possible to recapture Khartoum, but that was more an upwelling of senti-ment than a change in policy. In a subsequent debate in the House of Commons, Gladstone made it clear that he had no intention of keeping Britain in Egypt, let alone retaking the Sudan. Government policy was still to withdraw from Egypt as soon as conditions allowed, and to evacuate the Sudan.

In April 1885, when tempers had cooled and other imperial concerns— above all on the northwest frontier of India—were uppermost in people's minds, the government gave orders to stop all offensive actions in the Sudan. Lord Salisbury's Conservative government, which in June 1885 took over from Gladstone's for a brief span, did nothing to change that policy, notwithstanding its earlier protestations. The frontier of Egypt was drawn where it had been before Mohammed Ali had started Egypt's adventure in the Sudan, that is, near Wadi Halfa, on the second cataract.

Now started a period of great expansion by the mahdist state under the mahdi's successor, the khalifa Abdullahi, the man who had discovered the mahdi. This expansion was directed to all four points of the compass: to the west, where Darfur was captured; to the east, where the Ethiopians were defeated; to the north, where Anglo-Egyptian border troops were challenged, although without much success; and to the south. Only in the west did it meet with opposition. There the mahdists clashed with another expansionist force, the rulers of the Congo Free State.

Two years after Gordon's death, the mahdists were firmly established. The expeditions dispatched against them had been beaten back. The khalifa reigned over an empire half the size of Europe. He wrote a letter to Queen Victoria inviting her to come to Omdurman, to submit, and to convert to Islam. Similar letters were addressed to the khedive and the sultan of Turkey. Envoys took these letters to Cairo, and were told that the monarchs had no wish to reply.

# 6
# CONCLUSION

France began the partition of Africa. Whether we date this beginning to the new policy in West Africa or to the occupation of Tunisia, the French were the first. Nor was the policy altogether new. French intervention in Senegal was the resumption of an older policy of conquest, the incursion into Tunisia the logical consequence of the occupation of Algeria and of growing European interest in that country. That Tunisia would some day fall into the European sphere of influence had been apparent, but not that it would become French. The competing Powers kept one another in check for a time, but after the Congress of Berlin Britain had to offer France something in exchange for Cyprus. Tunisia was suggested, and Bismarck agreed. Against all the odds, therefore, the Regency went, not to Italy, but to France.

The French presence in Tunisia was thus the result of a number of special circumstances: the consent, indeed the encouragement, of the Powers, a patriotic lobby, and above all an auspicious political situation. To strike during an election year was a daring feat, but in the event it succeeded. A year later, during the Egyptian crisis, things were different and the French government held off. The British, for their part, did strike on that occasion. This came as a surprise. Traditionally, Great Britain considered that the greatest strategic threat in the eastern Mediterranean came from Russia and that this threat would have to be warded off from Constantinople, not from Cairo. But this did not mean that Great Britain had to allow Egypt to become a French sphere of influence. After all, Britain had considerable financial and commercial interests in that country, and then of course there was the Suez Canal.[100] British policy was accordingly aimed at maintaining the status quo in Egypt. That, however, proved impossible. Growing European influence inevitably transformed internal conditions, modernization altered the social structure, and the debt question influenced Egypt's foreign relations. The establishment of Anglo-French "dual control" of Egyptian finances in 1876 was a consequence of the last of these factors, the revolution of Arabi Pasha in 1888 the result of the first.

The hard-liners in the British cabinet insisted that something be done about it. But what? Gladstone would have liked to restore the Porte's authority. That solution appealed to his legalistic mind. However, it was unacceptable to France, which feared that it might pave the way for a Turkish return to Tunisia. For the British cabinet, the preservation of the Anglo-French entente, and in its wake international approval of joint Anglo-French intervention in the name of a European consensus, was of prime importance. French unilateral action had to be avoided at any cost. The French wanted to intervene. Gladstone was painfully surprised by the lack of liberal conviction shown by his fellow liberal Gambetta, and by the latter's refusal to stand by the parliamentary movement in Egypt. "Think of Bismarck & the Turk fighting the battle of representative and popular principles against us!" he wrote to Granville, his foreign secretary.[101] Conditions at home, however, left him no choice. Reluctantly, he followed his French colleague along the path of intervention. The fact that at the crucial moment France failed to turn up was also a consequence of domestic politics, this time in France. Gambetta's cabinet fell on 27 January 1882 over the question of electoral reform. Freycinet, his successor, was afraid to take the risk, and rightly so. The French Chamber was not in favor.

The British cabinet had thus to make a solitary decision, though it cannot be properly called a decision. Britain's hand was being forced by the British representatives in Egypt who had been at the receiving end of Arabi's challenge, and who now had the choice either of striking back or of allowing themselves to be humiliated. Put like that, the decision was not hard to make. The crucial fact was that, thanks to the Anglo-French alliance on the one hand and local initiatives on the other, Britain had no alternative to military intervention.

The Egyptian question was dominated by Anglo-French rivalry. That, incidentally, did not mean that the other Powers had no interest in the matter. The sublime but bankrupt Porte did not, of course, play a significant part. Its sovereignty was invoked or overridden as the situation demanded. Italy and Russia stood on the sidelines, gnashing their teeth and powerless. For as long as Britain and France steered the same course and Bismarck gave his blessing to this tandem, they had but one role to play, that of spectator. That much the 1878 Congress of Berlin had, in any case, made clear. Bismarck had no objection to the turn affairs were taking. He did not want to see France humiliated further, but neither did he want to see it strengthened. As for Great Britain, he was pleased to hold out a protective hand over what he considered to be its legitimate business in a region where German interests were as good as nonexistent. British friendship was certainly worth that much. Thus in 1882 Great Britain stepped inadvertently and reluctantly into Egypt, and so matters would remain until 1951. That had certainly not been the intention. Great Britain wanted a neutral and independent Egypt without French influence and under informal British control. Even the French—beaten rivals though they were—did not believe that Britain had intended to establish itself in Egypt all by itself and permanently so. In 1877 Britain sent the diplomat Sir Henry Drummond-Wolff to Istanbul offering a British evacuation and the restoration of direct Turkish rule over Egypt. The sultan was afraid that this might lead to even greater interference by Britain in Turkey, and he accordingly declined. Various British governments repeated the promise given by Gladstone's administration, namely, that Britain would withdraw from Egypt at the earliest possible opportunity. Between 1882 and 1922 this promise was repeated sixty-six times.[102] It was given by word of mouth and in writing and enshrined in conventions, but never put into practice, for the "earliest possible opportunity" meant that peace, order and security had to be guaranteed, and these conditions never prevailed. Great Britain remained in Egypt as an occupying power and de facto ruler, but one whose legal position was not defined until 18 December 1914, when Egypt became a British protectorate.

Its occupation of Egypt placed Great Britain in a difficult position: it became responsible for the country's finances, then in a perilous state. To remedy the situation the financial system would have to be changed. Revenues that should have been paid into the Caisse de la Dette Publique for the benefit of bondholders would have to be diverted into the treasury, which could only be done with the consent of the Powers involved in the settlement of the debt. On 28 June 1884 the British government convened a conference in London in an attempt to find a solution to this problem.

The attempt failed, mainly because of the opposition of Bismarck and Ferry.

In March 1885, however, agreement was finally reached. The new regulations, laid down in the London Convention of that year, amounted to continued international supervision of Egypt's finances. The Caisse de la Dette was continued but enlarged with a Russian and a German member. France and Great Britain together thus no longer held the majority, and Germany came in practice to occupy a key position. It could now, if it wanted, put Great Britain under pressure by waving its "Egyptian stick." It was yet another problem for Britain. All extra revenue—what was left over after paying the bondholders' coupons and covering the minimum state expenses—had to be divided between state and debtors. This meant that if the administrators of Egypt wanted to spend ten pounds on improving roads or the army, they had to raise twenty pounds in taxes. That was something not even the able financier Sir Evelyn Baring, who pulled the financial and other strings in Egypt as British agent and consul general from 1883 to 1907, was able to accomplish. Egypt's finances thus never recovered. This particular arrangement was not the better of two evils for Great Britain, but rather a combination of two evils: sole political responsibility, but financial dependence on the agreement of other countries. The Whigs in Gladstone's cabinet were opposed to the arrangement, but they were outvoted by the progressive members of the cabinet. The latter did not worry overmuch about the disadvantages because they did not mean Great Britain to stay very long in Egypt. For them the good relations with France following this settlement were more important than the drawbacks. The London Convention presented various British governments with a difficult dilemma: either the British taxpayer had to pick up the Egyptian bill, with all the electoral consequences that entailed, or else the Powers must be made to "clip the coupons," with all the diplomatic consequences stemming from that. Britain had become the prisoner of Egypt.

France could not stomach the loss of its influence in Egypt, and it refused to recognize the British occupation. For more than twenty years it would try to reopen the Egyptian question, to challenge Britain on the Nile and to seek compensation elsewhere. Britain, for its part, felt compelled to protect not only Egypt but also Egypt's lifeline, the Nile. Its influence spread, first to the Sudan, then to the great lakes, and finally, as Gladstone on one somber occasion had predicted it would, as far as the Cape and Zanzibar.

The British occupation of Egypt, unwanted and unplanned though it was, thus had a marked influence on the partition of Africa. It determined its course and its form. However, it was not its cause. For that would have meant that, without the Egyptian question, there would have been no partition of Africa, which is of course nonsense. The trend of enmeshing the black continent in the European diplomatic network was irresistible. The desire for a slice of the African cake was alive not only in Great Britain and in France but also, and increasingly so, in other countries. Their rivalry would make itself felt all over Africa. Great Britain had put this process in motion. Before long it would be accelerated, thanks to the actions of France and of King Leopold of Belgium.

# II

# THE CONGO AND THE CREATION OF THE FREE STATE, 1882–1885

*Nous devons être à la fois prudents,
habiles et prompts à agir . . .
[afin de] nous procurer une part
de ce magnifique gâteau africain.*

We must be careful, skillful
and ready to act . . .
[to] get us a slice of
this magnificent African cake.

Leopold II

In the 1870s the Congo was "discovered" by Europeans. The travels of Brazza (1875–1878) and above all those of Stanley (1874–1877) captured the imagination of a European public avid for knowledge. Geographical societies enjoyed great popularity. Stanley's journey was sponsored by two newspapers, one English and the other American. His account of his expedition through Africa, entitled *Through the Dark Continent*, became an international bestseller. In it Stanley extolled the great promise of the Congo, which he said was more fertile than the Mississippi valley, and spoke of a "new India," highly suited to trade and colonization. In addition to scientific and commercial considerations, however, there were also humanitarian motives for opening up the region. The slave trade, cannibalism and paganism in this part of Africa were rife, inviting European intervention. Central Africa thus became the object of keen European interest, not least politically. This was a novel development, since scarcely anything had been known until then about the region save that it was dreaded for its appalling climate.

The Congo region is part of what goes by the name of Central or Middle Africa, a somewhat confusing label because it can be applied in different ways. Broadly speaking, it refers to the area between the Sudan and South Africa, stretching from Cameroon to Angola in the west, and from Mogadishu to Mozambique in the east. The term is seldom used in that sense, however, because the area east of the great lakes is usually treated as part of East Africa. In fact, therefore, what we are particularly concerned with here is the western part. The center of the area consists of tropical rainforest. To the north lies savannah and to the south a zone of open forest. The whole of this region is dominated by the Congo or Zaire, a river which, with a length of some 3,000 miles, is one of the longest in Africa. Its basin, too, is immense, the river drawing its water from an area measuring nearly 1.5 million square miles, that is, from an area bigger than India. At Boma the river discharges into an estuary which, though wide, is no match for the gigantic deltas of the Niger and the Nile. Upstream the Congo quickly becomes unnavigable because of the large cataracts at Matadi. The region has a sparse population characterized by great variety. More than 200 languages are spoken, and there were once hundreds of independent communities. There were no large towns and markets, no riches to attract traders from distant parts. Economic life was not very highly developed, consisting as it did, in addition to hunting and gathering, of nomadic animal husbandry and sedentary agriculture.

Little is known about the political history of the region. Our sources are scant, and African historiography is in its infancy. Historians distinguish various kingdoms such as those of Lunda and Luba, but our knowledge of these is limited. In the nineteenth century the eastern part was largely dominated by traders and colonists from East Africa, at the time referred to as "Arabs," though they were in fact what we nowadays call Swahilis, that is, East Africans from an area nominally under the control of the sultan of Zanzibar. The leading potentate in the area, the man who had subjected a large part of eastern Zaire, was Hamed ibn-Mohammed, better known as Tippu Tip.

Tippu Tip (1837–1905) was born in Zanzibar. His father was Arab, his mother Swahili. He had gone to the Congo at an early age, and founded his empire on the Lualaba. From about 1870 to 1890 Tippu Tip was the most powerful man in the eastern Congo. His lieutenants ransacked large parts of the country in search of ivory and slaves, while he presided over a veritable regime of terror. Tippu Tip was nominally answerable to the sultan of Zanzibar, and when Europeans began to penetrate the region he did his utmost to have the sultan's sovereignty over the interior recognized by the Great Powers, an attempt which failed. He then decided to side with Leopold II, on whose behalf he governed the eastern Congo from 1887 to 1892. The great slave trader thus entered the service of the great antislavery champion.[1]

European interest was in the main, of course, focused on the western Congo. It went back to 1482, when the Portuguese navigator Diogo Cão first came across the mouth of the Congo. In 1485, during another voyage, he sailed up the Congo as far as Matadi. In 1492 and 1493 the Portuguese advanced as far as what is now called Pool Malebo—formerly known as Stanley Pool—where Leopoldville (Kinshasa) would later rise up. Europeans were not to advance much further in the next few centuries. The Portuguese came into contact with the king of the Congo, whom they were able to convert to Christianity. His kingdom was considerable in size, taking in all of northern Angola and parts of the Congo and Gabon. Relations were given a fresh boost with the rise of the Atlantic slave trade, that part of the African west coast becoming an important slaving center. The slave trade, however, aroused increasing moral revulsion, and its economic importance decreased with the advent of the industrial revolution. In 1804 the Danes, then ensconced in West Africa, were the first to ban the slave trade. More significantly, the British followed suit in 1807—at the time of the Napoleonic wars when the British navy ruled the seas—and the British seized the slave ships, freeing the slaves. The British colony of Sierra Leone was settled with these freed black slaves, as the name of its capital, Freetown, reminds us. The French set up so-called *villages de liberté* for their former slaves, and in 1848 founded a French Freetown, Libreville, in Gabon. The struggle against slavery was, however, long and arduous. Following the Napoleonic wars, the slave trade even expanded, and until the 1860s slaves continued to be shipped across the Atlantic. In the first half of the nineteenth century slavery was still big business, dominated by the Portuguese. About one-half of all slaves came from the Angola-Congo region.[2]

Between 1858 and 1878, when slavery was in the gradual process of being abolished, even in the Portuguese colonies, a legitimate form of trade developed in these parts: trade in agricultural products. Just as in West Africa, it was based mainly on palm oil and palm kernels and to a lesser extent on ivory and rubber. Many trading companies were set up on the coast or in the Congo delta. The French and Portuguese, but also the British and Dutch, were involved, the last two being the most successful. In political terms, however, France and Portugal dominated the coast. The Portuguese sphere of influence in particular was very extensive, stretching as far as Cabinda to the north of the Congo and to the south of it from Ambriz to Benguela, and later to Mossâmedes, which they founded in 1840. Luanda was the center, the only genuinely European town between Senegal and Cape Town. The French were to be found mainly to the north, on the coast of Gabon, although the French colony had declined to such an extent by about 1860 that the French seriously thought of abandoning it. Matters never came to that, however.

As elsewhere in Africa, there were thus several European settlements along the coast of central Africa during the nineteenth century. The usual pattern was for Europeans to consolidate their respective spheres of influence on the coast and then extend their authority to the hinterland. That would in all likelihood have been the case here as well, if an extraordinary phenomenon had not arisen: the emergence in the 1880s, out of nothing as it were, of a European colony in the African interior. Here the Belgian king, Leopold II, founded, not as king but as a private individual, a state the borders of which he was able to persuade the European Powers to recognize. As a result the French and Portuguese colonies on the coast were prevented from expanding inland, their path blocked by the newly formed Congo Free State, later to be the Belgian Congo, and later still Zaire, the second largest state in Africa. This extraordinary development came about as the result of the obsessions, ambitions and political genius of just one man, King Leopold II of Belgium.

# 1
# BELGIUM AND LEOPOLD II

## BELGIUM AND THE COLONIES

Of the many strange events that occurred during the partition of Africa, events in the Congo were perhaps the most incongruous. The upshot of all the confusions surrounding them was that Belgium, one of the smallest countries in Europe, acquired one of the largest and richest colonies in Africa, and that despite the fact that Belgium had decided to have no truck with colonies.

In nineteenth-century Europe Belgium was an unusual phenomenon. Before 1830 it did not exist as an independent state, but was part of the Kingdom of the Netherlands, founded in 1814. Its creation reflected the anti-revolutionary sentiments of the Powers and their determination to keep France in check. Nationalism, however, appeared to be stronger than this objective, and the United Kingdom of the Netherlands broke up, after a brief and not very harmonious union, to the relatively muted accompaniment of operatic music and scuffles in the streets. The Belgian rebels of 1830 were politically inspired by liberal and nationalist ideals, but needed a monarchist state to render their objectives acceptable to Palmerston and Metternich, the legitimist and anti-revolutionary guardians of the European peace. They chose as their candidate for the throne a man who might have become the British prince consort had his wife not died prematurely, and king of Greece had he wanted to. But Leopold of Saxe-Coburg wanted no such thing; what he had set his sights on was the Belgian throne, and he discharged his exalted duties with as much zest as success.

His kingdom was and is small but not insignificant. Belgium's strategic position was important enough to preoccupy the Powers, and Great Britain in particular, so important in fact that they guaranteed its neutrality by treaty. Economically, the situation of Belgium was no less remarkable. The population was not large. In 1865 the country had nearly 5 million inhabitants, but that number was to rise fairly quickly. Belgium was one of the most highly developed countries in Europe, a land of railroads, mines and blast furnaces. One-third of the population was engaged in industry. The Belgian economy was open and vulnerable and affected by the turbulent fluctuations of the European economic climate. This meant that in 1865, when Leopold II acceded to the throne, Belgium became sucked into the great economic boom, only to be drawn then into the long depression that lasted from 1873 until the end of the century.

Although the Scheldt was open once more to navigation and the maritime activity of Antwerp was far from negligible, Belgium was geared more to industry than to trade, to the continent than to overseas business. In that respect, it differed from its northern neighbor. Moreover—and that was another great difference—it had no colonies. There were a number of reasons for this. To begin with, the new liberal economic doctrine taught that colonies served no purpose. The old monopolistic practices were anathema to the new disciples of free trade. If colonies, according to the economic gospel of the day, had to be open to the services and goods of all countries, then they were nothing but a burden to the home country, which after all had to pick up the bill for administration and defense without receiving very much in return. In the middle and also during the third quarter of the nineteenth century, anticolonialism was a trend to be reckoned with. Not only did such small countries as the Netherlands and Denmark reject the possession of African colonies as futile, but such big countries as Great Britain and France were giving consideration to doing the same. Belgium had additional reasons for eschewing colonial adventures: it lacked a navy to protect any overseas possessions. Were it to take any bull-like steps into that international china shop it might easily jeopardize its neutrality, and hence its very existence. Its attempt at colonization in Guatemala in 1845 had proved a fiasco. Small wonder, then, that Belgium was an anticolonial country.

### LEOPOLD II

The second king of the Belgians had different ideas, however. Leopold II (1835–1909) was a strange character. To begin with, he was a man of gargantuan proportions. He was big and had big ideas, albeit he often acted in petty ways. He was tall and sturdily built, with a flowing beard and far too large a nose, of which his mother spoke slightingly.[3] The love she bore him was not very great, but considerable by comparison with that of his father, whom he was not allowed to see without a formal request for an audience. Not surprisingly, then, Leopold lavished his own overflowing affections on persons outside his marriage and family circle. His appetite was as insatiable in bed as it was at the table—and as indiscriminate. The precise number of his mistresses was unknown, but only too well known were his countless visits to brothels, where his predilection for minors caused a scandal even in a world renowned for its tolerance of royal excesses. For Leopold this turned out to be a special advantage: his reputation was so scandalous as to disguise the fact that his many visits to the capitals of Europe had objectives beyond the untiring search for new sensations in bed or at the table.

Leopold felt no less passionate about and generous to his country than he did about some of his mistresses. In a sense he forced his love even upon Belgium. Unlike other mistresses, however, his subjects put up some resistance.

From early youth, Leopold had taken a keen interest in everything connected with trade, navigation and overseas expansion. His model was the

King Leopold II

Netherlands, particularly the Dutch possessions in the East, and quite especially Java. On 17 February 1860 he delivered his first great speech to the Belgian senate, where, as heir to the throne, he had had a seat ever since his eighteenth birthday. The subject of this maiden speech was the encouragement of overseas trade and exports. He concluded with a veiled but unmistakable plea for colonial expansion. His evocation of the glorious past of the great trading companies ended with a reference to the profits Java was then pouring into Dutch coffers.[4]

This was the first of Leopold's many professions of faith, the beginning of a long but vain missionary campaign among his compatriots. It was also the result of Leopold's long intellectual preparation as Duke of Brabant. His interest in overseas countries dated back to his honeymoon in Egypt and the Near East, where he had gaped in admiration at the spectacular projects and plans for dams and canals. During the ten years between his minority and his accession to the throne in 1865 he had spent much time weighing up the chances of a Belgian incursion into the same field. His alacrity reflected the lack of discrimination so characteristic of him in other fields. Young Leopold expressed his thoughts so openheartedly that their very shamelessness had something disarming about it. His many correspondents were swamped with suggestions and enticements, with questions and requests. "Are the Philippines for sale?" he asked a Spanish correspondent. "Would you perhaps consider organizing an expedition to China?" he wrote to Queen Victoria, offering her Belgian troops as an afterthought. His mentality was more that of a buccaneer or a mafioso than of a king. Thus he wrote in 1859, "Incredible riches are to be found in Japan. The Emperor's treasury is immense and *poorly guarded.*" The emphasis was his own.[5]

Leopold's thinking bore witness to so crude an exploitative drive that it is astonishing how successful he was in putting up a facade of virtue, investing the start of his African adventure with an aura of missionary and philanthropic beneficence shammed with masterly skill. The turning point on his path to a more down-to-earth, but no less self-seeking, colonial doctrine came in 1861. At the end of that year Leopold came across a book that provided him with fresh ammunition for his colonial ideas, J.W.B. Money's *Java or How to Manage a Colony.* The author was a British lawyer who in 1858, after a four-year stay in India, had traveled to Java, mainly because he had heard that it was a beautiful island, "with a fine climate, easy travelling and an opera."[6] But Money found more than that in Java. He was particularly impressed by the achievements of the Dutch colonial administration and especially by the cultivation system, which poured impressive funds into the Dutch treasury. Money hoped that his book might serve as a lesson for his British compatriots in India. In that it failed. The Dutch agricultural policy, based as it was on forced labor and state monopoly, was far too illiberal, too much in conflict with the spirit of the times to appeal to Britain, that bulwark of free trade and free enterprise. For the illustrious reader in Brussels, however, the book proved to be a godsend. Java was to become his great model, his colonial paradigm. "Java," he wrote, "is an inexhaustible gold mine. The question can therefore be put as follows: is it advantageous to own a gold mine?"[7]

At first, his thoughts focused on the East. "Do you know of an island in Oceania, the China Sea or the Indian Ocean, which might suit us?" he asked a Belgian naval officer in 1861.[8] He also had a penchant for Borneo; at a later stage, New Guinea was to attract his attention, and so were Formosa, Tonkin, Sumatra and others. One after the other they led to plans, projects, probes, all of which ultimately came to nothing. Following Leopold's accession to the throne, however, a marked change took place.[9] The end remained the same, namely, to give Belgium a colony, but the means were different. Leopold now realized that his country, or at least his government, wanted nothing to do with colonial expansion. *Fortiter in re, suaviter in modo* (strong as far as the principle is concerned, but flexible in the execution), he remained true to his dream, but changed his tack. From now on he would operate as a private individual, with the prestige of sovereignty and his family fortune behind him of course, but free of government and parliamentary constraints. A constitutional prince in Belgium, an independent entrepreneur outside—such was Leopold's new strategy.

In 1869 he wrote grandly, "I promise solemnly to ask nothing from the Minister of Finance."[10] He did not quite keep that promise, but it was indeed the basis of his further operations. Henceforth these would take place in a unique world of societies and committees, companies and enterprises founded by himself. In name always international and almost always philanthropic, they became increasingly opaque and complex in practice. "L'Union fait la force"—"Unity is strength"—is the motto of the Belgian state. But Leopold himself lived more in accord with words taken from Schiller's *Wilhelm Tell*: "Der Starke ist am mächtigsten allein"—"The strong is mightiest alone."

## 2
# THE BRUSSELS CONFERENCE AND ITS CONSEQUENCES

All Leopold's colonial ambitions in the Indian and Pacific oceans having come to nothing, he eventually acquired a colony in the heart of darkest Africa, an area in which there seemed to be small scope for modern agricultural methods or surpluses. Thus a yawning gap lay between the king's dream and the reality. Leopold had come by a colony he had never dreamed of, and one in which he, great traveler though he was, would never set foot. The history of this strange course of events is a tale full of surprises, coincidences, changes of tack and turns of fate.

It is hard to tell precisely when it was that Leopold first turned his thoughts to Africa. As early as 1863 he mentioned a Belgian "domain" that might be set up, "be it in China, be it in Japan, be it in Borneo, be it in Central America, be it on the coast of Africa."[11] A wide choice, indeed. In 1873 there was a plan for, or at least the idea of, founding an East Africa Company in Portuguese Mozambique and then taking over the territory in which it traded.[12] However, for the time being this African domain was not to be taken wholly seriously. Until 1875 Leopold's thoughts remained fixed on far horizons in the East. The reluctance of the colonial powers to respond to Leopold's somewhat indiscreet advances was so great, however, that even the impetuous and persistent king grew discouraged. On 22 August 1875 he wrote to his confidant, Auguste Lambermont, that the Spanish authorities would not hear of ceding the Philippines—his old dream. The situation seemed bleak. "Neither the Spaniards, nor the Portuguese, nor yet the Hollanders are prepared to sell. I am planning to find out discreetly if there is anything to do in Africa."[13] Although not everything was to happen very discreetly, Leopold did find "something to do" in Africa in the years to come.

### EXPLORATION AND EXPLORERS

That Africa was gradually to attract Leopold's attention need not surprise us. In the 1870s Africa was as exciting a destination as the moon was in the 1960s. It was also very nearly as unknown. There were fewer travelers in Africa then than there are astronauts today, and they were at least as famous. The most famous of them all were of course Livingstone, Stanley and Brazza.

David Livingstone (1813–1873), physician, missionary and explorer, had little to do with the partition of Africa in the narrow sense, though the problem that occupied him during the last years of his life certainly did. Livingstone had been on a number of great journeys—his travels through Africa from Luanda on the west coast to Quilimane on the east coast constituted the most famous of these—before he decided to explore the sources of the Nile in 1866. During one of his journeys in 1871 he followed the course of the Lualaba, the long and mighty river which is in fact the western headstream of the Congo. Livingstone, however, was convinced that it was a continuation of the Nile. He was mistaken, but the result was that central Africa became the focus of the exploration effort, to be probed from West Africa as well as from East Africa.

Livingstone had crossed Africa from west to east. The first explorer to cross the continent from east to west was Lovett Cameron. It took him two and a half years to cut through from Bagamoyo in East Africa to the west coast, arriving in Luanda at the mouth of the Congo on 22 November 1875. He had not managed to follow the Lualaba and the Congo all the way—something Stanley was to do soon afterwards—but he had become convinced that the Lualaba was the continuation of the Congo and not of the Nile. In passing, he took possession of these regions for Britain in the name of the queen, but he had not counted on mid-Victorian revulsion for colonial obligations. That feeling was still strong enough at the time to lead to the rejection of all such annexations out of hand. The last thing Great Britain needed, the Foreign Office opined, was more jungles and more savages.[14]

The man who continued Cameron's work, Henry Morton Stanley, was to become the most famous explorer of his day and the greatest in the history of African exploration. He gained his fame above all as "the man who found Livingstone," but he has remained famous as the man who uttered the bizarre, "Dr. Livingstone, I presume." The life of this unusual man has been the subject of many biographies.

Henry Morton Stanley (1841–1904), whose real name was John Rowlands, was born on 28 January 1841 in Denbigh, Wales. The baptismal register states that his mother's name was Elizabeth Parry and that John Rowlands acknowledged paternity. Although this seems clear enough, the word "bastard" was added to make doubly certain. John Rowlands was a farmer and a drunkard, Elizabeth Parry a butcher's daughter who worked as a maid in London and now and then returned to her native village to be confined. She was to have another three illegitimate children, and accordingly earned a certain reputation in her birthplace. John Rowlands junior was first boarded out with his grandfather, and after the latter's death with neighbors. This arrangement proving unsatisfactory, in 1847 the boy was sent to the St. Asaph Union Workhouse, nowadays still in use as the H. M. Stanley Hospital. Charles Dickens has left us a description of the nineteenth-century workhouse as poignant as Dante's description of hell, and the resemblance between the two was indeed remarkable. Not surprisingly, the boy ran away from the place. After some wanderings he signed on in December 1858 as a cabin boy on a ship bound for New Orleans.

In America he discovered not only a new homeland but also a new father in the person of a rich cotton merchant, Henry Hope Stanley. This man adopted the young Welshman, who from his nineteenth year took the name Henry Morton Stanley. The old merchant died intestate just as the American Civil War broke out, and Stanley did not therefore go into the family business. He fought at first with the South, was taken prisoner, and then re-enlisted with the North. His true calling, however, was not soldiering but being a war correspondent. In this capacity he made a name for himself, but when the Civil War was over there was not much to report in America, and he became a roving reporter. He saw Spain, Ethiopia, Greece, Turkey—at the time there were wars, expeditions and adventures enough. Then his new employer, the owner of the *New York Herald*, gave him the assignment that was to make him famous: "Find Livingstone."

Livingstone was the darling of the British public, mainly thanks to his noble fight against the slave trade and his missionary fervor, albeit he converted only one African, who later abandoned his faith.[15] Like so many others, Livingstone had searched eagerly for the sources of the Nile and, again like so many others, in the wrong place. In 1870, after years of searching, he had vanished into the wilderness without a sign of life. Early in 1871 Stanley left from Zanzibar to start his great adventure. On 10 November 1871 he did at long last find Livingstone, and spoke the words that were to take their place among the most famous in history. After the meeting, glasses were raised with the champagne Stanley carried on all his travels. On 14 March 1872 the paths of the two explorers parted again. Stanley returned to the civilized world; Livingstone, in bad health, remained behind, determined to continue the search for the sources of the Nile. He died in May 1873. That month, Stanley returned to the coast a famous man. Soon afterwards he set out on the great journey that would make him even more famous. On behalf of the *New York Herald* and the *Daily Telegraph* he led what became known as the "Anglo-American" expedition, a journey from coast to coast intended to solve all the remaining mysteries. How big was Lake Victoria? Was it the source of the Nile? Was the Lualaba, discovered by Livingstone, the headstream of the Nile, of the Congo or of the Niger?

Stanley claimed to have completed the journey in precisely 999 days; the actual figure was 1,002. He reached Boma, in the Congo estuary, on 9 August 1877. For the history of the Congo this journey was of first importance. Stanley had shown that, past Stanley Pool, the river provided excellent access to central Africa. He recognized a great opportunity here for his native Britain, which had always remained dear to him but which held him in little esteem in return. Stanley's reputation was far from spotless. Unlike the universally revered Livingstone, he was considered a dubious character. His achievements might be impressive, but his methods were open to question. During his expedition he often acted ruthlessly. He himself traveled in almost boundless luxury. He never went anywhere without a portable bed, a silver toilet set and ample supplies of champagne.

The British did not think very highly of Stanley in other respects, either. His looks were not very striking. He was short, corpulent, and had a red face. Queen Victoria called him "a determined, ugly, little man—with a strong American twang."[16] His manners were vulgar. But he was strong and exceptionally healthy, and was as a rule the only white man to survive the expeditions he led. A famous photograph depicts him as the superman, Bula Matari, the "Breaker of Rocks." The British Geographical Society at first considered him a charlatan, but was later to acknowledge its error. Stanley's poor reputation in Britain was due not least to his enmity with John Kirk, the British consul and uncrowned viceroy in Zanzibar who had much that was unfavorable to say about him, and called Stanley's journey "a disgrace to humanity."[17] A great deal was written about the harshness and brutality of Stanley's actions, and there was much speculation about his character, the deficiencies in which were not surprising in a man with his childhood experiences. He is said to have been aggressive and domineering, but also sentimental, hypersensitive, unbusinesslike and frustrated. "Repressed homosexual" and "sado-masochist" are but two of the many epithets used about him.[18]

Kirk's campaign and the lack of interest in Africa's interior shown by Disraeli and Salisbury explain the cool reception Stanley's plans received in Great Britain. The warm attention paid him by King Leopold must therefore have been balm for the soul of the hard-pressed explorer. Stanley entered Leopold's service and stayed with the king until 1885, after which he was to lead the Emin Pasha Relief Expedition before returning to his beloved Britain. He gave lectures all over the world and became a member of the House of Commons and even of the Athenaeum Club. In 1899 he was knighted. He married, adopted a child and retired to a country estate in Surrey, turning its garden into a mini-Free State, complete with jungle and Stanley Pool. Stanley's taste continued to be controversial. He died in 1904.

Our third Congo explorer, Savorgnan de Brazza, was an entirely different type. Brazza (1852–1905) was a man with as confusing a background as Stanley's, albeit a very different one. While Stanley was an illegitimate child, brought up and kept down in a British workhouse, Brazza was the son of a Roman nobleman, grew up in a prosperous and respected home, and enjoyed patronage all his life. Just as Stanley was a British citizen who became a naturalized American but remained a British patriot, so Brazza, too, was a man torn between two countries: an Italian with a fiery French patriotism, who was never to be accepted in his chosen milieu, the French navy.

Pierre Savorgnan de Brazza was born in Rome in 1852, the seventh son in a family of twelve. His father and a friend of the family, the French admiral Louis de Montaignac, steered the young man's interest toward the navy—the French navy, that is—at an early age. That was because no Italian navy existed at the time, any more than Italy did itself. His parents were ardent supporters of the Pope and hence opposed to the House of Savoy. They did not want Pierre to serve in Victor Emmanuel's fleet, and unfortunately there was no papal equivalent. All the same the Roman Catholic Church did its best to advance the career of this young Roman gentleman, the papal nuncio in Paris acting as his faithful protector.[19] Fate, moreover, decreed that his other protector, Admiral de Montaignac, was made naval minister in 1874. Thanks to the admiral's intervention Brazza was allowed to enter the French naval academy in 1868 as a foreign student. At the time he was sixteen years old. Two years later he went on his first naval tour, but he could not become an officer without being a Frenchman, and he could not become a Frenchman until he was of age. Biding his time, he was finally naturalized on 13 August 1874, but once again the rules were against him: the seniority of a naval officer depended on the date of his naturalization. Once more, protection came to his aid when the rules and the hostility of the French naval establishment put obstacles in his path. Montaignac was able to have him commissioned and placed in charge of an expedition to Africa. That was in 1875. Brazza's great passion was voyages of discovery, so much so that while still at the naval academy he had gone on a strict diet to inure himself to the hunger all explorers had to face sooner or later.[20]

The Ogowe estuary had been in French hands since the 1840s, and the possession would later grow to become the colony of Gabon. That lay in the future, however, and in the early 1870s the colony even seemed doomed. There was little trade, and that entirely in British hands. Colonial administration was costly. For these reasons France was planning, during the very year of Brazza's expedition, to wind the colony up or, better still, to make a deal with Great Britain.[21] The Africans along the lower reaches of the river were causing problems, protecting their trade monopoly with success. Brazza's brief was to sail up the Ogowe, find the source of the river, and try to make contact with more hospitable tribes along its upper course. He was granted a year's salary in advance, a credit of 10,000 francs, and the help of two white traveling companions, one a doctor, the other a quartermaster. The minister of education then added a biologist. Thus four white men and seventeen black men arrived in Lambaréné on 13 November 1875 for a journey that was to take three years.

Brazza's expedition took him up the Ogowe, through the tropical rainforest to the upper reaches of the river, where Franceville would later be founded. There he came upon an area of savannah inhabited by sedentary farmers. The Bateke, as these people were called, also practiced weaving and maintained trading links with tribes along the Alima. Brazza advanced into the basin of this tributary of the Congo. The regions he crossed appeared to be rich in desirable raw materials, especially rubber and ivory, while the natives for their part seemed keen on European products. Brazza had discovered an unknown and relatively simple access route to the Upper Congo basin. A new future beckoned in Gabon.

Brazza's expedition heralded a fledgling colonial development in typical French style, neither political nor commercial, but romantic, military, exotic and adventurous. It sprang from the ambition, application and tenacity of a single man. The credit issued to Brazza had been intended to cover an expedition lasting one year, which in the event lasted for three. The money was not nearly enough, therefore, but the French government refused to provide any more. Fortunately, Brazza's mother sent him funds from Rome. In the end, Brazza paid more than half the costs out of his own pocket.[22] Though France showered him with honors, admitted him to the Legion of Honor, and decorated him with a variety of ribbons and medals, the navy refused to grant him the promotion he was owed. The famous explorer remained outranked by his classmates, which did not, however, diminish his burning French patriotism. Indeed, he was to take a step on behalf of his adopted country even richer in consequences: unasked, he claimed the Congo for France. However, this step brought him into direct conflict with France's great rival in central Africa, Leopold II.

### THE GEOGRAPHICAL CONFERENCE OF 1876

In 1875, when Leopold began to hatch his African plans, these explorers were all still out in the bush. Cameron surfaced again in November 1875. Brazza sailed for Africa that same month and was not to return until three years later, in Gabon. Stanley's journey through darkest Africa took from 1874 to 1878. News of these travels, however, did filter through to Europe,

and Leopold followed the reports with keen interest. In August 1875 the
Congress of the French Geographical Society was held in Paris. Leopold
used the occasion to collect detailed information on the exploration of
Africa,[23] and this persuaded him to convene another geographical conference, this time in Brussels, the better to discover what, if anything, could
"be done" in Africa. The conference would, of course, have to have clear
scientific objectives and be humanitarian in spirit, that is, to come out specifically against the slave trade. It would also have to be international,
avoiding all forms of rivalry. The resulting international, humanitarian and
scientific assembly met on 12 September 1876 in the palace of the king of
the Belgians in Brussels. The meeting was to become known as the Brussels
Geographical Conference.[24]

It was an impressive company that Leopold had brought together. There
were delegates from Russia and Austria, Italy and Germany, France and
Great Britain, and from Belgium itself came his faithful collaborators, Lambermont and Banning. Most of those taking part were geographers and
explorers, with very few businessmen or merchants present. The spirit of
Brussels was exalted, no less exalted than the address with which the Illustrious President opened the proceedings on 12 September 1876.

The subject that had brought them together, the king declared, was the
examination of one of the greatest tasks then facing mankind: the opening
up to civilization of the last part of the globe that had yet to benefit from
it, Central Africa. That task would have to be tackled through collaboration and consultation in order to obviate duplication of the work. The
concrete proposals on the agenda included the establishment of operational
bases in Zanzibar and at the mouth of the Congo, the assignment of access
routes to the interior, and the appointment of an international committee
to organize all the benevolent work.

The conference set to work immediately, and in accordance with modern
practice even split up into working groups. The idea of setting up stations
in Africa was warmly received. All explorers were agreed on their usefulness. The stations would first of all dispense hospitality to travelers. Next
they would have a scientific purpose, namely, to collect information about
the country and its people. Ultimately they would have to expand to become centers of civilization and strongholds in the war on slavery. Slightly
more difficult to obtain was agreement on the location of these stations.
Needless to say, there would have to be one on the west coast and one on
the east coast, that is, one at the mouth of the Congo and one in Zanzibar.
Luanda and Bagamoyo seemed the most suitable sites. When it came to the
interior, however, there was a difference of opinion between the "maxi-
malists," who demanded an ambitious network of stations that would ultimately be linked to the Nile and the Zambezi, and the "realists," who
wanted no more than an east-west linkage. The second group was to have

its way, and the conference finally agreed on four provisional stations, situated roughly along the route taken by Cameron.

There remained the third point on the agenda, the nature of the society about to be founded. The conference agreed on the formula of an international association with national committees in the various member countries. Thus on 14 September 1876 the Association Internationale Africaine (AIA) was founded, with its headquarters in Brussels and with King Leopold as its president. With all due modesty the king accepted the post, provisionally for just one year. He was at the same time to head the executive committee, which also included the German explorer Gustav Nachtigal, the British diplomat Sir Bartle Frere and the French biologist J.L.A. de Quatrefages, all of whom were present at the conference. The committee thus had a balanced composition. The president, finally, was entitled to appoint a secretary-general to help with the day-to-day running of the association. Leopold originally chose his confidant Baron Jules Greindl for the post. However, the disillusioned Greindl saw through Leopold's plans, and Leopold thought it best to replace him with Colonel M. Strauch.

Nothing was ever to come of the national committees. The British thought little of them, the proud Royal Geographical Society having no wish to act as a branch of a Brussels creation. Enthusiasm cooled even further when Leopold—oddly enough in an attempt to please the British— began to stress the humanitarian nature of his enterprise, namely, the fight against slavery.[25] The British did not seek an African monopoly in commerce or exploration, but they would have no one rob them of their abolitionist birthright. They accordingly founded their own African Exploration Fund, and that was that.

In France there was at first greater sympathy. No less a person than Ferdinand de Lesseps, once called "canaille" by Leopold, agreed to head the French committee.[26] At the 1878 World Exhibition he even gave readings in support of its aims and suggested a national lottery on its behalf. Nothing much came of all this, and most of the money had to be provided by government subsidies. The French committee did set up two stations, with the help of the state and of Leopold, but these stations flew the flag of France and not that of the Association. The German committee, too, opened a few stations that would eventually fly the German flag. Unlike the French, the Germans did contribute some money to the International Committee in Brussels, just once, and a modest sum at that. The only countries to pull their weight were the smaller ones, chief among them the Netherlands (which had not been represented at Brussels but had joined the AIA soon afterwards).

Internationalism stood a poor chance in a world where, certainly after 1870, patriotism had become the great passion. Economically, too, this was not the time for idealism or internationalism. In the 1870s an economic depression descended upon Europe, and governments adopted an increasingly interventionist stance. All the stories about fantastic commercial prospects and unprecedented investment possibilities told by enthusiastic travelers and ambitious engineers could not simply be brushed aside. The economic crisis cried out for a solution. In these circumstances Africa could not for long remain an object of exploration fever and philanthropy alone—commercial and political considerations were soon to play their part as well.

National passions thus put an untimely end to Leopold's international plans. But did the king really mind? Was this whole philanthropic and international rigmarole not just a form of window-dressing disguising Leopold's own commercial and national ambitions? Was Leopold not really after a colony of his own? Despite appearances, matters were a bit more complicated than that. Naturally Leopold never lost sight of his colonial ambitions, but at the same time he was genuine in his declared internationalism. When all was said and done, the task of opening up Africa was something quite different from his old design of buying a colony outright. Perhaps, now that all else had failed, he was being forced to look for such a colony, but that could not be done in the old way. After all, no developed colony was for sale in Africa. Here everything had to be built from scratch, and that needed a major operation, far above Leopold's financial means. On the other hand, anyone taking the lead in opening Africa up would not be too late for the eventual division of the spoils. And as for the humanitarian aspects, had not the president of the chamber of commerce in Lyons declared, "Civilizing in the modern sense of the word is to teach people to work so that they can buy, barter and spend"?[27] Clearly, the line between civilizing and exploiting was a very thin one.

The reputation of a rather dissolute and not very practical, yet basically idealistic and enlightened, ruler that Leopold acquired in Brussels in 1876 would in any case stand him in very good stead in the years to come. He maintained it until the turn of the century, when the Congo atrocities transformed his image for good from humanitarian prince into colonial villain-in-chief. That re-evaluation made little impact on the partition of Africa. The Congo State had been recognized by the Powers as early as 1885. Before then, during the years from the Brussels Conference in 1876 to the Berlin Conference in 1884 to 1885, Leopold's reputation rendered him inestimable service in the acquisition of that state and the international recognition of its borders.

# 3
# EUROPEANS IN THE CONGO

### FROM ASSOCIATION TO COMMITTEE

In 1876 Leopold had had an idea; by 1885 he ruled over a country almost a tenth the size of Africa. Something must therefore have happened in those ten years. Leopold's objectives had not changed. Even in Africa Leopold clung to his conviction that a colony was there for making money. For Leopold, "colonial profits" were not the icing on the cake but the cake itself. Even so, the way to that goal was a maze, most of whose paths led into a blind alley. Leopold's strength was that he never tired of seeking new paths. During these ten years he made two important changes. In November 1878 came the first, his conversion from the idea of an international philanthropic association to that of a private commercial enterprise; in November 1882 came the second, the change from a commercial plan to a political reality: the Congo Free State.

As an international entity, the Association Internationale Africaine was stillborn. Very few were fooled by the word "international"—the only country to take the Association seriously was Belgium. Even so, the Belgian state did not want to shoulder responsibility for Leopold's African plans. As a result, the AIA's activities were few. A new dynamic was added when Stanley turned up on the west coast after his long trek through Africa. That was in August 1877. The news reached Europe in September, and Leopold sprang into action at once. He wanted to win Stanley over to his cause. In a letter to Henry Solvyns, the Belgian ambassador in London, Leopold set out his view of matters. They would have to set to work carefully, he wrote, as they could not risk a clash with Britain, but they must also not miss the chance of acquiring a slice of "this magnificent African cake."[28] He accordingly proposed (1) a meeting with Stanley to find out if he liked him; (2) to raise enough money to enable Stanley to explore the Congo and to set up stations; and (3) as soon as conditions allowed, to develop these stations into Belgian settlements. Of this last point nothing should be allowed to slip out for the time being, as Great Britain would be certain to oppose it.[29]

On the evening of 13 January 1878, when Stanley arrived in Marseilles on the train from Italy, he was rather taken aback to be welcomed onto French soil by two "ambassadors" of the king of the Belgians, who without further ceremony invited him to enter the king's service. The former workhouse boy was undoubtedly overwhelmed by this display of illustrious interest. However, his British patriotism prevailed. He wanted first to hear the response of the British government to the proposals he had made to them. When the response came it was discouraging: the Colonial Office considered his plans too vague; the Foreign Office thought them interesting but impractical.[30] In short, there was little British enthusiasm for Stanley's ideas.

Brussels took quite the opposite view. The explorer who had been greeted so coolly in England was received here with open arms, and his ambitious projects were given a warm royal hearing. These projects amounted to nothing less than the opening up of the Congo. To that end a railroad would have to be built around the unnavigable section of the Congo River, that is, around the cataracts whose dangers Stanley had experienced at such close quarters. On the upper course, where navigation was again possible, trading stations would be set up and served by steamboats.

It was a grandiose plan, cut to Leopold's measure, but of course it needed vast sums of money. Who would be prepared to invest such sums in so risky a business? Leopold knew just the right people, a company that, in African trading circles, was known as the "Dutch House." In 1857 this company had begun operations in the Congo delta under the name of Kerdijk & Pincoffs. In 1868 it had been turned into a limited company: the Afrikaansche Handels-Vereeniging or AHV (African Trading Company). It owned forty-four trading posts in the Congo and was thus by far the largest enterprise in those parts. Not surprisingly, Leopold tried to interest this commercial giant in his plans. The reason the two Rotterdam traders welcomed his advances was not because of a particularly philanthropic bent or a soft spot for royalty. Rather, it was the nature of their business.

Trading in Africa was not only complicated, it was risky. There were rarely large profits to be made, not even in the good years, and the future was exceedingly uncertain. On the demand side, the behavior of the black buyers was capricious to say the least. The supply side (palm oil, palm kernels, groundnuts and coffee) was also beset with problems, because the raw materials constantly suffered losses due to poor harvests or natural disasters. In short, credit was badly needed, and credit depended on trust, which in turn—certainly at that time—meant a solid reputation.

Kerdijk and Pincoffs were not the scions of old families. They were, it is true, called "the aristocrats of the Congo trade," but that was the only aristocratic thing about them.[31] They were, to put it rather crudely, nouveaux riches, and what was more, of Jewish descent. Nevertheless, they were extremely successful—or rather Pincoffs was. His commercial acumen, his sweeping vision and tremendous powers of persuasion had made him one of the leading entrepreneurs of his day, a man who had to be listened to, not only in business circles but also in the Rotterdam city council and in the Dutch Upper House. In 1879 he was even offered the finance portfolio. Pincoffs's social position was thus ambiguous and the business game he played risky, since it was based on credit and trust. To gain that trust and to keep it, Pincoffs persuaded such prominent and even royal personalities as Marten Mees and Prince Hendrik, the brother of the Dutch king, to join his board of directors. No less princely were the dividends he declared, 9 and 10 percent. To make these possible, he doctored the books, practiced kite-flying, and shifted large sums of money from one company to another and back again. For Pincoffs was not only involved in African trading, he was also president of the Rotterdam Trading Association, the Dutch-Indian Gas Company and the Commanditaire Bank. All in all, he controlled a capital of 24 million guilders, an unheard-of sum of money at the time. In 1875, when his business in Africa was doing badly, Pincoffs started to rig the books of the "African lady," as his business was affectionately called in market circles. Soon after that King Leopold made contact with him.

On 27 April 1877 the Netherlands Committee of the AIA was founded. Its members included Prince Hendrik, Henry Kerdijk and Lodewijk Pincoffs. Leopold noted the royal and above all the Rotterdam interest with satisfaction. Anyone wanting to have a finger in the Congo pie could only profit from Rotterdam know-how. Leopold accordingly sent the secretary-general of the AIA to Rotterdam and invited Pincoffs to his palace in Brussels, seating the entrepreneur by the queen's side. Pincoffs for his part saw the AIA as his last chance of washing his hands of his calamitous African adventure by palming it off on the AIA or any successor enterprise. He thus offered his support in a most generous manner: free transport to, and on, the Congo on his ships, hospitality in his trading posts, and the help of his agents. It was all just a little too good to be true, and Stanley kept a suspicious and watchful eye on the Dutch influence in the planning process.

These plans were given tangible shape at a meeting held in Leopold's palace on 25 November 1878 with the decision to set up a Comité d'Etudes du Haut-Congo (CEHC) in the form of a *société en participation*—a kind of syndicate. The authorized capital was 1 million Belgian francs, in shares of 500 francs. The eighteen assembled founders participated to the tune of 742,500 francs. The rest would have to come from elsewhere. The main subscribers were Leopold himself, through his banker Lambert, who took up more than a quarter of the shares (260,000 francs), and the Afrikaansche Handels-Vereeniging, which took up half that amount, that is, shares worth 130,000 francs. The objectives of the company, according to the statutes, were "essentially philanthropic and scientific," though the company was also interested in markets for trade and industry.[32] The addition of these last few words highlighted the difference between the purely scientific purposes of the old AIA and those of the new CEHC.

This new creation thus brought commerce into the picture. In particular the statutes stipulated that, if field studies should reveal favorable market prospects, the shareholders would be entitled to participate in two new enterprises. The first was to be based on the construction and exploitation of a railroad, the second on trade and navigation on the Upper Congo. One of the articles, however, stated explicitly that any new enterprise must not compete with the Afrikaansche Handels-Vereeniging—it must not trade below the Yellala Falls, that is, on the Lower Congo, the area reserved for the AHV. Pincoffs had gained his objective. There would be—and quite quickly in all likelihood—a commercial enterprise to which he could bequeath his bankrupt but apparently flourishing business, and one that would in any case not compete with the AHV. Matters were not to reach that stage, however, because soon afterwards Pincoffs's bubble burst.

Meanwhile the Committee set to work. Stanley was given instructions to lead an expedition to the Upper Congo, to set up posts there and to establish shipping links. On 2 January 1879 the necessary funds were voted, and a few days later Stanley left for Africa. His journey was no short excursion. He had first to go to Zanzibar, the traditional point of departure of expeditions, in order to recruit labor, then back to the Congo via Suez and the Mediterranean. On Stanley's arrival at Aden on the return journey, he received a telegram from which it became clear that everything had changed. On 15 May 1879 a press report had appeared stating that the AHV had suspended all payments, that one of its directors, Kerdijk, had been arrested in Antwerp following a suicide attempt, and that the other director, Pincoffs, was a fugitive.

To Leopold, the fall of his most important partner was not a dramatic setback. On the contrary, it gave him a chance to take personal charge of the whole business without the involvement or objections of the gentlemen on the study committee. Henceforth Stanley would be acting under Leopold's own orders, although the public, which had little inside knowledge of the workings of the study committee, would continue to believe that Stanley continued to take his orders from the philanthropic AIA. The reality was quite other. Between Pincoffs's fall in May and Stanley's arrival in the Congo on 14 August 1879, a complete reorganization took place. The Committee was, in fact, put out of action—not very long afterwards, on 17 November 1879, it was to be formally wound up—and Leopold left in sole charge.

The directions he issued at first seemed to be based on a political plan. Great play was made of "free Negroes" who would be manning the trading stations. These stations would have to exert a good influence on the neighboring chiefs and lead to their association in a "republican federation of free Negroes," answerable solely to a president who would be resident in Europe and appointed by Leopold. This political scheme was so vague that Stanley rejected it out of hand. He did, however, agree that the stations might be regarded as states—or rather as statelets—and all of them together as one state. For the time being, however, trade remained the chief objective.[33]

Stanley arrived in the Congo on 14 August 1879. On 13 June the following year he signed the first of the treaties he had been instructed to conclude. It mentioned the sole and exclusive right to engage in agricultural activity, the exclusive right to build roads, and so on. The other treaties Stanley was to sign in the years to come were similarly worded. During this early period there was as yet no mention of ceding territories or sovereignty. Monopolies—that was what motivated the man who was to acquire the Congo with the promise of free trade. This motive was quite understandable. To tackle the enormous task of opening up the Congo, large capital investments were needed, and these would only be made available if economic advantages could be derived in the form of monopolies and concessions in areas with proven and attractive mineral resources and commercial prospects. Political aspirations had to be shelved for the time being, and there they would probably have remained for some time had the actions of another Africa explorer not stirred things up again.

### BRAZZA AND THE MAKOKO

Brazza, too, had of course been received in Brussels, and Leopold had tried in vain to recruit him. But Brazza was far too patriotic a Frenchman to work for Leopold's international concern. He noted the secrecy surrounding Stanley's activities and distrusted his plans. He himself was anxious to return to the Congo and was trying for a commission from the French navy in order to do something for France. Nothing was to come of this, the navy remaining resentful of this successful young officer. Nevertheless, the minister could not really refuse a favor to so important a man as Ferdinand de Lesseps. When the latter asked him to grant Brazza special leave of absence to enable him to lead a mission on behalf of the French committee of the AIA, the request was granted. Brazza was asked to set up two *stations hospitalières et scientifiques* for the committee. He was granted a subsidy by the ministries of foreign affairs and education, though he was not treated as a government employee and did not work under government instructions. He was the agent of a private association. Nor was his mission political. He had not been asked to establish a colony, but stations for the enhancement of knowledge, the propagation of Christianity, and the fight against slavery.[34] In the event, however, Brazza was to engage in quite different activities in the Upper Congo.

Brazza made great haste. As was his custom, he traveled light and hence quickly. He sailed from Europe in December 1879, left Libreville in March 1880, founded Franceville at the confluence of the Ogowe and the Passa in June, and on 10 September 1880 signed the treaty that would change the history of the Congo. It has become known as the Brazza-Makoko treaty, because it was thought for a long time that Makoko was a name and not an office. In fact, however, "makoko" was the title of the local ruler, King Iloo of the Bateke. By the treaty, the makoko ceded his land and his hereditary rights to France. As a token of this solemn act he asked for, and was presented with, a French flag.

Brazza in conversation with the makoko

In his report to the French government, Brazza mentioned the "protection" France had extended to the makoko's territory. The treaty itself refers to the makoko's sovereignty and to his ceding his territory and his inheritance rights of supremacy. The words differ, but the meaning is clear: the territory was to be treated as a protectorate. This also emerged from the next treaty Brazza signed. He traveled from Nduo to Stanley Pool and looked there for a piece of ground on the right bank of the Congo that might serve as a French settlement. He eventually chose a small but strategically placed area at the head of the navigable Congo. Next, on 3 October, he summoned the local chiefs, whom he described as "makoko's vassals," and took possession of the area "in the name of France and in accordance with the rights acquired on 10 September 1880." He told the assembled company that he had been sent by the "chief of the French." He later admitted that he had told a white lie ("un petit mensonge"), but that he could not possibly have explained in a manner comprehensible to Africans what the French committee of the AIA actually was.[35] In that he was surely right. Brazza hoisted the French flag and issued the assembled chiefs tricolors so that they might fly them in their villages as a sign of the French presence. The chiefs then recognized the transfer to France of the territory and signed the treaty. There were six signatories altogether: Brazza and the five black chiefs.[36]

It is important to be quite clear about what exactly happened here. Brazza was a naval officer on leave who had vainly tried to obtain government backing for his expedition. He was traveling in the service of a French committee which was a branch of an international philanthropic organization. His orders were to set up two scientific stations. What he set up instead was a French colony. He was acting, in his own words, "in the name of France," and considered himself "the representative of the French Government." It is hard to deny that Brazza took a most original view of his instructions. In his treaties he introduced such concepts as "sovereignty" and "hereditary rights to supremacy," which were alien to the political realities of Africa. This raises a number of questions. First of all, what were the real powers of the makoko? Whom did he really reign over? Were the other chiefs really his vassals? Different opinions have been expressed. A French missionary called the makoko "an insignificant king of the kind you meet every few kilometers in Africa."[37] Such modern and authoritative historians as Jan Vansina believe that we can indeed speak of the makoko's sovereignty over all the Bateke and hence of a degree of subordination.[38] Interesting though the question is, it was not of much practical importance. Far more important was the question of how Europeans viewed the matter at the time. If they recognized the makoko as a ruler, then the treaties he signed were sound.

Another question is what the makoko and the other Congolese chiefs really thought they were doing when they signed the treaties. In the course of the next few years hundreds of these and similar treaties were entered into. Stanley and his associates alone concluded some four to five hundred of them in the name of Leopold and his associations.[39] The same thing was also happening elsewhere in Africa. Thus the Royal Niger Company entered into 389 treaties with African chiefs within a span of eight years.[40] Why did the chiefs sign them? To begin with they were often put under some pressure. Brazza let it be known that the whites would be arriving in their big canoes and that the chiefs had to choose between peace and war.[41] Even so it would be wrong to claim that the treaties were imposed by force.

There were genuine negotiations. What we are entitled to ask is if the Africans fully understood what they were doing. Some African historians have spoken of blatant deceit: "The whites managed to cheat the blacks and take away their rights of sovereignty."[42] This is an old story. For that very reason France had explicitly laid it down in a treaty with the ruler of Coumanda, entered into as early as 1687, that he had "perfectly understood" the text, "word for word."[43]

It is, of course, an open question what exactly such terms as "taking possession," "surrender of rights," "transfer of sovereignty," and the like might have conveyed to the Africans. In West Africa contacts had been made over a fairly long period, and the local rulers were more careful. In the interior of the Congo, by contrast, Western expansion was an unknown phenomenon. The Africans there probably looked upon a treaty with the whites as some sort of trade agreement, which they would normally have sealed with a blood brotherhood according to African usage, but, because the Europeans seemed to like it so much better, sealed instead with a treaty according to European usage.[44] To their mind they were not ceding territory to the foreigners, but sealing a bond of friendship.[45] The question of what they thought of these treaties does not therefore have a simple answer. Some African chiefs seemed to have gone thoroughly into the subtleties of sovereignty and suzerainty. It is also certain that on several occasions conflicts arose about the meaning of these terms, and that differences in interpretation resulted from differences in culture and mental outlook. What mattered in practice, however, as we saw, was recognition of the treaties by the European Powers. As Stanley seems to have realized, Brazza, who had at his disposal nothing more than a flag and a walking stick, was better placed than he was with all his followers and weapons, at least so long as Stanley's treaties had not been recognized in Europe.[46]

Brazza was only too aware of the impact and potentially explosive nature of his treatment of, and treaties with, the chiefs. That is why he kept them secret, both from Stanley, whom he met in Vivi, and later from the French authorities in Libreville, where he arrived on 16 December 1880. Brazza remained in the Congo for some time, and it was to be another year before echoes of his activities reached Paris. At the end of December 1881 the French prime minister, Gambetta, received a detailed report about what was happening in the Congo. The report, compiled by a French naval officer, covered Brazza's and Stanley's expeditions. It also mentioned that there were problems because Stanley had been refused passage by a sergeant whom Brazza had left behind at Ncouna (the French station). Together with two sailors, that sergeant made up the entire defense force of the new French colony. At the beginning of the following year, in April 1882, came the first diplomatic troubles. The Portuguese, who had the oldest claims to the area, were becoming agitated. Moreover, a British Baptist mission which had reached Stanley Pool in July 1881 had made a copy of Brazza's treaty and had sent it on to London. The British ambassador in Paris was instructed to request information concerning the authenticity of the treaty from the French authorities.[47]

Thus the question of what the French government was to do about Brazza's annexations became increasingly pressing in the course of 1882. It was one thing to annex a territory, but quite another to ratify the treaty covering the annexation. The French government, in the person of Brazza's chief, the naval minister, came out against ratification. In his letter dated 27 June 1882 to the new prime minister, Freycinet, he made it clear that Brazza had no mandate from his department and that he was accordingly not acting on behalf of the French government.[48] Brazza had meanwhile realized that it was time to break his silence. He knew that there was no future in following the formal route to ratification, namely, through his superiors in the navy. He also realized that the other way, through his patron, de Lesseps, the president of the French committee, would put de Lesseps in an awkward position. After all, the French committee was run by a wider body of which King Leopold was the head. Only one way was thus left open to him: to go to Paris in person and to exert direct pressure on the small but influential circle of colonial enthusiasts. He arrived in the French capital on 7 June 1882 and launched his propaganda campaign without delay.

The seed fell on fertile soil. Brazza's return to Paris was a triumph. The Société de Géographie received him in the amphitheatre of the Sorbonne, Brazza being accompanied by two young black men wearing the uniform of French naval cadets. One banquet followed another. Brazza waged a concentrated publicity campaign and exerted tremendous pressure. The press was enthusiastic about the Congo. It painted lyrical pictures of the prospects and riches of an area described as "a virgin, luxuriant, vigorous and fertile land," a somewhat surprising combination of qualities.[49]

FROM COMMITTEE TO ASSOCIATION

King Leopold watched these goings-on with growing concern. The key to the area on which he had fixed his sights seemed to be slipping out of his hands. Leopold did not underestimate the strength of nationalist sentiment in the Paris of 1882. The British occupation of Egypt was a source of much French resentment. What could be done? Dismayed, Leopold even asked the Belgian ambassador in London to intercede with the Foreign Office. "Ask the British to send a warship to the Congo," he wrote, adding mollifyingly, "a very small one will do."[50] Luckily the ambassador had the good sense to do nothing of the kind. Leopold then sought refuge in what one might call forward flight. Anything Brazza could do, Stanley could do as well—and even better. In October 1882 Stanley received a large number of blank treaty forms that needed only to be filled in and signed. Upon putting a cross on one of these, a black chief transferred his sovereignty to the Association Internationale du Congo (AIC), Leopold's third and last creation. Unlike its two predecessors, the AIA and the CEHC, which had been genuinely international bodies, even if mainly in theory, the international label of the AIC was pure fiction. The AIC was nothing other than Leopold himself, under a new name. The name had been chosen with care in a deliberate attempt to confuse it with the other two bodies. As a result, the AIC was able to usurp the halo of philanthropic altruism and disinterested research borne by its two forerunners.

In October 1882 Leopold therefore adopted the purely political approach which had been latent for so long. Perhaps it would be better to speak of a return to his original dream of a colony, albeit in Africa this time instead of Asia. Moreover, the king now expanded his conception. "Free towns" in the form of stations were supplanted by "free towns and territories," then by "free states," and finally, in January 1884, by "the Free State."[51] The words changed more quickly than the reality, for the "new state" to which Leopold would first refer in January 1884 was really no more than a series of small stations with "sovereign" rights over the surrounding territory. There was no state as yet, let alone a state with recognized borders, but the road to the Congo Free State had been opened up and was about to be traveled at high speed.

During 1882 two rival political movements had thus been launched. In October 1882 Leopold adopted Brazza's method of getting treaties signed. In November the French government, too, after long hesitation and initial opposition, stepped in. On Saturday, 18 November 1882, Eugène Duclerc, the French prime minister, who also held the foreign affairs portfolio, submitted a draft law empowering the president of the republic to ratify the agreements made by Brazza, namely, the Brazza-Makoko treaty of 10 September 1880 and the agreement of the following 3 October whereby the makoko ceded his territorial rights. The French prime minister, and later Maurice Rouvier, the *rapporteur*, explained the background to these documents. They insisted that France had a vocation in Africa, and stressed the disinterested and peaceable character of Brazza's mission and his popularity with the indigenous population. International repercussions need not be feared because France had primary claims and moreover would put no obstacles in the way of trade by other countries. A single parliamentarian tried to spoil the festive mood. This senator remarked cynically, "At last we are no longer alone. We have an ally."[52] But the Chamber was easy to sway, and the treaties were ratified unanimously on 22 November 1882. *Le Temps* wrote next day with obvious satisfaction, "The Chamber . . . proved to be truly French."[53]

International repercussions did, however, follow, and quickly at that. The ratification of the treaties was a clear signal that Central Africa had entered a new phase.[54] Brazza had, as King Leopold somewhat oddly put it, "introduced politics into the Congo."[55] The French Chamber, for its part, had introduced the Congo into European politics. The consequences were not slow in coming. The genie had escaped from the bottle and was to haunt Europe. In the next two years, 1883 and 1884, the Congo assumed an increasingly important place on the European diplomatic agenda.

# 4
# THE CONGO QUESTION, 1882–1884

### PORTUGAL AND THE COLONIES

No matter what treaties were being signed in the Congo, one thing was certain: the Portuguese had first claim to the territory. They could trace their title back to the oldest of all, that of the discoverer. No one could challenge such patents. True, in the many centuries that had gone by since then, there had been scores of new agreements, but even in the nineteenth century the Portuguese title to the mouth of the Congo was still recognized explicitly or tacitly by the Powers. The big question was what Portugal would do about Stanley's and Brazza's incursions.

Portugal was a weak and backward country, but it was less behind the times than has often been alleged. Portugal may have teemed with men bearing titles as noble as they were long, but that did not mean that Portugal was a feudal society. In Portugal, too, the middle classes had in fact become the leading social group. The power of the church had been curtailed, and there was a strong republican current. In short, Portugal was a capitalist country, even if a weak and backward one. That meant that many more people clamored for special privileges and saw the future of the economy in an expansion of the colonial empire as a protected market. Such an empire also offered prospects for Portuguese emigrants. Both motives helped to shore up imperialist sentiment. Nationalism, pride in bygone achievements, and hopes for a new future went hand in hand with missionary zeal.[56] Of course, there were cynics and critics as well. They pointed out that Portugal's civilizing influence was a fiction and that Africans were unsuited to Christianity. "You might just as well try teaching the Gospel to gorillas and orang-utans," one critic wrote.[57]

In any case the Portuguese presence in Africa during the 1880s was extremely limited. There were even calls for a complete withdrawal from the interior, where attempts to extend Portuguese power had come to little. In Mozambique, apart from Lourenço Marques on the coast, the Portuguese could boast no more than a few settlements peopled by a handful of Portuguese soldiers and petty traders. In Angola Portuguese activities were confined to just a few towns, Ambriz and Luanda in the north, Benguela and Mossâmedes in the south. Luanda, the capital of Angola, lived on its old reputation of being the most beautiful town on the west coast of Africa, but its former prosperity, based on the slave trade, was no more, and its economic prospects were gloomy. Hence no matter how dire conditions were in Portugal itself, hardly any Portuguese went voluntarily to the African possessions, and most of Luanda's thousand white inhabitants were in fact criminals.[58]

The boundaries of the Portuguese claims to West Africa were vague, and so were those in the east. In the south the eighteenth parallel was generally taken to be the limit. Not that it mattered greatly, for the land there was desert and the next settlement was distant Walvis Bay. In the north the situation was less clear. The northernmost Portuguese province was Ambriz on the eighth parallel. In the territory north of that, especially in the gigantic Congo delta, lay scattered settlements belonging to several countries. This region stretched about as far as the Equator, where the French colony of Gabon began. The Portuguese also laid claim to the entire mouth of the Congo. All these boundaries and claims, incidentally, were in respect of coastal strips alone. In the interior, the situation varied from place to place, the Portuguese sometimes extending their influence far inland.

The Portuguese were not very popular. Their heyday had been during the slave trade, and their casual attitude to its abolition had earned them a bad name in abolitionist Britain. Above all, under the influence of Livingstone they had become known as "pedlars in human flesh" and "the curse of the Negro race."[59] There were also, of course, the notorious Portuguese customs duties. The reputation of Portugal in the nineteenth century could be summed up in two words: protection and corruption. The Portuguese were renowned protectionists. "That fearful tariff-loving people, the Portuguese," Stanley called them.[60] The Dutch chargé d'affaires in Lisbon spoke of a "spirit of outrageous protectionism and the exclusion of foreigners."[61] Worse still was the corruption. With the Portuguese, first the duty was paid, and then the customs officers. No wonder that their claims to African territory fell on deaf ears in Britain, which, incidentally, was Portugal's traditional protector on the European diplomatic scene.

Before the Congo became an international issue in 1882, rivalry in the area had been largely Anglo-Portuguese. The French were not yet interested, and the Dutch relied on British free-trade policies. Great Britain refused to recognize any Portuguese claims north of Ambriz, countering the Portuguese discovery argument by stressing the absence of effective occupation forces. The Portuguese claims had been superseded by their failure to give these claims any tangible form. The British countermove was to make treaties with native chiefs. The latter promised to abolish the slave trade, in exchange for which Great Britain recognized their sovereignty, thus repudiating that of Portugal. The British negotiators gave tangible expression to these arrangements by presenting the chiefs involved with a velvet cloak and a crown; to be on the safe side, London explained that a stage crown made of imitation gold was more than adequate.[62] The slogan was still "Empire on the cheap."

Attempts by the Portuguese to reach an Anglo-Portuguese agreement ended in failure in 1881. Thus at the time there was nothing to indicate an Anglo-Portuguese entente. Early in 1882, when the Brazza-Makoko treaty became known in Britain, things started to look quite different. The French prime minister may have described French policy as "eminently liberal"[63] during a discussion of the treaty in the Chamber of Deputies, but Great Britain knew better. "We should not be so annexionist," Lord Salisbury told the French ambassador, "if you were not so protectionist."[64] That was, in fact, the crux of the matter. The specter of French protectionism drove London back into the arms of Lisbon. Sir Charles Dilke summed up British policy very succinctly: "In order to keep France out, we were glad to put forward Portugal."[65] Installing Portugal in the Congo in order to hold back France was, commercially speaking, tantamount to driving the devil out with Beelzebub. But France was a mighty devil and Portugal a very small Beelzebub, and that made a world of difference. Ironically it was Gladstone's liberal cabinet that engaged in this peculiar form of exorcism, an act as alien to its principles as the occupation of Egypt had been a little while before.

### GREAT BRITAIN AND PORTUGAL

Anglo-Portuguese negotiations began in November 1882. Portugal suddenly found a receptive audience. The British negotiators treated their Portuguese counterparts tolerantly, and in so doing ignored the mood at home and in Parliament, where it could not be forgotten overnight that Portugal was as monopolistic in its commercial policy as it was in its missionary activities. But though British commercial and missionary circles voiced determined opposition to a treaty with Portugal, the treaty was nevertheless signed, albeit in a form much less favorable to Portugal than it looked at first sight. This was a consequence of a marked hardening of the British attitude in February 1883, thanks largely to the initiative of Sir Percy Anderson, the new head of the African department at the Foreign Office.

Henry Percy Anderson (1831–1896) was one of the great architects of Britain's Africa policy in the last quarter of the nineteenth century. His influence began to make itself felt in 1883 upon his appointment as head of the African department, and did not end until his death in 1896. He was a true champion of the new imperialism, changing the name of his section from the Slave Trade to the African department. This was more than a mere change of name, for it also involved a change of objectives. The days of humanitarian crusades were over. Africa had become a chessboard on which every move had to be answered with a counter-move. At stake was nothing less than Britain's power and renown.[66] There were admittedly too many players for a proper game of chess, but that did not matter because as far as Anderson was concerned there was only one real opponent, France. He treated the rest more as pieces than as players. This did not always succeed—it did not, for instance, with Leopold II or Bismarck—but it certainly had the desired effect on Portugal.

Anderson was aghast at the draft of the Anglo-Portuguese treaty he had been shown. To his mind it was far too vague and much too weighted in Portugal's favor. In a sharp note to the Portuguese ambassador he insisted that the point at issue was not the confirmation of old Portuguese claims but British recognition of Portuguese sovereignty over a territory to which Portugal had not the least title. For that reason complete freedom of trade had to be a *conditio sine qua non* of any treaty. The upshot of Anderson's intervention was a treaty that offered Great Britain many more advantages than had the original draft. Even so, it was not enough in British eyes, as will shortly be seen.

The British mood was and remained very anti-Portuguese. In addition, a powerful lobby was pressing the claims of Leopold II. Its leaders were James Hutton, a cotton trader and local celebrity from Manchester, and the Scottish shipping tycoon Sir William Mackinnon, a lifelong friend and collaborator of the second king of the Belgians (see pp. 137–139). They organized a powerful campaign against the draft treaty and forced the government to promise that it would submit the treaty to Parliament.[67] That placed the British government in a quandary. The chief and best argument for the treaty was its anti-French bias, but this could not be acknowledged in public, as the treaty would only be of use if it was recognized by the other Powers and by France in particular.[68] France could therefore not be antagonized. However, the British government could not easily go back on its earlier commitment. The Anglo-Portuguese treaty was signed on 26 February 1884. Britain recognized Portuguese sovereignty over the coast from 8° to 5°12' S, that is, from Ambriz to Pointe Noire—in other words over the entire mouth of the Congo. The hope was that Parliament would swallow this arrangement. However, resistance made itself felt at once, not only in Great Britain but on the continent as well. The chambers of commerce in Manchester and other British cities started a campaign against this "attack on our trade and industry," and church and humanitarian circles such as the Baptist Union and the Ladies' Negroes' Friend Society made common cause with them. Needless to say Leopold did not sit by idly either, while France and Germany found themselves united in their opposition to the treaty.

### LEOPOLD'S REACTION

By 1883 Leopold had clearly drawn ahead of France in the race for the Congo, thanks to Stanley's activities. The blank forms Leopold had issued had proved their worth. Local chiefs jostled one another to sell their "sovereignty," not for a mess of potage but for more attractive things such as bottles of gin and uniforms. In one year Stanley signed hundreds of treaties with over 2,000 chiefs who, according to him, reigned by "real divine right."[69] This sounds as if Bossuet had come to Africa.

At the same time he consolidated his presence with a military force of several hundred men, a thousand rifles and eight steamboats. Gradually he moved this mighty machinery up-river, until at the end of 1883 it arrived at the Stanley Falls, where he founded Stanleyville. He was now more than a thousand miles from the sea, which constituted the strength as well as the weakness of his operation. For what were the prospects of an empire, however large, which was cut off from its only link with the seven seas by a foreign power at the mouth of the Congo? To Leopold, therefore, the Portuguese claims, now that they were being taken seriously by Britain, posed a deadly threat. He found the answer by changing course in accordance with the motto "aux grands maux grands rémèdes"—great ills demand great remedies. If Britain preferred Portugal to France for fear of losing out commercially, Leopold could easily put British fears to rest by letting it be known that there would be untrammeled freedom of trade in his free state. The man who had always been in favor of state control and monopolies, who had always thought in terms of "sole and exclusive" rights, had suddenly been transformed into a champion of free trade! Chameleons were as nothing by comparison.

Needless to say, Leopold was asked to explain how this change would be effected. How could his free state exist without revenues? Leopold's new creation, the AIC, now came into its own. The AIC, he let it be known, would meet all the costs. This body—which existed on paper only—was so philanthropic, he wrote to the *Times*, that it could only be compared with the Red Cross.[70] This resulted in something of a quandary, as the first treaties signed in Leopold's name spoke quite a different language, being litanies of monopolies and of "sole and exclusive rights." The thwarted Portuguese were, of course, quick to publish some of these compromising documents. Leopold, never at a loss for an answer, reacted with the barefaced riposte that he had been compelled to demand these exclusive rights first before handing them back to all mankind in due course.[71] Not even a Marxist trained by Jesuits is a match for such dialectical skills.

Leopold's tactics proved successful. Great Britain would drop Portugal in the end and, as a "state without customs duties," Leopold's creation would eventually sail into the safe harbor of international recognition. But things had not yet come to that at the beginning of 1884. On the contrary, matters seemed very fraught for Leopold. On 26 February 1884 the Anglo-Portuguese treaty was signed, and Leopold's access route to the proposed Free State cut off. Driven into a corner, he now made overtures to his other great opponent, France. The French government naturally treated him with suspicion, since Leopold's own objectives were obscure, and behind him and his foreign committees France feared the hand of Britain. After all, Leopold's chief agent was Stanley, the renowned British patriot, who had openly declared that the region he had opened up would have to become a British protectorate.[72] The French therefore had little faith in Leopold's autonomy. If Britain was not already behind his projects, then the Free State would in any case, after its expected collapse, end up in British hands. There could thus be no question of a French recognition of the AIC claims, certainly not until the possibility of a transfer to Great Britain had been unequivocally eliminated. Leopold had no difficulty in reassuring the French on this point. For him the British threat had been no more than a diplomatic move against France. He even went a step further now and offered France first refusal. If the AIC should unexpectedly be forced to "realize" its possessions, that is to dispose of them, then France would have a *droit de préférence* over them. In other words, France was offered an "option" on the Free State. This astonishing move was not intended to rally the French to Leopold's side. It was aimed at the Portuguese.

The idea was as simple as it was effective. The best way to have his claims respected by the Portuguese was to confront them with an even greater danger. And who besides the AIC was Portugal's greatest rival in those regions? None other than France. Well then, if Portugal could be made to realize that if the AIC foundered, France would take its place, Portugal would think again.[73] The best way of making this point was thus to confer upon France priority claims to any estate left by the AIC. Portugal would then have an interest in ensuring that such a bequest was not handed over by striving to keep the patient alive. In 1884 France's first claim on Leopold's African estate was set out in letters between the French prime minister, Jules Ferry, and Colonel Strauch, the secretary-general of the AIC. Leopold's proposal was astonishing, not only because France had never asked for such a favor, but above all for the levity with which it had been granted. Not even the possibility that Leopold might bequeath his estate to the Belgian state had been overlooked. Leopold's imperialism is best characterized, in a variant of Lenin's famous phrase, as "the highest stage of opportunism."

The import and consequences of these charades were great and varied. In the short term the Anglo-Portuguese treaty was a red herring. Opposition to it, in Great Britain and outside, was so great that the British Parliament was unable to ratify it. Leopold's desperate measures were therefore nothing but overkill, although in the long run they would cause him serious problems. The Free State had been saddled with an irksome inheritance. Thus General de Gaulle informed the Belgians in 1960, during the preparations for Congolese independence, that in France's view the *droit de préférence*—first refusal—still held.[74] In the medium term, however, Leopold's steps proved crucial to the creation of his "free" state and to the recognition of its borders by Great Britain and France. With his free-trade promise Leopold gained the support of Great Britain, which considered him a more reliable champion of international commerce than the discreditable Portuguese. With his *droit de préférence* he eventually gained the support of France as well, a country that felt it had only to sit back and wait for the inevitable collapse of this philanthropic enterprise to take possession of the Congo. Moreover—and this was the most important point of all—his two promises, free trade and preferential rights, gained him the support of Bismarck, who saw advantages in both, economic in the first, and political in the second.

On 24 April 1884 Bismarck first discussed the Congo with the French ambassador in Berlin.[75] That discussion raised the problem to a higher, though not necessarily a more exalted, plane. Bismarck was to take a personal interest in the matter, and so the Congo was drawn into the wider sphere of international politics. Germany had, in fact, decided to set out on the colonial path itself. Within two years it was to acquire a colonial empire five times the size of Germany. To retrace this development we must now turn our attention to Bismarck and to the beginnings of Germany's colonial approach.

# 5
# GERMANY AND IMPERIALISM

### GERMANY UNDER BISMARCK

Germany's entry into the colonial race in 1885 came as a surprise. The chancellor had often declared that he had no interest in it, indeed, that he thought it madness. Nevertheless, his new approach was logical. Germany had become a great power, the most powerful country in Europe. How could such a country not participate in the international competition? Germany, after all, was an exceptionally dynamic country. Its population was growing fast: from 41 million in 1871 to 60 million in 1914. Demographic expansion went hand in hand with a change in the character of Germany itself. It became the leading industrial power in Europe. Great Britain alone was left as a serious rival. But its fast growth also rendered Germany vulnerable. The agrarian sector, the foundation of the old Germany, was caught in a structural market crisis, because it could not compete with cheap American grain. Industry, too, was subjected to a host of critical shocks, cyclical movements, and the periodic tensions so typical of this phase in the development of modern capitalism and of "unbalanced growth" in general. Unlike Great Britain, where commerce was the mother of all economic activity, the commercial sector in Germany was of relatively small importance. In Germany, too, the gospel of free trade was being preached but, again unlike Great Britain where it was a deeply held, almost mystical, faith, Germany merely paid lip service to it.

Although the political organization of the Reich was complicated, Germany faced the outside world as a single unit, led by the Kaiser and the Iron Chancellor. It had no such thing as a parliamentary system in the normal sense of the word, that is, an executive responsible to parliament. Nevertheless, support in the Reichstag was needed for new legislation, and the government also depended on the Reichstag when it came to voting money for new initiatives. This was one of Bismarck's many problems.

### Bismarck

Otto von Bismarck (1815–1898) was fifty-five years old when he achieved German unity. He was born on 1 April 1815, the year in which "Metternich's system" was established at the Congress of Vienna in order to maintain peace in Europe and to keep German nationalism in check. Bismarck was to disrupt both objectives. He came from a family of Prussian officers and Junkers, but studied law and chose politics and diplomacy as his career. He was a member of the Prussian Landtag (parliament) and of the Frankfurt Bundestag (assembly), and later ambassador to St. Petersburg and Paris before becoming Prussian prime minister and minister of foreign affairs. He governed in the name of the king but against the will of the parliamentary majority, and sought to achieve German unification, "not by speeches and majority decisions but by iron and blood." After three wars, with Denmark, Austria and France, he attained his goal: the king of a triumphant Prussia was proclaimed emperor of Germany in the Hall of Mirrors at Versailles. Bismarck himself, previously a count, was elevated to prince. Until the new Kaiser, Wilhelm II, dismissed him in 1890, he was to be the unchallenged leader of the new Germany. His moral authority, as the founder of the united Germany, was almost as unbounded as his political power based on the three offices he held jointly: chancellor of the Reich, Prussian prime minister and Prussian minister of foreign affairs. He was of impressive stature and robust constitution. His energy was boundless. As the Russian minister of foreign affairs, Gorchakov observed, he ate too much, drank too much and worked too much. Not surprisingly, he suffered from stomach and gallbladder complaints all his life.[76] Yet he remained in power until his seventy-fifth year and lived to the age of eighty-three.

The most important group in the Diet on whose backing Bismarck relied were the National Liberals. It was they who had stood behind his creation of the German Reich and who had remained his leading parliamentary support in the 1870s. However, the effects of the long economic depression had shaken German faith in liberal ideas in general and the free-trade doctrine in particular. In 1878 Bismarck broke with that doctrine and forged a new parliamentary majority out of the Conservative Liberals who had split from the National Liberals and the equally conservative Roman Catholic Center Party. This new group was anti-socialist and advocated the protection of German agriculture and industry, that is, of grain and steel.

In 1878 Berlin also became the diplomatic capital of Europe, something it had never been before. Even after the spectacular victories of 1870–1871 Bismarck had at first kept a low profile in the diplomatic field. For a time he did not consider it Germany's task to direct European diplomatic activity. The Balkan crisis of 1878 changed all that. Bismarck invited the Powers to Berlin to discuss the affair, and it was then that Germany accepted the mantle that had fallen to it upon its unification in 1870. Bismarck ruled over Germany, and Germany ruled over Europe.

Bismarck's diplomatic talents were legendary. He had an exceptional intelligence, an amazing gift for languages, and great familiarity with Europe. He was hard to outdo in cynicism or misanthropy, be it by word of mouth or in writing. His diplomacy was consistent but opportunistic. Its foundations were patience and caution, but these qualities went hand in hand with resolution and quickness of action, for Bismarck believed firmly that chances did not come twice.[77] He was enough of a diplomat not to eschew equivocation, sowing confusion whenever he thought it possible and desirable, and keeping three rather than two balls in the air at once. But he was also statesman enough to realize that trust is indivisible, and that in the long run a statesman's greatest possession is his reputation. He was enough of a gentleman to observe the code that diplomats do not lie to one another, but there was also something grasping and boorish in his behavior. In the diplomatic world Bismarck, like his country, was an upstart, with all the upstart's characteristics. As Lord Salisbury, whose family had been associated with diplomatic activity since the sixteenth century, put it, "He is rather a Jew, but on the whole I have as yet got my money's worth."[78] Bismarck—just like Lord Salisbury, for that matter—had a strong sense of duty and responsibility coupled to detachment and a sense of proportion. These were the qualities he also displayed when he came face to face in the 1880s with a new and to him unfamiliar development: the German colonial movement.

### THE GERMAN COLONIAL MOVEMENT

The two spiritual fathers of German colonialism were neither politicians nor businessmen. They were a missionary and a lawyer. Friedrich Fabri

(1824–1891) was a clergyman whose interest in overseas affairs was linked to his post of inspector of the Rhenish mission. However, in his book *Bedarf Deutschland der Colonien?* (Does Germany Need Colonies?), published in 1879, he used selfish rather than pious arguments, arguing with a host of figures and statistics that colonies were a source of prosperity. For Germany, moreover, colonies were a question of life and death, since they would represent a fatherland in foreign parts where the German nation could dispose of its surplus population without losing it to others, as was happening in non-German settlements. The other champion of colonialism, the lawyer Wilhelm Hübbe-Schleiden (1847–1900) from Hamburg, was an out-and-out imperialist. According to him, the world of the future would be run by just a few gigantic empires. His book *Deutsche Kolonisation*, published in 1881, was, unlike Fabri's, based above all on political and nationalistic concepts. Colonization, he claimed, was not so much a commercial as a political affair. In particular, colonies were an instrument for spreading German influence and culture, for the preservation of *Deutschtum*—Germanness.[79] That these ideas fell on fertile soil may be gathered from the rapid rise of the German colonial movement.

As in other countries, the movement could trace its origins to geographical societies and to commercial circles, especially in the Hanseatic towns. The idea of a large national organization was first put forward in 1882. The initiators were not businessmen, but a biologist, an explorer and a politician.[80] Business and industrial circles were not slow to pick up the message, however, and lent support to a manifesto stressing both the economic importance of colonization (the provision of new markets) and the fact that it was in the national interest to strengthen bonds with Germans overseas. These were the declared ideals of the Kolonialverein (Colonial Association) founded in Frankfurt on 6 December 1882. This association was singularly successful, recruiting more than 3,000 members within a year. It had branches in nearly 500 towns in Germany, and in some 20 towns overseas. By 1895 it could boast more than 10,000 members, enabling it to publish a journal, the *Kolonialzeitung*, a mouthpiece of the colonial message. Leading academics such as Schmoller, Sybel and Treitschke took up the call, the last-named even calling colonialism a *Daseinsfrage*[81]—a question of life and death.

The society did not set its sights primarily on economic profit or direct annexation, wanting merely to prepare the German people for Germany's new role in the world. That was the main difference between it and the other, smaller, society in the same field, the Gesellschaft für deutsche Kolonisation (Society for German Colonization). The latter had been founded in Berlin on 3 April 1884 and had a more practical objective, the raising of the capital needed for establishing a German colony in East Africa. Though the two organizations started out as rivals, they were to be amalgamated on 19 November 1887 into the Deutsche Kolonialgesellschaft. By then, however, the German colonial empire had been well and truly established. It had all happened very quickly in 1884 and 1885, once Bismarck had decided to adopt the objectives of his colonialist compatriots he had previously so despised and to lend their paltry claims and possessions the protection of the Reich. Many people were astonished and fascinated by this volte-face.

### BISMARCK'S COLONIAL CONVERSION

That historians should be so fascinated by Bismarck's conversion is due first of all of course to their being fascinated by Bismarck himself. Bismarck was the kind of man whom one would not normally have associated with rash and uncontrolled behavior. His actions had always been seen as part of some great plan, his diplomacy as forming a consistent whole, and his judgment as being infallible. That may be slightly exaggerated, but we may take it that Bismarck's actions were no mere whims and that there must have been good reasons for his conversion. This question is of particular importance, for in no other case did the colonial policy of a country coincide so fully with the policy of one man. Through Bismarck's actions Germany acquired 99.9 percent of its later colonial empire. To gain some understanding of that process, we must therefore try to come to grips with Bismarck's motives.

To begin with the most important of them, there can be no doubt that, at heart, Bismarck was not a colonial expansionist. He himself put it quite plainly as late as 1889: "I was not born to be a colonialist."[82] This statement was of course also an expression of his disappointment with the outcome of all those colonial doings and dealings, but it was more than that. Bismarck had expressed similar views in the past. "Colonies," he declared in 1871, "are to us Germans what silk-lined sable coats are to the Polish nobility, who have no shirts to wear underneath." And: "We are not yet rich enough to afford the luxury of colonies."[83] The import of these words was quite clear: Germany, just like those Polish noblemen, lacked an infrastructure. It lacked a navy strong enough to protect colonies. It had no commercial companies to exploit them. It had no need for raw materials or for markets. In addition colonies meant spending money on administration and defense. These funds would have to be voted by the Reichstag. Colonial expansion would therefore lead to the strengthening of the Reichstag and thus of the liberal parliamentary regime Bismarck had come to detest so much. In short, Bismarck had a variety of reasons for opposing colonialism, and in the 1870s he categorically turned down all requests for annexations. Why, then, did he act so differently in 1884 and 1885?

There are some explanations attributed to Bismarck himself. The first, noted by Friedrich von Holstein, was, "That whole colonial business is a sham, but we need it for the elections."[84] Here we are thus proffered an electoral, that is, a domestic-political, motive. The other explanation was given by Bismarck in a conversation with Eugen Wolf, an enthusiastic colonialist and explorer: "Your map of Africa is very good, but my map of Africa lies in Europe. Here is Russia, and here . . . is France, and we are in the middle; that is my map of Africa."[85] This was a foreign-political explanation. All the extensive literature on Bismarck's motives consists essentially of variations on these two themes, domestic-political motives such as electoral advantage, and foreign-political motives such as relations with Great Britain and with France.

It is true that Bismarck strove for reconciliation with his mighty neighbor. It is also true that at the Congress of Berlin in 1878 he had urged France to look to horizons beyond the blue line of the Vosges. But Bismarck knew only too well that the rigid confines of French nationalism did not allow that change of perspective—for the time being. However, the colonial vista also held attractive electoral prospects at home. It could contribute to a national consensus, and promised to deflect attention from social and economic problems and focus it instead on national successes. Hence it is not necessary to assume that there was a conflict between home and foreign considerations. What motivated Bismarck was the national interest as he saw it. Peace and order, calm at home and abroad, were of equal importance in furthering it.

Bismarck's actions in 1884 and 1885 can therefore be explained quite simply. Bismarck was almost seventy when he embarked upon his colonial adventure. He recognized that he was elderly and that his thinking about Germany and about politics was dominated by the past. His horizon was a European one, but the future might look different, and a statesman had to think of the future. This line of thought was clearly reflected in his address to the Diet on 26 January 1889, when he declared, "I have to think in decades, of the future of my compatriots, I must remember that in twenty or thirty years' time I might be reproached for having been that timid chancellor who lacked the courage to secure for us what has turned out to be so valuable a possession."[86] And he added that, "though no one can prove the benefit of colonies to the Reich, I cannot prove that they are harmful either." That was the crux of the matter. No one knew precisely what Africa could provide, but many thought that it had much to offer. In 1884 there was suddenly a chance to secure some of it at no great cost. Bismarck had learned during a long life that chances have to be seized whenever they appear. That is why he acted in 1884 and 1885 as was his wont: wary as a serpent and bold as a lion.

### THE BIRTH OF THE GERMAN COLONIAL EMPIRE

The birth of the German colonial empire is easy to date precisely. It took place on 24 April 1884, when Bismarck extended *Reichsschutz* (the pro-

tection of the Reich) to "Lüderitz-land" (see p. 283). That act was the
beginning of German South-West Africa. Other colonies were to follow in
quick succession. During the "Congo-Year," that is, the year between the
Anglo-Portuguese treaty of 27 February 1884 and the end of the Berlin
Conference exactly one year later, Germany acquired South-West Africa,
Togo, and on 27 February 1885, one day after the end of the Berlin Conference, German East Africa. This sudden development can be understood
against the background we have just sketched out. The colonial movement
had become an important factor of political life in Germany, one that was
to play a considerable role during the elections held that year. There was
thus good reason to give that movement satisfaction, provided it cost no
money and the diplomatic situation allowed it. Both conditions were satisfied in 1884. The diplomatic situation was favorable, and Bismarck had
found a way of acquiring colonies without having to apply to the Diet for
funds. This way had been mapped out for him in a memorandum drafted
by Heinrich von Kusserow, privy councillor at the Auswärtiges Amt, the
German Foreign Office. Kusserow had presented it to the chancellor on 6
April 1884.

Heinrich von Kusserow was a relatively unimportant civil servant and a
known colonial propagandist. He was therefore not taken very seriously,
the less so as he had previously presented a series of memoranda of inor-
dinate length that had irritated Bismarck as much as the man's long-winded
arguments. As a result Kusserow had been considered unsuitable for
important work, and after a short trial period at the "high school" of the
Foreign Office—the political department—he had been sent down to the
"nursery"—the legal-commercial department.[87] But Kusserow was not a
man who could be easily ignored. He was related, if not to the best, at
least to the richest families in Germany. He was the son of a Prussian
general, the grandson of the banker Oppenheimer, and the son-in-law of
Adolf von Hansemann, director of the mighty Disconto-Gesellschaft. On
top of that he was a man of ideas and hence managed to gain Bismarck's
ear occasionally, even after his relegation, provided he did not take too
long over it. His biggest idea was the need for Germany to have an overseas
empire. This provoked laughter among those of his colleagues who knew
better than Kusserow what power politics was all about, and to whom the
world outside Europe was a series of diplomatic posts to be shunned. Kusserow's public interest in Oceania caused his colleagues to refer to that
region as "Kusserowia."[88] To avoid further jokes at his expense Kusserow
kept his map of Africa, on which he had marked the future German possessions of his daydreams, in a secret drawer of his desk. Yet he was a real
zealot, one who passionately believed in a great and mighty overseas Germany, not to the greater profit of his brothers-in-law but to the greater
glory of the Fatherland.

The memorandum Kusserow drafted in 1884 bore witness at one and the same time to his enthusiasm, his familiarity with the subject, and his understanding of Bismarck's problems. In fact, he showed the way to acquire colonial possessions without having to shoulder administrative responsibility with all the costs that entailed. This miracle solution consisted of a chartered company. This was something out of the past, a relic from the days of the *ancien régime*, which had, however, recently been resurrected when the British government had granted a charter to the North Borneo Company. In essence a charter company held sovereign rights or, to put it another way, had the duty of ensuring order and providing the administration. In exchange it was granted a trading monopoly in the region assigned to it.

Kusserow considered this the answer to Bismarck's problem of how to grant the German colonist Lüderitz, who wanted to found a German colony in South-West Africa, permission to do so without the Reich's having to bear responsibility for the administrative costs. The German government would confine itself to providing diplomatic and military protection. Now, such protection was the business of the government and not of parliament, and hence needed no endorsement by the Diet. The path to the great objective—colonies without costs and without parliamentary interference—had thus been cleared. We do not know the precise influence of that memorandum on Bismarck; what we do know is that shortly after its presentation, Bismarck changed tack.[89]

Bismarck's other reason was diplomatic. The British attitude in the colonial sphere in general and in South-West Africa in particular irritated the chancellor. He had enquired several times whether the British were making any claims to South-West Africa. The British response had been slow and disdainful. No, Britain did not lay any claims to the territory, he was told, but would consider claims by others as infringing its "legitimate rights."[90] That smacked of a British Monroe Doctrine for Africa. The British attitude, incidentally, was due to confusion rather than arrogance. There was in fact little reason for the latter. The years 1884 and 1885 had been catastrophic for Britain. As Lord Granville, the foreign secretary, put it, it had all been "dreadful, jumping from one nightmare into another."[91] In Egypt, everything, absolutely everything, was going wrong—politically, militarily and financially—culminating in the tragedy of Gordon's death in Khartoum. In Asia, a major war with Russia was looming. Hence the last thing Britain wanted was to irritate Germany for no good reason, but Britain could make neither head nor tail of Bismarck's real intentions. Had Germany suddenly decided to become a colonial power after all? That seemed unlikely, but then what was Germany really after?

Bismarck, for his part, had no intention of vexing Great Britain, certainly not for the sake of the shores of some West African desert, but he did want Great Britain to take him seriously. Moreover, here was a situation in which he apparently could not lose. He could join France in making life a burden for Great Britain: he with colonial claims in Africa, France with complaints about the Congo, and both together with the financial sword over Egypt. This possibility posed a sizable threat to Britain in 1884, and no one could tell where it might lead. If France were tempted enough to join Germany and to forget all about the *ligne bleue des Vosges*, so much the better. But that was unlikely. Bismarck knew only too well that friendship with Germany spelled suicide for any French government. But even without a Franco-German entente, Britain could in any case be put under pressure. In fact Franco-German cooperation in Africa did not last long, although just long enough for Bismarck to found the German colonial empire. Franco-German collaboration was therefore not of strategic, but of tactical importance.

Bismarck thought long and hard before deciding on colonial expansion, but once the die had been cast he acted vigorously and with dispatch. He hid the dice under the cup for a little longer, but then he struck. On 7 June 1884 he let it be known that he did not recognize the Anglo-Portuguese treaty. That same month he sent his son Herbert to London to convince the British government of the seriousness of his intentions. Nachtigal, the German consul, was meanwhile given instructions to convert his West African scouting expedition into a political campaign. On 5 July Togo was declared a German protectorate, with Cameroon following on 12 July. On 7 August the area around Angra Pequeña was annexed, followed shortly afterwards by the entire coast from Angola to the Cape Colony. At the same time invitations to the Berlin Conference went out.

# 6
# THE BERLIN CONFERENCE

### TOWARD AN INTERNATIONAL CONFERENCE

On 26 April 1884, two days after the Reich had extended its protection to Lüderitz's possessions in South-West Africa, Bismarck had a talk with the French ambassador in Berlin. He let it be known that Germany was keen to discuss colonial affairs, and particularly the Anglo-Portuguese treaty, with the other Powers and especially with France. Germany had already protested to Lisbon against that treaty and now sought French cooperation in opposing the "policy of invasion and exclusivism of which England has just given fresh proof."[92] Bismarck thus started out very cautiously. He did not protest directly to London, but looked first for support elsewhere. The best form of protest was to internationalize the whole affair. The initiative had come from the Portuguese government. Once it had appeared that opposition to the London treaty was so great that international recognition was out of the question and London accordingly hesitated to present the treaty to Parliament for ratification, Portugal had lost interest in the agreement. Internationalization was now the best chance Portugal had of breaking its exclusive link with Great Britain.[93] That explains why Portugal began on 13 May 1884 to take soundings about the possibility of an international conference. Bismarck was quick to respond. He declared that a bilateral treaty had no international validity, for which international recognition was needed. He also insisted that an international waterway such as the Congo had to be placed under international control, as had been done with the Rhine and the Danube. Bismarck did not in fact hesitate to call the Congo the "Danube of Africa."[94] Free trade in the area had to be guaranteed.[95]

Bismarck thus assumed responsibility for settling the Congo question. During August and September he made contact with Paris, and finding support there for his conference plans, he invited London and Lisbon to attend an international conference to be held in Berlin. It would deal with the following subjects:

1. freedom of trade in the basin and mouth of the Congo;
2. freedom of navigation on the Congo and the Niger based on the same principles as applied for the Danube;
3. the definition of the formalities to be observed when taking possession of new territory on the African coast.[96]

Reactions were favorable. Other countries, too, could now be invited to the conference, beginning with those having interests in the regions concerned. These countries included, in addition to those already mentioned (Great Britain, France, Germany and Portugal), the Netherlands, Belgium, Spain and the United States. The rest were invited purely for show, or, as the letter of invitation more elegantly put it, "to ensure general agreement on the conference resolutions."[97] These countries were Austria-Hungary, Sweden-Norway, Denmark, Italy, Turkey and Russia. The invitations went out in October. There was thus one month for preparation and clarification of views before the conference opened.

### THE BERLIN CONFERENCE, 15 NOVEMBER 1884–26 FEBRUARY 1885

Bismarck opened the conference at two o'clock on the afternoon of Saturday, 15 November 1884 with a short but lofty address. He stressed the disinterested objectives of the conference. Its task was to bring Africa the benefits of civilization in general and of trade in particular. He then listed the main points on the agenda and insisted that the conference would not concern itself with sovereignty but would lay down rules for the occupation of new territories on the African coast in the cause of peace and humanity.

The Berlin Conference

The British ambassador, Sir Edward Malet, was the next speaker. His own lofty sentiments and thoughts certainly measured up to those of the Iron Chancellor. Sir Edward stressed that the conference should not dwell on the commercial prospects alone, but also bear the welfare of the native population in mind. He accordingly proposed a ban on the import into the Congo of such harmful commodities as alcohol, guns and gunpowder. However, altruism was not the only point on the agenda for Her Majesty's ambassador. He made one thing clear immediately: Great Britain refused to allow the Niger to be discussed on a par with the Congo. In the Congo, Great Britain was just one of the interested parties; on the Niger it was the "paramount power."

Even before the conference the British press had stressed how important this point was to Great Britain, and had expressed indignation over French plans to internationalize the Niger. The Niger was as British as the Senegal was French, and if the Niger had to be part of the negotiations, then the Senegal would have to be as well. This question was to linger between Britain and France for a long time (see p. 194), but the first round, fought over the Lower Niger, was quickly ended. Britain's position here was so strong that no one could challenge it. Nor did Bismarck even want to do so. He saw only too clearly that German interests were much closer to those of Great Britain than to those of France. Germany itself had no claims in that region, and free trade served it well. Germany thus stood behind Great Britain, and that was enough to settle the matter.

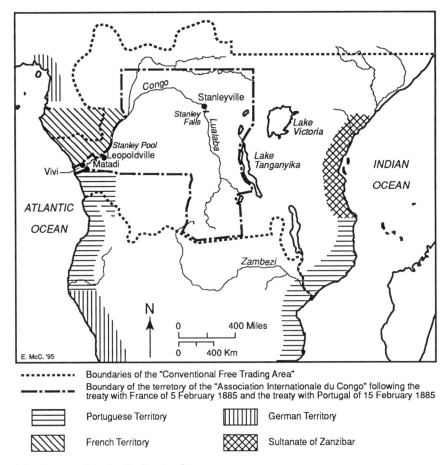

Boundaries of the "Conventional Free Trading Area"

Boundary of the terretory of the "Association Internationale du Congo" following the treaty with France of 5 February 1885 and the treaty with Portugal of 15 February 1885

Portuguese Territory                    German Territory

French Territory                        Sultanate of Zanzibar

The Congo after the Berlin Conference

The Niger question having been put out of the way, the conference could turn its attention to the region that was really at issue, namely, the Congo. The most important point here was to determine the size of the free trade area. The conference wanted to make it as large as possible. Stanley, who was nominally a member of the American delegation but was in fact acting as Leopold's agent, argued for an area stretching from the Atlantic to the Indian Ocean, right across Central Africa. He called the area the "geographic and commercial Congo basin," a splendid term, although the first adjective in particular bore a distant relation to the real situation. "You might as well consider the Rhine part of the Rhône basin,"[98] a nonplussed British diplomat remarked. Moreover, it was West Africa that appeared on the conference agenda, not the east coast. On the other hand, apart from geographical and procedural complaints, there were no great objections to Stanley's proposal. France and Portugal, both of which had claims in the area, were of course put out and tried to whittle part of the free trade area on the west coast away. Britain supported the claims of the sultan of Zanzibar in the east.

The final result was a compromise. Two free trade areas were approved. The first was defined as "the basin of the Congo and its tributaries" and stretched from the Atlantic to the great lakes. On the coast the northern boundary was fixed at 2°30' S, while the mouth of the Loge River was adopted as the southern limit. This coastal outlet was therefore fairly narrow, but immediately behind it the region fanned out broadly to the north as well as to the south. To the east of it lay the other free trade area, termed the "eastern maritime zone," which stretched from the great lakes to the Indian Ocean. Its northern coastal boundary was fixed at 5° N and its southern boundary at the mouth of the Zambezi. At Great Britain's request it was agreed that the Berlin Act would be binding on the signatories only and not on any independent African state. This, of course, was in deference to Britain's protégé, the sultan of Zanzibar. The two "free trade" territories, the Congo basin and the eastern zone, were jointly referred to as the "conventional Congo basin." The whole looked like a gigantic sausage, thick in the middle, tapering at one end and with a huge bite taken out of the other end by the sultan of Zanzibar.[99]

The conference also discussed a few other issues, among them humanitarian obligations toward the African population, a point the British ambassador had raised at the first session. Christian missions would enjoy protection and the slave trade be—once again—banned, as would the sale of strong liquor to the natives. This last was at least proposed by Great Britain. But Germany and Holland, feeling that charity should begin at home in Bremen and Schiedam rather than with Sir Edward's humanitarian concerns, demurred. Three-fifths of all German exports to West Africa were hard liquor. Bismarck himself owned three distilleries.[100] The Germans could hardly object to the principle as such, but kept referring back to the overall theme of the conference, namely, free trade. The resolution in question was accordingly changed to the effect that the local authorities would regulate the liquor trade. That was a roundabout way of saying that nothing would be done about it.

The most important item on the agenda, however, was the third: the settlement of new claims to the African coasts. Although Bismarck had stated in his opening address that the conference would not concern itself with sovereignty, the subject did of course arise behind the scenes. After all, the conference had been called to deal with the problems resulting from the Anglo-Portuguese treaty, and in the corridors the constant talk, as we shall see, revolved about the recognition of flags and the fixing of boundaries. The map of Africa had not been put up on the wall for nothing. But since this item on the conference agenda has become a source of myth and confusion, we must try to clarify what exactly was decided and what was not.

To that end we can do no better than start by taking a careful look at the letter of invitation. In the passage dealing with the topics for discussion there was mention of "new occupations on the African coasts." It thus expressly excluded existing possessions and the interior. When this matter was broached, the British delegate proposed that the same rules should also apply to new acquisitions in the latter. However, the French and the Germans objected. How could one possibly set up rules for regions about which next to nothing was known? As long as one kept to the coast, everyone knew what the discussions were about. Boundaries there could be simply fixed: from latitude x to latitude y. But what was to be done about the interior? For that matter, where did the coast end and where did the interior begin? To establish this, one would have to take an inventory of all the claims to sovereignty and make a survey of all the regions involved. That sort of operation, the French ambassador remarked, would be tantamount to a "partition of Africa." That was not what the conference had been called for. Its task was simply to establish rules for new occupations along the coast, not to discuss existing agreements nor to concern itself with the interior.[101] The conference had not been convened to divide up Africa, but to open it up to free trade and civilization, in the spirit of European co-operation and harmony. No one could object to that, and so the question of partition was brushed under the carpet. In the final Act of Berlin it was merely laid down that anyone taking possession of a new coastal region or setting up a protectorate over it had to notify the other signatories and to exercise a measure of effective authority. Since, however, scarcely any coastal parts remained unoccupied, in practice this proviso meant virtually nothing.

The conference closed on 26 February 1885. It had done its work. Three and a half months had passed since the opening, during which the delegates had met eight times, each session lasting some two and a half hours. With the opening and closing sessions, therefore, they met ten times in 105 days, for a total of about twenty-five hours. The congress had been no holiday, it is true, but nor had it been hard labor. There had been working sessions for the preparation of proposals, of course, and time had been set aside for consultation and taking instructions, but that was not the real reason for the slow progress. That reason must be sought elsewhere, not in the hall, but in the corridors. During the conference these were the scene of feverish discussions concerning the recognition of the Congo Free State, at their most difficult, of course, when they involved the two main rivals in the Congo, France and Portugal. Not until 5 February 1885 did France sign a treaty recognizing the Free State. Portugal followed soon after, on 15 February.

Even before the final Act of Berlin was signed, the Free State had declared its adherence to the conclusions of the conference. Bismarck could thus end his closing speech on a note almost as exalted as that of his opening address. He welcomed the new state and concluded with the following words: "The new Congo state is destined to be one of the most important executors of the work we intend to do, and I express my best wishes for its speedy development, and for the realization of the noble aspirations of its 'illustrious creator.' "[102] It was for the culmination of this diplomatic display that the conference had had to wait and the illustrious creator to work so hard. With the Free State the conference saluted an infant who, following many birth pangs, had just seen the light of day in a small, dark side room.

# 7
# THE BIRTH OF THE FREE STATE

### THE ROAD TO RECOGNITION

The Berlin Conference was thus held not only in the large assembly room but in corridors and small side rooms as well. While diplomats and ministers devoted their attention to noble principles and the finer points of international law, quite a different game was being played outside the hall, the game of diplomatic horse-trading and quid pro quo. The result, as we have seen, was the Congo Free State. The birth of that state, as behooves a creature of such vast girth, had been preceded by a long period of gestation. In October 1882—as we have also seen—Leopold took the crucial step of changing his commercial approach to a political one, that is, by advancing from the idea of running a business to one of running a state. What mattered next was to have that state recognized by the Powers, and Leopold had left no stone unturned to attain that end. In an attempt to gain British support on one hand, he had avidly embraced the gospel of free trade. Britain had approved. On the other hand, there was his no less surprising decision to grant the French priority rights, which admittedly gained him French sympathy but also aroused British suspicions. There were other problems too. What was the legal validity of his creation? What was its political future? Could one really claim sovereignty on behalf of an international society? The great Oxford jurist Sir Travers Twiss was asked for his opinion on the matter. He claimed that it could be done, mentioning such precedents as the Knights of Malta and the Teutonic Order.[103] That was a rather far-fetched argument. Moreover, to British eyes, Leopold seemed nothing more than a somewhat confused, benevolent philanthropist whose house of cards was bound to collapse very soon under the pressure of the international balance of power. All in all, feelings in Britain were mixed. But in the course of 1884, between the rejection of the Anglo-Portuguese treaty and the opening of the Berlin Conference, public opinion in Britain veered in Leopold's favor.[104]

Here Stanley played a major role. He was the great authority on the Congo and made ready use of that reputation. In a number of speeches delivered in England he attacked Portuguese misrule and praised the work of the disinterested king of the Belgians. He pointed in addition to the enormous prospects these regions held out to British trade. In a famous address to the Manchester Chamber of Commerce on 22 October 1884 he dwelled at length on these prospects. If every inhabitant of the Congo basin were to buy just one Sunday suit, 300 million yards of Manchester cotton could be used for that alone. If they were to buy one Sunday suit and four everyday ones, Stanley continued his "curious calculation," this would amount to many more millions of yards of cloth, to the tune of many millions of pounds.[105] Leopold's promise of free trade would make all this possible.

The Foreign Office, however, was not taken in by Stanley's paeans of praise to the disinterested Belgian ruler. "The King of the Belgians' Co. [is] a gigantic commercial monopoly," wrote Sir Percy Anderson.[106] He, for one, preferred the Portuguese. But once the Portuguese card had been played and trumped, there was nothing for it but to take the king of the Belgians in as a partner. Thus on 16 December 1884 Great Britain decided to recognize the AIC and so helped Leopold to take an important step on his laborious path to international recognition.

The Americans, incidentally, had been the first to grant this. As early as 10 April 1884 the Senate had decided to recognize the flag of the AIC, a gold star on a blue field—another bequest from the defunct AIA—as that of a friendly power. The Americans, of course, had no interests in Africa, and as Leopold, who could sometimes put things rather bluntly, expressed it, "The Americans are not greatly interested in Negroes."[107] That explained much of their attitude. But there was more. The recognition of the Association's flag had had as its most important advocate the American Henry Sanford, who was U.S. ambassador to Belgium and had business interests in the Congo.[108] He started lobbying on 27 November 1883 and at first came up against the inevitable skepticism of the State Department, which had little faith in the stability of the AIC. Then a philanthropic smoke screen was put up. Americans were told that the AIC was the successor of the altruistic CEHC, which in turn was said to be an offshoot of the humanitarian AIA.[109] The AIC would, moreover, do no more than act as temporary administrator of the "free states"—note the plural—that had been set up or would be set up in the Congo, more or less in the same way that the American Colonization Society had temporarily administered the newly created state of Liberia. This was incorporated into the declarations signed by the United States and the AIC on 22 April 1884, and subsequently endorsed by the Senate. The Americans thought that they were helping to found another Liberia. What they were founding in fact was the Belgian Congo.

### THE BOUNDARY QUESTION

Recognition by the United States, however welcome, did not count for much on the international scene. What Washington did was not very important at the time, what Berlin did all the more so. Two days after American recognition, thus on 24 April, Bismarck discussed Leopold's case for the first time with the French ambassador in Berlin. "I'm not really sure what that Association is exactly," he remarked.[110] Bismarck then made enquiries, and Leopold was only too pleased to assist him. The Association, the king explained, was an organization founded to set up stations with the purpose of linking the Atlantic to the Indian Ocean and of establishing a free state. To function properly, the state would have to stretch from coast to coast. Indeed, it would be best if it also comprised the Sudan, just ceded by Egypt, for here the slave trade was at its worst and the Association was better suited than anyone else to put a stop to it.

Here we find the first comments on an important new theme: the boundaries of the Free State. Having one's flag recognized was all very well, but it was not the same thing as gaining recognition for a territorial state. What Leopold possessed was a series of scattered stations. What he was asking for was a vast area of land. As the Belgian historian Jean Stengers has pointed out, it was rather like possessing a number of villages on the banks of the Rhine between Rotterdam and Basel and then demanding sovereignty over the whole of western Europe.[111] Yet, however fantastic Leopold's demands may have been, what he received was even more fantastic. The Congo Free State was more than twice the size of western Europe.

In this process, Leopold's negotiations with Bismarck had been of crucial importance, for Bismarck would be the first to recognize not only the Association but also the boundaries of its territory. Originally, this had not seemed likely. Bismarck was not a man to be taken in by daydreams or to be blinded by humanitarian eyewash. "*Schwindel*"—humbug—he had written in the margin of Leopold's note, next to a passage on fighting the slave trade.[112] In any case, he had insisted that free trade would have to be guaranteed first. Leopold was only too happy to oblige. Then Bismarck had asked him the crucial question: what were the boundaries of the Free State to be? Leopold's first reply was evasive. Could Germany not recognize the AIC and agree to accept the borders the AIC would specify at a later date? That was asking for carte blanche, literally and figuratively, and Bismarck, of course, had refused to grant it. He wanted a map on which the boundaries were clearly marked. So Leopold and Stanley together had applied themselves to a map of Africa at their meeting in Ostend on 7 August 1884. With bold strokes they had produced a first sketch of the Congo Free State. Compared with the dream of a region stretching from coast to coast and from Angola to Egypt, it was a modest plan—not even Leopold dared to commit such a dream to paper. For all that, the territory was massive enough, about two-thirds of the later Belgian Congo, or, to put it another way, the Belgian Congo minus Katanga.[113]

Bismarck examined the map. "Not all that stupid," he noted.[114] He did not know quite what to make of it all. On the one hand it was a great deal to ask. On the other he found Leopold foolish but not uncongenial. Moreover, Leopold posed no threat to Germany, and his plan had certain advantages. The presence of such a state might help to reduce international tensions in the region and keep more dangerous forces at bay. Even so, Bismarck hesitated at first about recognizing the proposed boundaries. The whole proposition was absurd and misconceived. But in the end he gave in. He knew that France would raise no objections because it had been offered privileged rights. He felt that Germany, too, ought to make some gesture. The result was a draft treaty between Germany and the AIC containing a whole series of articles summing up the obligations of the AIC toward the German Reich: the Free State would guarantee free trade, the Free State would protect German subjects, the Free State would do this and the Free State would do that. In return, Germany promised no more than the recognition of the flag. That was indeed very little, and so Article 6 was added: "The German Reich recognizes the boundaries as shown on the attached map."[115] This convention was signed on 8 November 1884. The crucial step had been taken. Now only France and Great Britain remained to be brought round.

Not much trouble was to be expected from France. After all, its privileged rights were such as to make it wish for the largest possible Free State, provided, of course, the territory did not impinge on regions to which France itself had claims. One such region was the "Niari-Kwilu," so called after two rivers in the Lower Congo. On the map presented to Bismarck, Leopold had cautiously marked that region as subject to "further adjustment." In his negotiations with France, he had to relinquish his claim to it. But Leopold was a man who, having lost something here, was anxious to recover it there. He accordingly presented a different map to France on 24 December 1884. On it the Free State lost the disputed territory but gained something else in exchange, namely, Katanga. Thus on that day Leopold annexed Katanga, at least on paper. It was to become the Congo's richest and most important province. However, according to Stengers, it was not its mineral riches that Leopold was after. What impelled him was a general imperialist urge, the desire for compensation for the "loss" of Niari-Kwilu and the objective of making the new state as large as possible and filling as much of the Congo basin as possible.[116] It was the result of an impulse and a way of putting out feelers. "If there is any opposition to it, we shall drop it," Leopold's delegate in Paris explained.[117] But Jules Ferry had no objections. Why should he have had? The larger the Free State, the more France stood to "inherit." On 5 February 1885 the map was accordingly recognized by France as an appendix to its convention with the AIC. Ten days later a treaty was also signed with Portugal, the other rival. As the Berlin Conference had dragged on, the Powers had become sick and tired of Portugal's procrastination and had ordered it bluntly to surrender the right bank of the Congo. In exchange, it was granted the left bank and a small area above the mouth of the Congo, the Cabinda enclave.

### "WHILE ENGLAND SLEPT"

Now Great Britain alone was left. Despite Hutton's and Mackinnon's active lobbying, there was little sympathy for the AIC in Great Britain. Sir Percy Anderson had few illusions about the Association, which he called "a private enterprise of a very abnormal kind."[118] There were, however, few objections to substituting the creation of the king of the Belgians for Portugal as guardian of the Congo. And opposing the Association would only benefit the country that posed the real danger, France. Moreover, Bismarck was a supporter of the AIC, and collaboration with Germany was particularly important for Great Britain, especially when it came to claims to the Niger.[119] Bismarck had left Britain in no doubt about that. The fact was that the Niger was more important for Great Britain than the Congo. Anderson therefore gave Leopold the green light fairly quickly: the AIC could count on British recognition. This was formally granted in the treaty of 16 December 1884, that is, shortly after the start of the conference. However, Great Britain left the boundaries of the Free State unspecified. That remained to be done, and when it was, some time later, it was in a most surprising way.

On 1 August 1885 Leopold agreed to become sovereign of the Free State. After some hesitation he decided against the title of Emperor of the Congo and made do with the more modest title of sovereign king.[120] He also drew up an act of neutrality, in accordance with Article 10 of the Act of Berlin, laying down that neutrality would apply to the entire area of the Free State as specified in the treaties with Germany, France and Portugal. In accordance with the Act of Berlin all the signatories to the act had to be notified of his declaration. If they raised no objections, their agreement could be assumed in accordance with diplomatic practice. Bismarck had meanwhile agreed to the new frontiers laid down in Leopold's treaty with France. The king thus had nothing to fear from Paris, Berlin or Lisbon. He awaited the crucial British decision with great suspense.

It was August. The African experts at the Foreign Office, including Sir

Percy Anderson, were on vacation. The civil servants they had left behind were not fully au fait with the latest developments. They compared the latest map they were sent with the map in their possession, which showed the borders of the Free State recognized by Germany, France and Portugal. That map had been published in Berlin after the conference and sent out to all concerned. The British civil servants had added it to the Congo dossier. Britain had been a signatory of the Act of Berlin. The civil servants accordingly assumed that all the maps accompanying the act, including the one with the Free State frontiers, were also recognized by the signatories of the act. That was not the case, however, for the act was not concerned with frontiers and territorial claims. The only maps to accompany the act were those referring to free trade zones and associated matters. But everything had been put in a single dossier, and meanwhile there had been so many maps, so many agreements, so many Congos, so many Congo basins and so many Congo associations that the civil servants' confusion was easy to understand. In any case, the Foreign Office decided that the two maps were identical, and let it be known on 1 September 1885 that the declaration had been duly noted.[121] In diplomatic language this signified acceptance, and was a matter of crucial importance. In later years, Katanga was to become a most desirable possession in the eyes of such British imperialists as Cecil Rhodes and Harry Johnston. When they approached the British government on the subject, it stuck to its guns. Anderson let them know that Leopold's map had been recognized in 1885 and that his territory unmistakably comprised the mining region of Katanga.[122] What was done was done. So the whims of Bismarck, the greed of Ferry and a "stupid blunder" by Whitehall, as Anderson was to call it after his return from leave, led to the inclusion of Katanga in the Free State, a state that, transplanted to Europe, would have stretched from Barcelona to Istanbul and from Sicily to Sweden.


# 8
# CONCLUSION

The Congo played a special role in the partition of Africa. On the whole, the partition took place against a background of bilateral rivalry, bilateral diplomacy and bilateral agreements: Anglo-British treaties, Franco-German conventions, Anglo-German pacts, and so on. In the Congo, by contrast, more than two parties were involved from the very outset. At first, these comprised the best known, namely, France and Great Britain, Powers we meet time and again during the partition. To a lesser degree, Portugal, too, was involved by virtue of its ancient rights, claims and possessions. But there were also several newcomers, the most important of which was Germany. Its sudden and unexpected decision to enter colonial politics was *the* political event of 1884. Even so, the most original newcomer was unquestionably Leopold II. He played a bizarre role in history: he was the constitutional ruler of a small but respected country which wanted no part of colonies, and at the same time a colonial conquistador in his private capacity and before long sole ruler over a gigantic colony, a constitutional Dr. Jekyll in Belgium and an authoritarian Mr. Hyde in Africa.

This new factor introduced yet another original element. Traditionally the partition of Africa had been dominated by Anglo-French rivalry. There had been Franco-German rivalry alongside it on the European continent since 1870. But during the Congo affair that rivalry seemed to have made way for Franco-German cooperation, which was, however, short-lived. The shadow of the Vosges remained stronger than the sun of colonial reconciliation. Even so, the short honeymoon in 1884–1885 had a crucial influence on the course of events. Bismarck's intervention meant the entry of a new player, and that called for a reshuffle and redeal of the cards and introduced a new element of uncertainty. Bismarck was used to taking the lead, not playing supporting roles. Germany was a force to be reckoned with. The same thing could not, of course, be said of Leopold. He did not direct the play that would end in his untrammelled possession of a fine colony. However, he profited from the existing tensions and offered an alternative: the Free State. This was not only an original solution, but at various moments offered each of the Great Powers considerable advantages over the alternatives.

The result of these new developments was a new form of diplomacy, no longer bilateral but multilateral, in the form of an international conference at Berlin. No wonder that this solution had so strong an appeal. The idea of an international conference of all European countries meeting under the leadership of Germany and discussing the future of an entire continent was appealing enough. It inevitably evoked such congresses as those of Vienna and Paris, where the political map of Europe had been reshaped, where boundaries had been redrawn, spheres of influence staked out, and territories divided or amalgamated or given away. Not surprisingly, therefore, it was widely believed that Africa was carved up in Berlin. Thus the Dutch paper *Algemeen Handelsblad* wrote on 21 November 1884: "No one can complain of monotony in politics, of plodding along carefully marked out state highways, while the chancellor of the *Reich* remains Europe's greatest and mightiest statesman. Original in everything he does . . . he has now taken the stage as the peace-loving commander of continents, one who distributes African empires right and left, just as the Pope once shared out America amongst the faithful." The writer then turned to the "youth and young men now being taught at secondary and high schools, commercial colleges, and universities" with this admonition: "Pay heed to what is happening now. In later years, thinking back to your youth, you will be able to say: We probably witnessed the last share-out of a continent amongst the states of Europe. West Africa in Bismarck's day was amicably and proportionally divided among the interested parties."

The belief that the Berlin Conference had divided Africa could therefore be found even in the newspapers of the time. Later, the idea took root more widely. Thus the Ghanaian president Kwame Nkrumah wrote, "The original carve-up of Africa was arranged at the Berlin Conference."[123] Many textbooks, too, have expressed this point of view. It is a mistaken one for all that. As we have seen, Africa was not only not divided at Berlin, but the subject was not even on the agenda; indeed, the partition of Africa was explicitly rejected by the conference. It is true the idea was in the air. The large map of Africa did not adorn the wall for nothing, and the conference had of course been called because here and there in Africa a fierce race for colonies, protectorates and spheres of influence had been started. The conference aimed to stop this process, or at least to keep it in check. It was a "holding operation," an attempt to calm matters by reaching agreement on principles and codes of conduct. One is rather reminded of later conferences to usher in the Year of the Woman, to draw up codes of conduct for multinational companies, or to pass resolutions against racism. That aspect lends the conference an air of unreality. Here the spirit of Geneva, not of Vienna, reigned supreme, the spirit of Woodrow Wilson rather than of Bismarck, of Grotius rather than of Machiavelli. The delegates discussed principles and procedures. They drafted resolutions and motions; they wore themselves out in hairsplitting arguments and elegant formulations, in defining navigation channels, points of international law and humanitarian duties. No wonder that Bismarck hardly put in an appearance. "The whole business bores him," Holstein noted in his diary on 13 December 1884.[124] In Bismarck's own memoirs the Berlin Conference is not even mentioned.

The conference therefore did not so much preside over the partition of Africa as serve as a symbol of it. The partition of Africa had been placed on the agenda of European diplomats and refused to go away for some time to come. The conference may have been a holding operation, but it was one that misfired, because, even as the conference was weighing its words, agreements recognizing the Free State and fixing its borders were signed, and the African gamble was greatly speeded up.[125] During the next few years many more treaties were concluded and a veritable race for protectorates begun. To keep that race under some control agreements were desperately needed. Arrangements for these had been tried in Berlin as well. Hence it has often been said that the Berlin Conference drew up the rules of the African game. It did no such thing. What rules it laid down under the heading of "formalities" referred to the African coast, not to the interior, but it was in the interior that the game would be played out in the next few years. The coastal regions had been almost entirely divided up already. If rules were needed, they were needed for the interior, but such rules were not drawn up. It is of course true to say that, here as elsewhere, when it came to it, the dictum that might is right applied. Yet there was a wish, if only on paper, to establish something like principles. That wish gave rise to the framing of several diplomatic principles that could be applied to international competition for territories about to be acquired, or to spheres of influence—a concept that entered international law soon after the conference—about to be defined.

The first of these principles was the so-called hinterland doctrine. According to it, a power with claims to the coast had a right to its hinterland. It has often been said that this doctrine was adopted during the conference.[126] That is another mistake—the Berlin Act contains no mention of the hinterland concept. But because it emerged so soon after Berlin, the mistake is understandable. In any case, the hinterland concept was not all that unreasonable. Any country trying to avoid trouble must make sure not to establish its sphere of influence directly behind another country's possessions. It was exceedingly difficult, however, to determine where a hinterland began and where it stopped. How serious a problem this was became clear when the French suddenly demanded Nigeria, insisting that it was the hinterland of Algeria.[127] Lord Salisbury called it a "doctrine . . . which they [the Germans] have to a great extent invented,"[128] but which was not recognized in international law.[129] Britain would have no truck with the hinterland theory. Lord Selborne, the British under-secretary for the colonies from 1895 to 1900, voiced this complaint: "I do not understand how it is that the hinterland doctrine always works against us. If the French or Germans have a strip of coast they claim, and claim successfully, everything behind it to the North Pole."[130] Yet Britain recognized it as a principle during negotiations, for instance with Germany over East Africa.[131] For all that, the hinterland theory was of small importance in practice.

More important was another principle of earlier provenance, namely, that of effective possession, based on treaties. The legal validity of Afro-European contracts was, as we saw earlier, highly questionable; as Bismarck put it in his inimitable way, in Africa it was only too easy "to come by a piece of paper with a lot of Negro crosses at the bottom."[132] European diplomats therefore knew only too well that such agreements were of little value. Yet such documents had a considerable effect in practice, as no country was anxious to cast explicit doubt on them. If it did, another country might well challenge the validity of the doubter's own treaties. That was to be avoided at all costs, which explains why these spurious treaties could prove of great importance and were generally taken at face value. Things were of course quite different when two parties had tangible cause to argue about treaties. Then there would be a legal battle over their validity, as we shall see when we come to West Africa.

The most important principle in international recognition was not, however, the hinterland doctrine, nor the existence of treaties. That principle was and remained the oldest of all "laws," namely, effective occupation.[133] Great Britain had done its utmost in Berlin to weaken that principle since it was not keen on the costly obligations its acceptance might entail. Thus what was put down on paper meant very little in the end. "Effective occupation" was held to be obligatory for new claims alone, not for old ones; on the coast alone, not in the interior; and only when creating colonial possessions, not when establishing protectorates. Paradoxically, however, this very principle had a kind of normative effect. In practice, the need for some form of effective occupation or presence when pressing one's claims became an important question. This explains not only why the Berlin Conference failed to put an end to the race for the interior, but why, on the contrary, that race continued at an accelerated pace.

The partition of the interior of Africa and of the continent as a whole was ultimately a matter of bilateral diplomacy. In the years to come, whenever a piece of the map was marked out as British or French, it would no longer mean that the countries interested in that territory, that is, the countries with claims to it or to its neighborhood, had recognized the claim. Such maps said nothing about the reality in Africa. The treaties had been framed in very general terms and showed that those responsible for them knew very little about the geography of the area. Frontiers were fixed in accordance with the course or aspect of rivers and mountains, or at least that was the general idea. The picture on the ground was different. As Lord Salisbury put it in a famous sally, "We have been giving away mountains and rivers and lakes to each other, only hindered by the small impediment that we never knew exactly where the mountains and rivers and lakes were."[134] Sometimes the mountains, lakes and rivers turned out not to exist. If still less was known about the area, the boundaries were fixed along degrees of longitude and latitude. The resulting treaties were treated as skeleton treaties, to be rectified by boundary commissions. The results of their surveys would then be incorporated into boundary agreements. In that field there was, not surprisingly, a great deal of activity. In less than twenty-five years, from 1882 to 1905, France and Great Britain signed 249 such boundary treaties covering West Africa alone.[135] Bilateral diplomacy thus had a heyday—the congress-diplomacy experiment would not be repeated. This unique feature of the Congo question was thus of short duration.

The other special element of the Congo question, too, proved to be short-lived. The Franco-German entente lasted for just one summer. It was over before it was properly begun, unable to prevail while the mortgage of 1870 remained unredeemed. With Alsace-Lorraine in German hands no lasting reconciliation was possible. Clemenceau called Ferry, following the latter's diplomatic collaboration with Bismarck against the Anglo-Portuguese agreement, "*le protégé de M. de Bismarck.*"[136] A more deadly epithet could hardly have been devised in France at the time. Bismarck saw the futility of further overtures. "I give up my attempt to reconcile France," he said as early as September 1885.[137]

Between Germany and Britain, by contrast, there was no fundamental clash of interests. Once the British had recovered from their surprise and their first shock at Bismarck's strong-arm tactics, they quickly came round. There was enough for everybody in Africa, and Britain already had more than it could cope with. That explains why Gladstone declared in the House of Commons on 12 March 1885, "If Germany is to become a colonizing power, all I say is 'God speed her!' She becomes our ally and partner in the execution of the great purposes of Providence for the advantage of mankind."[138] The *Daily Telegraph* extended "a hearty welcome . . . to the development of the Teuton abroad."[139] Here, too, the normal pattern thus returned soon enough: the partition of Africa would continue to be played out against the background of Anglo-French rivalry.

Bismarck was quickly disillusioned with his colonial adventure. The chartered companies proved to be a fiasco. They were kept alive artificially, very much against the wishes of German financiers. Bismarck's banker, Hans von Bleichroeder (junior) expressed "sound banking instincts" when he declared that investment in Africa was sheer nonsense.[140] But the Bleichroeders had to play along from time to time lest Bismarck be made to look ridiculous. In the long run even that proved of no avail. The chartered companies were wound up, and the Reich took over the colonies. What Bismarck had not wanted had thus come to pass: Germany assumed political and financial responsibilities in Africa. Not surprisingly, therefore, Bismarck declared in 1889 that he was sick and tired of the colonies.[141]

Leopold II, by contrast, was far from disappointed. For him 1885 was only the beginning. The borders of the Free State were a minimum, not a maximum. The Free State would therefore become a token, not of international reconciliation, but of conflict. That was the case inside Leopold's creation as well. Nothing came of free trade. The state claimed all uncultivated land. Now, such land just happened to be the source of the products of the greatest commercial interest: ivory and rubber. Those who traded in them thus became thiefs or fences. That explains why Stengers characterized the commercial policy of the Free State as follows: "Article 1) Trade is completely free; Article 2) Nothing can be bought or sold."[142] Leopold's financial problems were nevertheless considerable. He himself had to contribute, so much so in fact that his wife complained, "But Leopold, you will ruin us with your Congo."[143] He had to pawn his overseas decorations and the livery of his lackeys, and even resolved as a last resort to forego one course of his luncheon.[144] All to no avail. Belgium organized a state lottery. It did not help, and the Belgian state had to lend Leopold money.

Still the problem was not solved. Then, just in the nick of time, Leopold was saved by rubber. The growing demand for it was driving the price up, and the hunt for "red rubber" in the Congo finally yielded the requisite revenue. The chase, however, led to such excesses that it caused one of the greatest scandals in colonial history, the Congo atrocities. International indignation at the methods used in the Congo grew so loud that Leopold, under pressure from Belgian politicians, was forced to abandon his personal regime in the Congo. In 1908 the Belgian state took over. The atrocities also gave the lie to Leopold's philanthropic pretensions. The former embodiment of humanitarian ideals and altruism was transformed into a symbol of the purest imperialism and the most brutal exploitation. While Ferdinand de Lesseps had still been able to call Leopold's creation "the most humanitarian work of our century,"[145] the king of the Belgians had turned the Congo, in Joseph Conrad's famous words, into Africa's "heart of darkness."

# III

# "COOL AND COURAGEOUS": GERMANY AND GREAT BRITAIN IN EAST AFRICA, 1885–1890

So geographers, in Afric-maps,
With savage-pictures fill their gaps;
And o'er uninhabitable downs
Place elephants for want of towns.

Jonathan Swift

G eographically, East Africa is a very broad concept. It comprises the entire western shore of the Indian Ocean, from Obock to East London. Historically, however, it refers to a much smaller area. Ethiopia and the Red Sea area do not fall within it. Their history is closely bound up with that of the Sudan and the Nile and will be examined in that context (see p. 242). The northern border of East Africa thus lies in Somaliland, the southern border in Mozambique. The latter can equally well be considered part of East, Central or southern Africa. Because the final delimitation of the Portuguese colonies in southern Africa—not merely of Mozambique but also of Angola—was so closely linked to that of southern Africa as a whole, the history of these colonies will be considered in the appropriate chapter (see p. 297). In the history of the partition of Africa the concept of East Africa therefore has a special meaning. In pre-colonial terms, it referred to an area that can be included in the sphere of influence of Zanzibar over East Africa; in colonial terms it was part of British and German East Africa; in post-colonial terms, it comprises the modern states of Kenya, Uganda, Tanzania, Rwanda and Burundi. Even in this very limited sense, it is still an area the size of western Europe. In Africa nothing is small.

The heart of East Africa is the highland around the great lakes, which stretches almost as far as the coast. Even in the nineteenth century the coast and the interior were almost entirely divorced from each other. The people in the interior shaped their own destinies. They lived in political units of varying sizes. The coast, by contrast, lay open to overseas invaders, among whom first the Arabs and the Portuguese and later the British and the Germans were the most important. The coast actually belonged more to the world of the Indian Ocean than it did to Africa proper, Arab influence being of very long standing. The most important factor in the Arab presence in East Africa was the prevailing wind. For many centuries, the north-northeasterly monsoon had carried Arab ships southwards along the east coast of Africa from December to February. From April to September the south-southwesterly monsoon had carried them back again. There had thus

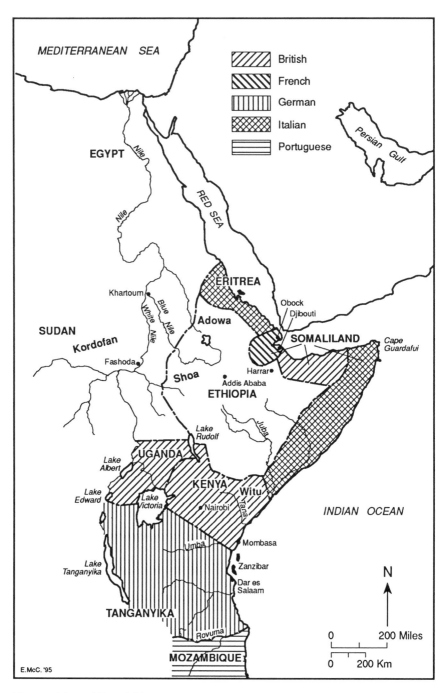

The partition of East Africa

always been trade, and for close on a thousand years there had also been Arab and Persian colonies along the coast from Mogadishu to Cape Delgado. The Portuguese took over the Arab sphere of influence for a time, just as they did its very heart in Arabia, but in 1651 they were driven out of Muscat and Oman and later out of East Africa as well. The fall of Fort Jesus in Mombasa put an end to their presence north of the Rovuma, and the Portuguese sphere of influence was henceforth confined to Mozambique. To its north the coast was controlled by Arabs, theoretically by the imam of Oman but in practice by independent sheiks. Such was the situation in 1806 when Said ibn-Sultan seized power in Muscat, the most important seaport of Oman.

# 1
# THE RISE OF ZANZIBAR AND BRITISH INFLUENCE

### SAID AND BARGASH

It took Said many years to consolidate his authority in Oman. When he eventually succeeded, he also paved the way for the ultimate surrender of that authority. In 1840 he moved his seat to the island of Zanzibar. There were several reasons for doing so. The island was more fertile than the dry sands of Oman. It had a good harbor and adequate supplies of drinking water. Moreover, its location was very favorable to trade, and Said had his mind set on that. He was a true merchant-prince, and had the foresight to introduce the cultivation of cloves to Zanzibar, the island proving to be so well suited to the crop that it quickly acquired a world monopoly in it. He also introduced a new coinage, reformed the customs duty, and made trade agreements with America and several European countries. Trading companies and consuls took up residence in Zanzibar, and the result was a spectacular renaissance of what had been a forgotten island. Zanzibar became a veritable bazaar, a kind of Afro-Asian Singapore, with a mixed population of Arabs, Africans, Indians and Europeans. It had the largest slave market in East Africa and was the center of the ivory trade. Under Said, Zanzibar's authority was extended to virtually the entire coast. But Zanzibar did not merely dominate the coast of East Africa, it also exerted control, if in an informal commercial way, over the hinterland as far as the great lakes. Said remained imam of Oman, but he had also, and above all, become sayyid, sultan of Zanzibar.

The political side of his rule was quite another matter. Borders did not concern him greatly. All the coastal towns had governors officially representing him, but they were in fact their own masters. In the interior, too,

The port of Zanzibar

there lay Arab settlements along the Arab trade routes which recognized Said's authority. But that was as far as it went. No political structure was ever imposed. Effective occupation was not Said's concern.

When Said died in 1856, his empire was divided, his elder son receiving Oman, his younger son Zanzibar. The elder was understandably dissatisfied, but the arrangement was confirmed, that is imposed, by Great Britain. The two thrones were separated, and in 1862 France and Great Britain solemnly confirmed the independence of the two rulers by treaty. An Anglo-French condominium seemed to be in the offing, but British influence on the small island became dominant, while the French were more interested in a much larger island, Madagascar. Hence European intervention here, unlike elsewhere, did not lead to Anglo-French rivalry. Britain was the undisputed master in Zanzibar. The only other European Power it would have to contend with was Germany, but that would not be until 1885. Moreover, the Germans, unlike the French, were not interested in trading monopolies. Consequently, therefore, East Africa was not to become the scene of great international tensions.

Anglo-Zanzibar collaboration was confirmed and consolidated by the team of Bargash and Kirk. Sultan Bargash, who came to power in 1870, was an energetic ruler in Said's mold. He brought Zanzibar even closer to the Western world than Said had done by developing shipping and telegraph links. No less energetic was the British representative in Zanzibar, Sir John Kirk (1832–1922), a medical man attached to the consulate as a doctor. Kirk does not seem to have been an exceptional physician, for he was unable to cure the British consul of his complaints, but he seems to have been good at diplomacy, becoming consul himself in 1866 and later consul general. He stayed at this post until 1887, a year before Bargash's death. As consul general, Kirk became Zanzibar's strong man, the sayyid's *éminence grise*. The price Bargash paid for his increasingly close collaboration with Great Britain was the abolition of the slave trade. In 1872 Sir Bartle Frere conducted the negotiations, and in 1873 the slave trade was finally abolished. A matter of hours after the signing of the treaty the Zanzibar slave market was closed down. As a reward Bargash was invited to England, which he visited in 1875. He met the Queen and the Prince of Wales, visited seaports, buildings and museums, attended the Ascot races, and was treated to choral music in Crystal Palace and a performance of *Lohengrin*. His words of thanks were simple but emphatic: "What can I say but thank you, thank you, thank you?"[1] In 1875, Anglo-Zanzibar relations had their finest hour.

ZANZIBAR AND EAST AFRICA

This collaboration extended to the sultan's possessions on the African continent, where his claims stretched as far inland as the great lakes. Others, too, had staked their claims to this area, among them the khedive of Egypt, on whose behalf Gordon had even tried to join the province of Equatoria to the Indian Ocean at Mombasa, albeit in vain. In 1877 a group of British entrepreneurs suggested to Bargash that they take possession in his name of the land lying between the coast and Lake Victoria. The area was, after all, without protection, and might easily fall prey to the khedive. The businessmen were prepared to tackle this project with all vigor and at no cost to the sultan. The sponsor of this grandiose plan was "a little Scotsman" called William Mackinnon.

## Mackinnon

William Mackinnon (1823–1893) was a self-made man. The son of poor parents, he had enjoyed little education and went into business at an early age. In Glasgow he worked for an employer engaged in trade with the East, and in 1847 he traveled to India to become a partner of his old schoolmate, Robert Mackenzie, then engaged in coastal trading in the Bay of Bengal. The firm of Mackinnon & Mackenzie developed into a considerable enterprise. Mackinnon himself concentrated on the shipping side, and the British India Steam Navigation Company he founded expanded rapidly, so much so that its ships became a familiar sight everywhere east of Aden, as well as in Zanzibar, where Mackinnon was responsible for the shipping, mail and telegraph links. He became an important figure, active in a number of enterprises. Many people had cause to appeal to him, and few did so in vain, especially when it came to charitable or church activities. It was this combination of business acumen and missionary zeal that put Mackinnon on the road to the African interior, where he became involved in a number of African adventures, almost invariably frowned upon by British politicians and civil servants, who considered Sir William an altogether too enthusiastic and unpractical dreamer.

This view was not entirely unfounded, since some of his many plans proved quite unworkable. That was the case, for example, with his elephant-importing project, based on his study of the differences between Indian and African elephants. While Indian elephants were put to use in their native land for all kinds of work, African elephants were not, which suggested to Mackinnon that it would be an interesting idea to ship Indian elephants to East Africa and get them to teach their African brethren how to make themselves useful as mounts and beasts of burden. A shipload of elephants was accordingly dispatched from Bombay. The problem was that there were no harbors suited to the landing of elephants in East Africa. The attempt to disembark the animals close to the shore in the hope that they would make for land by themselves ended in disaster: the elephants pulled the ships back into the sea, the animals drowned, and the ships foundered. Mackinnon's experiment thus failed before a single African elephant had been taught its first lesson. The scheme did not do very much for Mackinnon's reputation.[2]

The project he came up with in 1876 was both more ambitious and more realistic. Mackinnon and his friends asked for no more and no less than commercial and administrative control over all the sultan's possessions on the mainland. While their company would have all the rights normally enjoyed by a colonial administration, the sultan would share in the profits. Though that meant a considerable loss of prestige for him, the sultan was quite happy to agree, being only too well aware that his hold over these possessions was precarious while his authority in Africa remained as theoretical as it was. What was more, he himself had asked the British government for the help of British "capitalists" in the "development and civilization of Africa." But while British capitalists were only too happy to oblige, the British government was not. Lord Salisbury in particular was opposed to an operation that he felt would inevitably saddle Britain with fresh obligations. His personal opposition, however covert, had its effect on the sultan.[3] The negotiations were broken off. In 1878 the sultan may have been prepared to create a British East Africa, but Britain itself was not. Consular control of Zanzibar was quite enough.

Mackinnon did not abandon his interest in Africa, however, nor Bargash his desire for British aid. In 1879 Mackinnon applied once more for a concession, if in more modest form, namely, the lease of Dar es Salaam and a number of other territories on the way from Dar es Salaam to Lake Nyasa. But the sultan had not forgotten Salisbury's view of the matter and refused once more, in the most courteous terms. Mackinnon, disappointed, revised his African policy and turned to another Africa enthusiast, King Leopold. He became involved in a number of Leopold's committees and activities in East and Central Africa. In 1887 he founded the British East African Association, which was to play a considerable role in the partition of East Africa.

Bargash, for his part, asked openly for a British protectorate in 1881, but the liberal Gladstone government was even less inclined to shoulder that kind of obligation than its conservative predecessor had been. The request was thus politely turned down.[4] Influence, not annexation, was the primary aim of the British government, the preservation of the status quo the main pillar of its East Africa policy. This negative imperialism, formulated earlier in the Franco-British mutual nonintervention pact of 1862, was reaffirmed in 1884, when fear of German ambitions gripped the Foreign Office. British influence was used to force Bargash into making a solemn declaration that he would not cede his sovereignty or any part thereof to any foreign power, nor accept a protectorate, without first consulting Great Britain.[5] It was hoped that this pledge would avert the new German threat, but it proved powerless to do so. In 1884 Bismarck became converted to colonialism, and Great Britain was to feel the effects nowhere more than in East Africa.

## 2
# GERMANY AND EAST AFRICA

Even before Bismarck's conversion, Germany had not been wholly absent from East Africa, German traders being particularly active in Zanzibar. A merchant from Hamburg, for instance, had discovered that while the cowrie shells that were found in the area had no value there, they served as money in West Africa. This came as close as one could get to realizing the old alchemists' dream of turning base metals into gold. The Hamburg contingent thus did good business, many of them settling permanently in Zanzibar. In the 1870s roughly half of all Zanzibar's exports were in their hands, more than twice as much as Great Britain could command.[6] However, the first German plans to acquire territory in East Africa came not from these traders but from the Gesellschaft für Deutsche Kolonisation—the Society for German Colonization—founded in Berlin on 28 March 1884. The society was run by a triumvirate: Count Behr-Bandelin, a reactionary landowner, Friedrich Lange, publisher of the *Tägliche Rundschau*, and Carl Peters, who was the greatest of them.[7]

Carl Peters

### THE PETERS EXPEDITION

Carl Peters (1856–1918) was one of the most bizarre characters in the history of imperialism in Africa, a history so rich in strange figures. He was the son of a clergyman, and the year of his birth, 1856, was not, sadly for him, divisible by three. For Peters was a firm believer in Pythagorean number mysticism. All the important events in his life, he wrote, took place in years divisible by three. "In 1878 I was awarded the gold medal for arts and science by the University of Berlin; in 1881 I went to London, the most important experience in my life—that date is divisible not only by three but even by three times three; in 1884 I went to Africa for the first time."[8] And so it went on. It is not surprising, therefore, that Peters believed not only in numbers, but also in ghosts, a belief which, after all, was in keeping with his love for England. In 1881 he paid his first visit to London, staying with an uncle and aunt. The ardent German patriot fell deeply under the spell of that gigantic metropolis, the center of a proud, old, powerful and worldwide empire.

In 1882, back in Germany, he published a philosophical book with the elegant but not particularly lucid title *Willenswelt und Weltwille* (The World of the Will and the Will of the World). Shortly afterwards he went to London once again to hold a vigil for his recently deceased uncle, who was considerate enough to revive temporarily that night and smile at his nephew for fully twenty seconds.[9] Peters stayed on in London for a while, made an attempt at swimming the Channel, failed, but managed to reach the continent, albeit by ship, and to devote himself wholeheartedly to his colonial vocation.

Learned man though he was, Peters did not look upon German colonization as a matter of study and scientific advancement. His slogan was "words *and* deeds." It will not, however, be a surprise to learn that this philosopher laureate, who believed in number mysticism, ghosts and predestination, was not taken very seriously by a chancellor who believed in iron and blood. Nor was he treated with great respect by the diplomats in the Wilhelmstrasse, who believed in telegrams, memoranda and cautious moves on the chessboard of international politics. They made short shrift of the learned doctor's plans and projects. Peters had to fend for himself, but eventually received enough money from his Society for German Colonization to equip an expedition. An advance party, consisting of Peters and three traveling companions (a lawyer, a count and a farmer) left in the greatest secrecy, but Peters's ideas had by then become so notorious that Bismarck felt impelled to let him know that, no matter what his plans might be, he must not count on support from the Reich.[10]

Peters was the undisputed leader of the expedition. His aim, in his own lapidary formulation, was "to acquire an empire to my own taste."[11] That taste was not very specific, since as far as Peters was concerned his empire might equally well have been in South America or West Africa, though in the end he settled for East Africa. On 16 September 1884 came the decision to equip an expedition for the purpose of acquiring land "somewhere across from Zanzibar."[12] The expedition set out under the motto "cool and courageous."[13] "Swiftly and stealthily" would have been more accurate, for the group departed in great haste so as to avoid embarrassing questions. Moreover, to help keep their secret, Peters and his men gave out that they were English. They had notified the German Foreign Office, but did not ask for its blessing,[14] knowing as they did that the German government was opposed to their enterprise. The German consul in Zanzibar, alerted by his Foreign Office, informed them that he could accord them no protection whatsoever. They were there at their own expense and risk. Bismarck was anything but keen on precipitate interference with British Zanzibar policy.

On 10 November 1884 the expedition set off. It was made up of forty-seven men, a small contingent, and was, moreover, badly equipped: not enough food, no tropical kit, no medicines. They nevertheless felt, Peters wrote, like the conquistadores who had conquered Mexico.[15] On 23 November they signed their first treaty. Another eleven were to follow during the next few weeks. All of them were more or less the same as the first, the "Treaty of Eternal Friendship" concluded with a village chief whom Peters referred to as "Mafungu Biniani, ruler of Quatunga, Kwindokaniani, etc., sultan of Nguru."[16] Peters's method was simple. A village chief, generally designated "sultan" but sometimes simply "highness," would declare that he held sovereign rights to a given territory. He would then go on to state that he was ceding all the rights flowing from that sovereignty to his friend, sometimes referred to as his blood brother, Peters. The deeds were always in German, and there was only one copy, signed by Peters with the sovereign adding a cross. The signing ceremony was usually preceded by a merry-making session, during which guns were fired, German songs sung, schnapps was drunk and sometimes—more in keeping with Karl May's cowboys and pioneers than with Carl Peters himself—blood brotherhoods were sealed. This, incidentally, caused the German Foreign Office to ask its lawyers to make an analysis of the meaning of blood brotherhood in international law. Peters took great care to persuade the village chiefs to declare that they were not dependents of the sultan of Zanzibar. On one occasion he even went so far as to get the chief to declare that he did not know that such a person as the sultan of Zanzibar existed.

The Peters expedition traveled across the hinterland of Bagamoyo and Dar es Salaam, that is, through Usagara, Ukami, Useguha and Nguru. All that can be said with certainty of this last territory is that it was annexed, but not that the expedition ever set foot in it. The expedition was, after all, short of manpower, and quickly began to feel the handicap of inadequate equipment. Many of the men fell ill, and there were quite a few fatalities. After just thirty-seven days, the sick and worn-out travelers were back at the coast. Although by African standards five weeks was more of an excursion than an expedition, the cool and courageous travelers had been able to take possession of nearly 55,000 square miles, almost as much land as the Netherlands, Belgium, Switzerland and Denmark combined. That was on paper only, of course. The legal validity of such contracts was nil, unless, that is, they were recognized by the international community, meaning Great Britain.

It was 17 December 1884 when Peters reached the coast with his treaties, and 5 February 1885 when he arrived in Berlin. The Berlin Conference was still in full swing. Peters presented his documents to the German Foreign Office with accompanying memoranda in which he explained that the annexed territory was "sublimely beautiful." It would make a splendid nucleus of a "German India" in Africa.[17] In fact it was not altogether unlike Heidelberg, he added.[18] That was quite enough to make the German leaders lose their hearts, though not their heads: it would never do to spring such late acquisitions on the Conference at the last moment. Once the Berlin Conference was over, however, Germany lost no time. The conference closed on 26 February. The next day a *Schutzbrief*, an imperial charter, was issued, placing Peters's territories under German protection and vesting authority over them in the Society for German Colonization. The Kusserow formula—protection without cost to the German Reich by means of chartered companies—once again proved its worth.

Germany had now moved into East Africa, acquiring a taste for more. This new interest was reflected with much feeling in the "Song of the Germans over the Sea":

*Noch manches Eiland lockt und lauscht*
*Aus Palmen und Bananen:*
*Der Seewind braust, die Woge rauscht,*
*Auf! freudige Germanen![19]*

Such a tempting island was, of course, primarily Zanzibar itself. But Zanzibar was ruled by the Kirk-Bargash team. The new German consul, Friedrich Gerhard Rohlfs (1832–1896), was resolved to put a stop to that. Rohlf's career was a peculiar alternation of medical and military roles. A member of the Schleswig-Holstein Volunteer Corps, a medical student, an Austrian soldier, a French legionnaire, an army and harem doctor in Morocco, and finally an Africa explorer[20]—Rohlfs had been all of that by the time he left for Zanzibar in 1884 as German consul. Since his colonial ambitions were well known, they caused considerable anxiety in Great Britain and gave rise to rumors about an impending German protectorate. The sultan, however, would have nothing to do with German patronage. He declared that he trusted in "the Most High God" and in "Her Gracious Majesty the Queen," and rejected Rohlf's overtures out of hand.[21] Bismarck, too, counseled moderation. Great Britain must not be provoked. Even so, a naval demonstration was organized to persuade the sultan to recognize the German protectorate over Peters's territories, which the obdurate sultan claimed as his own. On 7 August 1885 five German gunboats dropped anchor in the roads off Zanzibar. That was enough. On 20 September the sultan recognized not only all Peters's territories but also the district of Witu as German protectorates.[22]

### WITU

Witu was an area on the East African coast, lying at the mouth of the Tana and at the margin of the sultan of Zanzibar's sphere of influence. Its center was a fortress in the bush, a few days' march from the coast. The state of Witu—inasmuch as one could call it a state, for it was more of a robbers' nest—stretched a few dozen miles into the interior, and its head was Ahmed the Lion. His territory happened to be the next place "somewhere" in East Africa to attract the attention of German colonists, although in the event not that of Carl Peters but of the Denhardt brothers. These explorers had succeeded in raising enough money to mount an expedition to Tana for the purpose of acquiring land and studying the commercial prospects. On 29 December 1884—the month Peters returned to the coast—they disembarked in Africa and set out for Witu. If Peters's expedition had been an adventure story, then the Denhardts' was a picaresque novel.

In Ahmed the Denhardts discovered a lion at bay. The sultan of Zanzibar was determined to root out this thorn in his flesh, and Ahmed knew that the only way to stop him was to obtain the protection of a European Power. Hence he was only too happy to enter into a pact with the Germans. In April 1885 he signed a series of treaties with them giving them possession of some twenty square miles of territory and appointing them sole representatives of his sultanate both in Zanzibar and in Europe. At the same time Ahmed called for a German protectorate over the entire "Witu empire." This request opened up unheard-of prospects. Germany accordingly granted it, and during the naval demonstration of August 1885 forced the sultan to recognize it. The Denhardts now made a strange discovery: they found that Ahmed the Lion was not only the ruler of an area measuring a few square miles, but was actually the sovereign of all Swahilis. According to this interpretation his dominion stretched from Mozambique to the Red Sea. The German government, the Denhardts claimed, had only to adopt that view and Germany would be lord and master over East Africa.[23]

But Bismarck knew better than that. He realized that the key to East Africa was Zanzibar, not Witu, and that Zanzibar was held by Great Britain, not by Ahmed the Lion. British opinion was divided. Gladstone was not interested. He called the regions concerned "the mountain country behind Zanzibar with an unrememberable name."[24] Granville, his foreign secretary, took much the same view. He also remembered that Bismarck could wave his "Egyptian baton" even in East Africa. Both men were therefore keen to avoid trouble with Germany over this issue. There was, however, an opposing current in British politics, determined on framing a new strategy in Africa. Its views were first presented in a Foreign Office memorandum drafted by Clement Hill, a senior official, on 9 December 1884. His approach was geopolitical—he viewed African affairs in the framework of British imperial policy. "Is it not worth considering," Hill asked, "whether in view of the European race for territories on the West Coast . . . we might not confine ourselves to securing the utmost possible freedom of trade on that coast, yielding to other Powers the territorial responsibilities . . . and seeking compensation on the East Coast?"[25] That approach would later become known as the "British lake" theory. The northern and eastern shores of the Indian Ocean, India and Australia were already in British hands. If the East African coast were added, then the Indian Ocean might be considered a British inland sea, a British Mediterranean.

That was a splendid geopolitical view. But for the time being good relations with Germany came first. Bismarck for his part kept a cool head. He realized that British support was needed if he were to gain the goodwill of the sultan of Zanzibar, and that such goodwill was essential for the commercial exploitation of the new colony. Moreover, British capital would also come in handy.[26] Negotiations opened and were eventually crowned with success. The settlement reached was set down in the form of an exchange of notes between Germany and Britain dated 29 October and 1 November 1886. In them, the sovereignty of the sultan of Zanzibar over the islands of Zanzibar, Pemba, Mafia, and Lamu, and over the East African coast from about the Rovuma (the border with Mozambique) to the Tana (the border with Witu) was recognized, all to a depth of ten nautical miles from the coast. The hinterland was divided into a German sphere of influence in the south and a British sphere of influence in the north, with the Umba, which joined the sea at Vanga, as the boundary. Above the British sphere of influence lay the German protectorate of Witu. The British sphere was thus cut off by German territory above and below it. Britain also undertook to help Germany obtain a lease of the ports of Pangani and Dar es Salaam, thus providing the German region with "windows and doors" to the coast.[27] Sultan Bargash asked for six months to think matters over but was not granted it. On 7 December 1886 he signed the treaty. That month the borders with Mozambique were settled as well.

All in all, the first Anglo-German partition treaty in East Africa was a triumph for Bismarck. His moderation had gained Germany a large protectorate without alienating Great Britain. Germany had gained access to the coast through two leased harbors. The British sphere of influence had been cut off on two sides. Of these, the northern frontier with Witu was the most threatening for Britain: it gave Germany access to Uganda and to the Upper Nile. The German success had been the result of extremely able diplomacy. The *Schutzbrief* of 27 February 1885—coming as it did so soon after the drama of Khartoum—was proof of excellent timing. Britain was in a weak position and could not dispense with German support in Egypt. Once again it had become clear how closely bound up European diplomacy was with African expansion. That very link was, incidentally, to lead to the opposite result a few years later: by the second partition treaty, in 1890, Germany had to surrender Witu, and Britain was thus rescued from the German threat to the Nile. Then it was Germany who was anxious to keep on the right diplomatic side of Great Britain and hence had to be generous in Africa. But a great deal was to happen before that, both in Berlin and in Africa.

# 3
# GREAT BRITAIN AND GERMANY IN EAST AFRICA, 1886–1890

After the treaty of 1886 Great Britain and Germany both had a sphere of influence in East Africa, but the coast was still in the hands of the sultan.

Without the coast little could be done, and access to the sea was thus essential. Germany and Great Britain set about the matter in the same way. They delegated the exploitation and administration of their territories to private companies, which tried to gain access to the coast by means of leasing agreements. The German company concerned was the Deutsche Ost-Afrika Gesellschaft (DOAG), or German East Africa Company, in which the Kaiser was the largest shareholder. In 1887 that company assumed the rights of the Society for German Colonization, with the reins remaining in the hands of Carl Peters. The British counterpart was the British East African Association (BEAA), founded by William Mackinnon in 1887. It was granted a concession by Bargash by the treaty of 24 May 1887 giving it complete authority over the stretch of coast in the British sphere of influence, that is, between the Umba and the Tana, on condition that it would exercise that authority in the name of the sultan and under the Zanzibar flag. The BEAA was also granted legislative and executive powers, including the right to levy tolls and taxes, together with the right to dispose of all land not in private hands. In return, the association guaranteed Bargash the income he currently received from the customs duties imposed at the coast plus 50 percent of the anticipated rise in that income.[28]

Needless to say, the DOAG refused to make do with less, and Bargash, who was in financial difficulties, was ready to give them what they asked, doing so on 28 April 1888. The treaty was more or less the same as that signed with the British. The German coastal stretch ran from the Umba in the north to the Rovuma in the south. However, the DOAG's administrative record was poor. The capital at its disposal was small, and in any case not enough to establish an effective authority or the machinery needed for the commercial exploitation of the territory. The capital could of course have been augmented by the collection of customs duties, but effective authority was required for that. There was thus a vicious circle—just how vicious will be shown below.

### THE DOAG AT WORK

On 15 August 1888 the DOAG took over the administration of its territories. It employed fifty-six agents, all from Carl Peters's ruthless school. The German government provided a naval squadron to cover the transfer of power. The agents started at once to fill the company coffers, and to that end introduced a series of taxes compared with which the collection of the tenth, the twentieth and the hundredth penny by Philip II was mere child's play. Among many other taxes, they levied a burial tax, a transport tax, a cocoa tax, a poll tax, and in addition created concessions and obligations, measures, orders and regulations, papers, seals, dues and stamps, all in the best Prussian tradition. Small wonder, then, that the astonished Arabs and Swahilis, who as far back as anyone could remember had been

A station of the DOAG

used to nothing more than simple import and export duties and even simpler bribes, looked upon the actions of their new masters with amazement and horror and rebelled against them.[29]

The uprising began on 22 September 1888 in Bagamoyo and spread to the other coastal towns, especially to Pangani, where the movement found its leader in Abushiri ibn-Salim, a slave trader and sugar plantation owner and member of a prominent local family.[30] The rebels refused to recognize the authority of the sultan of Zanzibar. By the end of 1888 the entire region ostensibly under DOAG control was in revolt, trade was paralyzed, and European staff went in danger of their lives. The company was clearly unable to run the colony. The German government now had a simple choice: they could wash their hands of the whole business or step into the breach. Bismarck viewed the mess the DOAG had made of their colony with great dismay. The chartered company formula, so splendid on paper, did not seem to work in practice. Yet state intervention meant applying to the hostile Reichstag for credits, an operation Bismarck loathed. In the event cunning and providence offered a way out. The Catholic antislavery campaign happened to have reached its climax in 1888 with the Pope's encyclical *In pluribus*. The leader of that campaign was the French cardinal Charles Lavigerie. The Vatican was second only to Britain in its abolitionist zeal. So, since East Africa was the last great hunting ground of the Arab slave traders, here was an opportunity of turning the fight against the rebels into a war on the slave trade. In so doing, Bismarck was able to gain the support not only of the British government, but also of the German Catholic Zentrum Party.

In a long address to the Reichstag, he explained that what he was asking was not support for a private colonial enterprise, but the fulfillment of a humanitarian and moral duty, a stand for "civilization, Christian conversion and national duty." By signing the Act of Berlin, Germany had assumed that obligation.[31] The Reichstag voted the necessary credits on 30 January 1889. A state commission would be appointed to take charge of the operations.

Bismarck also received British support, though not without opposition, the German competitors not being greatly loved in Great Britain. It was, however, obvious that the rebels would be unable to distinguish between white men who were British and those who were German. Moreover, the antislavery rhetoric was irresistible to British ears. For Lord Salisbury there was an additional, political, motive: he was not at all keen to see Germany going it alone in East Africa. The French had allowed Britain to do this during the Egyptian crisis, and as a result had disappeared from the Egyptian scene. The same thing could well happen to the British in Zanzibar. Salisbury was afraid of sudden German, and perhaps even Italian, forays against the sultan.[32] Britain therefore chose to give Germany maritime support during the East African crisis, thus contributing to a German success.

The German state commissioner, Major Hermann von Wissmann, recruited an army consisting largely of African troops, and in May 1889 launched his operations from Bagamoyo and Dar es Salaam, the two bridgeheads besieged by the rebels. The siege was relieved and the German-led troops moved inland. On 8 and 9 November they took Pangani. The local chiefs gave Abushiri little support, his movement began to falter, and he eventually became a ringleader on the run. In December 1889 his camp was attacked and his men overpowered. Abushiri was one of the few to escape. After roaming the bush for several days he appeared before a village chief who took him prisoner and handed him over to the Germans. They sentenced him to death, as they had sentenced most of his followers, and he was hanged on 15 December 1889.[33] During the next few months the rest of German East Africa was gradually pacified in the brutal and barbarous way that was to become so typical of the German presence in East Africa.

Developments in the British sphere of influence took a different course. The British company proceeded more cautiously, preferring the carrot to the stick and so avoiding major uprisings. The British East African Association, too, was a modest enterprise with little capital, but its leader, Mackinnon, was nevertheless a most ambitious man. His sights were set on the hinterland, the region above Lake Victoria—in other words, on Uganda. The Foreign Office, which was gradually preparing a Nile strategy, was also interested in the region, but it was skeptical and cautious too—skeptical because it doubted Mackinnon's ability, and cautious because the territory was vulnerable to a German thrust from Witu and the 1886 treaty had not established any spheres of influence there. Salisbury, in particular, was suspicious of Mackinnon, whom he considered a nuisance. "He has no energy for anything except quarreling with Germans," he said of him.[34] Even so, the 1887 agreements between the British company and Bargash were recognized by the British government, and the East African Association, having turned itself into the Imperial British East Africa Company (IBEAC) on 18 April 1888, was granted a concession on 3 September for exploiting the sultan's territories, from Kipini in the north to Umba in the south. Now the race for the interior, for Uganda, could begin in earnest.

The Germans were the first to arrive in Uganda and to establish a protectorate there. The man responsible for that was Carl Peters. There had been a special reason for his going there: Peters was one of many who had set their mind on rescuing Emin Pasha. In the event, Peters was to fail in that mission, for others preceded him with greater success. However, his rescue mission had an unexpected effect, namely, the German annexation of Uganda.

### THE RESCUE OF EMIN PASHA

Emin Pasha (1840–1892) was actually Eduard Schnitzer, born in Silesia of Jewish parents who had converted to the Lutheran faith. Eduard studied medicine in Berlin, Königsberg and Breslau, and in 1864 left for Albania, which was then still under Turkish rule. He converted to Islam, adopted the Turkish title and name of Dr. Hairoullah-Effendi, took employment as a quarantine officer, and from then on wore a fez.[35] He caused something of a scandal when he returned to his birthplace with the widow of a Turkish official, her four daughters and a number of female slaves. However, he left soon afterwards for Egypt, where he enlisted as medical officer under Gordon, governor of Equatoria since 1874. He then adopted the name Mehemed Emin. When Gordon became governor-general of the Sudan in 1877, Emin succeeded him as governor of Equatoria province and became Emin Bey. The khedive made him a pasha in 1886, and he was henceforth known as Emin Pasha.

Emin Pasha was a man of many talents. He was a brilliant chess player, a pianist, and could speak more than twenty languages. He was also an accomplished botanist and ornithologist and regularly dispatched specimens to museums in Europe. Last but not least, he was a competent administrator, and under him Equatoria became a financial success. The fall of Khartoum in 1885 and the collapse of Anglo-Egyptian authority over the Sudan put a stop to his idyllic existence. The mahdists fanned out across the Sudan, and Emin Pasha retired to the southern part of his province to

Emin Pasha

escape their clutches, living there on what the land could provide. Now and then reports of his fate reached Europe. According to these he was completely isolated and was unlikely to be able to carry on for much longer.

Such reports of the trials and tribulations of the last lone standard-bearer of European civilization, in danger of perishing like a second Gordon in the middle of a mob of howling dervishes, appealed to the public imagination, especially in Great Britain. London was thus faced with the problem of what, if anything, to do about it. Lord Salisbury considered that the military and diplomatic dangers were too great. Moreover, in his opinion, "It is really their business, if Emin is a German."[36] But since the German government was not keen to intervene either, a private initiative was clearly called for. It was taken by William Mackinnon on the British side. He and another businessman, the merchant James F. Hutton, founded the Emin Pasha Relief Committee in November 1888. Their concern was not, however, wholly humanitarian. The 1886 Anglo-German agreement on East Africa had opened up new prospects for British expansion in the area, without fear of hostile German reactions. A relief operation would kill two birds with one stone: it would serve a good popular cause and also open up a trade route from East Africa to Lake Victoria and the Upper Nile. The syndicate set up by Mackinnon was fittingly called the Syndicate for Establishing British Commerce and Influence in East Africa and for Relieving Emin Bey—in that order.[37] The money was found. The Egyptian government contributed £14,000 to regain the lost province. Stanley was asked

Stanley watching a war dance

to lead the expedition, but the syndicate had counted without King Leopold.

Stanley was still in Leopold's employ, and anyone wishing to make use of his services had to ask the king's permission first. Leopold, who was also very interested in the Nile, gave that permission only on condition that the expedition left from the Congo and not from East Africa. The expedition would then open up the route, not from British territory, but from the Free State and hence help carry Leopold's flag closer to the Nile. There was no way of ignoring the king's wishes. Stanley, having been sounded out about the plan, had meanwhile left for a lecture tour of America, but had stipulated in his contract that, if the king should need him, he would have the right to cut his tour short. On 11 December 1886 he received the following telegram from Mackinnon: "Your plan and offer accepted. Authorities approve. Funds provided. Business urgent. Come promptly." Stanley at once sent a no less concise telegram to his impresario. "Must stop lecturing. Recalled. Sail Wednesday at 4 a.m." Stanley failed to mention that the summons had come from Mackinnon, and intimated that he had been called back by his royal master in Brussels.[38]

In Zanzibar Stanley recruited the men he needed for his expedition and arrived with them in the Congo in March 1887. Soon afterwards the real adventure began, one that was to turn into tragedy. Of the nearly four hundred men with whom he had left, only one-half would make it to Equatoria. Sickness and hunger wiped out the rest. In April 1888 Stanley finally encountered Emin Pasha near Lake Albert, and was somewhat disap-

Stanley meets Emin Pasha

pointed to find that he looked appreciably healthier and better-kempt than his rescuer. Emin was grateful for all that. "I owe you a thousand thanks, Mr. Stanley." he exclaimed, "I really do not know how to express my thanks to you."[39] Stanley then brought out the three half-bottles of champagne he still had left, and they drank to Emin Pasha's health. Emin had been found, and now a start could be made on his rescue.

Rarely in history has there been anyone so reluctant to be saved as Emin. He was determined to hang on to Equatoria. He refused to abandon his province and rejected Leopold's offer to let him stay on as governor of Equatoria, though on behalf of the Congo Free State. The arrival of other Europeans had, however, undermined Emin's local standing and authority. His troops rebelled against him, and in the end he had no option but to follow Stanley. In April 1889, exactly one year after Stanley's arrival, they left Equatoria for the east coast, reaching Bagamoyo on 4 December. "There, Pasha, we are home!" Stanley exclaimed. "Yes, thank God," was Emin's response.[40] Stanley and Emin rode proudly, on horses belonging to the German officers stationed there, to the officers' mess, where a banquet was held that night. Emin, who had a cataract and was under the influence both of alcohol and of a special message of welcome from the Kaiser, fell from a balcony, was badly injured, and was taken to hospital. He survived the fall and, though by now nearly blind, decided to return to Equatoria, to reclaim his province and to offer it to Germany. The man who had been rescued with so much effort and at British and Egyptian expense now exchanged the Egyptian service for the German and left in the direction whence he had come. He did not get very far, however, for he was attacked and murdered on the way. Stanley returned to Europe in triumph, where King Leopold immediately proposed that he make his way to the Nile at the head of an army of 20,000 Congolese soldiers in order to recapture Khartoum. Things did not come to that, however, for Stanley turned the offer down.

Stanley had rescued Emin Pasha. But in the meantime others had had similar plans. In Germany there was also a call to form a Save Emin Pasha Committee, though it was not until June 1888 that it actually saw the light of day. By then, however, Emin had already been saved by Stanley, though news of the rescue had not yet reached Europe—Stanley did not return to the "inhabited world" until December 1889, by which time a German expedition under Peters was well on its way, having left in March 1889.

When Peters eventually reached the borders of Equatoria, he discovered a camp built by two Britons who were temporarily away hunting in the forest. Being no Englishman, he saw nothing wrong with reading their mail, including a letter from Stanley mentioning his rescue of Emin Pasha. That was a bitter blow, but luckily Peters read on and learned that Mwanga, the kabaka of Buganda (part of what would later become Uganda), was in difficulties and had asked for British help.[41] Resolved to rescue someone come what may, Peters now decided to save Mwanga in Emin's stead. He made for Buganda, restored the king to his throne, and *en passant* declared Uganda a German protectorate. This was done by means of a treaty—described as a "preliminary treaty" to be on the safe side—signed on 28 February 1890. However, only the German version of the treaty mentioned a protectorate. Fortunately for him, Mwanga had enlisted the help of a French missionary, who testified that the French text —the only legitimate one—spoke merely of *amitié*, friendship.[42] This subtle difference did not, however, matter greatly in the end. The crux of the matter was that Germany was proposing to seize Uganda, and its annexation was unacceptable to Lord Salisbury and his government. Salisbury held clear views on British policy in Africa, among which British control of the Nile held pride of place. These views had far-reaching repercussions, since Salisbury was to play a crucial role in shaping British Africa policy and hence also in setting the course of that continent's partition.

### LORD SALISBURY

Lord Salisbury was British prime minister from 1885 to 1902, with a few short interruptions, and as such had a crucial influence on British foreign policy. These years formed the critical phase in the partition of Africa, orchestrated by Salisbury in person. It is to his great credit that this process

Lord Salisbury

took place without much conflict, or at least without major clashes, between the European Powers. This was certainly due in part to his detached attitude to diplomacy in general and to African adventures in particular. Salisbury was possessed of considerable intellectual ability and mature judgment. He considered leading his country the self-evident duty of men of his birth. After all, his family had been doing it for centuries.

Robert Arthur Talbot Gascoyne-Cecil (1830–1903) was the ninth earl and the third marquis of Salisbury, and as such a member of one of England's most eminent families. His ancestors had been chief ministers of the crown under Elizabeth I and James I. He lived in Hatfield House, which had come into the family in 1607 following an exchange of houses between James I and the first earl of Salisbury. Hatfield, where Queen Elizabeth I had spent her youth, was one of the richest and most beautiful estates in England. The owner was a very unusual aristocrat who shared almost none of the traditional interests of the English aristocracy. He did not like sports, hunting, horses, clubs, or receptions and was not, indeed, overfond of human beings. He was a deeply religious man and attended his own chapel every day. He also took a keen intellectual interest in philosophy and the natural sciences. He performed chemical experiments in his private laboratory and himself brought electricity to Hatfield House, unfortunately electrifying the lawns in the process. His favorite reading included Tacitus, Virgil, Euripides, Shakespeare, Goethe and *The Count of Monte Cristo.*[43]

Lord Salisbury was, of course, educated at Eton and Christ Church, Oxford. He had no fond memories of Eton, calling it "an existence among devils," and refused to set foot there ever again.[44] At the age of twenty-three he was elected to the House of Commons for a constituency that was firmly in the hands of his family. He sat there for fifteen years, and, after his father's death in 1868, in the House of Lords for another twenty-seven years. For seventeen years he was leader of the Conservative party, shepherding it through five elections and winning three of them. In the 1860s, while still a young man, he set out his political philosophy in a series of articles published in the *Quarterly Review*. He was opposed to equality, democracy and the extension of the franchise. On the last issue, he broke with Disraeli, the Conservative prime minister, who introduced the second Reform Bill in 1867. That opposition nearly cost Salisbury his political career. He had an even greater aversion to atheism, to the class struggle and to socialism. He considered enfranchising the Irish to be as ridiculous as giving the vote to Hottentots, and once referred to a politician from India as "that black man."[45] Hence it is not an exaggeration to call him, not just a conservative, but a hidebound reactionary.

Salisbury was a great orator and wit, far too witty for a politician. He did not suffer fools gladly, and did not watch his tongue. His first leader, Disraeli, called him "a great master of gibes and flouts and jeers."[46] His tendency to commit gaffes was so great that an ill-advised remark used to be called a "salisbury." In diplomatic life, too, his facetious bent and sarcasm would sometimes get the better of him. These handicaps did not, however, impede his remarkable career in national as well as international politics.

Salisbury's first ministerial appointment was that of secretary of state for India. He held that office from 1866 to 1867 and again from 1874 to 1878. In 1878 he became Disraeli's foreign secretary and stayed at this post until June 1885, when he became prime minister for the first time. His first cabinet was not long-lived—it lasted until February 1886—but the Gladstone Liberal cabinet that took over from it was even more short-lived, disappearing from the scene again in August of that year. The Conservatives then came back into power. Lord Salisbury led the government twice more, and this time for longer spells: from 1886 to 1892 and from 1895 to 1902. He combined the office of prime minister with that of foreign secretary until he surrendered the second office in 1900 on political and health grounds. He was, incidentally, not a strong leader of his cabinet, at times giving his colleagues too much leeway.

Salisbury has often been compared with Bismarck, but unlike the Iron Chancellor he was not a man of "great designs." He did not believe that world politics could be imposed from on high; one had to take events as they came, trying to make the best of them. "British policy is to drift lazily downstream, occasionally putting out a boat-hook to avoid a collision," he observed.[47] He had a remarkable sense of timing. His statesmanship was a mixture of realism, Machiavellianism, opportunism and pessimism. It was his deepest conviction that world history was unpredictable and ironic. Diplomacy, according to him, was the last political arena not yet invaded by the masses, but he was afraid that happy state could not last. He considered passion and sentiment so many pitfalls of political life. The press and public opinion were further threats to good, that is, to secret and cautious, diplomacy.

He took very little interest in Africa, and although African affairs were to dominate his diplomatic life, he never changed his attitude to that continent. "Africa was created to be the plague of foreign offices," he once remarked.[48] And he was to be plagued by it constantly. His interest in the partition of Africa was purely academic. He considered it an intellectual exercise, a subtle game of move and countermove, of bid and counterbid. He felt that the "constant study of maps is apt to disturb man's reasoning powers."[49] Yet peering at African maps was something he was forced to do constantly, that and the partition of unknown territories into spheres of influence, and the giving away of rivers and mountains of which no one could say where they were. He liked to make fun of the whole thing and realized full well how chimeric the partition of Africa really was.[50] Harry Johnston, who played an important role in it, refers to it in his novel, *The Gay-Dombeys*. The leading character, based unmistakably on Lord Salisbury, takes a guest for a walk over his estate one Sunday after church and luncheon, and having arrived at a peaceful spot, says, "Now let us settle the fate of the Niger." The same leading character then muses at length over the peculiar fact that the fate of the Niger should have been discussed and decided under a beech tree in Hertfordshire.[51]

In 1889, after much study, Salisbury decided that a British evacuation of Egypt was no longer feasible: the result would be chaos and anarchy, perhaps even war with France. The Suez Canal would be threatened, and British influence in the eastern Mediterranean would collapse. Britain thus had to remain in Egypt. On 9 November 1889 he declared publicly that the British government, regardless of the stand of the other Powers, was determined "to pursue to the end the task which it had undertaken in Egypt."[52] A little later Salisbury drew a conclusion that was as logical as it was weighty: to safeguard Egypt, Britain would have to control the entire Nile valley, or at least prevent any other Power from establishing itself there.[53] Otherwise that Power would be able to blackmail Britain or put it under pressure. Egypt was and would continue to be dependent on the Nile. Hence East Africa, and Uganda in particular, was of vital importance to Britain. Peters's treaties in Uganda and the German claims based on them posed a threat to British control of the Nile valley. For that reason Germany would have to be kept out of, or where appropriate expelled from, Uganda. There was yet another reason for preventing German East Africa from spreading too far westward. If it was allowed to do so, it would be endangering a British north-south linkup. That linkup was not very important to Lord Salisbury, but it was a passion with the great British public, for it was nothing more nor less than the great dream of Cecil Rhodes and other influential imperialists, the "all-red route" from the Cape to Cairo.


# 4
# THE CAPE-TO-CAIRO DREAM AND THE ZANZIBAR-HELIGOLAND TREATY

### THE DREAM

The Cape-to-Cairo route was to enter history as Cecil Rhodes's great dream. He also claimed to have been its intellectual father. The idea had, however, been conceived, formulated and propagated earlier by that other passionate and avid imperialist, Harry Johnston, and earlier still by Sir Edwin Arnold in a pamphlet published in 1876. In fact, the idea was older still, for it had been propounded as early as 1798 by the Brazilian explorer Dr. Jose Lacerda. But Lacerda had been against the idea, for he was pro-Portuguese and preferred a west-east linkup between the Portuguese colonies of Angola and Mozambique. That link would be threatened by a Cape-to-Cairo route.[54] Yet hard though they fought against it, it was not the Portuguese but the Germans who would ultimately foil Rhodes's plan.

The Cape-to-Cairo route held a great appeal for the British public, which was much taken with the grandeur of the concept, but it failed to excite the experts. Sir George Goldie said that trade sought the shortest route to the sea. Lugard called it "claptrap" and "a mere sentimental jargon."[55] Sir Percy Anderson thought it an extremely unpractical proposal.[56] Lord Salisbury treated it with utter contempt. He called it "a curious idea, which has lately become prevalent," pointed out that "trade does not willingly go across a continent," and added that he could not imagine a "more inconvenient possession" than ownership of a narrow strip of land in the interior of Africa, a three months' journey from the coast, and wedged between German East Africa and Leopold's Congo.[57] He was therefore opposed to it, but he could not afford to ignore Rhodes's influence and was therefore unable to shelve the idea without further ado. Nor could he ignore the ambitious territorial claims of Mackinnon and his IBEAC.[58] The plan accordingly figured in his first proposals to Germany.

On 22 December 1889 Salisbury invited the German government to talks on the outstanding Anglo-German colonial disputes. This invitation followed hints by Herbert von Bismarck that his father was "sick and tired" of the perils of Zanzibar.[59] Uganda was the real point at issue—thanks to

Peters and Mackinnon it had become a focus of Anglo-German rivalry. The Germans treated Uganda as the hinterland of Witu; the British treated it as part of their sphere of influence. As far as Salisbury was concerned a strategic issue was involved: British possession of Uganda would keep Germany out of the Nile valley.

On 18 March 1890 Bismarck unexpectedly disappeared from the scene. He and the Kaiser—since 1888, the youthful Wilhelm II—had differed on domestic as well as on foreign policy, and especially in their attitude to Russia. The Kaiser was anxious to take charge of foreign policy himself. The upshot was that, after Bismarck's departure, the Reinsurance treaty between Germany and Russia was not renewed. Caprivi, Bismarck's successor, had little understanding of foreign affairs, no more so than Marschall, the minister of foreign affairs. As a result the handling of foreign affairs fell to Baron Friedrich von Holstein, a senior counselor in the foreign ministry. This grey eminence of the Wilhelmstrasse was to become the most powerful German diplomat and to remain so until the Moroccan crisis of 1905. In any case, a new phase in German *Weltpolitik* began in 1890, known as the "new course" and characterized by a more deliberate policy of expansion, a more aggressive style, and unstable leadership.

Caprivi, the new chancellor, was no more keen on colonies than Bismarck had been. In an address to the Reichstag on 12 May 1890 he poked fun at the colonies. "People thought, if only we owned colonies, bought an atlas and painted Africa blue in it, we should be great people."[60] This approach and the pro-British nature of the new course simplified the negotiations. On 13 May 1890 Salisbury unexpectedly came up with a whole packet of new proposals. Germany was to give up Witu and hence Uganda as well. It could keep its other territories, but would have to provide what territory was needed for the Cape-to-Cairo route. Britain would establish a protectorate over Zanzibar. In exchange for all this, Germany would receive Heligoland.[61]

It was asking too much. Heligoland was of interest to Germany in the context of its maritime ambitions, and the construction of the Kiel Canal had lent it a fresh importance. But while it was of great moment to Germany, it meant very little to Great Britain and could hardly be considered adequate recompense for unobstructed British hegemony in East Africa. For that was what the Cape-to-Cairo link really amounted to. Moreover, the German colonies would be virtually surrounded by British possessions, and cut off from the Congo Free State. That state was still thought to be in danger of imminent collapse and due to be taken over by others very shortly, probably by one of the neighboring countries. If it accepted the British plan, Germany would cease to be one of these neighbors. All in all, therefore, the British demands were unacceptable.

Salisbury did not really mind. What he was really concerned with was Uganda. The Cape-to-Cairo route was no more than poetic license. He accordingly dropped the idea, the more so as it was in the process of being resurrected in different form, for negotiations had been taking place at the same time between Leopold and Mackinnon, leading to the so-called Leopold-Mackinnon treaty of 24 May 1890. That treaty recognized Leopold's claims to the Lado Enclave in Bahr el-Ghazal, an enclave on which Leopold was anxious to lay his hands in connection with his wish to press on to the Nile. From the British point of view, that would have the advantage of keeping France out of the Nile valley. Mackinnon's company, for its part, was granted sovereignty over a narrow stretch of land between Lake Edward and Lake Tanganyika. The "all-red route" had thus been saved. The Leopold-Mackinnon treaty, however, was between private individuals and not between states, but when Mackinnon showed the document to Salisbury, the latter gave it his approval. Later, the British government was to say that Lord Salisbury had merely been giving his "private opinion" (see p. 228).

### THE TREATY

The Anglo-German negotiations of 1890 had thus led to the abandonment of the all-red route, sacrificed on the altar of Nile politics. The expansion of the British East Africa Company west of Lake Victoria was halted at 1° S. Cecil Rhodes's British South Africa Company was allowed to press on to a line between Lake Nyasa and Lake Tanganyika. Above that line lay German territory. The northern boundary of the German sphere of influence was a line running from the mouth of the Umba to a point east of Lake Victoria at 1° S. From there it ran westward to the borders of the Congo Free State.[62] All in all, German East Africa became roughly the size of contemporary Tanzania plus Rwanda and Burundi. On that basis Britain and Germany were able to see eye to eye, and on 1 July 1890 the agreement known as the Zanzibar-Heligoland treaty was signed. Germany gave up Witu and all other claims north of the Tana, recognized a British protectorate over Zanzibar, and received Heligoland in exchange. At the same time several less important border issues in West Africa and South-West Africa were settled.[63] The precise details were left to a commission of experts.

The treaty was a great triumph for Britain, which gained by diplomacy what it had been unable to obtain in the field: Kenya, Uganda and Zanzibar, in short, everything it had wanted. The danger of German expansion in East Africa had been checked. The treaty was the first in a series of major partition treaties, and had all the characteristics of European imperialism in its African heyday. Geographical knowledge of the territories involved was extremely scant. The treaty mentioned rivers and mountains that later turned out to be nonexistent. Protectorates were recognized that had still to be declared.

The negotiations and the treaty were thus typical products of European diplomacy, the work of political leaders who saw African problems in the framework of European diplomatic relations, and who attached little importance to Africa itself. They were not the work of colonial and imperialist fanatics, but of traditional *Realpolitiker*. The exchange of Heligoland for Zanzibar shows how much the partition of Africa was a part of international relations in the wider sense. For Germany, British friendship far outweighed African considerations in 1890.

The colonial enthusiasts in Germany were disappointed, especially Carl Peters, who declared that Germany had bartered two kingdoms for a bathtub in the North Sea.[64] That disappointment was the main reason for the establishment of the hyper-nationalist All-German Union (the *Alldeutsche Verband*). In Britain, too, murmurs could be heard about ceding British territory, even if it was only a bathtub. Queen Victoria declared that "giving up what one has is always a bad thing." The fact "that any of my possessions should thus be bartered away caused me great uneasiness," she also said. Salisbury explained that this deal had been unique, one that fell in the category of once only and never again.[65] The objectors would do well to remember that something much more important had been achieved: Britain had made the Nile safe, at least with respect to Germany. It was just too bad that other rivals were to appear only too quickly.

# 5
# UGANDA

The 1890 treaty turned out to be not the end of the Uganda question but the beginning. The British government had done everything it could and dared to do: negotiating with other governments and drawing lines on the map. The real work, however, would have to be done by private parties, in this event by the IBEAC. The problem was that that body was more of a philanthropic and political association than a commercial enterprise. This one-horse company, as Rosebery called it, owned little capital and, because its commercial prospects looked bad, was unable to attract much more.[66] The political situation in Uganda, moreover, was as complicated as it was tense. The British protectorate comprised the kingdoms of Buganda, Banyoro, Ankole and a few more. Buganda was the most important of these. The British government believed that it was the job of the IBEAC to administer and to manage it. The IBEAC, for its part, felt that it needed government subsidies to do the job. The great British public was not interested, but was torn between two conflicting desires, one almost as strong as the other: fighting the slave trade and paying minimal taxes. That conflict was to give rise to many a problem and in the long run lead to a kind of impasse.

### LUGARD AND UGANDA

The first attempt to set up an effective administration was made by Captain Frederick John Dealtry Lugard, a young officer in the service of the IBEAC. He would later become famous as the great empire-builder in Nigeria and be raised to the peerage as Baron Lugard. Lugard did what he could. On 6 August 1890 he left from Mombasa on an 800-mile expedition to Buganda, where he arrived in December. The situation there was complicated. Authority was vested in Mwanga, the kabaka. There were various rival religious groups, not only Muslims and Christians, but Catholics and Protestants, who also fought one another. On 24 December Lugard came up with the following proposal: he offered company protection to the kabaka, in exchange for which the latter would hand over suzerainty, abolish the slave trade, grant free trade and freedom of conscience, and place himself under the control of a British resident. That was asking a lot in exchange for very little, but the missionaries persuaded the chiefs, the kabaka's vassals, to accept the offer. This they did, and on 26 December 1890 the kabaka followed suit.

Lugard's position was now officially established, but his effective powers were still very few. That did not prevent him from continuing westward and from concluding further treaties, by which fresh territory was brought under British protection. Meanwhile, the situation in Buganda, where Lugard had left a second in command, continued to be confused, Catholics and Protestants continuing to fight one another and the kabaka regularly suiting his religious convictions to the latest changes in fortune. The situation, as a British observer remarked, was more reminiscent of the time of the Edict of Nantes than of the nineteenth century.[67] In the summer of 1891 Lugard returned, only to learn that the company had decided on 16 July 1891 to abandon Uganda and to recall him to the coast. But Lugard did not leave immediately, as a civil war between Catholics and Protestants had just broken out and order had to be restored. That was done, and the country was split into Catholic and Protestant areas, or more precisely, ten of the twenty counties went to the Protestants, nine to the Catholics and one to the Muslims.[68] The Peace of Augsburg was nothing by comparison. Lugard now departed from Buganda, leaving the kabaka behind as king of a British protectorate.

The reason for the company's decision to withdraw was an acute shortage of funds. Expenditure far exceeded income, and there was no prospect of better times to come unless a railroad was built with government funding. Salisbury was in favor of such a course. The Mombasa railroad suited his long-term strategy: control of the Nile and of the Sudan. The British

Parliament, by contrast, wanted nothing to do with so extravagantly expensive a project. The company's actual withdrawal was in fact delayed for some time because private individuals came up with some money at the request of the Church Missionary Society. In addition Salisbury was granted a small sum by Parliament, admittedly not in order to build the railroad, but to make a study of its feasibility. Something like an impasse had been reached: quitting was a financial necessity for the company and a political one for the government, but any official decision to pull out would have unleashed a flood of protest from antislavery and missionary circles at home. The result was a stay of execution.

A withdrawal from Uganda, however, seemed definitely in the offing by the time Gladstone formed his fourth cabinet in August 1892. Gladstone and his second-in-command, Sir William Harcourt, the chancellor of the exchequer, were pre-eminently "little Englanders." However, the views of Lord Rosebery, the powerful foreign secretary, had to be taken into consideration as well. This popular, elegant, and wealthy Scot was beloved of the queen and of the Liberal party. He was considered their future leader, which he duly became, albeit with little success. His career, which had a most brilliant start, came to a sad end, but before then he was able to rescue the Africa policy of his predecessor, Lord Salisbury, and, moreover, at a crucial moment. However brief, his political intervention was thus of the utmost importance in the partition of East Africa.

### ROSEBERY AND IMPERIALISM

Archibald Philip Primrose Rosebery (1847–1929) was born a prodigy and would remain one all his life. His tutor at Eton called him "surely the wisest boy that ever lived."[69] Hereditary theory, incidentally, does not explain this remarkable gift. His father's only intellectual achievement was *An Address to the Middle Classes upon the Subject of Gymnastic Exercises*. His mother did not think much of her son, his teachers at Eton grew disappointed in him, and his university studies were not a great success. The master of his Oxford college finally gave him the choice of getting rid of his racehorse or being sent down. Rosebery opted for the second alternative and was not wrong to do so. His horses were to win the Derby three times. In short, Rosebery was rich by birth. Thanks to his marriage to a Rothschild he was to become one of the richest men in Britain, at a time when the rich were very rich indeed.

Rosebery entered politics more or less by chance after supporting Gladstone in the famous Midlothian campaign. He was a political anachronism even then: an immensely rich peer in the progressive Liberal party. In some respects, incidentally, Rosebery was a progressive, and in one respect he was even well ahead of his time. He was a liberal imperialist, and thus marked the breach of the Liberals with the "little England" tradition of

Cobden, Bright and Gladstone. Imperialism was a deep conviction with him, great idealist and patriot that he was. In his eyes the Empire was a blessing for the world and a necessity for Britain. He saw the danger of British isolation in a world of large, armed and hostile countries. Britain must stake its claim in the partition of that world, something it had not sought itself but into which it had been forced by others. Thus, it must join in the great game of "pegging out claims for the future," to quote a famous dictum of his.[70] Gladstone called that the "spirit of territorial grab," which was precisely what it was, but then it reflected the spirit of the age.[71]

Rosebery was far too rich to overexert himself, too intellectual for ambitions, and too much of a historian to harbor illusions. He did, however, prize the post of foreign secretary he was awarded in the last Gladstone cabinet, for it gave him the chance of maintaining Salisbury's foreign policy in a Liberal cabinet. He did not seek to become prime minister; that office fell to him because there was no other suitable candidate. His tenure was not a success. From the outset there was open antagonism between him and his great rival, Sir William Harcourt, the Liberal leader in the House of Commons, where Rosebery, being a peer, could not sit. His premiership thus became a personal tragedy for the highly strung Rosebery, ending in complete failure and causing him unbearable insomnia. He resigned after only fifteen months.

As foreign secretary, however, he did prove a success. His policy was Salisbury's, if with more passion. Rosebery, who, according to Bernard Shaw, "never missed a chance of missing an opportunity,"[72] was resolved not to miss any chances in Uganda. He was to have his way. On 20 September 1892 he presented a memorandum to the cabinet, drafted by Sir Percy Anderson, insisting that Uganda must be preserved for Great Britain, partly as a springboard for the possible reconquest of the Sudan. "This is Jingoism with a vengeance," Sir William Harcourt fulminated. "We are to have a 'Wacht am Nile' and our drum and fife band is to play: 'Sie sollen ihn nicht haben, den freien britischen Nile' "[73] (a parody of the German patriotic hymn "The Watch on the Rhine"). But Harcourt and Gladstone and Morley might rage for all they were worth, they could not dispense with Rosebery and the imperialists. Rosebery had his way by threatening to resign. He sent Sir Gerald Portal to East Africa with orders to review the situation on the spot, one result of his findings having been anticipated by Rosebery: Uganda would not be surrendered. The other results of Sir Gerald's inquiry were positive as well. He depicted East Africa as a region of great strategic importance and with unique commercial prospects: the inhabitants needed shoes, socks and opera glasses, and every day new market prospects appeared.[74] That was enough. Toward the end of 1893 Sir Gerald's conclusions were accepted by Parliament. Soon afterwards Gladstone resigned and Rosebery took his place as prime minister. On 12 April 1894 a British protectorate over Uganda was officially declared.

That protectorate put an end to the period of chartered company rule in East Africa. On 1 July 1895 the British government also took charge of the region between Buganda and the coast and established the British East Africa Protectorate there. The coastal strip was placed under the control of the British Zanzibar Protectorate. The IBEAC was rescued from bankruptcy: it was given £250,000 for expenses incurred, surrendered its charter, and was wound up in 1895.[75] Meanwhile the role of the German East Africa Company had also been played out. It, too, had proved to be too weak financially to meet its administrative obligations. The German government assumed control on 1 January 1889, when it founded the crown colony of German East Africa. The DOAG was most generously indemnified and continued its existence as a private trading enterprise.[76] The time of chartered companies in East Africa was over.

# 6
# EPILOGUE:
# THE FRENCH OCCUPATION OF
# MADAGASCAR

The great absentee in the game of the partition of East Africa was France. Unlike Germany, it had no trading interests of any importance there; unlike Portugal, it had no claims to, or settlements along, the East African coast; and unlike Great Britain, it had no strategic interests in the region. In short, France had no business in East Africa, but since the partition was a game played by all the Powers, and France happened to be one of these, it was nevertheless sucked in. What Britain and Germany were after in East Africa were spheres of influence and protectorates. These were at first defined on paper only and did not gain practical importance until later. In the beginning the whole game was about diplomatic recognition, not about effective control. In that game, the crucial factor was the diplomatic rather than the geographic reality. Neither the sultan of Zanzibar nor the king of Witu, but the German and British leaders determined that. They had made agreements and in so doing had left France out in the cold. However, to play the diplomatic game properly French recognition was needed as well, the more so as France had been a party to the 1862 Zanzibar treaty. In diplomacy, after all, the simple principle of quid pro quo was considered to be the ultimate piece of wisdom. France had therefore to be bought off. Luckily, its ambitions in East Africa did not clash, or clashed hardly at all, with those of the other two parties. For the French sights were set on Madagascar.

French claims to that island were among the least well founded of all, even by the wildest stretch of the imagination. Louis XIII had officially taken possession of the island, and Richelieu had handed it over to the Compagnie d'Orient, but there the matter had rested. The seventeenth century was long past. In the nineteenth century, Madagascar was an independent island to all intents and purposes, one where Europeans were lowly foreigners subject to the harsh local laws. Madagascar was not a political entity, though it was dominated by one state alone. The heartland of that state was found on the island's central plateau, and was called the Hova kingdom. That was, however, a misnomer. The Hova were in fact no more than a caste, albeit the dominant one, in an ethnic group of Pacific origin, the Merina, a Polynesian group that had arrived 2,000 years earlier. In the course of those long years, the Merina had intermarried with other groups and could thus be considered, together with a number of other peoples, as indigenous to the island. In any case, they were the most powerful group. In the course of the nineteenth century the Merina kingdom extended its authority over roughly two-thirds of the island. Madagascar was known as "la grande île" for good reason—it is as large as France and Belgium combined—and the Merina kingdom was therefore one of the largest in the world at the time of the partition of Africa.

Moreover, it was a modern kingdom. It had become that under King Nampoina (an abbreviation of Andrianampoinimerina, a name too long even by Malagasy standards), who had reigned from 1782 to 1810, and under his son Radama (1810–1828). They had reorganized the army and acquired firearms in exchange for the abolition of the slave trade, although slavery itself was by no means abolished. These rulers, the Mohammed Alis of Madagascar, had also opened up their island to modern technology and, to a certain extent, to modern ideas. Missionaries, teachers and technicians were admitted. Compulsory education was introduced, and by the end of the nineteenth century proportionally as many Merina children went to school as did children in western Europe. In 1880 the first Malagasy doctors returned home after having been trained in Edinburgh.[77] British Protestant and French Catholic missionaries fought a fierce struggle for the possession of Malagasy souls. The Protestants took the lead: by the end of the nineteenth century there were roughly half a million Protestant as against a little more than a hundred thousand Catholic converts. Moreover, in 1868 the queen, the prime minister and several other leaders converted to the Protestant faith, which also became the state religion. All this enlightenment exerted some, but not much, influence on the morals and customs of the Hova kingdom, which remained renowned for its brutality and coarse ways. Queen Ranavalona I (1828–1861), nicknamed "the Cruel," was also known as the "female Caligula."[78] The political system was dictatorial oligarchy centered on the court, coupled to sole ownership by the monarch of all the land, together with slavery, punitive military expeditions and general oppression. The Hova kingdom may have succumbed to the lures of modernization, but thanks to its central government and military strength it was better able to stand up to foreign domination than most. After Ranavalona's death in 1861 there was a fierce struggle for power from which Rainilaiarivony emerged as the island's prime minister and strongman. He consolidated his position further by marrying three successive queens, and remained in power until the French intervention in 1894.

France, as we have seen, had set its sights on the island. It already owned the neighboring island of Réunion, a colony represented in the French parliament, together with several smaller islands off the coast of Madagascar. The imperialism of the Réunionnais added fuel to the flames of the French expansionist urge, which was further increased by the Catholic *députés* in the French parliament who had taken the Catholic missionaries on the island under their wing. As a result of all these pressures, the French right, normally staunchly anti-colonialist, called for intervention.[79] Tension mounted in 1881 when the Hova adopted "Law 85," which outlawed land ownership by foreigners. Seeing that a treaty signed in 1868 had granted Frenchmen in particular the right to own property on the island, the new law was a source of bitter conflict and was even a *casus belli*.[80] The clash came in 1883 when France demanded compensation for its wronged citizens as well as a protectorate over Madagascar. That demand was rejected by the Hova government. A French naval squadron then appeared, and several coastal towns were bombarded, but the time was not yet ripe for a major operation. France was involved in conflicts in Tunisia, in the Congo and—most important of all—in Tonkin. A war in Madagascar was not on the cards at that time. The French commander was accordingly instructed to refrain from invading the island and to confine himself to naval shelling operations. On 17 December 1885 the conflict was settled by the Treaty of Tamatave. It was a most unusual treaty, because France recognized the sovereignty of Queen Ranavalona III over the entire island, an authority that she had never possessed or exercised. In return, Madagascar handed over control of its foreign affairs to a French resident, which was tantamount to accepting a protectorate without putting it in so many words. The treaty was therefore ambiguous and lent itself to all sorts of interpretations, the more so as there were considerable differences between the French and the Malagasy texts. Small wonder that it failed to end the conflict between the two parties and simply provided for a decade's respite.

The turning point in this ten years' truce came after five years. In 1890 Britain and Germany recognized the French version of the Tamatave treaty. They were, in fact, recognizing a French protectorate over Madagascar in exchange for French recognition of their protectorates in East Africa.

France and Madagascar were thus left to fight it out by themselves. The harassment of the French inhabitants had meanwhile been stepped up, and a number of them were murdered at regular intervals. In 1894 the French had had enough. A motion put forward by a deputy for Réunion for a stop to Malagasy intransigence was adopted unanimously. Hanotaux, the minister of foreign affairs, was asked to take action. He first tried diplomacy and an ultimatum, but the diplomatic approach failed and the ultimatum was rejected. The red Hova banner was raised on the island's twelve sacred mountains. The French representative lowered the French flag and took it with him to the coast. In November 1894 the French left the island. That same month both Chambers voted credits for a major expedition. French imperialism had won out after having vacillated in Madagascar for ten years.

On 12 December 1894 the French navy took Tamatave and went on to capture other seaports, among them Diego Suarez and Majunga, where a large expeditionary force was assembled: 15,000 troops, mainly Senegalese infantrymen, and 6,000 auxiliaries, bearers, muleteers and drivers for the thousands of *voitures Lefebvre* (light vehicles drawn by horses and mules).[81] The march to Tananarive, the capital, took them 250 miles inland. The expedition was a military stroll but turned into a medical martyrdom. The Hova had just two generals with which to fight the French, namely, Hazo and Tazo, the bush and fever.[82] There was no quinine, and "General Fever" struck down a third of the troops within a short time. Instead of launching a massive attack it was decided to send forward a column of 4,000 men, 1,500 drivers and 3,000 mules who covered the remaining stretch in fourteen days. They reached the capital on 26 September, and brought it to its knees in a few days. One day later a treaty was signed by which Madagascar was declared a French protectorate. The queen kept her throne and her red parasol—symbols of her sovereignty—but not for long. The protectorate formula did not prove effective because it afforded small satisfaction to the French colonists and because the Merina did not play by its rules. The upshot was rebellion and anarchy. On 20 June 1896 Madagascar was annexed and in September a governor-general, Joseph Gallieni, was appointed, invested with every military and civilian power. His second-in-command was Hubert Lyautey. Together these two men were to pacify the island, and together they were to become France's most famous colonial soldiers.

# 7
# CONCLUSION

The partition of East Africa was played out against a background of peace and sweet reasonableness—at least as far as the Europeans were concerned. Anglo-French rivalry, which used to give so sharp an edge to relations after the British occupation of Egypt, played no part this time round. France had no stake in East Africa, and Portugal hardly any. The demarcation of the northern border of Mozambique was a matter between Germany and Portugal, and that was quickly settled. What tension and rivalry remained was thus confined to Germany and Britain, with King Leopold playing a modest supporting role. The German and British pioneers in East Africa, Peters and Mackinnon, were keen and ambitious enough, but control of the whole enterprise was in the hands of two very cool, and as far as Africa was concerned, very detached statesmen, namely, Bismarck and Salisbury. The crucial events, moreover, took place in the 1880s, when public interest in Africa was still slight. In the 1890s the atmosphere was to become much more tense, and concessions would be harder to make. This would become clear when East Africa came to the fore once again in connection with Anglo-French rivalry for the Nile.

Britain obtained all it had set its heart on in East Africa. It alone had a clear conception and a clear strategy: the Nile valley must be protected from foreign taint. The rest was open to discussion. The East African coast, too, was of course of strategic importance, but there was room enough for others as well. Salisbury's policy thus came down to Harcourt's reviled "Wacht am Nile." The cabinet that followed, and in which Harcourt had so important a post, thought of giving up this policy, but nothing came of that. The influence of imperialists in Rosebery's mold had meanwhile become too great even among the Liberals. The "little Englanders" were being forced to bow out. Imperialism became part of the national consensus.

For Germany, the division of East Africa proved to be a matter of some satisfaction as well. The German position had, after all, resulted from no more than a whim of that strange adventurer, Carl Peters. The result of that impulse, which the government had originally greeted with so much skepticism, was German East Africa, one of Germany's largest and most important colonies. By the treaty of 1890 Germany had renounced further ambitions in the region in exchange for Heligoland. From the colonial point of view, that may have been a retreat, but from the more exalted perspective of international politics it was an advance. Heligoland was closer than Zanzibar.

Viewed from the African angle, these events looked quite different. For when all was said and done, the partition treaties laid the basis for European conquest and occupation, which culminated in an extremely violent form of oppression. From 1888 to 1902 the Germans launched eighty-four major military campaigns in Tanganyika, one every two months on average. In 1901 they also started on the southeastern part of the colony. The upshot of this policy was the Maji-Maji rebellion, so called after the magic water (maji-maji) alleged to change bullets into water.[83] In the event, the magic failed to work, since according to the official Reichstag report 75,000 Africans were killed. Other estimates give twice, or even four times, that figure. Some tribes lost 90 percent of their members.[84]

The British were faced with similar problems. They tackled them somewhat more calmly, not least because they had fewer military resources. Yet they, too, were drawn into a great many conflicts. In western Kenya alone some fifty armed clashes took place from 1894 to 1914, 40 percent of them leading to punitive expeditions, or one expedition per annum on average.[85] The French for their part launched large-scale pacification campaigns in Madagascar. Gallieni, who commanded them from 1896 to 1905, worked hand in hand with Lyautey, applying a method they had perfected in Tonkin. That method was a combination of military subjection with the creation of an administrative and socioeconomic machinery. Lyautey himself summed it all up in a metaphor that was to become famous: "With pacification, a great wave of civilization spreads out like an oil slick."[86]

# IV

# SOLDIERS AND TRADERS: FRANCE AND GREAT BRITAIN IN WEST AFRICA, 1890–1898

Great Britain . . . has adopted the policy of advance
by commercial enterprise. She has not attempted to
compete with the military operations of her neighbour.

Salisbury

$W$est Africa is a term that on closer examination proves to be less obvious than it seems. What precise area does it cover? The western boundary is easy enough to define. It is the Atlantic Ocean. The eastern boundary is more difficult. Where does West Africa end and East Africa begin? It is hard to tell, and was even harder at a time when very little was known about the interior. The northern and southern boundaries are also not easy to define. Strictly speaking, West Africa stretches from Ceuta to Cape Town, but in practice the term has a much more limited application. Morocco and the Sahara are considered part of North Africa; South Africa, Namibia and Angola as part of southern Africa (Angola is a borderline case); Zaire, the Congo, Gabon and Cameroon as part of Central Africa. What remains is therefore a relatively small area, though large enough for all that, even in its truncated form. At present it comprises fifteen independent states: Mauritania, Senegal, Gambia, Mali, Guinea, Guinea-Bissau, Niger, Ivory Coast, Burkina-Faso (formerly Upper Volta), Benin (formerly Dahomey), Togo, Nigeria, Ghana, Sierra Leone and Liberia. That is the area with which we are concerned here, that and Cameroon, whose history is closely bound up with it.

During the partition of Africa into colonies and protectorates, two terms were used to refer to this region: Guinea and Sudan. The word Guinea comes from the Portuguese and is probably derived from Akal n'Iguinawen, the Berber for "Land of the Black Men."[1] It was applied mainly to the coast, the area with which Europeans were most closely involved. This coast was divided into Upper Guinea, the part which runs from north to south, from Cape Blanco to Sierra Leone, and Lower Guinea, the coastal region from Sierra Leone to Cameroon. The interior was generally referred to as the western Sudan.

The area south of the Sahara is one of pronounced geographical and climatic contrasts. In the north lies the Sahara, to the south the Sahel, an area of steppes and savannah, with vast open spaces, half desert, half grassland. The lowermost and largest part of the coast, by contrast, consists of tropical rainforest, so dense as to be nearly inaccessible. The two areas—

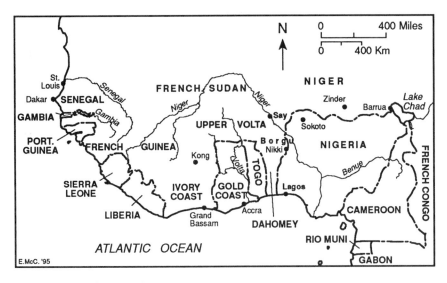

The partition of West Africa

leaving the Sahara out of consideration for the moment—are also clearly distinct in historical and cultural respects. The savannah was Islamized before the sixteenth century, which led to the emergence of Islamic states, some of considerable size. The tropical rainforest, by contrast, being difficult to penetrate, saw little Islamic missionary activity and was not suited to the formation of large states. Here, political structures were generally small and rarely grew beyond the scale of a few village groups.

But however sharp the contrast between the two areas may be, the division is not clear-cut. Two great river systems provide a measure of unity and of cohesion. The first of these systems is formed by the Senegal and the Gambia, two rivers running chiefly from east to west and giving access to the interior in a way that is almost unique in Africa. The mighty Niger, 2,600 miles long, is the hub of the other system. These waterways provide natural access to, and the most important means of communication within, this gigantic territory. They are also the nucleus of the two great economic systems in the region, the trading system of Upper Guinea and western Sudan, linked by the Senegal, and that of Lower Guinea and central Sudan, access to which was provided by the Niger. The Senegal and the Niger were also to serve as approach routes for the two most important European colonizers of West Africa: the Senegal for the French and the Niger for the British.

Contacts between West Africa and Europe go back to the fifteenth century, when the Portuguese began to explore the area. Other countries followed suit, notably Spain, the Netherlands, Great Britain and France. The center of European commercial activity lay in Lower Guinea, whose coast was distinguished from west to east into the Grain, Ivory, Gold and Slave Coasts, after the most important products. For a long time, slaves were the chief West African export. To further that trade, the Portuguese, French, British, Dutch and other Europeans established a network of forts and entrepôts along the Guinea coast.

Following the abolition of slavery, a period of "legitimate trade" ensued even here. The industrial revolution had created a new form of servitude, that of wage slavery, and the new economy hinged on machines and industrial workers. The machines had to be greased and the workers washed. Hence Europe needed both lubricants and soap, for which palm oil provided the raw ingredient. Houses and streets in the new Europe also had to be lit, and for the time being this was still done by candles, also made from palm oil. British manufacturers could thus combine profit and conscience in the memorable slogan, "Buy our candles and fight the slave trade."[2] Palm oil was found in West Africa in abundance, and trade in palm kernels grew up alongside it, yielding oil of a higher quality for the manufacture of margarine, another product of considerable importance in urban life. Groundnuts, cotton, cocoa and coffee completed the picture. Europe for its part supplied Africa mostly with textiles, but also—and to the dismay of humanitarian circles—with gin and rifles.

Contacts between Europe and West Africa were thus of very long standing. By the time the "scramble for Africa" began, Europeans had been in West Africa for more than four centuries, although their presence bore little resemblance to colonialism. Relations were based on mutual interest. While the Europeans traded on the coast, the Africans carefully guarded their control over trade with the interior. The European presence remained confined to a few coastal settlements, which sometimes laid claim to some authority over the interior, but were usually in no position to press these claims home. In any case the Europeans were not many in number; few could stand for long what was to them a murderous climate. West Africa was rightly known as "the white man's grave."

Not surprisingly, therefore, European political interest in the area was slight. The trend was toward withdrawal rather than expansion. The Danes retired as early as 1850, and the Netherlands in 1872, ceding its possessions on the Guinea coast to Great Britain. The British were not very enthusiastic about their new acquisition; they, too, tended to favor political withdrawal from West Africa. That trend was further strengthened by the various Ashanti wars Britain fought in the hinterland of the Gold Coast. Trade, yes, administer, no, was the British motto. In 1865 a select committee of the House of Commons even recommended a change of policy toward the settlements in the region "with a view to an ultimate withdrawal from all, except, probably, Sierra Leone."[3] In France, there was no great wish to expand in Africa either. After the defeat of 1870 France could, in any case, entertain few colonial ambitions. Recovery and reform had to come first.

Small wonder, then, that in about 1880 European settlements in West Africa should have been no more than an extremely meager collection scattered over a long coastline. French possessions (on the Senegal) and British possessions (on the Gambia) were the most important European colonies on the Upper Guinea coast. To the south they were followed by Portuguese, and then by further French and British, possessions, ending with Liberia, a country created by U.S. President James Monroe for black Americans who wanted to return to Africa. In Lower Guinea, France and Britain made up the only foreign presence; Europeans here were strictly confined to the coast. The interior was under the control of the African rulers of Dahomey, Benin, Ashanti, and of the neighboring territories. There was nothing to suggest that twenty years later Europeans would have colonized the whole of West Africa, laying claim to all the land between the Atlantic Ocean and Lake Chad. Yet that is what happened, the process being completed, moreover, in a very short time, roughly between 1880 and 1900, with the main race being run from 1890 to 1898. Two countries, France and Great Britain, took a leading part in that race, while Germany played a sometimes noisy but largely subsidiary role. It all started in 1879 with the new French policy of expansion in Senegal, admittedly a continuation of the old policy, but with new methods and fresh vigor.

# 1
# FRANCE IN THE SUDAN

### EXPANSION

The French presence in West Africa goes back to the seventeenth century, to be precise to 1659, when Louis Caulier founded the town of St.-Louis on a small island in the mouth of the Senegal. The French colony of Senegal developed from this outpost, and consisted of four towns, St.-Louis, Gorée, Dakar and Rufisque. These so-called *quatre communes* were considered to be an integral part of France, a piece of France overseas, electing their own deputies to the French parliament. In economic respects the colony was almost completely dependent on the slave trade and seemed to offer few prospects once that trade was abolished. The only economic alternative was the trade in groundnuts, and these came from the interior, that is, from regions outside the French sphere of influence. The economic fate of Senegal was thus dependent on regions beyond French control, and which France was afraid Britain might occupy by advancing from Sierra Leone. That fear lay at the heart of a policy of military expansion unprecedented in the history of Africa.

The remarkable thing to begin with was that this policy should have emerged at such an early date: it was first applied to Senegal in the 1850s, that is, under the Second Empire. The architect of French military policy in West Africa was an officer in the engineering corps, Louis Faidherbe, who was to serve as governor of Senegal twice, from 1854 to 1861 and again from 1863 to 1865. When he was first appointed to the post he was just thirty-six years old. He had the reputation of being a difficult and demanding man, but competent and painstaking as well. Faidherbe was a dynamic and imaginative soldier and was to become a famous figure in French military and colonial history. His aim was to turn Senegal into a viable colony. To that end, he believed, it was essential to subdue the Islamic states in the western Sudan by military force. In Algeria, too, where Faidherbe had served earlier, he had found it necessary to crush Islamic resistance. Only when Islam had been subjected would it be possible to initiate the commercial activities that would lay the basis for Senegal's prosperity.[4]

However, Faidherbe's great expansion plans had to be put to one side for the time being. The ministry refused to allocate adequate funds, even though it agreed that military expansion was a prerequisite of further colonization. It was, in fact, to become the basis of French West Africa policy in later years. Faidherbe was also the founder of the famous Senegalese Rifle Corps, the *tirailleurs sénégalais*. He personally designed their dashing uniform: black cloak and hood, short blue cloth jacket and waistcoat, red sash, blue cotton Turkish trousers, boots and white gaiters, and a red zouave cap. This colorful corps was to grow into one of the most important sectors of the French colonial army, even when the black riflemen had long ceased to come from Senegal and were being recruited throughout the Sudan.

The fall of Napoleon III's empire and the shock of defeat in 1870 put a temporary halt to French expansion in West Africa, but at the end of the 1870s it was given a new lease on life. In 1876 Colonel Brière de l'Isle was appointed governor of Senegal. He was to remain at his post until 1881. With his arrival, a new urgency made itself felt. Brière de l'Isle was an officer in the *infanterie de marine*, a far from prestigious unit also known as "the Cinderella of the French armed forces."[5] It consisted in the main of the worst cadets turned out by St. Cyr, and was looked down upon by fashionable cavalrymen as a *ramassis de voyous*—bunch of louts. Nearly half of them were of humble origin.[6] The corps nevertheless proved to be an outstanding fighting machine, one of the best tools for conquest ever used in the colonies. What Algeria had been for the army, the Sudan became for the navy: a private hunting preserve. Brière, as one of his successors, Gallieni, was to put it in early *franglais*, was an advocate of "le go-ahead des Américains."[7] Brière's aim was essentially the same as Faidherbe's: establishing a French empire in West Africa by military expansion. This tempestuous soldier presented Paris with an ambitious plan for a railroad linking St.-Louis and Dakar to the Upper Niger. It was the age of railroad fanatics and other makers of wild plans. There was even a scheme for a railroad right across the Sahara, from Algeria to the Sudan. Still more fanciful was the plan to put the Sahara under water so as to create an inland sea fit for navigation. Ibsen's Peer Gynt dreamt of this idea as early as 1867:

> And the waters would rush like a life-giving river
> In through the gap and fill the desert.
> Soon this whole white-hot grave would lie
> Fresh as a dimpled sea. . . .
> Steam will drive factories in Timbuctoo,
> Bornu will speedily be colonised, . . .
> Around a bay on rising sand,
> I'll found my capital Peeropolis.
> The world's degenerate. Now comes the turn
> Of Gyntiana, my new land!

"A little money and I could do it," Peer Gynt continued.[8] The French engineers had the same problem. The money was not forthcoming. Compared with these projects Brière de l'Isle's ideas were modest, but for the time being nothing came of them either. The railroad enthusiasts fought one another in Paris and were fought in turn by the Tuareg in the field. On 16 February 1881 a reconnaissance party under Colonel Paul Flatters was wiped out in the Sahara. That put a temporary stop to the trans-Sahara railroad and similar dreams and schemes.

However, the French plan to advance into the Sudan survived and became increasingly well defined. It received fresh impetus in 1879 when Joseph Simon Gallieni, a captain in the French navy, was appointed *directeur politique* in St.-Louis. Gallieni (1849–1916), who was go on to gain fame in Madagascar, had begun his colonial career in the western Sudan. He was born on 24 April 1849 in a small village in the Pyrenees. His father, an Italian, had taken out French nationality and became a French officer. Gallieni junior followed in his footsteps, and after attending the military academy at St. Cyr, which he left in 1870, he fought in the Franco-German War and was taken prisoner. In 1872 he started on his African career, first in Réunion, and then in the western Sudan. On 1 January 1877 he arrived in Senegal. Here he was to serve twice, first from 1877 to 1881 as a young officer, and again, after a period spent in France and Martinique, from 1886 to 1888, this time as Commandant du Haut Fleuve—commander of the upper river. Gallieni's greatest triumphs then followed: he pacified Tonkin (1892–1896) and Madagascar (1896–1905). Later still, in 1914, he became even more famous as governor of Paris and organizer of the celebrated "Marne taxicabs." After a brief and frustrating spell as minister of war in 1915, he died in 1916.

Brière de l'Isle and Gallieni played a crucial role in the new French approach to Senegal. More important, however, were the changes in Paris, where the Freycinet cabinet took office in 1879, with Admiral Jauréguiberry as minister of the navy and colonies. That cabinet introduced a new French policy in West Africa. Freycinet and Jauréguiberry were political allies and friends. Charles de Saulses de Freycinet (1828–1923) was undoubtedly the more influential of the two, and played an important role during the early years of the Third Republic. He may appear somewhat pale in comparison with such colorful contemporary politicians as the popular Gambetta and the hated Jules Ferry, but he nevertheless played a prominent part in French politics. In the early 1880s he was foreign minister for three years. He was also prime minister and minister of war on several occasions, and during the First World War, by then almost ninety years old, he was to become a minister once more, albeit without portfolio. Freycinet, who had been educated at the Ecole Polytechnique, was a firm believer in technology and industry. He first took ministerial office in 1877, appropriately in the department of public works. In this capacity he made his name with the so-called Freycinet plan, which was designed to reverse the economic crisis that had held France and Europe in its grip since 1873, using public works and the construction of a railroad in particular to do so. For Freycinet firmly believed that civilization progresses along railroad tracks, or, as he himself put it in a ministerial declaration, "Civilization spreads and is firmly established along its lines of communication."[9] Freycinet was also a fervent colonialist, fully convinced that the Sudan would prove of great value to France. Here, where it was assumed there was nothing but desert, there actually lived 100 million people, "in a state more or less close to semi-civilization," he informed the French president.[10]

Admiral Jauréguiberry, the new naval minister, had similar ideas. He had succeeded Faidherbe as governor of Senegal and he, too, favored French expansion into the Sudan, painting glorious pictures of an inexhaustible new market of 80 million people and of an abundant flow of raw materials in the opposite direction. Jauréguiberry was no great intellect and no economist, but he was also not a dreamer. Practical engineers such as Freycinet and sober businessmen such as Rouvier shared his vision. In the Sudan they saw "a new Canada," or perhaps a "French India," belated compensation for colonies lost to Britain in the eighteenth century.[11]

With Freycinet and Jauréguiberry these ideas became government policy, and that was a decisive change. Until then the advocacy of expansion in Senegal and Sudan had been the work of such local imperialists as Faidherbe and Brière, or of lone colonial enthusiasts in Paris. It was now adopted as official policy by the French government. As a result Brière's position was considerably more comfortable than Faidherbe's had been. Brière, in fact, did no more than continue Faidherbe's policy, but he knew that he had the backing of ministers ready to stand by him and prepared to ask parliament for the necessary funds. The unusual, or at least the new, feature was the acceptance by the French government that colonial expansion could no longer be left to the free play of social forces, but demanded intervention by the authorities. This new conception of the role of the state in colonial affairs was the crux of the new imperialism. It reflected a transition from "informal," that is, private, to "formal," that is, state, imperialism. This transition would make itself felt later among other colonial powers, but France was its pioneer.

In 1879–1880 Freycinet and Jauréguiberry decided that it was time for the French government to act on the ground in West Africa. Jauréguiberry took the decisive step in September 1880: he placed the western Sudan under military control, appointed Major Gustave Borgnis-Desbordes Commandant-Supérieur du Haut Fleuve, and gave him supreme authority over all operations on the Upper Senegal. This was the beginning of the period of military government that was to continue in the western Sudan until 1899. It was a far-reaching step, for it shifted the center of power from the governor in St.-Louis to the commander in the interior. The all too lax control by Paris of the activities in the colony became slacker still, not to say nonexistent. Jauréguiberry and Freycinet had at first taken personal charge of the French expansion, but had gradually allowed it to slip out of their hands by vesting full authority in a military commander they could neither control nor even keep under observation. Hence no one in Paris really knew what was happening. Western Sudan became the playground of the French navy. Borgnis-Desbordes, the new commander, was the very man for this job. Unlike Gallieni or Lyautey, he was a real saber-rattler who knew but one solution for everything: the military one. Not surprisingly, he very quickly became involved in a series of large military operations.

### WAR

European expansion in West Africa had been preceded by another expansion spearheaded by Islam. The nineteenth century in the Sudan was one of jihads, holy wars, aimed at the spread of Islam and the creation of Islamic states. The great caliphate of Sokoto in northern Nigeria, with which Britain was to become involved, was a product of the renaissance of African Islam. Another famous jihad was that waged by al-Hajj Umar. Umar made the pilgrimage to Mecca in 1826, visited Cairo on the way back, married the daughter of the sultan of Sokoto, and returned to his birthplace in Futa Toro in 1837. In 1852 he proclaimed a jihad against all pagans in the western Sudan. It led to the emergence of the Tukolor empire, which stretched from Timbuktu in the east to the frontiers of French Senegal. After Umar's death in February 1864 his oldest son Ahmadu took over his father's realm. However, his authority was always shaky.

### The Tukolors

The Tukolor empire presented the French with a problem. At first the problem was of a political kind, namely, whether the Tukolors should be treated as enemies or as potential allies. Faidherbe had already had to face this problem, and his successors had to do likewise. Because the French did not know the answer, their policy was a succession of alternating wars and treaties. The Tukolors were shrewd negotiators and did not hesitate to play the French against the British, as became clear, for instance, during the negotiations conducted by Gallieni in 1880. "We do not know the English," said Ahmadu's envoy, "and for various reasons we prefer the French. But," he added, using a striking metaphor, "a man who cannot get drink from his mother, must get it from his grandmother."[12] In other words, if the French did not cooperate, the Tukolors might have to turn to the British. The French took the hint. At the Treaty of Nango, signed on 4 November 1880, they were granted trading and maritime rights in exchange for rifles and fieldguns and for recognizing Ahmadu's authority. The treaty was thus a political victory for Ahmadu, although the French, too, considered it a success because the assumed British threat had been averted.[13]

With the arrival of Borgnis-Desbordes a new period began, diplomacy making way for force. In February 1883 he occupied Bamako, the capital on the Niger. Just one year later a French gunboat, the parts for which had been brought overland, was launched on that river. Ahmadu watched this French incursion into his territory stoically. Later, when the French found themselves in military difficulties elsewhere, they reverted to diplomatic consultation, and in 1887 a new treaty was signed. In it Ahmadu accepted a French protectorate over his territory.[14] It was only a paper protectorate, but the clauses of the Act of Berlin lent diplomatic importance even to such treaties, something that mattered greatly to France in its competition with Britain for spheres of influence on the Upper Niger.

The man who negotiated this treaty, Gallieni, had first parleyed with the Tukolors as early as 1880. Since then he had been promoted to lieutenant-colonel and commander of western Sudan. However, he too was to come round to the view that diplomacy was not enough. Ahmadu and Samori— another enemy of France—would have to go, he told his successor. But he left it to him to pick the right time and meanwhile ignored the instructions issued by the ministry in Paris. "Do as I do," Gallieni advised, "take no notice of the officials and follow your own ideas."[15] This lesson fell on fertile soil, for Louis Archinard was a real fire-eater in the mold of Borgnis-Desbordes. Entirely in the spirit of the latter, and on his own initiative, he launched a successful attack on one of Ahmadu's fortified towns in February 1889. During a visit to Paris the following summer he persuaded the minister of colonies to agree to a major expedition against Segu, the Tukulor capital. The attack came as soon as weather permitted, in February 1890. Segu was taken by the French without much difficulty. Ahmadu's power was broken, and the Tukulor empire in effect came to an end. Ahmadu himself retired to the east, where he enjoyed a short breathing space in a remote corner of his former empire. In 1893, however, even this last remnant of his former realm was swallowed up by France. Ahmadu fled and found shelter with his father-in-law, the sultan of Sokoto. Archinard sent Ahmadu's grandson to France, where he was taught at a lyceum and later at the military academy of St. Cyr. He died, however, while still young, so that nothing much came of this interesting experiment in assimilation.[16] The French had meanwhile become involved in a much lengthier and more arduous conflict with the man who was to become their most formidable opponent in West Africa. His name was Samori.

### Samori

Samori is a legendary figure in the history of West Africa. His French colonial opponents painted him as a savage dictator and pitiless oppressor, and nicknamed him "Samori le Sanglant," Bloody Samori. But even they admired his military prowess and freedom-loving spirit, as witness some of the other nicknames they gave him, "the Bonaparte of the Sudan" and the "African Vercingetorix."[17] In post-colonial, nationalist historiography, Samori is described as the greatest hero and freedom fighter of West Africa, the embodiment of African resistance. Be that as it may, Samori was in any case the greatest military organizer and empire-builder in the history of West Africa.

Samori was a product of the so-called Dyula revolution. The Dyulas were Islamic long-distance traders who had at first been content with the financial and commercial power they had gained as a result of their mercantile prowess. For they did not hold political power, which remained vested in the traditional animist chiefs. Samori himself was born in about 1833 to a family who had renounced Islam to return to so-called paganism. His mother was captured by a hostile family and enslaved. Because he had no money to buy her freedom, he took service with the family as a soldier and was promised in exchange that in due time his mother would be set free. Samori threw himself into his new calling with enthusiasm. He was a born leader and had considerable military and organizational skills. In about 1861 he and six comrades swore an oath of friendship.[18] Twenty years later he was ruling over an empire of 300,000 subjects.

By 1873 he was ready to make his move. He had created an army and trained it by applying what by African standards were unprecedentedly strict rules of discipline. The army was made up in the main of infantrymen, each armed with a rifle, a saber and a dagger. A cavalry corps was added later. Meanwhile Samori had started to build his empire. First came conquest, then consolidation. For the latter he sought and found support in religion. He converted to Islam and turned his realm into an Islamic state, from which it derived its cohesive strength. He himself took the title of almami, a rather vague term, which, however, implied that he was spiritual as well as temporal ruler over his people. Samori's empire emerged in the 1870s and continued in various forms until the French brought it to an end in 1898. Its size fluctuated and cannot be precisely determined, since political power in Africa was based on power over people, a scarce commodity, and not on possession of land, which was plentiful.

Samori was not only a great strategist but also a gifted diplomat. In 1885 he sought contact with the British in Freetown, the capital of Sierra Leone. Its governor was happy in the knowledge that Samori was ruling with a firm hand in the hinterland of the British colony, something that was bound to help the trade with the interior on which the colony's economy depended. Samori's envoys informed the governor that their almami's control of the roads was so complete that even a woman could walk alone and in perfect safety from the interior to the coast. Governor Sir Samuel Rowe was most impressed and sent to the Colonial Office for the silver medal Great Britain kept in store for most favored chiefs. In the summer of 1885 Samori sent him a petition, requesting the governor to ask the Queen of England to take his country under her protection. Rowe's response was guarded. "I must tell you that the great Queen of England only extends her friendship to such persons as deserve it."[19] The almami would first have to prove his merit in the queen's eyes by opening his roads to British traders.

Rowe's reaction was cool because he knew that this request for protection had little practical importance. It was, as he explained to the British foreign secretary, something like the politeness of a Spaniard who tells you that his entire house is at your disposal. That sort of thing must not be taken literally.[20] Rowe was quite right, but he underestimated the importance that protectorate treaties had meanwhile acquired in the diplomatic game of the European Powers. Their real value might be small, but no one was prepared to challenge their validity. In 1885, in any case, the Berlin Conference had just been considering the subject, and such a treaty would have had tangible political implications. That was to become clear soon afterwards, when Samori signed a protectorate treaty with France.

In practice Samori had many more dealings with France than he had with Britain, and relations were generally less amicable. For the French were not only after trade, but also and above all after political power. The upshot was a series of campaigns and battles in the years from 1881 to 1885 that proved none too favorable for Samori. French fire power was too great, and the war became one-sided. In one short campaign alone during the first two weeks of June 1885 Samori lost 900 men while the French lost just two.[21] On 28 March 1886 he therefore signed a peace treaty and a trade agreement, in which the borders between the French sphere of influence and that of his empire were laid down. Samori was left with an empire of considerable size (approximately two-thirds as big as France). Samori for his part acknowledged a French protectorate over that empire, but did not accept that this gave the French any authority to rule over it, behaving in fact rather like Rowe's polite Spaniard. The French, however, gave the treaty a literal interpretation and insisted on that in the years to come.[22] Things had not come to that pass in 1886, however, when relations were still good and Samori sent his favorite son to Paris as a sign of his goodwill. The young prince was received personally by President Grévy, Prime Minister Freycinet and General Boulanger, and taken to the opera, to the Longchamp races and to "le music-hall."[23] In 1887 and 1889 the treaty was once more elaborated and confirmed by both parties. However, in the end it proved to have been no more than a stopgap. Ahmadu's fate gave Samori a clear hint of what lay in store for him as well.

In May 1891, following a succession of border incidents, Samori broke with France. That marked the start of the "Seven Years' War" against him. During the first phase, from 1891 to 1894, the French fought a series of campaigns that proved successful for them inasmuch as they took possession of Samori's empire. But Samori conducted a systematic scorched-earth policy so that the French had little joy of their conquests. He refused to give them battle, thus keeping his army intact, evacuated his people, and built a new empire in an entirely different part of the Sudan. This was a remarkable feat, rather as if Frederick the Great had withdrawn from occupied Prussia to found a new kingdom near Moscow.

The French had no real interest in the region at the time and allowed their war with Samori to draw to an end, not so much *faute de combattants* as *faute de contact*. By 1894 they lost all track of Samori and had virtually forgotten him. Things might easily have continued in this fashion had not one of Samori's sons, acting on his own initiative, attacked a French column and wiped it out. That sealed Samori's fate, for such a thing could not, of course, be left unavenged. In the spring and summer of 1898 fresh campaigns were launched, and early on the morning of 29 September Samori himself was unexpectedly taken prisoner as he sat under a tree reading the Koran. The French governor banished him to Gabon, where he died of pneumonia on 2 June 1900. That was the end of the Samori era, except that a long time later his grandson, Sekou Touré, was to become president of the Republic of Guinea.

Samori in captivity

### IMPORTANCE AND RELEVANCE

The French penetration of the western Sudan tells a story different from that generally associated with the partition of Africa. It was achieved by means of systematic campaigns of conquest and almost permanent warfare, and happened because French expansion in this area reflected a clear political plan. The original objective had been to turn Senegal into a viable colony, but that had quickly developed into a much more ambitious project: the creation of a great French empire in western Sudan. At the root of this project lay not only economic ideas—the assumed commercial prospects of the region—but also strategic considerations, namely the desire to link up three French possessions, Algeria in North Africa, the French Congo in Central Africa and French West Africa. For the success of this scheme the eastward extension of Senegal, in the direction of Lake Chad, was essential. This so-called Chad strategy began to find favor in French colonial circles in about 1890, and gave a fresh impetus to the French policy of conquest in the Sudan. The policy was thus not a case of the flag following trade, but rather the opposite: a state opening up a territory by force in the hope that trade would follow the flag.

The most striking element in this story is the systematic use of military force. Elsewhere European expansion generally took place by means of treaties, in which sovereignty was surrendered for protection. In the Sudan, too, such treaties were signed, but their importance was relatively slight since resistance to the spread of European influence was strong. Young and powerful states were to be found here, with a strong military machine and an ideological cohesion based on Islam. However, save in one case, these states failed to make common cause. In their division lay their weakness.

The French left political decisions in the region almost entirely to their men on the spot. Since these local leaders were generally pugnacious and ambitious soldiers, they rarely looked for diplomatic solutions and more often than not resorted to military strength. Just like Algeria, the Sudan was placed under a *régime du sabre*, though this time not the saber of the army but that of the navy. These wars were no easy victories for France, not so much because of their opponents as because the terrain, especially during the rainy season, was virtually inaccessible, and the climate murderous all year round. The advances were, as Colonel C. E. Callwell wrote, first and foremost "campaigns against nature."[24] French losses in battle or during advances were relatively slight, however, because the French were so vastly superior in fire power. Death by disease, of course, does not make the headlines.

Paris saw little cause, therefore, to trouble about clashes in which there were so few casualties, at least on the French side. Whenever the authorities tried to intervene, they generally did so with little success, not least because of the complicated political situation in Paris. Ministerial instability, inter-ministerial rivalry—the departments of war, colonies, the navy and foreign affairs all vied for leadership of colonial policy—and an unclear command structure ensured that politics lost its grip on African affairs. The press and the public complained about the reign of a "pouvoir occulte."[25] So western Sudan became the playing field and parade ground of *officiers soudanais*, not a few of whom laid the foundations for their future career in this region. Many a famous French marshal and general in the First World War had made his name in the fight against Samori, Ahmadu or some other West African ruler. For in the long run French military expansion would not remain confined to the Sudan but would spread as far as Lower Guinea. To follow this development, however, we must first look at the British presence in West Africa.

# 2
# GREAT BRITAIN AND THE NIGER

With the fall of Samori in 1898 we ran ahead of the main events, because it was in that year that the partition of West Africa was settled with the help of the Anglo-French agreement. We must therefore return to the 1880s to appreciate how Anglo-French rivalry in this area had come about. While France was busy conquering an empire in the Sudan, Britain was laying the foundations for Nigeria, its most important colony in West Africa. It all began on the coast, in the gigantic delta formed by the Niger and its tributaries. The bounds of this delta are two rivers, the Benin in the west and the Cross in the east. The whole is a huge area measuring some 250 miles along the coast and extending to more than 120 miles inland. The region used to be as unhealthy as it was infertile. Yet by 1830 this spot, so badly served by nature, had grown into one of the greatest trading centers in West Africa, largely thanks to the trade in palm oil. The interior was rich in the oil, and the rivers provided easy access to it. In Britain the area became known as the Oil Rivers. The British traveler and writer William Winwood Reade called it the "Venice of West Africa."[26]

Africans played an important role in the palm-oil trade because Europeans were not allowed to trade directly with the interior. Contacts with the oil producers had to be made through African middlemen, who thus held monopoly control over this link in the commercial chain. The middlemen were concentrated in a number of such city-states along the coast such as Brass, Bonny and Calabar. City-states were fairly unusual in Africa; in them, power and prestige depended entirely on success in business. In the Oil Rivers, every trader carried not only a marshal's baton but a royal scepter in his knapsack. A slave could rise to become a ruler, as witness the career of King Jaja of Opobo. The American dream was as nothing by comparison.

The Oil Rivers constituted one center of brisk British commercial activity in the area. The other center was the kingdom of Lagos further to the west. Lagos was important to Britain for two reasons: first because the slave trade was being brazenly continued in the face of British opposition, and second because of the growing importance of the palm-oil trade—here just as in the Oil Rivers. For that reason, Britain appointed a consul to the "Bights of Benin and Biafra" as early as 1849. His influence, however, was small, and in 1861 the king of Lagos was persuaded to cede his kingdom to Britain against an annual pension of a thousand pounds sterling. In 1861 Lagos thus became a British crown colony. The Colonial Office, incidentally, did not think much of the change and called it a "a deadly gift from the Foreign Office,"[27] because it meant the addition of yet another poverty-stricken colony for which money would have to be begged from Parliament.

In the Oil Rivers the British presence remained confined for a time to a British consul. To make an impression the consul would now and then send a gunship upriver, which instilled some healthy respect in the local population, although not very much, certainly among those who did not live right on the banks of the river. The British government was content to leave things at that. It was the period of "informal empire" and of "moral suasion." The Niger was important enough to be kept open for British

trade, but not for shouldering the costs associated with a colonial administration.

This attitude was to dominate British policy for a long time. "We have
already quite enough territory on the West Coast," wrote the secretary for
the colonies, Lord Kimberley, to Gladstone as late as January 1882.[28] A
few months later, in April of that year, when the British consul, Edward
Hewett, urged the establishment of a protectorate over the Niger coast,
Kimberley let him know without hesitation that no such thing could be
considered. "The coast is pestilential; the natives numerous and unman-
ageable," was his terse but unequivocal view.[29] Occupation could only lead
to war with the black population and to higher taxes in Britain. Both were
out of the question. The fact that Britain nevertheless gained a dominant
position on the Niger was thus not the work of the British government but
of a British subject, the merchant and empire-builder Sir George Goldie.

### GOLDIE AND THE NIGER

"All achievements begin with a dream," Goldie is said to have declared
when he was asked later how it had all happened. "My dream as a child
was to colour the map red."[30] Goldie became the head of a great commercial enterprise, although at heart he was not a trader but a true imperialist in the romantic vein, a kind of Cecil Rhodes. The comparison is
obvious and has been made often enough: both great imperialists founded
a country, and both of them made a fortune. However, there were also
considerable differences between them. To begin with Goldie was more
down-to-earth than Rhodes, and did not, for instance, believe in Rhodes's
Cape-to-Cairo dream. "Trade seeks the sea by the shortest route," was his
laconic assessment of that idea.[31] Goldie relied on trade. Unlike Rhodes,
he owned no gold or diamond mines. Goldie's romantic sentiments, moreover, were not confined to business and politics, as Rhodes's were. For,
unlike Rhodes and many other British empire-builders, Goldie was not
afraid of women. On the contrary, his life, or at least the earlier part of it,
was dominated by them.

George Dashwood Goldie Taubman (1846–1925) was a Manxman
whose family had grown rich on the Isle of Man by smuggling tea, wine
and spirits. It was not of purely British stock, as the name Taubman suggests, and when he was knighted in 1887 Taubman changed his name to
the more British-sounding Goldie. Little is known about his youth, except
that it was wild and turbulent. "I was like a gunpowder magazine," he
declared later.[32] He went to the Royal Military Academy at Woolwich but
left halfway through his course, when an inheritance made him financially
independent. He left then and there for Egypt, fell almost as quickly in love
with a beautiful Egyptian, and moved with her to the Egyptian Sudan.
There he learned to speak Arabic, read many books about Africa, and lived,

Sir George Goldie

as he himself put it, in a "Garden of Allah." After three years this para-
disiacal existence came to an end and Goldie returned to England. The
reason is not entirely clear. According to some, his Egyptian mistress had
died of consumption, but according to others, she lived for many years
more, albeit unhappily, in Cairo on the money Goldie had settled on her.
He himself led "a life of idleness and dissipation" in England, before thinking better of it all and returning to The Nunnery, his rather inappropriately
named parental home on the Isle of Man.[33]

There it did not take Goldie long to fall in love with the family governess
and to carry her off to Paris, where they lived discreetly in sin for some
time. However, it was 1870, the year of the Franco-Prussian war, and the
lovers were willy-nilly sucked into the maelstrom of international politics.
The Prussians were laying siege to Paris, and no one could get out of the
city, except for Gambetta in his famous balloon. It looked as if Goldie and
his governess would be in for a long stay, and since this irredeemably compromised them both there was nothing for it but to get married. The wedding took place in 1871, in London, but Goldie remained without a career
or plans for the future until he was nearly thirty. Then in 1875 he and his
brother heeded the appeal of the latter's father-in-law for them to take
charge of an ailing London company trading in palm oil on the Niger. The
two brothers reorganized the business and renamed it the West Africa Company. In 1877 Goldie went out to Africa to take charge of its affairs on
the spot.

Goldie was a man with striking if not very prepossessing looks, with an angular face and piercing blue eyes. A former girlfriend described him as someone halfway between a vulture and a mummy.[34] His behavior was eccentric and his opinions forceful; he was a convinced atheist and materialist, and believed that the future of mankind lay in work, trade, industry and technology. He took these ideas with him to Africa.

In the 1870s trade on the Niger witnessed a new development. The Europeans had gained access to the river and had started trading there directly. The result was the coexistence of two markets, the traditional one in the delta, where merchants from Liverpool did business with African traders, and a second one upriver where trade was done directly with the producers. Here both the British and the French were very active, and engaged in cutthroat competition. Mergers were clearly the only way to survive. Goldie, just like Rhodes, seemed to be a master in that field. In 1879 he formed the United African Company (called the National African Company from 1881), which comprised all the British companies trading on the river. Next he turned to the French and began a trade war with the two main French trading companies, which gave up the struggle in 1884 and sold their interests to the National African Company. On 1 November 1884 Goldie became the undisputed master of the Lower Niger.

The Berlin Conference acknowledged this state of affairs: it accepted that the Niger was an exclusively British sphere of influence. However, Goldie's plans went much further than that. He was not interested in the Lower Niger alone but in the whole river, not only in trade but also in political power. His objective, in short, was to add a new colony to the British Empire. To that end he now focused all his energy on the interior, expanding his riparian empire into a network of more than a hundred posts with more than fifteen hundred employees. Twenty of his gunboats patrolled the Niger. At the same time he signed treaties with various African chiefs—thirty-seven in all by 1887. Each of these treaties stipulated that the chief "ceded the whole of our territory to the National African Company (Limited) and their descendants for ever," and that he granted the company a trading monopoly.[35] The clause ceding territory in perpetuity was so unprecedented that the Lord Chancellor considered Goldie's treaties suspect for that reason alone.[36] In practice, however, the company had been acting as a kind of government in the hinterland ever since 1884, albeit without the official blessing of the British authorities. Yet official recognition in the form of a charter was what Goldie was after, because that was the only way of achieving his political objective, the incorporation of Nigeria into the British Empire. Everything thus depended on London.

### THE BRITISH POLICY

The British government adopted a hesitant attitude to the Niger question. True, the need for some form of political action was becoming increasingly clear at the beginning of the 1880s, but Britain continued to feel apprehensive about the financial and political consequences and tried to put matters off for as long as possible. However, pressure from British traders to break the power of the African middlemen in the delta by political intervention continued to grow. French competition was another important spur. The old view that new protectorates were so many unwelcome burdens still held, but as Sir Percy Anderson observed in 1883, the situation had changed. It was now "a question between British Protectorates, which would be unwelcome, and French Protectorates, which would be fatal."[37] At the end of 1883 the British government therefore changed its mind and instructed Edward Hewett, the British consul, to sign protectorate treaties in the Niger region. However, in Britain, as elsewhere in the world, the official mills grind slowly. It was not until 16 May 1884 that Hewett was provided with the blank protectorate treaties. He set to work as quickly as he could, but by then it was too late. Bismarck had anticipated the British, and in 1884 had sent Dr. Gustav Nachtigal, the German consul and explorer, on the gunboat *Möwe* to the west coast of Africa, ostensibly on a trading mission but actually to sign treaties. On 5 July 1884 Nachtigal signed a number of these in Togoland, and on 14 July he sailed up the Cameroon estuary and signed a protectorate treaty there as well. The French could, no doubt, have imagined a better *quatorze juillet*, but the hardest blow was struck at the British. When Hewett sailed up the Cameroon estuary on HMS *Flirt* on 19 July, he discovered that the German flag had been hoisted there already. The combination of the *Möwe* and Nachtigal had been too quick for him—which gave rise to the nickname "Too-Late Hewett."

Now an Anglo-German treaty-signing race was started, naturally to the irritation of both contenders. The issue was not, however, worth a major conflict. Gladstone had other priorities, and so Bismarck had his way: Germany acquired Cameroon. His efforts were later recalled by a young Cameroonian in an elegant quatrain:

> *Ich bin ein Bub' von Kamerun*
> *Der deutschen Kolonie;*
> *Fürst Bismarck hatte viel zu tun*
> *Bis er erworben sie.*[38]

Bismarck, in turn, then supported the British claims to the Niger at the Berlin Conference. Shortly afterward, in May and June 1885, the British and German governments reached agreement on the demarcation of their respective spheres of influence in Nigeria and Cameroon.

These events all went to show that the British government had indeed changed course, if reluctantly. Now it was the turn of a more active policy. On 5 June 1885 Britain let it be known, in accordance with the new rules issued at the Berlin Conference—that is, by notifying the Powers—that it had established a protectorate over "the Niger Districts." These did not merely include the entire coast between Lagos and Cameroon, but also a large part of the hinterland, roughly as far as the confluence of the Niger and the Benue. A protectorate was not enough, however. What increasingly mattered in practice, after Berlin, was effective occupation, of the interior as well, although the Act of Berlin did not say so specifically. Britain had just one practical, that is cheap, method of achieving this end, and that was to grant a charter to Goldie's company. Unfortunately, that posed a grave problem. Such charters, by which a company acquired sovereign rights and could act as a government, more or less implied granting it a trading monopoly in exchange for its assumption of such onerous duties. In any case Goldie's company needed such a monopoly if it was to survive economically.[39] Both parties, Goldie and the British government, were thus interested in a charter. The problem was that the Act of Berlin had just laid it down that navigation on the Niger had to be free to all, and such freedom was in conflict with Goldie's monopolistic ambitions. Goldie accordingly gave that clause a peculiar interpretation. The act, he argued, spoke of freedom of navigation. Yet anyone who went ashore had obviously ceased to navigate, hence forfeiting the right to free trade. In order to trade it is necessary to go ashore from time to time, so Goldie's version of freedom was not worth a great deal.[40] What Goldie was in fact trying to do was to square the circle: to achieve a monopoly in free trade.

A conflict with the British government ensued. Goldie did not refrain from pointing out that Britain's special position on the Niger, as recognized in Berlin, was based on his company's de facto monopoly. If the British government did not toe the line, he let it be known quite bluntly, he might well be forced to sell his business to the French. That looked suspiciously like blackmail and did little to improve relations between the crown and the company. In the end, on 10 July 1886, the charter was granted all the same. The Royal Niger Company had been established.

The Act of Berlin had to be respected, hence there could be no question of granting Goldie a trading monopoly. However there was no reason why levies should not be imposed to pay for the administration, and Goldie was given permission to impose these. He was also granted a refund of all the expenses he had incurred in asserting his authority. The geographical area covered by the concession was not very clearly defined. It naturally comprised all the territories for which Goldie had signed treaties, but the boundary with the delta was not specified, any more than was that with Lagos. A possible expansion of the concession was thus allowed for. The British government was keen to see the delta, too, under private administration and hoped for an amalgamation of Goldie's company with trading companies there, but nothing came of that. The differences between the two groups of traders was too great, and the conflicts between them could not be settled.

Britain now had a protectorate and the company a charter, but the old urge of the British government to avoid as much responsibility as possible still prevailed. The establishment of the protectorate had been a defensive measure in the main; it had not been an attempt to spread British influence, but one to stop other countries from spreading theirs. In 1886 Harry Johnston, the British vice-consul in the Oil Rivers, summed it up as follows: "So long as we keep other European nations out, we need not be in a hurry to go in."[41]

Great Britain nevertheless became increasingly enmeshed in the Niger affair because of a growing series of trading problems. The Liverpool merchants in the delta were being hard pressed not only by Goldie but also by their African competitors, of whom one of the most formidable was King Jaja of Opobo, the ruler of a city-state in the delta. Jaja was a very shrewd man, one who had risen from slave to king. He had a sharp nose for business and a good understanding of Western methods and techniques. He lived in Opobo in a Western-style palace and sent his sons to school in Glasgow. When the Liverpudlians complained that Jaja was hampering their trade, Jaja replied that he had every entitlement to do so. He had indeed accepted a British protectorate by signing a treaty on 1 July 1884, but, wily ruler that he was, he had, before putting pen to paper, asked the British consul to specify precisely what such protection entailed. Hewett's reply had been that the British queen had bestowed her "gracious favour and protection" upon him, but that for the rest, the country would remain under his rule. "The Queen," Hewett had explained, "does not want to take your country or your markets, but at the same time is anxious that no other nation should take them."[42]

This splendid formulation of what would later be called "preventive imperialism" had undoubtedly reflected the true feeling of the British government at the time, but the mood had changed, and not even the Foreign Office could continue to turn a deaf ear to the plaints of British merchants. Jaja's position was not to be envied. He was Hewett's bête noire, and the foreign secretary had called him "a false and cruel chief."[43] In 1866 the foreign secretary informed Hewett that the former, far too restrictive, interpretation of the treaty would have to be dropped. Britain would now claim sovereignty over the entire region. Individual treaties with such ministates as Opobo would not be allowed to stand in the way and would have to be redefined. As a result, the term "protectorate" acquired a new and far broader meaning.

For a time, however, nothing happened. Hewett fell ill that same year and went home on leave. His replacement, Vice-Consul Harry Johnston, took over in January 1887. At the time he was still a young man, no more than twenty-seven years old. He was an ambitious and impetuous member of the new imperialist school, and believed firmly that nothing must be allowed to stand in the way of progress. Now, there could be little doubt but that Jaja was just such an obstacle. He would have to go. On 12

September 1887 Johnston accordingly asked London for permission to get rid of him. Salisbury, the prime minister, was not very keen on that sort of thing, but he was on vacation in the south of France. The instructions Johnston received from Salisbury's staff were so vague and confusing that he read them as approval of Jaja's deportation. He accordingly persuaded Jaja to meet him with a promise of safe-conduct, and then offered him the choice between exile and war. As the guns of a British gunship were trained on the town at the time and his favorite son was in Britain,[44] Jaja chose the first alternative and was escorted to the Gold Coast. From there he later departed for the West Indies.

Lord Salisbury was not pleased. "In other places it would be called kidnapping," he observed.[45] Yet he did nothing to revoke Johnston's orders. Jaja's deportation was not the end of the affair. A commission was sent out to the delta to look into the best form of administration for the area. The "consul and gunboat stage" was past.[46] The outcome, arrived at in 1891, was a compromise. The territory remained a protectorate in name, but became a directly administered colony in fact. In other words the delta was given its own form of administration, the details of which were elaborated in 1893 in the articles of the Niger Coast Protectorate. With this, the idea of a single British administration on the Niger run by Goldie's company was dropped. The Liverpudlians had refused to bow to Goldie's rule, and the conflicts of interest had proved to be unbridgeable. For a time there would be two rulers on the Lower Niger: the British government in the delta and Goldie's company upriver.

# 3
# THE PARTITION: PHASE I, 1890–1895

The old system, marked by very little European involvement in West Africa, thus came to grief in the 1880s. The new policy ushered in by France in the Sudan in 1879, and Goldie's operations on the Niger that same year, had started a process that would unavoidably force West Africa onto the agenda of European diplomats. The Berlin Conference provided a first demonstration of that. In Berlin, the hub of international politics at the time, there had been much talk of West Africa. A new era had dawned. The partition of West Africa had become a matter of concern for European diplomacy.

### THE CALM BEFORE THE STORM

Yet the Berlin Conference was not followed by an explosion of activity. On the contrary, there was a calm before the storm, a "loaded pause," as the British historian J. D. Hargreaves called his book on this period.[47] That calm lasted until 1890. On 1 July of that year Germany and Britain signed the Zanzibar-Heligoland treaty. The French, who also had rights in Zanzibar, protested against being excluded. "What point is there in spending a few thousand million francs a year on the army and the navy if we allow ourselves to be treated like the republic of Andorra?" a French deputy complained in the Chamber.[48] These protests led to political démarches, and these in turn to Anglo-French negotiations conducted by Lord Salisbury on the British side and by Ambassador Waddington on the French. William Waddington was in fact almost as English as Salisbury. He was the son of an English industrialist, but had been born in France and, after Rugby and Trinity College, Cambridge, had settled in the country of his birth. His main interests were archeology and numismatics, but he ended up in politics, where he did so well that he became minister of foreign affairs and even prime minister of France.

Waddington was no more interested in Africa than Salisbury was. Hence the negotiations did not take long. On 5 August 1890 a Franco-British agreement was signed. It was in fact a package deal in which the main issue was East Africa, the starting point of the whole discussion. France recognized the British protectorate over Zanzibar in exchange for British recognition of the French protectorate over Madagascar. The agreement also included a number of clauses about West Africa. The most important of these was British recognition of a French sphere of influence from France's Mediterranean possessions to a line stretching from Say on the Niger to Barruwa on Lake Chad, but excluding everything "that fairly belongs to the Kingdom of Sokoto." The excluded part fell into the sphere of influence of the Royal Niger Company.[49] This agreement was to prove of great importance during later Anglo-French disputes in West Africa, and in the ultimate partition of that area.

The agreement was in fact a sort of emergency alliance, an attempt to keep the threatening Anglo-French tensions in West Africa at bay. The threat was real enough, as eastward French incursions from Senegal and the northward expansion of the British Niger Company could easily have led to confrontation. The partition into spheres of influence laid down in 1890 was meant to prevent just that. In both countries the immediate question was of course who had gained more from the partition. There were different answers. The critics of the British government insisted that Britain had conceded too much. They pointed to the many thousands of square miles assigned to France. Lord Salisbury naturally felt it incumbent upon himself to defend his policy. In doing so, he gave in to the temptation to adopt something of an ironical approach. His propensity for skepticism was great, especially when it came to African affairs, and he had a pronounced weakness for quips. He was well aware of this, as witness his declaration, "I dislike speaking when I am tired, not because I am afraid of being dull, but because I am afraid of not being dull enough."[50] The night the issue was being debated in the House of Lords he was evidently tired. In any case his address was far from dull. He told his critics to look not just at the quantity of the land acquired by France but also at the quality. "I will not dwell upon the respective advantages of places which are utterly unknown not only to your lordships but to the rest of the white race," he remarked. All he himself had to add was that while France had indeed been assigned a large area, it was "what agriculturists would call 'very light land', that is to say, it is the desert of the Sahara."[51]

Next morning, the *Times* congratulated France on "the splendid possibilities" and the "really magnificent sphere of influence" it had acquired in the Sahara.[52] The French ambassador had followed the debate from the gallery, and Waddington was still enough of an Englishman to grasp the full import of the ironic tone. He gently drew Salisbury's attention to the rather tactless character of his remarks when he wrote to him. "No doubt the Sahara is not a garden and contains as you say much 'light' land; but your public reminder of the fact was, perhaps you will allow me to say so, hardly necessary. You might well have left us to find it out."[53]

The ambassador was, of course, perfectly right; Salisbury's remark spoiled French satisfaction with the agreements and poked fun at the result of negotiations on which the French had so prided themselves. Not surprisingly, French critics argued that France had been caught napping and had given away too much. They claimed that the Royal Niger Company enjoyed no authority over the enormous lands it had laid claim to. They were certainly right—the French government had taken a highly exaggerated view of the Royal Niger Company's sphere of influence. Ironically enough, the myth of that company's might had been spread not by the British but by the French themselves. French colonial enthusiasts had made much of the tremendous expansion of Goldie's company, but for the express purpose of drawing the attention of the French government to the resulting threat and hence putting it under pressure to counter that threat. They had now fallen into the pit they had dug themselves, for Goldie's company had, in fact, not yet set foot in that part of Nigeria, and Britain thus had the territory thrust into its lap, so to speak.

The truth about the Anglo-French treaty of 1890 is that there were no winners and no losers. Both parties gained, each in its own way, simply because their approach was so different. Salisbury's policy was to help the British merchants who helped themselves.[54] The Niger Company was not only helping itself but was also helping the British government by playing the part of British agent. Hence it deserved state support. Of course, the Niger question did not hinge exclusively on the trading interests of Goldie's company. It was at heart about a nascent colony, but as far as Britain was concerned the basis of the whole operation was and remained a commercial one. Ultimately it was all about the economic prospects of the Niger. E. D.

Morel put it very succinctly in 1902: "Commerce took us to West Africa; commerce keeps and will keep us in West Africa. It is the *fons et origo* of our presence in West Africa."[55] The French approach was altogether different: in France the initiative came from the state and not from private companies. The basis was a strategic and geopolitical plan, not commercial considerations. The French were out to build an empire in West Africa. These distinct starting points made it possible to reach a compromise satisfying to both parties, not just in 1890 but even later, when France and Britain were to have an even sharper confrontation on the Niger. For the treaty of 1890 did not so much bridge the differences between them as lay the foundations for a new and greater conflict.

### THE NEW COURSE IN FRANCE AFTER 1890

The Anglo-French agreement of 1890 was doomed to failure from the outset. This outcome was inevitable because Europe was witnessing the emergence of a keener and more aggressive form of imperialism, supported and carried forward by public opinion. While expansion in Africa had originally been the concern of individual soldiers in France and traders in Great Britain, by the 1880s it had been elevated to cabinet policy and diplomatic démarches. In the 1890s, moreover, it was also to become the platform of increasingly powerful colonial pressure groups. As a result West Africa acquired a new importance. As always in that part of the world, it was France who took the initiative, gaining a lead of several years over Great Britain. The new course France began to follow in 1890, which was bound up with the rise of the *parti colonial*, did not have an echo in Britain until 1895, when Joseph Chamberlain became colonial secretary.

In 1890 the political climate in France was quite other than it had been during the preceding years. In the 1880s France had been in the grip of the great internal crisis following the attack on the republic by the royalist general Georges Boulanger. If the general had had his way, the continued existence of the republic would have been in doubt. That danger was scotched for good when the hopeful kingmaker failed to answer the call "A l'Elysée!" at the crucial moment. The chance of a royalist coup had been thrown away. The Boulangist movement went into a steep decline, and Boulanger himself went not to the Elysée palace but to Brussels, where he committed suicide at his mistress's grave. French home affairs then entered calmer waters.

At about the same time Germany switched to its *Neue Kurs*, and that new course created fresh possibilities for French foreign policy. In 1892 a Franco-Russian treaty was drawn up, although it did not receive its final form, that of a military alliance, until sometime between late 1893 and early 1894. It offered France at long last the safety from Germany it so badly wanted. It also gave it the self-confidence it needed to pursue a more active colonial policy and to face Britain, its main rival in Africa, with greater boldness. Finally, it was also in 1890 that the so-called *parti colonial* was founded; this colonial pressure group was to exert a strong influence on French foreign policy in general and on French colonial policy in particular. The *parti colonial* was not a political party in the normal sense of the word. It was a collective name for the many colonial and propaganda groups that emerged in France during those years and that grew into a powerful colonial lobby. The first of these groups was the Comité de l'Afrique Française, founded in November 1890 by the author and journalist Hippolyte Percher, who wrote under the pseudonym Harry Alis.

Henri-Hippolyte Percher (1857–1895) died as the result of a duel he fought in connection with persistent rumors that he, the great French colonialist, had sold his pen to Leopold II and hence served the Free State rather than France. Later that rumor proved to have been correct: Harry Alis had indeed been Leopold's secret agent. His colonial career was as colorful as it was brief. It lasted a mere five years, from 1890 to 1895, but in these few years he achieved a great deal. Nothing, incidentally, had presaged his colonial vocation. Percher's previous interests had been chiefly literary. He had published a collection of short stories, of which eight copies were sold; had founded the *Revue moderne et naturaliste*; was a friend of Maupassant, with whom he traveled in Algeria and Tunisia; and had been involved in several literary scandals. Later works such as *Hara-kiri* and *Quelques fonds* were more successful, but did not provide enough for him to live on. Journalism proved more financially rewarding, especially his editorial work on the prestigious *Journal des Débats*. As a result he met Eugène Etienne and other politicians, and that led to the establishment of the Comité de l'Afrique Française. Alis preached the colonial cause not only in newspapers but also in such works as *Nos Africains* and *A la Conquête du Tchad*. It was soon afterwards, at the end of 1891 or the beginning of 1892, that he sold his services to Leopold and put himself forward as a "disinterested intermediary" between France and the king of the Belgians, both of whom had ambitions to advance upon the Nile.[56] The persistent rumors about his venality finally led to the duel that was to prove fatal to him.

The Comité de l'Afrique Française was not the only one of its kind. Other committees were to follow in quick succession (Comité de l'Egypte, Comité de l'Asie Française, Comité de Madagascar, and others). For all that, the French colonial movement was not very large. It had a total membership of about 5,000, which was not a great deal when compared with the 40,000 members of the German Kolonialgesellschaft.[57] It was certainly no mass movement. Yet the *parti colonial* was influential thanks to the adherence of so many prominent and respected figures, most of them politicians, diplomats, army officers, journalists, geographers and writers. Business circles had their own Union Coloniale Française. As was usual in

France, most of these *comités* had started out as lunch societies (Déjeuner de Maroc, Déjeuner Etienne) and were to go on rallying their members mainly at dinners and banquets. Not surprisingly, therefore, the *parti colonial* was known as "the diners' party."[58] It would be wrong, however, to underestimate that activity. In colonial affairs, too, the French like to settle things "over the walnuts and wine." Apart from that, the committees published newspapers and journals (in the years after 1830, a new colonial paper was founded nearly every year), sent out expeditions, held congresses, and handed out diplomas, certificates, prizes and medals. Of special importance was the establishment of the Groupe Colonial de la Chambre on 15 June 1892, when 42 deputies formed the organization, which by 1893 had expanded to 120 members and to nearly 200 in 1902. In 1898 a Groupe Colonial du Sénat was also founded. It did not have a clear political party bias, although there was a slight preponderance of *modérés* (liberals) and later of radical members. The group was a collection of parliamentarians interested in foreign and colonial affairs. It reached the height of its power in the years from 1870 to 1905, and dominated French policy during the partition of Africa. Its influence then began to wane, having been based mainly on good personal contacts with ministers and government officials. The undisputed leader of the group and, in fact, of the entire *parti colonial*—their "chief, guide and master"—was Eugène Etienne, whom his admirers also called "Notre-Dame des Coloniaux."[59]

Next to Jules Ferry, Eugène Etienne was the most important figure in the colonial history of the French Republic. But although he had held many high offices and had been minister several times, he was less well known than Ferry. Ferry's name was linked to the great issue of modern French history, namely, the fight for secular education, while Etienne was principally concerned with foreign and colonial affairs, and to a lesser extent with trade, transport and economic affairs. He was the spokesman of modern colonialism, a capable manager and a shrewd businessman. British newspapers called him the "French Mr. Chamberlain," not merely because of his colonial enthusiasm and his powerful position but also because of his commercial acumen.[60]

Eugène Napoléon Etienne (1844–1921) was born on 15 December 1844 in Oran, Algeria, the son of a professional officer who had become a big property owner in Algeria. Etienne was therefore a *colon* and would remain one all his life. Originally bent on an officer's career himself, he changed his mind when he married young in 1865. He then joined a commercial house run in Marseilles by Maurice Rouvier, a man who was to make his mark in French finance and politics. Through Rouvier, Etienne met Gambetta and thus found his way into politics. In 1881 he was elected *député* for Oran, a seat he was to hold for nearly forty years, until 1919, when he became a senator. In the Chamber he was a *modéré*, a follower of Ferry and Gambetta. In 1887 he received his first important political appointment: under-secretary of state in the naval ministry—Etienne's first chance to "lay hands on the colonial pie," as he put it himself.[61] In 1889 he was again appointed under-secretary of state. The colonial department was then transferred from the naval ministry to that of trade. Not until 1894 did it become an independent ministry housed in the Pavillon de Flore, a wing of the Louvre. This time Etienne stayed on for three years (February 1889 to February 1892), and although he was to hold many more ministerial posts, his real power lay in the place in which real power happened to be vested during the Third Republic, the Chamber. In 1892 he became vice-president of the Chamber, an office he was to hold several times and in which he wielded great influence. From 1892 to 1905, when he became minister once more, he presided over the Groupe Colonial in the Chamber, which made him the most influential man in French colonial and foreign politics.

Despite all its shades of opinion and individual differences, it is true to say that the *parti colonial* had a clear vision of France's place in the world. It saw France as a Power, not with international but with wide regional interests. This explains why the *parti colonial* was not particularly concerned with Asia. *Lâchons l'Asie, prenons l'Afrique*—leave Asia, take Africa—the title of a well-known book by Onésime Reclus published in 1904, could have been the movement's battle cry. It considered France to be a Mediterranean Power, and Algeria the central pillar of the French empire. This bulwark would have to be strengthened and made safe by extending and securing the protectorate over Tunisia that France had established in 1881, thus safeguarding the eastern border. To protect the western flank a similar operation would be needed in Morocco.

To the *parti colonial* the Maghreb was the very heart of the French presence in Africa, with Black Africa serving as the hinterland of the North African empire. The two existing French bridgeheads, one in West Africa and the other in Central Africa, had to be linked not only to each other but also to North Africa. The junction of these links fell somewhere near Lake Chad. All three French possessions in Africa would have to be joined here. That meant penetration from the north, that is, from Algeria, via the Sahara; from the south, from Gabon, along the eastern border of Cameroon, meanwhile occupied by the Germans; and also from the west. In the west France already owned two bridgeheads, Senegal and western Sudan on the one hand, and several scattered French possessions on the coast of Guinea on the other. Two things had therefore to be done. The two West African regions had to be linked, and this body, in its turn, had to be linked to the French possessions in North and Central Africa. Maurice Barrès, the well-known nationalist writer, summed the plan up in 1890: "the foundation in Africa of the world's greatest colonial empire."[62]

The ideas of the *parti colonial* were adopted by the responsible ministerial officials. As a result France witnessed the rise in the 1890s of a sort of colonial consensus about the objectives as well as about the methods of colonial policy. Effective occupation of the regions involved had to be brought about speedily. International agreements and treaties with African chiefs were all very well, but effective occupation was more important, signifying the stepping up of military exertions. In the Sudan that amounted to the continuation of the traditional policy, in other words, subjugation of Ahmadu's and Samori's empires. That, as we saw, was achieved in 1893 and 1898, respectively. In Guinea it required a new initiative, the subjugation of the kingdom of Dahomey, which stood in the way of the French advance upon the Niger and hence also of the link to the Sudan.

### THE FALL OF DAHOMEY

European possessions along the Guinea coast in the 1880s still constituted a fairly insignificant collection. France had been established in Grand Bassam since 1842 and would use this settlement as a springboard for the Ivory Coast, over which France declared a protectorate on 10 January 1889. The frontier between it and the Gold Coast was drawn a few months later. This British colony had been in existence since 1850, to the great dissatisfaction of the British government, for the Gold Coast was to be locked in conflict with the mighty Ashanti empire in the hinterland for the rest of the century. The Ashanti were infamous, especially in Great Britain, where every Sunday school related tales of the bloodthirsty deeds of these barbaric people. Their capital, Kumasi, was renowned as the "metropolis of murder."[63] Britain fought a number of important Ashanti wars. The second of these, from 1873 to 1874, was led by General Wolseley, who fought a perfect campaign, defeated King Kofi, and put Kumasi to the torch. However, the Ashanti were not yet ready to submit. There followed another two wars, the last of which took place from 1895 to 1896, when the British government finally succeeded in proclaiming a protectorate over Ashanti.

To the east of the Gold Coast lay Togo, a colony acquired by Germany in 1884. Next came several French possessions on the coast of what is now Benin. In 1889 a Franco-British treaty laid down the boundary between the French territories and the adjacent British colony of Lagos, at least along the coast. The boundary extended some sixty miles inland, although what was more important was what happened beyond these sixty miles. That was where the kingdom of Abomey lay, not only barring French access to the Lower Niger, but also threatening the French possessions on the coast. Here France had two harbors, Ouidah and Cotonou, and it had also established a protectorate over the mini-kingdom of Porto-Novo in 1863. King Toffa of Porto-Novo was in effect a vassal of the king of Abomey, or at least was considered as such by that king. King Glegle of Abomey, as he was called, was a formidable man, a "Negro Louis XIV" according

The Amazons of Dahomey

to the French.[64] To drive home his claims to Porto-Novo he would launch annual attacks on the territory, thus infuriating the French. In fact, the entire kingdom of Abomey was beginning to pall on them because of its barbarous customs and vile practices.

Abomey—or Dahomey, as it was also called—was indeed an unusual state. It had a strong standing army. One of its most remarkable sections was the Amazon corps, created during the eighteenth century when the then king had decided to turn some of his many wives into soldiers. These Amazons had been a fixed part of the army ever since and, indeed, the most feared. In Dahomey women did the lion's share of the fighting. In exchange they also had all the privileges enjoyed by king's wives, living in palaces and eating food specially prepared for them. Less agreeably, they were not allowed to have relations with men other than the king, whom they did not see very often for obvious reasons. The punishment for breaking this rule was death. Psychologists, then as now, have traced the savagery of these Amazons to their enforced chastity.[65]

Fighting women and a spate of harsh sentences constituted but a small part of the strange practices for which this kingdom was famed. In Europe Dahomey was as notorious as Ashanti. There was an extensive literature on the subject of its "bloody customs." Widespread and frequent human offerings, especially during royal funerals, annual sacrifices of young boys and girls, torture and cannibalism, continuous hunts for new victims to satisfy the unbridled blood lust of the people and its rulers—all these subjects were given great prominence by the French press, especially when it was deemed necessary to appeal to outraged consciences in support of the French decision to move against Dahomey and its king.

That move began in November 1889, when the French government sent the famous explorer Dr. Jean Bayol on a diplomatic mission to King Glegle. The doctor was to persuade the king to stop the human sacrifices, to put an end to his raids against King Toffa, and to accept a clear boundary between the French sphere of influence and his own. Bayol's mission was a failure. King Glegle was on his deathbed, and Bayol, after first having been kept a near-prisoner for some time, was finally received by the king's son, who told Bayol that there was nothing to discuss. "The king of Dahomey gives his land to nobody. Whosoever tries to take it from him must die," he declared quite bluntly. To this warning he added a piece of advice for the French. To his utter amazement, he said, he had learnt that France was no longer a kingdom, but a republic. From that he concluded that the country was being governed by "rash young men." He recommended that the French put a stop to that and restore the monarchy. That might also prove to be a first step in the improvement of mutual relations. With this message, Dr. Bayol was sent on his way.[66]

Soon afterwards this prince, Kondo, "an admirable and shapely Negro,"[67] acceded to the throne, adopting the name Behanzin and the title "Shark of Sharks." He organized a magnificent funeral for his father, the undisputed climax of which was the sacrifice of forty-one boys and forty-one girls.[68] The French had now grown heartily sick of this "royal gorilla," as one deputy called Behanzin, and decided to march on Dahomey.[69] Their force was commanded by General Alfred Amédée Dodds, a doughty fire-eater from Senegal. Dodds led two campaigns against Dahomey, in 1892 and again from 1893 to 1894. Dahomey put up fierce resistance, much fiercer at any rate than the French had expected. The defenders used their artillery so effectively that the attackers thought the guns were manned by

Germans, Africans being clearly incapable of such gunmanship.[70] The Amazon corps was all but wiped out in this war, the men too suffering heavy losses. In January 1894 Behanzin surrendered. He took five of his wives and went into exile in the Caribbean, whence he would later go on to Algeria, where he died.

With the capture of Dahomey, France had taken an important step toward gaining access to the Lower Niger. All that still stood in its way was the sultanate of Borgu. Borgu thus became France's next objective, but because Britain was growing increasingly apprehensive about French plans and activities in the area, it too decided to move on Borgu. The result was the "race for Borgu," the climax of Anglo-French rivalry in West Africa.

# 4
# THE PARTITION: PHASE II, 1895–1898

### CHAMBERLAIN AND THE NEW COURSE IN BRITAIN

The new imperialist ideas that had become official government policy in France during the 1890s amounted in essence to assigning a greater role in colonial affairs to the state. Similar ideas were beginning to make headway in Great Britain as well, though British political parties were divided on the issue. Liberals such as Gladstone, Granville and Harcourt were traditionally "little Englanders," but Lord Rosebery, who followed Gladstone as prime minister in 1894, was a convinced imperialist. The Conservatives had been considered the leading pro-Empire party ever since Disraeli's Crystal Palace speech, even though most of the Tory establishment belonged to the landed gentry, who cared little for the British Empire. Lord Salisbury himself, the Conservative prime minister, was a diplomat of the old school, one whose main concern was maintaining the balance of power within Europe. Imperialist expansionism was strongest in a new party, the Unionists, consisting of those Liberals who, in protest against Gladstone's conversion to Home Rule for Ireland, had left the party in 1886. In 1895 their leader, Joseph Chamberlain, joined the Salisbury cabinet, which thus became a two-party cabinet made up of Conservatives and former Liberals. To the great surprise of many people, Chamberlain chose the rather unglamorous colonial portfolio, a decision that was to have wide repercussions. From 1895 to 1902 Chamberlain ran the office with energy and verve, and as leader of one of the two coalition parties he left a strong mark on Britain's foreign and imperial policy. As a result, this passionate social reformer and imperialist became the architect of the new British policy in West Africa and later in Africa as a whole.

## Chamberlain

Joseph Chamberlain (1836–1914) is one of the most important figures of nineteenth-century British politics. A social reformer and ardent imperialist, a self-made man and a professional politician, he represented the forces of progress and modernity in the conservative Britain of his day. Although Chamberlain's name is inseparably linked with Birmingham, the city that made him rich and later famous, he was born in London and grew up there, the son of a shoe manufacturer. Soon after leaving school he joined his father's office, where he worked until his eighteenth birthday. Then his father sent him to Birmingham to help run a screw-manufacturing company in which he had invested money. The energetic young businessman proved to be exceptionally successful there, and twenty years later, in 1874, was able to retire a rich man at the age of thirty-eight and to devote himself fully to his real passion, politics.

Chamberlain took his first political steps in Birmingham. From 1873 to 1876 he was lord mayor of the city, which he, in his own words, "parked, paved, assized, marketed, gas-and-watered, and *improved*."[71] Good management and good drinking water, that was what it was all about, according to Chamberlain, in Birmingham, in Britain and in Africa. The move from municipal to international politics was thus no more than a logical step. Chamberlain grasped the great political opportunities offered by the new electorate, enfranchised by the Reform Bill of 1867. The age of mass politics had arrived, and that meant that traditional forms of political organization had to be replaced. In 1877 Chamberlain founded the Liberal Federation, a political party machine with headquarters in Birmingham, thus laying the foundations of his political power. When Gladstone returned to government in 1880 he made Chamberlain president of the board of trade, and Chamberlain began his career in national politics.

He had meanwhile made his name as a great organizer, speaker, manipulator and agitator, but not as a political theorist. Nor would he ever become one. Chamberlain was a man of action, not a thinker. "You decide first and then find reasons" was his motto.[72] He had a passionate temperament, was a born fighter, and was not always overscrupulous. Gladstone called him "the prince of opportunists," and Salisbury, in whose cabinet he served later, said of him that "he had not yet persuaded himself that he has any convictions."[73] Yet in 1886 Chamberlain took a decision that could truly be described as based on principle, and which in any case ruined his chances of becoming prime minister, and indeed his whole political career. For in that year he broke with Gladstone on the Home Rule issue. Chamberlain, too, wanted reforms in Ireland, but not an Irish parliament that might become the nucleus of an independent state. When it came to the choice between reform and nationalism, Chamberlain chose the second.

Joseph Chamberlain

Gladstone's Home Rule proposals split the Liberals, and Chamberlain became the leader of those separatists in the party who called themselves Unionists. Home policy was now relegated to second place, while nationalism and imperialism became his central preoccupations. He genuinely believed that "the British race"—his favorite expression—was the best in the world, and that the spread of British influence was in the interest of all mankind, and of "colored" people in particular. He also believed that a new age had dawned, in which there was room for only a few large empires. These, according to him, were those of America and Russia and perhaps Britain as well, at least if it knew how to organize its empire properly. For this, "imperial federation," the close collaboration and mutual adjustment of politics and economics through closer union of the whole empire, was needed, and that is what he was working for. The time of laissez-faire was past. Chamberlain also realized that free trade had had its day, and became an advocate of tariff reform, that is, of protectionism and imperial preference.

No wonder, then, that he chose to become colonial secretary in 1895. The post was neither important nor prestigious, unlike, say, that of foreign secretary, chancellor of the exchequer, or first lord of the admiralty, but

Chamberlain did not care for honors or esteem. "I cared for power," as he put it himself.[74] As early as 1888 he had written to his future wife that he would be secretary for the colonies "some day," and seven years later that day had come. Chamberlain was used to having his way. As leader of the Unionist faction in Parliament he wielded considerable power in the cabinet. Together with Lord Salisbury, the prime minister and until 1901 also the foreign secretary, and Balfour, Salisbury's nephew and leader of the House of Commons, Chamberlain was part of the troika that governed his country for seven years, from 1895 to 1902.

With Chamberlain there appeared a completely new approach to African affairs, that of modern, economically motivated imperialism. Chamberlain's motto was "development." He did not believe in the hands-off politics of laissez-faire imperialism, either at home or in Africa. To him, imperialism was an extension of radicalism. The social reform of Britain would have to be continued with an economic development policy for the Empire. In that development the state would have to play an active role. Chamberlain thus resuscitated the ideas of Freycinet and Jauréguiberry twenty years later.

His new policy was one of investment and development. Railroads had to be built, capital attracted, production stimulated. The export of liquor would have to be fought much like the slave trade, for the future of Africa lay in its people. The goose expected to lay the golden eggs had to be protected. Administration would have to be improved and taxes introduced to pay for such improvements. Agricultural agencies would have to be set up to help in the growing of such export crops as cotton, cocoa and rubber. "Scientific administration" and "constructive imperialism" were the key concepts of the new regime. The approach was quite different from that of the prime minister under whom Chamberlain had to serve. Salisbury was a man of the past, Chamberlain of the new age.

Chamberlain's attitude to power was that of the political boss, his temperament that of the successful businessman, and his tone that of the boy who had gone from rags to riches. He brought a new style to British diplomacy and was quick to see concessions as a form of appeasement. Salisbury said of him that he "hated giving anything away," but Chamberlain explained that he merely hated giving something away when he did not get anything better in its place.[75] He did not play the game for the game's sake but for the stakes, and had a predilection for bluff and brinkmanship. Of Theodore Roosevelt's famous motto, "Speak softly but carry a big stick," he borrowed the second part only. G. M. Young's dictum might have been written specially for him: "Nothing is so bloody-minded as a Radical turned patriot."[76] It was thanks to the power relationships in British party politics that two such different men as Chamberlain and Salisbury had been thrown together into one cabinet in 1895. And it was the same relationships that ensured that this cabinet would continue for over seven years, despite its many tensions.

### BORGU

Following the German annexation of Togo, three great European Powers—France, Germany and Great Britain—now had possessions on the Guinea coast. What mattered was not to be locked into these possessions. If Britain could advance from the Gold Coast and out of Nigeria to the hinterland quickly enough and far enough, then it could unite these two possessions, and Togo and Dahomey would be cut off. If, on the other hand, France were to break through to the north from Dahomey and join up with the French thrust in the Sudan from the west, then it would have surrounded Togo and the Gold Coast. Expansion in the interior was thus the order of the day.

Whereas Germany played hardly any role in this process, Great Britain took a leading part. However, British expansion in the Gold Coast did not prove particularly successful. From 1893 to 1894 Britain was caught up in the Third Ashanti War. There were problems on the Niger as well, for though the British sphere of influence had been laid down by the Anglo-French convention of 1890, two French expeditions, led by Monteil and Mizon, respectively, had demonstrated that the British claims to this region had been based on bluff. The Niger Company had no real power in the area, and in the absence of effective occupation the British claims would be hard to maintain in practice. That constituted the weakness of the British position, and is why the subjection of Dahomey had been so important for France. The road to the north had been opened up as a result. The Say-Barruwa line had, of course, posed a problem, as it set a southern limit to French expansion in the Sudan. The French discovered a solution to that problem, however, as simple as it was sensible. They argued that the convention had indeed set a limit to French penetration from the north to the south, but not to penetration from the south to the north.[77] No one had thought of that at the time, but after the fall of Dahomey the road to the Niger, too, lay open to the French. If they could only take Borgu on the Niger, then they could create a link with the Sudan from there. A protectorate over Borgu, to be followed by effective occupation, thus became an important objective of French policy.

Borgu was a principality or sultanate whose borders were as vague as its constitutional position. It was even questionable whether such a state as Borgu really existed. Britain maintained that Borgu was part of Bussa, with which it had a treaty. Britain accordingly called the king of Bussa the "sultan of Borgu." The French asserted, first, that there was no such thing as a sovereign over Borgu, and second, that if there was, it was the king of Nikki. As the diplomats in Europe could not solve the problem, it had to be tackled in the field. The French accordingly sent an expedition to Nikki with instructions to sign a treaty with its ruler. The British, not to be outdone, also sent a mission to Nikki. The result was a race for Borgu, or rather for Nikki, for it was here that the ruler of the region was believed to reside.

The French expedition was led by Captain Henri Decoeur, which turned out to be an unfortunate choice. Decoeur was a kind of Fabius Cunctator, but not nearly as successful. He set out for Nikki at the end of January 1893 but was back again toward the end of January 1894, complaining about the unreliability of his bearers and the many dangers of the terrain. Such behavior was of course disappointing, but for all that he was entrusted with a new mission during a visit to Paris in the rainy season, and was also voted a subsidy by the Comité de l'Afrique Française. Decoeur, however, continued to dawdle as before, and the French advance never materialized.

The British expedition was led by quite a different sort of man, Captain Frederick Lugard, the "Maker of Nigeria," as he was often called, and rightly so. Lugard was to establish the British protectorate over northern Nigeria and was later to be made governor-general of all Nigeria. Later still Lord Lugard, as he was to become, also acquired great fame as a colonial theorist. He became the founder of the system of "indirect rule" and was the author of *The Dual Mandate in Tropical Africa*, a plea for colonial development that was to become the bible of British colonial administrators. Things had not yet come to that pass in 1894 when Lugard was instructed to beat the French in the race to Nikki.

Lugard (1858–1945) was then thirty-six years old and a man with a far from spotless reputation. He was the eldest son of a missionary in Madras, but had chosen to become a professional soldier. His reputation was controversial, and he was not much liked, especially by the French, both because he had sided against the French missionaries in Uganda and also because he had been unscrupulous enough to spy on and question Captain Paul Monteil at the Moulin Rouge on the eve of Monteil's mission to the Sudan.[78] The Liberals in Great Britain did not think much of him either. Their later leader, Sir Henry Campbell-Bannerman, wrote about him in a letter to Harcourt, "The general opinion of Lugard is that he is a lunatic, aiming at being a second Gordon—just what we thought."[79] That was in 1892. The British government was therefore clearly of two minds about Lugard, but Goldie had need of just such a man. Lugard reluctantly exchanged East for West Africa and left for Nigeria on a special mission for Goldie's company. The "steeplechase," or the *course au clocher*, as the French called it, had begun.[80]

The distance Lugard had to cover was longer than that faced by Decoeur, who had already left, but Lugard was traveling by river and not overland, which gave him the advantage of greater speed. Moreover, his orders were not to occupy territories but merely to come away with treaties. The precise

Lord Lugard

instructions Goldie gave him were to "zig-zag a good deal, so as to run a network of treaties across and between the few treaties obtained by the French."[81] On 5 November 1894 Lugard and his company reached Nikki. It quickly became clear that the negotiations would not be easy. The king let Lugard know that he did not wish to receive him before he had been sent a present. Lugard demurred and a few tense days followed. Then the air cleared, and on 9 November the standard treaty, "Form No. 12 (For Moslems)," was signed.[82] However, Lugard never saw the king, nor was the treaty signed by the king; it bore the signature of the imam and of a "minister" who bore the honorary title of "Butcher in Chief." They were acting on behalf of a former king of Nikki who had been dead for six years. Not surprisingly, the validity of this treaty was challenged by France.

On 12 November Lugard left Nikki, and a good two weeks later Decoeur arrived. He too was able to obtain a treaty, signed this time by the king himself, "le Roi de Nikki, capitale de Borgou." When the French discovered that Lugard had also come away with a treaty, they not only declared it invalid but also abandoned the idea that Nikki was the capital of Borgu.

The ensuing dispute between Great Britain and France was as heated as it was involved.[83] In the meantime, however, it became clear that the French were determined to advance to the Lower Niger and that it was thus time for serious negotiations. These opened in 1896. Six years earlier, in 1890, a Franco-British Niger Commission had been set up to look in greater detail at the agreement signed that year, but that commission was no longer active. It was now reassembled. The new negotiations did not, however, lead to any concrete results for some time because the Méline government, which favored a strong colonial expansion policy, had taken power in France in May 1896. Moreover, the Franco-British dispute over the Nile made itself felt behind the scenes. The French raised their claims to the Niger to levels that proved unacceptable to Britain. At the end of May, negotiations were broken off. The race began anew, and this time in earnest.

The French became extremely busy in West Africa, their activities culminating in the occupation of Bussa in March 1897. That was the straw that broke the camel's back. For though there was not a single Briton to be found in Bussa, Goldie's company had held clear and recognized contractual rights over the territory since 1885. The principle of effective occupation was thus in head-on collision with that of rights based on treaties. If Britain were to give in on this point, then the second principle and hence the entire foundation of British Niger policy, based as it was on treaties between the African chiefs and the Niger Company, would be jeopardized. Moreover, Bussa afforded access to the Niger, and hence the issue of the trading monopoly and with it the economic future of Goldie's company was at stake.[84]

Franco-British tension thus hinged on a question of principle, but what also played an important part was the fact that Britain, too, now had a colonial secretary who was prepared to use the resources of the state for the protection of imperial interests. Chamberlain was even prepared to throw in not only financial, but also military resources. The end of the period of company rule was in sight. Matters had grown too intricate and the ramifications too great to be left to the vagaries of private enterprise. On 27 May 1897 Chamberlain discussed the subject with Goldie. The point at issue was, in the first instance, financial support by the company for the West African Frontier Force (WAFF), which Chamberlain had established as the military instrument of his Niger policy. Goldie refused, not least because he was given inadequate guarantees that his charter would be extended. Chamberlain was exasperated by this and let his secretary of state know that if that were Goldie's attitude there was only one solution, namely, "to expropriate him at once, lock, stock and barrel."[85] It was not for nothing that Chamberlain had grown up in Birmingham business circles.

The West African Frontier Force was set up even without Goldie's support, and being 2,000 men strong, recruited from among the Hausa and the Yoruba, proved to be a formidable force. At Chamberlain's request, Lugard took command of it in late November 1897. He was given carte blanche when it came to the purchase of equipment and arms. As Chamberlain explained, "expense is no object—plenty of guns and everything."[86] Lugard's orders, this time, were to conduct a "chessboard policy" rather than follow Goldie's zig-zag course. Chamberlain's strategy was to set up a British settlement next to every French one, an extremely risky policy that invited incidents. Salisbury did not agree with it and advocated a more cautious approach, but he was overruled in the cabinet.[87] Even Lugard, the professional soldier, was more cautious and practical in this instance than the former manufacturer. He called Chamberlain's chessboard policy "mad and impossible."[88] His own suggestion was to concentrate on control of the river, the most important strategic and commercial factor in the region, rather than on the occupation of land, but Chamberlain insisted, and Lugard did not feel that he was in a position to ignore his instructions. The British chessboard policy on the Niger was launched in 1898.

The consequences were predictable. Incident followed upon incident. There was a veritable flag-planting race—wherever a tricolor flew, a Union Jack was quickly hoisted not too far away. On 7 June 1898 Lugard let Chamberlain know that a military clash was inevitable. In the event, however, neither party really wanted to go to war over Borgu or Nikki, certainly not Lord Salisbury, who had not the slightest desire to do battle "for the sake of a malarious African desert."[89] The two contenders thus cooled down, the Niger commission was reconvened, and on 14 June 1898 came the signing of the Anglo-French convention that put an end to twenty years of Anglo-French rivalry for the Niger.

The 1898 Niger Convention was a victory for Britain.[90] True, France acquired Nikki and thus gained access to the Niger at a much more southerly point than Say, but British claims to Nikki had always been weak, and the place itself was of small importance. Britain, for its part, retained political control over the Lower Niger and at the same time acquired the Sokoto caliphate. Chamberlain's "Birmingham screw policy," as Lugard called it, had thus proved successful.[91] Present-day Nigeria owes its large size to it. The French were disappointed. Much of what Decoeur, Monteil and others had acquired for France had gone by the board.

EPILOGUE

With the Anglo-French Convention of 1898, the partition of West Africa was largely completed. The rest was epilogue. For the British there still remained the task of the setting up of Nigeria, for the French the completion of their Chad plan. The British government held consultations with the Niger Company to arrange a transfer of authority. The Niger Coast

Protectorate, that is, the delta, was joined in 1900 to the Lower Niger, of which Goldie's company had had charge, and the whole renamed the Protectorate of Southern Nigeria. The name Goldesia had been suggested originally, but Goldie himself had insisted on rejecting that Rhodes-like honor. Negretia, too, had been proposed but turned down as poor Latin. So Nigeria it was in the end.[92]

On 9 August 1899 the British government took over the territory from the company, paying £865,000 for it, to the dismay of the chancellor of the exchequer, who was opposed to any such purchase, even though the company had brought Britain half a million square miles and 30 million people, and though it could therefore "fairly be said that the Company has founded an Empire."[93] The figure of 30 million inhabitants was no more than a wild estimate, and the half million square miles an exaggeration (the whole of Nigeria measures less than 400,000 square miles), but it was impressive enough nevertheless. Even so, the House of Commons approved the purchase with very bad grace, and only because it was persuaded in the end that further troubles with France might thus be avoided. Next to Southern Nigeria, the Lagos Colony and Protectorate was also retained as temporary administrative entity. Next to that came the new protectorate over Northern Nigeria.

British Nigeria thus consisted provisionally of three more or less independent components. Between 1900 and 1903 Northern Nigeria was effectively brought under British control. The man who did this was Lugard. With the subjection of the emirates of Kano and Sokoto on 3 February and on 15 March, respectively, the British protectorate had become a fait accompli. In 1906 Lagos was incorporated into Southern Nigeria. At that point there were just two administrative units, Northern and Southern Nigeria. They continued to exist side by side as independent entities for some time and were not combined under a single administration until 1 January 1914. The first governor-general of the united Nigeria was none other than Lugard.

For Lugard the end of Goldie's company thus marked a new beginning. He was no more than forty-one years old, and his career as the "Maker of Nigeria" was yet to begin. For Goldie, who was fifty-four, it meant not only the demise of his company but also the end of his career, though not of his fortune. Nor was that his only setback. His wife, the former governess, had died not long before. There were no prospects of a new career—those offers he received were unsatisfactory. Goldie became a private citizen, lived on for a long time and, having been reconciled to his fate, happily at that. He died in 1925 at the age of seventy-nine.

France threw itself passionately into the implementation of its Chad plan after the 1898 agreement. It sent out no fewer than three expeditions to Lake Chad from three different points of the compass, not as part of a great Napoleonic strategic plan but thanks to individual impulses and successful lobbying by the expedition leaders.[94] Their main objective was to get rid of Rahab, the ruler of that territory, who was acting like a new Samori and refusing to listen to reason or to heed French diplomatic pressure. Force was thus the only solution. The three expeditions set out for Lake Chad in 1899, the first led by Emile Gentil from the south. The second, led by Captains Foureau and Lamy, crossed the Sahara from Algeria, and the third, under Voulet and Chanoine, advanced from the west. This last expedition was to write the bloodiest and most bizarre chapter in the all too bloody and bizarre history of French Sudan expeditions.

Paul Voulet was a difficult man, a doctor's son who had been a failure at school, had taken service as a lowly marine, and had nevertheless been promoted to the rank of captain. Lieutenant Chanoine, by contrast, had been trained at St. Cyr. His father was a general and later became minister of war, if only for a month. Voulet and Chanoine's expedition turned out to be unexpectedly demanding. It took them through a region exhausted by the many wars that had recently been raging in this part of the Sudan. At first they separated into two columns, one under Voulet and the other under Chanoine, but joined up again near Segu on the Niger. Later their paths parted once more, only to join up again near Sansanna-Hausa on the Upper Niger, this time for good, before advancing to Lake Chad. The column was made up, as usual, of just a few French officers and NCOs. Most of the soldiers were *tirailleurs sénégalais*, accompanied by a much larger number of bearers and women who saw to the household chores. Altogether they constituted a train of fifteen hundred. This number gradually grew, mainly because many more women were being captured and carried off, and not only for domestic purposes.

"War feeds itself," Gustavus Adolphus, king of Sweden, had declared as early as the seventeenth century, and that old maxim still applied. The expedition lived off the land. There was no alternative. Men and beasts swallowed up not only nearly 8,000 gallons of water a day, but also vast quantities of food, for the expedition had been badly equipped and provisioned. In the poverty-stricken area they crossed this posed a grave problem, as, incidentally, it did for a great many similar expeditions. What Voulet and Chanoine did was therefore exceptional not in principle, but rather in the scale and manner in which they set about requisitioning what was needed. Anyone who refused to come forward with the required goods, or who otherwise offered resistance, was shot out of hand. Whole villages were put to the torch and their inhabitants killed or carried off.

In this way the expedition advanced through the land, pillaging and burning, leaving behind a trail of corpses and sacked villages. Voulet and Chanoine did not allow any of this to worry them unduly, as news of their doings was scarcely likely to reach Europe. The expedition was, after all, passing through unexplored territory, cut off from the outside world. The ends justified the means, and reaching Lake Chad, they believed, was so

The Voulet-Chanoine mission

important an end that what happened on the way would be forgotten.
Everything might therefore have gone well, so to speak, had there not been
a leak. The man responsible was Lieutenant Péteau.

Lieutenant Péteau had originally been a member of the expedition, but

The Voulet-Chanoine mission at work

had been sent back to Say, the French fort on the Niger, after a dispute with Voulet. From Say, Péteau wrote several letters to his fiancée, telling her about his experiences and about the excesses and crimes the expedition had committed. Needless to say, he placed his own role, that of horrified observer, in the best possible light, and that of his former commanders, the brutal Voulet and Chanoine, in the worst possible one. That started the ball rolling. Péteau's fiancée showed the letters to the *deputé* for her district, who passed them on to the minister for the colonies, who in his turn showed them to his cabinet colleagues. The latter decided there and then, even before any official reports had been received, to strip Voulet and Chanoine of their command and to send out a senior officer to relieve them.

This decision, taken on 16 May 1899, was probably based on political rather than humanitarian considerations.[95] The republican regime was experiencing a severe crisis in the wake of the Dreyfus affair, and after the recent failure at Fashoda colonialism was less popular than it had been. Moreover, General Chanoine, the captain's father, had left the government. In any case, the French authorities were determined to be rid of Voulet and Chanoine, and sent Lieutenant-Colonel Klobb out to take over command of the expedition.

Klobb was a serious and committed officer with considerable experience of the Sudan. He left immediately and, in order to make haste, traveled as light as possible, first by train and then on horseback to the Niger. From there he continued by boat and, whenever the river was too low, on foot or by canoe. On 13 July 1899 he arrived at Dankori, near Zinder, his objective in sight. Klobb sent a messenger to Voulet with a letter that Voulet considered insulting, and to which he returned an arrogant answer. He informed Klobb that he wished to retain his command and pointed out that he had 600 men armed with rifles at his disposal. Any attempt to approach would be met with force. Klobb could not believe his ears. This was rank insubordination. It was unthinkable for Klobb that an officer might disobey his superior. But then Voulet was no ordinary officer. He realized that his career would not survive the scandal he had caused, and could see only one alternative—nor was he the only European with such a dream: to establish his own kingdom in the Sudan. What Samori could do, Voulet could do as well. "I am no longer French, I am a black chief,"[96] he said to his men, who sang:

> Le grand capitaine
> Il pense à nous;
> Il nous emmène au paradis.
> Où ça les amis?
> A Zindiri, Zindiri.
> Le grand capitaine,
> Superb' Superb'
> Il est notre Samory.[97]

The next day—it was *quatorze juillet* 1899—Klobb made his way to Voulet's camp. Voulet ordered him to turn back. When Klobb refused, Voulet gave orders to open fire, and Klobb fell dying to the ground. Voulet's success was short-lived, however. The shooting down of one's superiors does not help to enhance discipline in the ranks. When Voulet told his men that they must not count on returning to the Sudan, they rose in revolt. Chanoine was shot on 16 July. Voulet was able to escape on horseback, but was discovered a day later and also shot. Thus, as in a Shakespeare play, all the main actors lay dead on the stage when the curtain came down.

This outcome suited the French government. Now that the culprits were no longer alive, there was no need for an inquiry. Voulet and Chanoine could be considered victims of tropical frenzy. They must have been out of their minds. They had, after all, shot Klobb, their superior. The Voulet-Chanoine mission could be written off as a regrettable but exceptional incident. The myth of France's *mission civilisatrice* thus remained intact.

Meanwhile, Joalland, a lieutenant with the Voulet-Chanoine group, and Lieutenant Meynier from Klobb's contingent had taken over command. The Voulet-Chanoine mission continued as the Joalland-Meynier column, for the great objective, Lake Chad, had to be reached at any price. Reached it eventually was. In February 1900 the three French columns made contact. Lamy had taken the long road through the Sahara on foot, Gentil had traveled north from the Congo, partly on foot and partly by river. Together they were able to settle scores with Rabah, the ruler of the territory. On 22 April 1900 the crucial battle took place and ended in the death of Rabah, whose head was cut off and, in accordance with custom, offered to the French commander. The great French Chad plan had been implemented.

The region was now in French hands and the three French colonies linked. However, the whole concept of adding an African hinterland to the North African possessions, which had been the basis of the Chad plan, could not amount to anything while the Sahara itself was not under effective French control. In the next few years the conquest of the Sahara therefore took pride of place in French strategic plans for the area, and in July 1901 Captain Laperrine was appointed "Commander-in-Chief of the Oases."[98] This *vieux Saharien* tackled the subjugation of the area with great vigor, but not even he was able to claim immediate successes. Resistance was stubborn and subjugation would prove to be a long-drawn-out affair.

The French conquest of Mauritania was also part of this overall scheme. This desert region, which on purely theoretical grounds was considered to be a dependency of Senegal, was not something in which any of the Powers was particularly interested. In 1900 a Franco-Spanish treaty assigned the area between the Senegal and the Rio de Oro to France, but it was to be a great many years before the French could claim it in practice. The desert and the nomads continued to be difficult opponents. By 1912 the greatest difficulties had admittedly been overcome, but the region was yet to be fully pacified at the beginning of the First World War.

The result of all these endeavors was that West Africa became a predominantly French sphere of influence. On the map the handful of Spanish, German and Portuguese possessions in this part of the world appeared as small islands in a large French sea. Of course, there were also the British possessions, ranging from such minute enclaves as Gambia—several attempts to exchange that colony for French territory were to come to nothing—through more important colonies such as Sierra Leone and the Gold Coast, to the gigantic protectorate of Nigeria. On the map, however, even these important British possessions were no more than pockets in a largely French area. The *parti colonial* had thus had its way. West Africa had become a French sphere of influence and was to remain one even after decolonization.

# 5
# CONCLUSION

West Africa is the part of Africa with which Europeans have had the longest contacts and the greatest difficulties. It might therefore have been expected that the partition of Africa should have begun here. In a sense that is in fact what happened, for it is possible to consider the new French imperialist policy toward Senegal and Sudan as the inception of the partition of Africa. But that is a rather artificial view. The new French expansion policy introduced in 1879 by Jauréguiberry and Freycinet was on the one hand not quite new, but rather the continuation of an old French expansion policy first applied in Senegal by Faidherbe under the Second Empire; on the other hand, it did not have many immediate consequences. International discussions on West Africa did not start until 1884, by which time quite a lot had been happening elsewhere. The Egyptian crisis had led to pronounced French bitterness at this unilateral British intervention, as well as to fresh colonial rivalry. Moreover, Brazza's expeditions had focused attention on the great prospects of West Africa, and Bismarck had started to interfere in the black Continent. Only after all these events did West Africa appear on the agenda of the European Powers, who would, in fact, be doing their utmost to get it off the agenda again. Bismarck soon lost interest in the area, and Germany would play hardly any part in it. The borders of Togo and Cameroon were settled by diplomats without too much trouble and remained unchanged. With Germany out of the way, only France and Great Britain were left on the scene.

French expansion proceeded from west to east and was aimed at control of the Upper Niger. The British proceeded from south to north and focused on the Lower Niger. Originally the two were more or less separate processes. However, the Upper Niger inevitably makes way for the Lower Niger, and vice versa. The dividing line was therefore not cast iron. With equal inevitability, the east-west and north-south lines were bound to intersect somewhere some day. A clash between French and British expansionist forces in West Africa was therefore inescapable. The partition treaty of 1890 had been a first attempt to separate the two river domains, but this attempt came to nothing. West African developments had reached too great a momentum to be stopped in that way. The French *parti colonial* put forward a strategic and geopolitical program in which West Africa held pride of place. The British continued to make it their primary aim to keep others out rather than to go in themselves, but this policy succumbed under the pressure of events. Paper protectorates were no longer enough. Private enterprise could not withstand the thrust of a foreign Power ranged against it. The old epoch of Britain's informal West African empire, in which the

Africans supplied the raw materials and there were no European rivals of any importance, was past. The European rivals had made fresh inroads and had therefore to be curbed, if necessary by force. Moreover, it was no longer enough to trade from day to day; there was also a need for investment in the future. The state had to see to that, as no one else could or would. Almost twenty years after Freycinet, this view became part of British policy, under the influence of Chamberlain.

During these years, Chamberlain's policies had a marked effect on British Africa policy. As a result, the British attitude changed and became more aggressive. Chamberlain was not, however, in sole charge, and at regular intervals was held back by the sober realism of Salisbury and other members of the cabinet. Chamberlain could be given his head when it came to playing chess or even poker with the West African Frontier Force, but Salisbury made sure that the diplomatic channels to Paris were kept open and that an agreement with France was not ruled out.

The final partition of West Africa was sealed in the 1890s. The steeplechase was run from 1895 to 1898, that is, from the Jameson raid to the Fashoda crisis. In other words the issue came to the fore just as the two most important British problems in Africa flared up. While Lugard was racing across Nikki and Borgu, Sir Alfred Milner, the British governor in Cape Town, was preparing to bear down on the Boer republics. At about the same time Marchand was marching on Fashoda in a last-ditch attempt, by establishing a French stronghold on the Upper Nile, to force Britain to reopen the Egyptian question. Their problems in the Transvaal and the Sudan so preoccupied the British government that West Africa became no more than a sideshow. It is remarkable that the swamps of the Bahr el-Ghazal should have been thought more important than the riches of the Niger, yet that was so in the context of imperial thinking at the time. It also explains the outcome of the West African steeplechase.

That outcome looks surprising at first sight. While Britain had traditionally taken a particular interest in West Africa and had had the most say in that part of the world, France would be wielding the greater influence in the end. This was a consequence of the difference in political priorities between Britain and France. That difference had been formulated most lucidly by Lord Salisbury as early as 1892. The French, he said, pursue a policy of empire-building through military conquest, while the British prefer a policy of "advance by commercial enterprise."[99] That was indeed the long and the short of it. To French colonialists, West Africa was a matter of vital importance. The French thus took the initiative and elaborated a coherent political ideology based on a wide political consensus. British policy, by contrast, remained for a long time one of waiting and seeing, of reacting to others. It was only late and with great reluctance that Britain eventually became converted to the exigencies of modern imperialism, and assigned to the state the role it necessarily had to play in this process. But even then the British approach remained primarily commercial. France could have as much territory as it liked, provided Britain had the areas of economic interest. Even at that late stage Britain's attention remained focused on other parts of Africa, parts more closely bound up with general imperial policy and the worldwide balance of power. In that sense the result of Anglo-French competition in West Africa may be considered a fair mirror of the general aspirations and activities of these two colonial rivals.

# V

# THE LONG MARCH TO FASHODA, 1893–1898

*Nous avons été comme des fous en Afrique,*
*entraînés par ces gens irresponsables*
*qu'on appelle les coloniaux.*

We have been like fools in Africa,
led on by those irresponsible people
known as the colonials.

Félix Faure

The great Anglo-French conflict in Africa began in 1882 with the British occupation of Egypt. Sixteen years later it drew to a spectacular climax in what nearly became the war for Fashoda. Fashoda itself was an insignificant place on the upper White Nile, just above its confluence with the Sobat. It had been founded in 1855 as an Egyptian antislavery control station among the Shilluks and was, in Queen Victoria's words, "so miserable and small an object" that going to war over it seemed inconceivable.[1] But the conflict was not, of course, about Fashoda. Fashoda was merely the culmination of a long process, a symbol of the final trial of strength between the two main colonial powers, Great Britain and France.

The history of the long road to Fashoda is complicated, but its basis was plain enough. In 1882 Britain had occupied Egypt and in the years that followed had decided to stay put. By the simple strategic precepts of the times it therefore had to be in control of the Nile and hence of the Sudan. Salisbury came to that conclusion in 1889, but France refused to acquiesce in Britain's unilateral intervention in Egypt and was determined to force Britain to reopen the Egyptian question. This needed military pressure, and that, in turn, could only be applied if France gained a foothold on the Nile. The British strategy led to the reconquest of the Sudan by Kitchener, that of the French to Marchand's advance on the Nile. In 1898 they met at Fashoda.

# 1
# THE BRITISH NILE STRATEGY

## EGYPT AND THE NILE

In 1889 Lord Salisbury declared that Britain intended to remain in Egypt. This implied British control of the Nile. "Egypt is the Nile and the Nile is

Egypt," as Sir Evelyn Baring never tired of repeating.[2] In fact, it was no more than a reformulation of an old truth. Since time immemorial, Egyptians had known that their livelihood depended on the level of the Nile and had believed that dark powers commanded the river. The seven lean and the seven fat years of the Bible were thought to have been caused by fluctuations in the level of the Nile. According to medieval chronicles and legends, the king of Ethiopia had the power of opening and closing the Nile at will. Ariosto's *Orlando Furioso* was a later version of that story. In the nineteenth century, what had once been legend and poetry became the subject of serious discussion. Charles F. Beke, lawyer, traveler and amateur geographer, was the first to consider the possibility of changing the course of the Nile and hence of destroying Egypt. In 1851 he sent Lord Palmerston his "Memoir on the Possibility of Diverting the Waters of the Nile so as to Prevent the Irrigation of Egypt." The planned desertification of Egypt had become a real threat.[3]

Being in control of the Nile was a complicated matter involving diverse geographical, technical and economic factors. The Nile has a high season and a low. During the first, Egypt obtains most of its water from the Blue Nile, which rises in Abyssinia, while the White Nile, which originates in the Sudan and Uganda, yields a negligible amount of water. In the low season, the opposite applies, the White Nile supplying the bulk of the water.[4] The White Nile was therefore of great agricultural importance. Now, in nineteenth-century Egypt, agriculture had made considerable strides thanks to new irrigation methods. In particular, the cultivation of cotton had become possible, and cotton exports had turned into a crucial aspect of the Egyptian economy. All in all, therefore, control of the Nile and of the White Nile in particular had become a matter of vital strategic importance.

The Egyptians were fully aware of this. "The Nile rules Egypt and the Nile means the Sudan. Egypt and the Sudan are therefore as inseparably bound together as body and soul," wrote an Egyptian statesman.[5] Following the British occupation the whole irrigation question became a British concern, Britain recognizing that modern technology offered unprecedented means of controlling the flow of the river. What had been no more than a specter was now perceived as a real threat: the fate of Egypt was in the hands of those who had control of the Upper Nile. Command of the Nile valley therefore became an important objective of British policy in Africa. In 1891 Salisbury wrote to Baring, "That we should insist on the command of all the affluents of the Nile, so far as Egypt formerly possessed them, is agreed."[6] The Nile would have to be defended. The outcome was the British *Wacht am Nile*—watch on the Nile. Danger could come from three sides: from the Red Sea (Italy), from East Africa (Germany) and from France and the Congo Free State in the west. Britain relied on diplomacy to ward off these dangers. The German threat was averted by the Zanzibar-Heligoland treaty of 1890, which had defined the respective British and German spheres of influence in East Africa (see p. 159). In 1882 Italy had acquired its first colony in the neighborhood of the Nile, that is, on the Red Sea. As we shall see below, the Italian threat, too, was averted by diplomatic means.

The German and Italian threats could therefore be warded off peacefully, but they were not, in fact, real threats. Neither Germany nor Italy had the will or the means to challenge Britain in an area it considered of vital importance. The only serious opponent was France, which refused adamantly to accept the permanent British occupation of Egypt and hence British monopoly rule over the Nile basin. Moreover, France had far better means than Germany or Italy of advancing on the Nile basin and of staking claims to it. France, too, had therefore to be placated, and preferably in the same way, that is, by diplomacy, consultation, exchanges and the delimitation of spheres of influence. The basis of British diplomacy was simple enough: continuing to cling inflexibly to the British sphere of influence on the Nile but being conciliatory in other areas, especially in West Africa. Thus Kimberley informed France in 1894 that if "a satisfactory arrangement is come to with regard to the British sphere in the Nile watershed, Her Majesty's Government will be prepared . . . to meet the French Government in a most conciliatory spirit" in all matters concerning West Africa.[7] Lord Salisbury was fully in favor of this policy. Having become prime minister in 1895, he was prepared to go even further than his liberal predecessor. He was convinced that in West Africa "there was no loot to get except in Goldie's dreams," and he was quite happy to make a number of concessions there.[8] This quid pro quo policy, generally so successful in all parts of Africa, failed to work in this case. As we have seen, Chamberlain, without whose support Salisbury's cabinet could not continue, did not like that approach, and the French, too, would not hear of it. Egypt was too important a prize for that.

### THE REOPENING OF THE EGYPTIAN QUESTION

No one could have explained precisely why France should have taken such strong exception to the British occupation of Egypt. It was, in fact, a matter of sentiment. Ever since Napoleon had set foot there, Egypt had been the chosen land of the French. Destiny had selected France to play a unique role here and to lead the country on the road to modernity. The British occupation of 1882 was accordingly viewed as a snub to France. Some even saw it as a second Sedan. The real Sedan of 1870 could not be avenged while Germany continued as strong as it was. Perhaps, though, there was a chance of undoing the Egyptian Sedan.

Meanwhile the Egyptian wound continued to fester. For a considerable time nothing happened on the Nile front, and the initiative was left to King

Leopold, who had set his sights on the Nile some time before. He had even visited Egypt on his honeymoon, and in 1880 he had had his mind concentrated upon the Nile for good by General Gordon. The Congo was not enough for His Majesty; he thought it too "prosaic."[9] The Nile, by contrast, was indubitably romantic, and so were Leopold's plans for it. Fighting the slave trade in the Sudan and at the same time creating a gigantic empire, joining the Congo to the Mediterranean via the Nile, and thus becoming a modern pharaoh, those were fantasies on a scale that appealed to the king of the Belgians.[10]

Leopold was fighting on two fronts, the diplomatic in his dealings with the European Powers, and another in Africa itself, where what mattered was effective occupation. In Africa, the Congo Free State had relatively strong military forces and provided an excellent springboard for further conquest. Leopold sought the support of such local rulers as Emin Pasha and the redoubtable slave trader Tippu Tip. He equipped military expeditions, his diplomatic moves having brought him a measure of success in the form of a treaty with Mackinnon's Imperial British East Africa Company on 24 May 1890. However, when Leopold ordered the Van Kerckhoven expedition to advance on the Nile soon afterwards, London let it be known that any attempt to cross the Congo-Nile watershed was unacceptable to Great Britain. Needless to say, Leopold now brought out his Mackinnon treaty and stressed that it enjoyed Lord Salisbury's approval. However, the Foreign Office retorted laconically that such approval had been no more than Lord Salisbury's "private opinion." The Imperial British East Africa Company had not been entitled to cede any rights. Moreover, the treaty had never been officially ratified and was therefore "unknown" to the Foreign Office.[11] For once there was someone more brazen than King Leopold, and the outbluffed sovereign had to leave it at that for the time being. Since his troops were meeting stiff mahdist opposition on the ground, he thought it best to halt his march on the Nile, though not for good. Never at a loss, the indefatigable king tried a new approach. He found it in French willingness to pursue an active policy in the Sudan.

Leopold now tried to win France over for a new initiative on the Nile, in the hope of harnessing his powerful neighbor to his little cart. In this he succeeded. He was the inspiration behind the 1893 Monteil expedition which drove France on to the road to Fashoda. But like a true sorcerer's apprentice, Leopold conjured up forces beyond his control, which would ultimately force him to drop his Nilotic ambitions. The Fashoda strategy ended in a direct Franco-British confrontation and brought an end to the twilight state in which the leader of a small European Power had been able to spread his wings.

# 2
# THE FRENCH NILE STRATEGY

## HANOTAUX'S POLICY

In May 1893 plans were drawn up for a French expedition to the Upper Nile under Major Paul Monteil. This was the first of a long series of attempts to force Britain to reopen the Egyptian question. The last of these would be Marchand's expedition culminating in the confrontation at Fashoda in September 1898. The man largely responsible for that expedition was Gabriel Hanotaux, appointed minister of foreign affairs on 30 May 1894. He was to remain at the Quai d'Orsay until 1 November 1895, when, during a cabinet reshuffle, he was succeeded by Marcellin Berthelot. Berthelot's term in office was, however, of short duration, and on 29 April 1896 Hanotaux was back at the Quai d'Orsay, where he remained until 15 June 1898, that is, until a few months before Fashoda. All in all, Hanotaux shaped French foreign policy for more than three and a half years, a record of ministerial stability exceeded only—and what is more, by a substantial margin—by his rival, Théophile Delcassé, colonial minister in Hanotaux's day and his successor in 1898. As foreign minister, Hanotaux was in charge of French Nile policy, although he was not its intellectual father.

Gabriel Hanotaux (1853–1944) had an unusual career. The climax, his ministerial post, came when he was just forty-one. Four years later he abandoned politics. He was to live for almost another half century, but was never again called to ministerial office. Instead he returned to the job for which he had been trained, that of historian, a field in which he proved to be productive though not great. Nor, for that matter, was he ever a great politician.

Hanotaux was the son of a respectable lawyer in a small town in northern France, but his way of life betrayed little of the rectitude of his parental background, and his character little of the calm and poise for which men from Picardy are renowned. He had a great many affairs, illegitimate children, flirtations and scandalous entanglements and was not to marry until he was sixty-one.[12] His character was unstable and his life was punctuated by moods, emotions, flashes of inspiration and depression. At crucial moments he lacked resolution and sound judgment. While dreaming one night, he discovered the solution to all Europe's problems—the break-up of the British Empire. More ominously, he elaborated the idea on awakening next morning and proposed to submit the resulting plan to the French president.[13] Despite his undeniable intelligence, these character traits rendered him unfit for the office he had come to hold at such a young age after a short but brilliant career.

Hanotaux's original passion was history. He studied at the Ecole des

Hautes Etudes and at the Ecole des Chartes and worked in the Quai d'Orsay archives on his magnum opus, a life of Cardinal Richelieu. A series of newspaper articles he wrote attracted the attention of Gambetta, who brought him into politics. Hanotaux became a civil servant and later *chef de cabinet* at the foreign ministry. In 1886 he was elected to the Chamber, but lost his seat in 1889 and returned to the foreign ministry, where he was soon afterwards offered one of the highest posts, that of director of commercial and consular affairs.

In 1894 he had his finest hour. Charles Dupuy formed his second cabinet, and was unable to find a minister of foreign affairs. Good candidates such as Paul Cambon and Delcassé refused or were vetoed by others. The choice then fell upon Hanotaux, who after some hesitation accepted the invitation. He thus became the chief of his former chiefs, earning for himself one of the most important and prestigious ministerial posts. But he had no party support and was the only minister without a seat in the Chamber. His relations with the president, the prime minister and Delcassé were strained. All this explains why his position in the cabinet was weak from the outset.[14]

Hanotaux's political ideas were a mixture of romantic nationalism and a strong belief in the French—or even the Latin—mission. Overseas possessions were important in giving expression to that mission and in displaying "French energy"—the title of one of his books. Social-Darwinist ideas played an important part in his policy. Hanotaux feared the rise of other countries. "Britain, Germany and Italy are ahead of us and Holland is catching up," he warned.[15] Colonial expansion made an emotional appeal to him; rational considerations took second place. He considered Britain a rival but—except in his dreams—not necessarily an enemy. There was room enough under the sun for both powers, but Britain would have to be forced to bow to French interests. The means for achieving that were diplomatic, and lay specifically in closer French relations with Germany and Russia.

Germany was undoubtedly France's main rival but in practice that did not have to be an obstacle to collaboration. France would simply have to reconcile itself to the reality of 1870. Meanwhile there were no objections to ad hoc collaboration with Germany against Britain. The same applied to Russia. Hanotaux had little love for that country and recognized the grave dangers of the Franco-Russian alliance, but it meant a great deal to the French people. First and foremost, it was proof that France was no longer isolated and so provided a sense of security. The alliance was an important political asset,[16] and Hanotaux was prepared to go a very long way to maintain it. Thus he banned a performance of *Hamlet* when the czar visited Paris in 1896 because he considered it wrong to stage a play about regicide before the czar.[17]

For Hanotaux, as for so many French people, French loss of influence over Egypt was a painful experience. He was anxious to restore that influence, preferably by diplomatic means and not by military pressure. Yet the second was the course for which he ultimately opted when he approved the Marchand mission, though France's adoption of this path had been decided earlier. The Marchand mission was the last of a series of French attempts to occupy the Upper Nile in order to force Britain to reopen the Egyptian question. Now the precise meaning of that oft-quoted phrase, "the reopening of the Egyptian question," was not clear, nor was the means of achieving it, or what a French expedition to the Nile could contribute toward it. But the basic idea was simple enough: British occupation of Egypt must not be allowed to become permanent. Britain must be forced to discuss its position, and that could best be done at an international conference on the ultimate fate of Egypt. France would have to play a leading role at that conference. A physical French presence on the Nile, the lifeblood of Egypt, would considerably strengthen the French bargaining position, hence the various French attempts to gain a foothold on that river. The first of these attempts was the Monteil mission.

### THE MISSION THAT WAS CALLED OFF: THE MONTEIL MISSION

Plans for the Monteil mission went back to the beginning of 1893. In January of that year, Théophile Delcassé became secretary for the colonies. He favored an energetic approach in support of French ambitions on the Nile, but he was not the first to come up with the idea of a mission. The original scheme was put forward by the Comité de l'Afrique Française, and more especially by its secretary, Harry Alis. Harry Alis, in his turn, had not thought of the idea himself, but had had it suggested to him by his master, King Leopold of the Belgians.

The decision-making process that led to the first step on the road to Fashoda was remarkable. King Leopold did not want to forfeit his ambitions regarding the Nile. He had asked for British recognition of his treaty with Mackinnon and hence of his sovereignty over Lado, but that, as we saw, had been rejected out of hand. Leopold then, as always, changed his course, but not his objective. He approached France and launched his plan for a Franco-Congolese campaign and for the delimitation of their respective spheres of influence in the Congo-Nile region, "une grande action commune," as Hanotaux was to call it later.[18] But the French hesitated. They considered Leopold a friend of Britain and were afraid of falling into a trap. Moreover, what did Leopold really have to offer? According to Hanotaux, no more than the "verbal support of a state that does not even exist."[19] But Leopold was not to be caught napping. His next step was as ingenious as it was unusual. He suggested that the French advance on the Nile from the Congo. Why? Because the expedition would then have to cross territory where large numbers of Free State troops were found, which meant that France would be forced to reach an agreement with the Free

State. Leopold had this plan proposed by Harry Alis, the man who called himself the most impartial person in the world and who perhaps was just that, for as we saw he was not only the secretary of the Comité de l'Afrique Française but also a secret agent in Leopold's service. The seed fell on fertile soil. The plan found favor in French colonial circles, and in February 1893 Delcassé began to think seriously about sending an expedition to the Bahr el-Ghazal. His first problem now was to find a suitable leader for it. The man he had in mind was Major Monteil.

Parfait-Louis Monteil (1855–1925) was a marine officer in the best *officier soudanais* tradition. He had distinguished himself in a successful expedition, from 9 October 1890 to 10 December 1892, which had taken him from St. Louis via the Niger and Sokoto to Lake Chad, and from there through the Sahara to Tripoli. The reputation he understandably gained from that feat made him the obvious choice.[20] However, Monteil was not anxious to accept the honor. Delcassé then asked Sadi Carnot, the president of the republic, to help him prevail upon Monteil. Carnot was a politician, but he was first and foremost an engineer, trained at the famous Ecole Polytechnique. He was interested in technical questions and fascinated by the problem of controlling the waters of the Nile.

At about the same time, to be precise, on 20 January 1893, Alexandre Prompt, one of Carnot's old classmates—"un de mes camarades de Polytechnique"—delivered a lecture to the French Institut Egyptien in Cairo. Prompt was a French hydraulic engineer who had had many years of experience of regulating the flow of the Nile in the Egyptian service. He therefore knew what he was talking about. In his address, he talked of the possibility of building dams for storing the water of the Nile in the winter and releasing it in the summer. He stressed two things: if the flow of the White Nile were stopped, Egypt could be laid dry during the summer, and if the dams were suddenly opened, Egypt would be washed away. He added two further pieces of information. It would not be expensive to build these dams, and Fashoda was the place to do it. Prompt clearly overlooked the fact that there was no stone to be found anywhere in the environs, near or far, of Fashoda.[21] Copies of Prompt's lecture were sent to Delcassé and to Carnot. Carnot was spellbound. He received Delcassé and Monteil, holding Prompt's brochure in his hand, and said simply, "Come on, Monteil, accept!"[22] And he added, "Fashoda must be occupied."[23] Monteil replied that, as a good officer, he took his president's wish for his command. Thus an informal talk between the president, the colonial secretary and an officer gave rise to the Monteil mission to Fashoda, without the knowledge of the foreign minister.

The decision having been taken in May 1893, the preparations were quickly begun. In June, credits were granted for the dispatch of an exploratory party. In July, Monteil went to Rotterdam to make transport arrangements with the Nieuwe Afrikaansche Handelsvennootschap. In

August, his stores were shipped out. Then nothing at all happened for a long time. One year later, in July 1894, Monteil was still in France. The reason for this delay was not only that he needed time to "fashion himself a Congolese soul," as he put it,[24] but to an even greater extent Leopold's strong position. Delcassé wanted to settle the border disputes with the Free State on the ground, but Monteil was not in favor of that. He knew that the Free State could muster a large military force, and was not prepared to shoot his way through Leopold's territory.

The border question would therefore have to be settled by diplomatic means first, but that was frustrated by Leopold's recalcitrance. The king was fully aware of his military superiority. Moreover, he saw the opportunity for a new move in his balancing act. Having played the French card against Britain, he now tried to play the British card against France. The situation in both countries seemed to him propitious for such a move. In France a tug of war was proceeding between Hanotaux and Casimir-Périer, the new president, a man as volatile and unstable as Hanotaux himself. The main issue between them was control of foreign policy, the president adopting a much more flexible attitude to Leopold than Hanotaux would have wished. As for Leopold, even while he was negotiating with the French, he was also making overtures to Britain.

Britain had dismissed Leopold's ambitions regarding the Nile out of hand. In 1894, however, London changed tack. There were two reasons for that. In the first place Britain was about to proclaim a protectorate over Uganda which, together with its ambitions on the Upper Nile, was bound to bring it into direct conflict with Leopold. The border question would thus have to be solved. In the second place, Britain had got wind of the French expedition plans. To the British policy makers, France was a greater danger than Leopold. By admitting Leopold to the Nile, the French could be kept out. This idea formed the basis of the Anglo-Congolese treaty of 12 May 1894.

That treaty settled three points. To begin with, Leopold recognized the British sphere of influence on the Nile, as laid down in the Anglo-German treaty of 1890. In exchange Leopold was given a lease, for the duration of his life, on the whole of the left bank of the Upper Nile from Fashoda to Lake Albert. The western boundary of the leased territory was longitude 30° E. A further slice of territory, to the west of this (between 25° and 30° E and south of 10° N) was leased to Leopold and his descendants. The entire area leased to Leopold covered two provinces, the Bahr el-Ghazal and Equatoria. In return, Leopold ceded to Britain a strip of land between Lake Edward and Tanganyika, roughly the same corridor he had assigned to Britain in the treaty with Mackinnon of 1890 (see p. 159).[25] The British concessions were aimed at keeping France from the Nile, and the small strip ceded by Leopold was to keep the Cape-to-Cairo route open. This last was a great mistake, for as a result opposition to the treaty would come, not only from France but also from Germany, as German East Africa was now surrounded by Britain, and its access to the Congo Free State cut off. That was quite unacceptable to Germany, as it had already hinted in 1890.

For Britain, the corridor served no real purpose. It was no more than a proof of Sir Percy Anderson's negotiating skills. Anderson was convinced that while Britain had been generous with King Leopold, the latter had given little in return. After a lifetime of diplomatic activity, negotiation had become a form of art for art's sake with Sir Percy. The game was more important than the stakes. All that Leopold had to offer was the corridor, and so Anderson asked for it and got it.[26] In the event it proved to be not a gift but a provocation. To Germany, it was a clear sign of Britain's hegemonic ambitions. German notes of protest were written in acid tones. Rosebery, the prime minister, said they were fit for negotiations with Monaco but not with Great Britain. Even so, Britain bowed to the pressure, surrendering the corridor on 22 June.

However, the strongest resistance to the treaty came from France, which had been conducting negotiations with Leopold on the same matters. As a result it was not until 12 May 1894 that the final Anglo-Congolese treaty was signed and not until 22 May that it was made public. It had been agreed upon as early as 12 April, but Leopold wanted to keep it secret and have it postdated in order to conceal from the French that, even while he was negotiating with them, he had already made a different agreement with the British. The response was furious. While Germany put Britain under pressure, Hanotaux aimed his heavy artillery at Brussels, threatening no more and no less than the settling of the "Belgian question." In so doing, he reminded the Belgians of the precarious basis of the very existence of their country, namely, its neutrality. He let it be known that France would look upon a conflict between so-called Congolese, but in fact Belgian, troops and the French army in Africa as a violation of Belgian neutrality. That shaft went straight home; as a Belgian newspaper put it, "Just imagine the reaction in France to a report that a French officer was killed by Belgian bullets before being eaten by Bangalas in the service of King Leopold."[27] Until then Leopold's strength in African affairs had lain in his weakness, in his being the sovereign of a little country. This time that weakness was no longer an asset but a real handicap. He gave in and asked Britain to waive the treaty.

Needless to say, Rosebery demurred, but his position was weak. Sir William Harcourt, his arch-enemy in the cabinet, was a true little Englander. As the Liberal leader in the Commons he had demanded to be kept informed of all important diplomatic steps. One of these was undoubtedly this perilous provocation of France and Germany. Understandably, therefore, Sir William was furious at the steps that had been taken and even more so at the outcome. He remarked bitterly that British foreign policy was being run by "two men unfit to manage a public house."[28] Now, while the cabinet probably did not agree with this assessment, it certainly did share his conclusion. The treaty was abrogated. On 14 August 1894 there followed a Franco-Congolese treaty in which Leopold promised not to meddle in the Bahr el-Ghazal. The French road to the Nile had been kept open.

All these diplomatic developments naturally delayed the Monteil mission considerably; in the end they would even lead to its tacit abandonment. Hanotaux had become convinced that Britain would strongly resent any French advance on the Nile, and he was determined not to allow Delcassé and the colonial party to force his hand. He believed that he could solve the difficulties with Britain by a mixture of diplomatic pressure and judicious actions on the ground, but without provoking Britain by a direct push to the Nile. On 13 July 1894 Monteil was given his definitive marching orders: he was to advance as far as possible in the direction of the Congo-Nile watershed, but he had strict instructions not to send even a single man into the Nile basin. His job was solely to settle border disputes with the Free State.

On 16 July 1894, then, Monteil finally departed, but as we have seen nothing was to come of his mission, so long in preparation. Hanotaux had set his seal on the new instructions, but Monteil was and remained in the service of the colonial department, and Delcassé had lost interest now that the Nile had ceased to be the objective. On 24 August, when Monteil was about to leave Loango, Delcassé informed him by telegram that his mission had become pointless now that France had reached agreement with the Free State.[29] The money and the troops were needed urgently for the struggle against Samori. Monteil was instructed to make for Grand Bassam on the Ivory Coast. So ended Monteil's expedition to the Nile.

Meanwhile, however, there had been serious political repercussions. The Upper Nile question had now been officially linked with the Egyptian question and hence with Great Power politics. Once brought into the open, it had become a matter of prestige and public concern, as those in charge of the French and British foreign services were quick to remark. Once again France took the initiative. Delcassé produced a new plan, a new mission and a new man: Victor Liotard.

THE MISSION THAT NEVER WAS: THE LIOTARD MISSION

The abrogation of the Anglo-Congolese treaty did nothing to reduce the tensions between Hanotaux and Delcassé. Their objectives may have been the same, but their tactics differed. While Hanotaux preferred a wait-and-see attitude, hoping that Britain might be persuaded to negotiate over the Sudan, Delcassé and the colonial party, to which he belonged, clamored for action. This difference in approach reflected a difference in their respective starting points. Hanotaux was responsible for foreign affairs, of which French Nile policy may have been an important part but no more than that. Other matters had to be taken into account as well. The Quai d'Orsay looked upon colonial affairs in the wider context of international relations in general. Delcassé at the colonial office was mainly concerned with colonial expansion. In the normal course of events, his policy ought to have been coordinated by the Quai d'Orsay, but circumstances were not normal. Hanotaux was an ex-civil servant, without much political backing, and moreover at loggerheads with Casimir-Périer, the president, who liked to exercise his prerogatives in the field of foreign policy. Delcassé, by contrast, enjoyed the support of the powerful lobby of the colonial party, which had three other cabinet members in addition to Delcassé. All in all, therefore, Hanotaux's position was weak, and grew weaker still when it emerged all too soon that his hope for results by negotiation had come to nothing.[30]

After the Anglo-Congolese treaty had been abandoned in June 1894, following international pressure, France and Britain remained locked in discussions of the Nile question for the rest of the summer. These discussions were conducted by Hanotaux and Lord Dufferin, the British ambassador, who used very forceful language and even spoke of war. His threatening stance was later softened under pressure from the British cabinet. In September his place at the negotiating table was taken by Sir Constantine Phipps, the British chargé d'affaires. The negotiations proved to be highly involved. Both parties harped on their respective spheres of influence, but whenever necessary also supported their cases by reference to Egyptian claims or even those of the Turkish sultan. While one side argued that Egyptian (or Turkish) control over the Sudan had been abolished and that, as a result, the Sudan had become *res nullius*, an area in which the right of conquest alone prevailed, the other insisted that Egyptian control of the Sudan had merely been suspended and could thus be restored. Hanotaux was prepared to issue a declaration that the Upper Nile lay outside the French sphere of influence, provided Britain made a similar declaration.[31] That sort of mutual nonintervention pact was however no longer acceptable to Great Britain. It might have been a way out had the old, purely defensive objective—warding off foreign threats to the Upper Nile—still prevailed, but things had changed, and a new imperialist spirit had come to dictate British foreign policy. Britain now considered the Nile an indisputable part of its sphere of influence, one involving not only its interests, but also its prestige.[32]

The situation was thus extremely complex. Both countries were nervous of each other's activities in the area, of which very little was actually known but a great many things were suspected. Both also had to cope with colonial pressure groups. Hanotaux might tell his British counterpart what he himself considered acceptable, but that was not worth very much unless he could guarantee that the French government and parliament would underwrite his views. That was something he could not do, because the colonial party was inflexibly opposed to France's turning its back on the Nile, certainly not without compensation elsewhere. The simplest solution would have been for Britain to offer France concessions on the Niger in exchange for concessions on the Nile. However, Britain was unable to concede a great deal of territory on the Niger—Sir George Goldie's Niger Company was too powerful for that—nor did Britain, knowing that it had the upper hand, feel inclined to placate France. The negotiations thus foundered. In October 1894 they were finally broken off. The consequences were not long in coming. On 20 October Delcassé decided to give the green light to the Liotard mission. It was the second attempt to implement French ambitions by a move on the Upper Nile.

### Liotard

Victor Liotard (1858–1916), *pharmacien de deuxième classe* in the French navy, had considerable experience of Africa. In 1891 Brazza had appointed him delegate for Upper Ubangi, Brazza himself having been elevated to commissioner-general of the Republic for the French Congo. Upper Ubangi was the most forward-lying part of the French Congo, close to the watershed with the Nile. Liotard's task was to expand French influence in the direction of the Upper Nile.[33] However, his actions in the area were fairly ineffectual. He did not enjoy much support from his own government and met strong opposition from the Free State troops present there in large numbers. In October 1894 he went on leave to France. On 20 October, Delcassé appointed him "State Commissioner for the territories the western boundary of which is a line drawn from Bangui to El Fasher." The definition was wide enough, but it lacked a most important specification, namely, the eastern boundary of the territories. That boundary was clearly at the back of Delcassé's mind: it was the Nile, but that was something he could not, of course, declare openly. In any case, the newly appointed commissioner departed on 25 October 1894.

On 17 November 1894 the matter was discussed in cabinet. Hanotaux still pursued the course of negotiations with Britain on the basis of a mutual nonintervention formula, while Delcassé voiced his opposition to it. Liotard would reach the Nile sooner than the British, or so he believed. The French position was too strong for such a concession. Delcassé was given his way, the vote of Casimir-Périer, the president, deciding the issue. Casimir-Périer was anxious to demonstrate his authority over Hanotaux, who in any case could offer no clear alternative. The negotiations with Britain had become bogged down. The cabinet accordingly instructed Delcassé to make arrangements for the occupation of territory on the Upper Nile.

In practice, little came of these instructions. Liotard was a cautious and patient man, not one for lightning raids or heroic expeditions à la Brazza or Marchand. In any case he was offered no more than modest resources. Delcassé promised the cabinet that Liotard would have reached the Nile within a year. The reality was different. After a year Liotard had advanced no further than the frontier of Upper Ubangi, and it was another three months before he reached the Nile watershed. By then he was on the edge of the Bahr el-Ghazal, and was never to get much further. Chautemps, Delcassé's successor at the colonial office, was not interested in the mission and withdrew Liotard's credits on 23 September 1895.[34]

The Liotard mission was therefore no real mission, no real march on the Nile. It was a mission that never was. And yet it had two important consequences. In the first place the Nile policy of the *parti colonial* became official cabinet policy, against Hanotaux's wishes. His prestige and influence on French Africa policy were to suffer badly as a result. In the second place rumors about the French expedition had leaked to Britain. French activities on the Nile and the British attitude toward them were raised in the *Times* in March 1895. On 28 March this led to questions in the House of Commons, answered by Sir Edward Grey, parliamentary under-secretary for foreign affairs.

Sir Edward Grey (1862–1933) was a young but promising politician, who was not only to become foreign secretary but was to hold that office for eleven years without interruption. He was on friendly terms with Lord Rosebery, the prime minister, and also enjoyed the trust of his chief, Lord Kimberley, the—incidentally not very influential—foreign secretary. As a peer, Kimberley could not defend his policy in the House of Commons, and so Grey spoke for him. When Grey asked him what he was to say about West African developments, Kimberley could tell him no more than "You must do the best you can but I think you should use pretty firm language."[35] When the matter was raised in the House at question time, Grey said in all honesty that the government knew nothing about a French expedition to the Nile. The debate on foreign policy and African affairs continued.

Grey expected that it would be mainly devoted to the Niger, the subject of recent negotiations mentioned in government policy statements. However, the debate concentrated not on the Niger but on the Nile. The same questioner pleaded for a firm British stand with regard to that waterway and asked for a statement on the government's position. Grey was forced to improvise. The matter had not been discussed in the cabinet, and he had received no instructions. However, he knew the prime minister's feelings and took it upon himself to interpret these to the House.[36] The "pretty firm language" intended for the Niger could also be used for the Nile. The result was the famous "Grey Declaration." Grey declared that he could not give credence to rumors about a secret French expedition in a territory over which British claims were so widely acknowledged. That, he added, would not only be "an inconsistent and unexpected act," but also an "unfriendly act" and would be so viewed by England.[37] The truth was out. Grey had spoken resignedly, but speak he did: "an unfriendly act." True, in diplomatic language that was not the same as a *casus belli*, but it came pretty close to it, and at any event it was taken for that by many.[38]

This was not the first time that the word "war" had cropped up during discussions of the Nile. Lord Dufferin, as we saw, had also said in a conversation with Hanotaux that a French advance on the Nile would mean war, but that had happened within the four walls of an office, and he had had his knuckles rapped for it by his government.[39] This time things were different: the threat had been uttered in the full light of a public debate. By his improvised comments Grey had forced the cabinet's hand. Harcourt and the other little Englanders were not happy about it, of course, but the prime minister, the queen, the press and the majority in the House of Commons stood behind Grey.[40] And repudiating that sort of declaration after the event was of course something quite other than ensuring that it was not made in the first place. The "Grey Declaration" was thus upheld, although its sharper edges were smoothed away. Grey's words, Kimberley informed the French ambassador, were, when all was said and done, no more than the views of "a simple under-secretary of state."[41]

So it was that between November 1894 and March 1895 the two Powers most concerned had come to adopt an official government Nile policy. In France that policy amounted to support for some future advance on the Nile, in Britain to the affirmation that any such advance would be considered an "unfriendly act." Both countries had thus committed themselves to the policy that was to culminate in the Fashoda crisis of 1898. In the summer of 1895 a new French Nile expedition was planned, the Marchand mission, but it was not until the spring of 1896 that anything came of it. Then France was faced with two startling developments: the Italians had suffered a crushing defeat at Adowa, and the British had begun the reconquest of the Sudan. The first development had been the occasion for the second.

# 3
# ITALY AND IMPERIALISM

## ITALY AFTER UNIFICATION

There was nothing wrong with Italian imperialism, except that it was Italian. It was only logical that Italy should want to play a part in the partition of Africa, a continent with which it was so closely involved. After all, Sicily is not far from the African coast, and one does not have to be a great historian to recall that centuries ago Rome's rise had begun with its struggle against Carthage. In the nineteenth century these facts were in any case known only too well. Italy, moreover, had enough would-be colonists to populate the whole of North Africa. Nineteenth-century Italians emigrated en masse. This great migration was an integral part of the history of poor and overpopulated Italy.

In the middle of the 1880s the exodus assumed dramatic forms. In all more than 1.3 million Italians left their homeland.[42] That wave was above all due to the economic crisis of the 1880s, which ravaged agriculture. In Italy the associated problems were aggravated further by the uneven distribution of the land and by the devastation of vineyards caused by vine phylloxera. The "emigration of the desperate" was an understandable concern of intellectuals and politicians, and the loss of *italianità* a particular scourge in an age of nationalist and Social-Darwinist fervor.

Italy had been unified in 1870, but its was a unity marked by division. There was a great contrast in development and mentality between the north and the south, the northerners looking down on the southerners with the contempt the average colonist reserved for Africans. To the leaders of the Italian *risorgimento*, Italy was moreover a flawed entity. It had an imperial capital but no empire, and such an empire was part of the Italian dream. At first little was done to implement these imperial and irredentist ideals. Consolidation and peace were the order of the day after 1870, that is, after the heroic years of the struggle for unification. Of course Italy, too, was interested in the estate of the "sick man of Europe," especially in North Africa, but it was in no position to strike a forcible note about it. The Congress of Berlin of 1878 had had nothing to offer the Italians. That had been a disappointment. The consequent French occupation of Tunisia in 1881 had been more than a disappointment, it had been a humiliation. The direct consequence was a reorientation of Italian foreign policy. Italy became reconciled to Austria, its hereditary enemy, temporarily shelved the *irredenta*, and on 20 May 1882 joined the Dual Alliance, thus turning it into a Triple Alliance: Germany, Austria-Hungary and Italy. The indirect result was a revival of Italy's colonial aspirations, which, though confused and even contradictory, were sublimated into a vague ideology, a Latin variant of the white man's burden.

CRISPI AND IMPERIALISM

Under Francesco Crispi (1818–1901), imperialist ideas in Italy became more clearly defined. Crispi was the Italian counterpart of Jules Ferry—he presided over the birth of Italian imperialism, and he perished from it. In fact, he was the only imperialist thrown up by Italian history—with the exception of Mussolini. Crispi's reputation has remained controversial to this day. His private and political conduct was punctuated by scandal, and his character flaws stood in the way of a successful political career. He was haughty, deaf to criticism, irascible, tight-lipped and very moody. Yet one thing was indisputable: his fervent nationalism.

Crispi started out as a lawyer and became involved in Italian politics at an early age. He was influenced by Mazzini's nationalist ideas and joined Garibaldi's movement. In 1870 he welcomed the unification of Italy with enthusiasm. He was elected a member of parliament in the new kingdom, and in 1877 minister of the interior. Ten years later he became prime minister for the first time, combining this office with that of minister of foreign affairs. He twice led the Italian government, first from July 1887 to February 1891 and again from November 1893 to March 1896, enjoying considerable support in parliament and in the country, and wielding great power for nearly six years. In domestic affairs he was a democrat in theory but displayed dictatorial traits in practice. His aim was to be the Italian Bismarck.[43] Strikes were forcibly suppressed and anarchists put down with a heavy hand. In foreign affairs he stood for grandeur and expansion. He was a staunch supporter of the Triple Alliance, but above all he was the father of Italian imperialism. His imperialist credo comprised a number of economic and demographic facets shored up with historical observations and messianic appeals.[44] Crispi's hymn to imperialism did not differ appreciably from the familiar refrain of Italian imperialists: Italy must have colonies. Its past demanded it and its future called for it. That refrain was first given practical expression when Italy's position in the Mediterranean was strengthened by a treaty with Britain (on 12 February 1887) and once the Triple Alliance had been extended with a Mediterranean clause (20 February 1887).

Italy took its first imperialist steps, not in the Mediterranean, where international rivalry was keen, but in the Red Sea. The Genovese shipping house of Rubattino had acquired the Bay of Assab in 1869, naturally with an eye to the opening of the Suez Canal. The Italian government then took over the rights to the territory, and on 5 July 1882 made it the first Italian colony. The capture in 1885 of Massawa, also on the Red Sea, was an event of greater importance. Italy now aimed at linking Assab and Massawa and at occupying the hinterland. In 1890 this attempt was crowned with success, and the colony of Eritrea was born. The Italians shared the western shore of the Red Sea with the French, who had settled in Obock in 1862, and with the British, who had been in Aden since 1839 and who relied for provisions chiefly on the Somali shore across the Gulf. After the Egyptian evacuation of the Sudan in 1887, Britain had also declared a protectorate over part of the western Red Sea coast. In 1888 the borders between British and French Somaliland were fixed, and in 1892 Djibouti became the capital of the French colony. In 1887 the sultan of Zanzibar granted Italy a protectorate over the entire east coast of Africa from Kismayu on the mouth of the Juba to Cape Guadarfui at the tip of the Horn.

Italian Somaliland was to emerge later from these concessions. After diplomatic consultations between Italy and Britain, two treaties were signed, on 24 March and 15 April 1891, delimiting their respective spheres of influence in East Africa. In essence these treaties stipulated that while Great Britain was willing to let Italy play the leading part in the Horn of Africa, it expected Italy to keep well away from the Nile. The Juba was to be the boundary between Italian Somaliland and British East Africa.[45] For the time being, however, Italy was far more interested in Ethiopia.

### ITALY AND ETHIOPIA

Ethiopia had once been a mighty country, but fell into steep decline during the eighteenth century. Emperor Jesus II (1730–1755) was the last ruler to exert any real authority over his empire. Then the downward slide had set in, one early nineteenth-century emperor even having had to suffer the ignominy of finding that the treasury was too poor to pay for his coffin.[46] However, the people still had high hopes in the future. There was the memory of a great past, there was the Christian church, which could play a unifying role, and there was a cultured and literate elite. The leader of the national restoration movement, Kassa, was a former bandit chief who rose to the rank of *ras* (prince) and ultimately, in 1833, to become the *negus*, or emperor. On that occasion, he adopted the name Theodore and the title "The Chosen of God, the Conquering Lion of the Tribe of Juda, the King of Kings of Ethiopia." It sounded more magnificent than it was. Theodore quarreled with Britain, which sent out an expedition against him under Sir Robert Napier. Theodore was defeated on Good Friday, 10 April 1868, whereupon he shot himself. After a power struggle, the ruler of Tigré became the country's new leader. In 1872 he was proclaimed Emperor John IV, and kept his crown until 1889. John's greatest problem was the expansion of Egypt under Ismail, against whom he had to defend a rather loose constellation of small states. Internally, too, he was threatened by a youthful rival, the ruler of Shoa, who was later to achieve fame as Menelik II.

The Italians had meanwhile learned that expansion into Ethiopia was no easy option. They first came up against the might of the Ethiopian troops in 1887—on 26 January of that year their army was routed at Dogali. The Italians reacted with a series of military and diplomatic measures. The humiliation at Dogali had of course to be avenged at all costs. As Crispi put it, "To begin with, we must show those barbarians that we are strong and mighty."[47] To that end it was decided to build up a powerful expeditionary force. The second weapon was diplomatic and involved playing off Menelik against his rival, Emperor John.

The Italian game paid off. By a secret treaty concluded on 20 October 1887, Italy as good as recognized Menelik as sovereign of Ethiopia. John's position grew increasingly precarious as he had to cope not only with fresh Italian troops but also with invading mahdists. He was killed during an otherwise successful battle with the latter on 10 March 1889. Most Ethiopian chiefs now recognized Menelik as their new emperor, a fortunate choice as Menelik was one of the most remarkable African leaders of his day. Under his reign, Ethiopia ceased to be a victim of imperialism and became its instrument. It now joined in the dividing process instead of being itself divided.

### Menelik

Menelik (1844–1913) was a descendant of the royal family of Shoa, a region in the heartland of Ethiopia, where the capital Addis Ababa (New Flower) was later to arise. His father's kingdom had been conquered by Theodore in 1855. When the father died, the son was taken to Theodore's court, whence he escaped in 1865. He returned to Shoa and regained his father's crown. He then launched a successful campaign to extend his power base, which came to a temporary halt when he was proclaimed emperor. Menelik was to reign until 1908 and to turn Ethiopia into a strong, centralized modern state.[48] He pursued an expansionist policy and spread Ethiopian influence far and wide. He was a modernist and as such gave his country a postal system—he even applied for membership in the International Postal Union—a coinage, a railroad and a newspaper. He was interested in military matters and built up a well-equipped army. A European, one of the many who underestimated Menelik, once showed him a rifle and explained that it went "boom-boom." Menelik took the man to his arsenal and showed him his weapons, including more than a hundred thousand rifles.[49] His military might was the basis of his success, though his diplomatic skills were perhaps even more important.

Ethiopia, like so many African countries, had fallen prey to foreign influences. Foreign advisers and schemers—not only British and French, but also Italian, Swiss, Austrian and Russian—had come flooding in. The Powers were vying for Menelik's favor. France let it be known that it felt a "very sincere and disinterested friendship" and "profound sympathy" for a proud nation that had for centuries so courageously defended its independence as well as the Christian faith.[50] The French press dreamed up an alliance between the Ottoman emperor, the khedive, the mahdi and the negus, naturally under French control.[51] Queen Victoria had a gramophone record pressed for Menelik with a message of British goodwill.[52] Russia stressed the religious bond between the Coptic and the Russian Orthodox churches and sent impressive gifts together with strange adventurers. Leopold, of course, refused to be left out and wanted to send a mission led by Menelik's former father confessor, a Belgian priest.[53] All this display of friendship may have been sincere, but it was certainly not disinterested.

Menelik II

Britain and France were trying to use Ethiopia as a pawn in their complicated game for the Nile. Russia and Italy saw a chance of playing some
part in Africa, however modest. All of them looked upon Menelik, as the
British diplomat J. R. Rodd put it, "as little more than an exceptionally
enlightened savage."[54] In fact, however, Menelik was an extremely skilled
diplomat, a man of near Bismarckian qualities.

His first great move on the diplomatic chessboard was the Treaty of
Everlasting Peace and Friendship concluded at Ucciali (called Wichale in
Amharic) on 2 May 1889. By it, Italy recognized Menelik as emperor of
Ethiopia in exchange for a number of strategic and commercial privileges.
The most important clause of the treaty was article 17, in which the King
of Kings declared that, if required, he would make use of Italy's diplomatic
services. That at least was what the Amharic text stated. Something that
sounded far less innocent could be read in the Italian text, however,
namely, that he *had* to make use of these services.[55] Now, that was a formula designed for protectorates, and a protectorate was precisely what Italy
wanted. How this confusion had come about is unclear; more important is
the fact that Menelik let it be known that he did not accept the Italian text.

Italy thus failed to acquire a colonial empire by the simple device of insinuating a mistranslation from the Amharic. More was clearly needed. Crispi was prepared to provide it, and ordered Italian troops under General Baratieri, the governor of Eritrea, to be brought up. In September 1895 Menelik declared war on Italy. The Italians commanded a formidable force of nearly 18,000 men including more than 10,000 Europeans, but the negus threw some 100,000 men into the field, of whom no more than 20,000 bore spears and swords alone. The rest were well armed. Menelik even commanded cavalry and artillery formations.[56] Yet not even these mighty contingents were able to overrun the Italian fortifications, and Baratieri was therefore right to adopt a policy of biding his time and exhausting the enemy. However, Crispi, his impetuous master in Rome, would have none of these Fabian tactics. He bombarded his commander with fiery exhortations and sarcastic telegrams. The tormented Baratieri went on the attack on 1 March 1896. The result would enter the history books as the Battle of Adowa. The Ethiopian army scored an overwhelming victory. Ras Makonnen, Haile Selassie's father and one of Menelik's ablest diplomats and generals, was the hero of the day. The outcome was disastrous for Italy: 6,000 killed, 1,500 wounded and 1,800 taken prisoner. More than half the Italian troops had been eliminated. Five days later Italy sued for peace. The consequent negotiations led to the Treaty of Addis Ababa, signed on 26 October 1896. The Treaty of Ucciali was revoked, and Italy recognized the sovereignty and independence of Ethiopia. The Italian expansion was over; the Ethiopian had begun.

Ethiopia's diplomatic position had also changed. As an independent nation, Ethiopia had become a serious negotiating force. The French now considered it well worth their while to accept the offer Menelik had made them in 1895. The resulting Franco-Ethiopian Friendship Treaty of 27 January 1897 recognized Ethiopian independence and French predominance, though France was not to reap its fruits. Aware that Britain was more powerful, the negus played a double game and soon afterwards signed a treaty with Britain granting it a number of rights that conflicted with those enshrined in the Franco-Ethiopian treaty.

Meanwhile the news of the Battle of Adowa had had other consequences as well. The British government was asked by Germany to do something in support of the Italians. That placed Britain in an awkward position. Germany's urgent request to come to the aid of its desperate ally could not be dismissed out of hand. Britain was at loggerheads with France and with Russia, France's ally. The Triple Alliance among Germany, Austria and Italy constituted a kind of counterweight to that bloc. For Britain, which stood alone, good relations with the Triple Alliance were therefore important, which meant heeding the German request. Another reason lay in the Sudan and its mahdist regime. Britain looked upon that dervish state as a model of barbarous backwardness, religious fanaticism and vicious oppression. To the British, it was more or less what Hitler's Germany and Stalin's Russia were to be to their twentieth-century descendants: an evil empire. Britain, moreover, had not forgotten Gordon's death. Revenge was not far from many people's minds. The reconquest of the Sudan thus had a considerable popular appeal.

Yet it was not that kind of sentiment that brought Lord Salisbury to his decision. He was not the man to allow his policy to be dictated by sentiment and emotion, and looked at international affairs from the point of view of *Realpolitik*. Seen in that light, the mahdists did not pose a great danger. They could destroy nothing, for there was nothing to be destroyed. When the time was ripe and if there was enough money, they could be brought to submission without too much trouble. Until such time, they could safely be left in peace; indeed, they were even doing Britain a service by keeping the Italians out of the Sudan. Salisbury therefore wrote to Baring in Egypt, on 21 November 1890, "These people were created for the purpose of keeping the bed warm for you till you can occupy it."[57]

That was in 1890, but in the next few years the situation began to change. Famine raged in the Sudan and decimated a population weakened by disease, war and slave hunts. The mahdists were on the point of collapse. For Britain, that was a mixed blessing. On the one hand, it would simplify British rule, on the other it would simplify matters for others as well and thus attract them to the Sudan. Who those others might be was only too obvious: Leopold, France and Ethiopia, or in Sir Edward Grey's words, "Belgians or French, or some devilry working through Abyssinian intrigue."[58] Italy had dropped out of the race after Adowa. A French-Ethiopian alliance by contrast was considered a real threat.

There were thus many reasons for proceeding to the long overdue revenge of Gordon and the reconquest of the Sudan. That cause was not only popular with the British public, but the weakening of the mahdist state made the work simpler and the French threat rendered the task more urgent. The Triple Alliance, moreover, was bound to be on Britain's side. Finally, Egyptian finances and the Egyptian army had greatly improved. The financial reforms had been the work of Baring and his young assistant, Alfred Milner, who wrote a successful book, *England in Egypt,* on the subject. The army reforms had been handled by the British commander-in-chief of the Egyptian army, the *sirdar* Kitchener, who had turned his Egyptian and Sudanese soldiers into a formidable fighting force. What could have been more appealing, therefore, than to start the reconquest of the Sudan under the guise of a relief operation for the hard-pressed Italians? And so it came about. On 12 March 1896 Salisbury announced the invasion of the Sudan. Now the French too awoke from their slumbers. The plan they had drawn up as early as 1895 was taken out of mothballs. It had been conceived and developed by an enthusiastic and audacious officer, Jean-Baptiste Marchand.

# 4
# THE MISSION THAT FAILED:
# THE MARCHAND MISSION

Jean-Baptiste Marchand (1863–1934) was born on 22 November 1863 in Thoissey, in the Bresse. His background was as humble as his education. He left secondary school when he was only thirteen to become a clerk and remained one until he was twenty. The rest of his career was to be considerably more adventurous. In 1883 he enlisted in the colonial army, the *infanterie de marine*. That was where the action was—and the chances of advancement. Marchand, who quickly rose from quartermaster-sergeant to lieutenant, distinguished himself in a country where the *infanterie de marine* was lord and master, namely, in the Sudan. He attracted the attention of Louis Archinard, the undisputed leader of the colonial troops. By the time he was twenty-six Marchand had been awarded the Legion of Honor, and in 1892 he was promoted to captain. His looks were impressive and romantic, and he had an iron constitution, an attractive personality, ambition and good connections. His patriotism was undeniable, but a hankering after money, promotion and esteem also played a part in his life. After the Sudan, the Ivory Coast became his chosen terrain. He earned renown with a voyage of discovery up the Baoulé in West Africa and developed a marked taste for expeditions and explorations.

### THE PLAN

Marchand spent the summer of 1895 in Paris, where he made contact with politicians and journalists and with the Comité de l'Afrique Française. He gained access to Hanotaux through the salon of Hanotaux's doctor, Louis Ménard, where Sudanese officers were regular guests. Here he first outlined his plans off the record, before formally presenting it to the colonial and foreign ministries on 11 September 1895. The plan for the "Congo-Nile mission," as the Marchand expedition was officially called, was written by Marchand himself in a thick school exercise book. It ran to four chapters. The first set forth the history of the Bahr el-Ghazal, the decline of the mahdist state, the role of the French and the strategic importance of the area. The second portrayed British ambitions. Britain was not only determined to establish a north-south link (the Cape-to-Cairo route) but also to forge an east-west link: the English "cross over Africa." Marchand pleaded for the protection of French interests from these machinations. In the third chapter he set out how this was to be done. The objective of his mission was to strengthen French influence in the hinterland of the Congo Free State, so that when it was eventually carved up, France, too, would be present and able to say, "Here we are!"[59] To achieve this, no occupation was needed, only the signing of treaties and the winning of friendships. The mission's goal was Fashoda. The last chapter, finally, specified the requirements and costs of the expedition.[60]

So much for Marchand's project. At first his main support came from the colonial ministry, where his old patron, Archinard, had meanwhile risen to become director of defense affairs, and where the minister, too, was an enthusiastic supporter of the plan and looked forward to the day when he could say that Captain Marchand "had pissed into the Nile upstream from Khartoum."[61] Such an operation was, of course, bound to have serious diplomatic consequences, and hence the views of the Quai d'Orsay had also to be taken into account. After some hesitation, Hanotaux seemed to have come round to the plan, but he was not given time to act on his decision because the Ribot cabinet fell on 28 October 1895 and Hanotaux with it. This was a great disappointment for Marchand. "The cabinet has fallen," he noted in his diary, "and we have to start all over again. *Comme Sisyphe je recommence.*"[62] But this French Sisyphus, for one, was not alone. It is true that Hanotaux was not included in the next cabinet, where two professors assumed responsibility for overseas matters, the chemist Marcellin Berthelot at foreign affairs and the Egyptologist Pierre Guieysse at colonial affairs, but the civil servants stayed on, and they were in favor of the plan. The Egyptologist, too, was won over. As a result, Berthelot came under strong pressure. The mission was presented to him as a nonpolitical voyage of discovery, "a kind of anonymous visit . . . without flag or mandate."[63] On 30 November 1895, a minister for less than a month, Berthelot gave his consent.

However, it was still to be some time before Marchand received his marching orders. These finally arrived on 24 February 1896, and had, of course, been issued by the colonial ministry. Berthelot received no more than a copy. There was no longer any mention of an "anonymous voyage of discovery." Instead, Marchand's mission—by analogy with the notorious action by Dr. Jameson in South Africa—was referred to as a "raid" on Fashoda. Marchand was to enter into "serious alliances" and to look for "indisputable titles."[64] The French government considered his project of the utmost importance, but insisted that the expenses be kept down, if only because large credits would draw attention to the mission and break the seal of secrecy surrounding it. The departure was thus delayed for a long time on financial grounds. However, Adowa and the British actions breathed new life into the enterprise. Bourgeois, the prime minister, became personally interested in the plan, but was to resign all too quickly. His cabinet fell on 23 April 1896. On 29 April the Méline administration took over and Hanotaux returned to foreign affairs.

And still Marchand was unable to leave, because the new cabinet insisted on scrutinizing and approving his orders. Approval finally came on 23 June 1896. His orders were modified in several minor respects, but the main plan had remained unaltered. Hanotaux, in fact, had no clear idea of what purpose the mission could serve. He only felt that "something had to happen" on the Nile, that France must act and that negotiations would follow as a matter of course. To Marchand he simply said, "Go to Fashoda, let France fire her pistol."[65] On 25 June 1896 Marchand left for Africa. On 8 December 1896 his credits were approved by 477 votes to 18. Even a number of socialists voted in favor. "Our vote is not political but national," Jean Jaurès explained.[66]

THE EXPEDITION

Marchand arrived in Loango on 24 July 1896. The expedition he was to lead was the largest France had ever mounted in Central Africa. It comprised six officers, including Marchand, four European noncommissioned officers, a doctor, an interpreter, a secretary, an administrative officer and a landscape painter. The last three were to turn back very quickly. In addition, there were some 150 native troops. The supplies were impressive. They included, in addition to arms, ammunition and traveling equipment, provisions and bartering material with which to gain as many new friends as possible—hence the 70,000 linear meters of cloth and the 16,000 kilograms of Venetian beads. Marchand personally placed the orders for truffles, for foie gras and for *tripes à la mode de Caen*. Cognac, Pernod, champagne and 1,300 liters of red Bordeaux were also carried.[67] All in all, the cargo weighed some 100,000 kilograms, comprising 3,000 loads. Small wonder that there were serious transport problems.

Marchand's journey took him over enormous distances, 3,000 miles all told. The first section, from Loango to Brazzaville, was known, but there was nevertheless a problem: the colony was in a state of near-rebellion. Brazza, the administrator of the French Congo, was not in a position to settle the crisis and to provide the necessary transport, which he proposed to leave to the mighty Nieuwe Afrikaansche Handelsvennootschap from Rotterdam. However, Marchand insisted on a military solution: order had to be restored first. He had his way. Thus the second half of 1896 was passed with the pacification of the caravan route between Loango and Brazzaville.

In January 1897 the actual expedition set out. Marchand wrote that he would be in Fashoda within a year, perhaps in ten months, and on 1 January 1898 at the latest. The reality was different—it was not until 10 July 1898 that he eventually reached Fashoda. The first part of the journey was relatively easy. Marchand followed the Congo to its confluence with the Ubangi. That part of the voyage was done by steamboat. The second part was covered by canoe, up the Ubangi as far as its junction with the M'bomore and then up that river. Marchand had really wanted to proceed northward before turning east and then making for Fashoda via Darfur

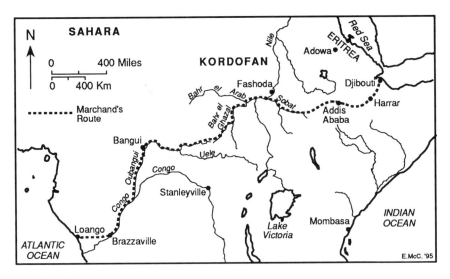

Marchand's route

and Kordofan, but Liotard, the French commissioner-general of Upper Ubangi and Marchand's immediate superior, instructed him to turn east as soon as possible and to follow the rivers. Liotard considered the northern alternative undesirable for political reasons. Marchand, by contrast, thought the river route unsuitable for technical reasons. To begin with, nobody knew if the rivers were navigable—the known parts were studded with rapids and cataracts, and the rest gave rise to the worst fears. However, Marchand submitted to Liotard's orders and requisitioned whatever river vessels he could lay his hands on, including the *Faidherbe*, an easily dismantled small steam launch. He would have preferred the *Leo XIII*, owned by the Catholic mission, but the missionaries refused to hand over their boat to what they considered an abominably irreligious republic, notwithstanding Marchand's appeal to their patriotism.[68]

The obstacles proved to be formidable. At times the river was unnavigable, and the *Faidherbe* had to be dismantled and carried overland. In 1897, after an arduous journey, the expedition reached the Sue, a tributary of the Bahr el-Ghazal. The objective was now close, and yet it was to be more than another six months before it was reached. Climate was the reason for this new delay: from November to May, the drought causes a drastic drop in the level of the watercourses and streams of the Bahr el-Ghazal. In that season the Sue consists mainly of sandbanks, and there could be no question of relaunching the *Faidherbe* or of traveling by water at all. This new delay and Marchand's caution led to tensions among members of the expedition; even so the last phase was begun on 4 June 1898. The

*Faidherbe* had to be abandoned, at least temporarily, and the journey continued by canoe. The first few weeks were desperate, the expedition becoming bogged down in the swamps. Dams had to be constructed to create the few centimeters of water that were the minimum required to float the boats. On some days the expedition advanced no more than a few hundred yards. Once again, the *sudd* was proving to be the impenetrable barrier it had been for centuries. But then, on 25 June, the Bahr el-Ghazal was reached at long last and the worst was over. On 30 June, Marchand stood beside the White Nile and on 10 July, at 1700 hours, he was in Fashoda.

Marchand had gained his objective, and yet he was not the first Frenchman to reach the Nile, nor even the first Frenchman to hoist the tricolor there. For the French had also made an attempt to reach the Nile from the east, from Ethiopia, and to send out a small expedition with orders to join Marchand at Fashoda. That expedition had left towards the end of 1897 and was led by the Marquis de Bonchamps. It had followed the Sobat, a river joining the Nile below Fashoda, and it had come to within a hundred miles of Fashoda but had been forced back by hunger and exhaustion. On the return journey, however, it had encountered another, Ethiopian, expedition, which included a Russian colonel attached to the Russian legation in Addis Ababa. Two members of the French contingent joined this group and once more traveled westward. They reached the Nile just below Fashoda on 22 June 1898. As there was still no sign of the Marchand expedition, they prepared to leave again, but only after raising the French flag on an island in the Nile. Unfortunately, one of the Frenchmen was ill and the other could not swim, so that one of the Africans was deputed to carry the flag across, braving the crocodiles. The Russian colonel decided this would never do, leapt into the water himself, reached the island, and raised the tricolor. Thus the first French flag over the Nile was hoisted by a Russian.[69]

On 12 July 1898 Marchand did it again: "The tricolor was solemnly raised over the *moudirieh* of Fashoda."[70] The solemn occasion did not, however, pass as serenely as it might have done because the halyard broke and the tricolor fluttered down, but despite this misadventure Marchand had taken possession of Fashoda on behalf of France. In France itself, no one knew anything about it. Marchand was completely cut off. The *Faidherbe* was still stuck fast in the *sudd*. News took eight to nine months to reach Paris, and the expedition was left wholly to its own resources. All too soon it would be put to the test.

The mahdists refused to acknowledge the tricolor, and on 25 August they launched their first attack, opening fire from two armor-plated steamboats. Although Marchand commanded a thousand troops, the exchanges of fire never went beyond an artillery duel. On 29 August the *Faidherbe* finally arrived in Fashoda. It was a moment of great emotion. "It's the Faidherbe. It's France," exclaimed one of those present.[71] The madhdists withdrew. On 3 September Marchand concluded a treaty that established a French protectorate over the local Shilluks.[72] The day before, on 2 September 1898, Kitchener had won the decisive battle of Omdurman.

# 5
# FASHODA

## KITCHENER OF KHARTOUM

Horatio Herbert Kitchener (1850–1916) was probably the greatest and certainly the best-known British colonial general. This is of course due chiefly to his appointment as secretary of state for war in 1914 and to his famous recruiting campaign. At the time, every young Briton was confronted with the face of the moustachioed field marshal staring at him from the well-known poster above the exhortation "Your country needs YOU." However, Kitchener had become a national figure long before that, during the Boer War. In the most difficult phase of this most difficult war in British history, he had been commander-in-chief of the British troops in South Africa. It was then that he had taken the title of Lord Kitchener of Khartoum, of Vaal and of Aspall, but he was to remain famous as Kitchener of Khartoum, for he was remembered above all as the man who had avenged Gordon and who had recaptured Khartoum. His victory at Omdurman was and remained his greatest triumph.

Kitchener was a controversial figure and a man of contrasts. He was a cool-headed leader and a great organizer, but also a man of strange outbursts and fits of rage. He posed as a model of indomitability, manfulness and impassivity and liked to be shown looking like a conqueror. His moustache was always trimmed to perfection and his uniform spotless, but his office was in chaos. He was known as "K of K" after Khartoum, but in South Africa he became known as "K of Chaos."[73] Some of this paradox may have sprung from his singular upbringing. He was the son of a colonel who had taken early retirement on an Irish estate where he ruled over his family in military style. His wife had been given permission to take breakfast in bed but only on condition that the maid carried it in at eight o'clock sharp—and what was more, on the first stroke of eight.[74] Kitchener senior had many other eccentric traits. He objected violently to blankets, which he considered unhealthy—the Kitcheners slept under newspapers alone— and was a great advocate of strict corporal punishment. Kitchener junior himself was never to marry. Needless to say, he was cut out for a military career and, like Gordon, he joined the Royal Engineers. He served, *inter alia*, in Palestine and Cyprus, and in 1882 transferred to the Egyptian army (Egypt was that year occupied by Britain). Two years later he took part in Wolseley's campaign in the Sudan to save Gordon, which came too late.

Kitchener

In 1892, at the age of forty-two, he was made *sirdar*, commander-in-chief of the Egyptian army. In March 1896 Salisbury charged him with the reconquest of the Sudan and asked him to lead the Anglo-Egyptian army. Kitchener's first great victory was the recapture of Dongola from the mahdists on 23 September 1896. It was greeted with expressions of joy and enthusiasm in Cairo and London. Lord Cromer, the strongman of Egypt, now called for the immediate reconquest of the entire Sudan. The time seemed ripe for it. The problem, however, now as ever, was to persuade the chancellor of the exchequer to approve the necessary credits. Kitchener went to London, was given a hero's welcome, organized a powerful lobby, and was granted the credits. He could now realize his military design: to build a railroad straight through the Nubian desert from Wadi Halfa to Abu Hamed and then on toward Khartoum.

Thus he arrived in Omdurman, a city on the White Nile, opposite Khartoum. On 2 September 1898, at the break of day, battle commenced. At eleven thirty that morning Kitchener put away his binoculars and remarked that "the enemy had been given a good dusting."[75] This was well observed. Some 11,000 mahdists had been killed and 16,000 wounded. The Anglo-Egyptian army counted 48 dead and 382 wounded.[76] Winston Churchill, who took part in the campaign as a journalist and as a soldier, called the battle "the most signal triumph ever gained by the arms of science over barbarians."[77] The mahdi's tomb was opened and his nails used as souvenirs. The remainder was burned. The khalifa fled and was not discovered until a year later, when he was killed on 24 November 1899 during the battle that ensued. Gordon had been avenged, and the revenge was sweet. "Surely, he is avenged!" Queen Victoria noted in her diary.[78] The British, it should be noted, were also very impressed by the courage of the "fuzzy-wuzzies," the mahdist soldiers. Rudyard Kipling's famous poem "Fuzzy-Wuzzy" included this line: "You're a pore benighted 'eathen but a first-class fightin' man."[79]

Omdurman signified the destruction of the mahdist army and the end of the mahdist state. On 19 September Kitchener was in Fashoda. He protested formally against the French presence there and raised the Egyptian flag. This was a brilliant move on his part, for the French had always insisted that Egyptian rights had to be protected from the British, even in the Sudan. Marchand therefore found it hard to protest against the flag-raising ceremony. He did, however, let it be known that he had taken possession of the western bank of the Nile on behalf of his government. In his proclamation, Marchand used his new seal, "Afrique Centrale Française—Mission du Congo-Nil," abandoning that of "Commandant des Troupes, Haut-Oubangui." The new seal had been handed to him by the colonial ministry when he had left Paris two years earlier.[80] His intervention was thus an act of government policy and the resulting crisis would have to be solved at government level.

### THE CRISIS

When Marchand met Kitchener in Fashoda, Hanotaux had ceased to be foreign minister—the Méline government had managed to hold on for a long time but had fallen more than a month before, on 27 June 1898. Hanotaux was succeeded by Théophile Delcassé, the spiritual father of French Nile policy. It was he who had devised the Fashoda strategy, and he was now left to clear up the mess.

During the two years Marchand had spent in the wilds of Africa, Hanotaux had been trying to strengthen the French negotiating position. He had hoped that the steps taken by the French would lead to greater British readiness to enter into negotiations. Fashoda could easily be ceded as a small concession.[81] He also believed that France had to take the lead in putting pressure on Britain. Other Powers, such as Russia and Germany, would undoubtedly follow suit. To him, the Egyptian question was an international, not an Anglo-French, problem. That was a fatal miscalculation.[82] The Russians were not at all anxious to be drawn into this trap. Their interests lay in the Straits and in East Asia, not in Egypt. The Germans, for their part, were interested in maintaining Anglo-French tensions, not in resolving them. On 30 August 1898 Britain and Germany reached agreement on a possible partition of the Portuguese colonies (see pp. 315), and became as good as allies. Hanotaux's last hope was to enlist Ethiopian support. On 20 March 1897 he had signed the White Nile convention with that country, by which both parties had agreed to accept the White Nile as the boundary between them.[83] Ethiopian support, however, turned out to be of no practical significance.

Yet Anglo-French negotiations might well have borne fruit had Salisbury and Hanotaux had their way, which they did not. Hanotaux was in a weak position because he was under constant pressure from the colonial party, the colonial ministry and his own civil servants. Salisbury was in a stronger position, but his cabinet depended on support from Chamberlain, who acted as a one-man British colonial party. Chamberlain, who was firmly opposed to Salisbury's policy of making concessions in West Africa in exchange for British sway over the Nile, dug in his heels. He believed that the French had to be made to eat humble pie, preferably in public and with a pistol to their head.[84] In both countries, therefore, the hawks had the last word, so much so that compromise seemed out of the question. Because of this, Fashoda became a confrontation with the gloves off, one in which might alone prevailed. It was, as Salisbury put it, "something to remember," a naked clash of force, in which technical details counted for little.[85]

Britain was the stronger of the two. It held all the trumps, political, diplomatic and military. While Kitchener had come to Fashoda at the head of a victorious army, Marchand commanded no more than a handful of French soldiers and a hundred Sudanese *tirailleurs*. Britain had a powerful navy, whereas the French navy was inferior and the Russian fleet could be of little help during the winter. Nor did Russia ever offer such help.[86] Britain had no allies, but then it had no need of any. Its relations with the Triple Alliance were good. France had its Russian ally, but the support of that ally was lukewarm. In practice, therefore, France stood alone. Salisbury headed a strong government, while the French government was weak and divided. In 1898 France, moreover, was being torn apart by the aftermath of the Dreyfus affair. But most of all, Britain had the political will to go as far as was required. For it, the Nile was of vital national importance. This was not the case in France. For France, Fashoda was a question of prestige, not a matter of life and death. The crisis may have been ominous, but the outcome was inevitable: Delcassé had to give in.

In legal terms, incidentally, the British position was not very strong. It may have cited Egyptian rights whenever it suited it to do so, but it forgot them just as quickly again to rely on the conqueror's rights. Delcassé showed considerable legal acumen in countering these claims. He also made passionate appeals to national honor and spoke of unacceptable humiliations. In response, Salisbury coolly retorted that Marchand's position was untenable and that his lines of supply would be cut off. Where Delcassé spoke of negotiations and compensation, Salisbury insisted on evacuation and unconditional withdrawal. The Brisson cabinet, in office for just a few

Kitchener meets Marchand in Fashoda

months, resigned in October and made way for the Dupuy cabinet. Delcassé
remained in office. French public opinion began to realize how absurd the
whole affair really was: a war with Britain was threatening over Fashoda,
while Alsace-Lorraine was still in German hands.[87]

On 1 November 1898 the new cabinet was sworn in. Next day Delcassé
let it be known that he had decided to recall Marchand. Within a day the

cabinet approved the decision. On 11 December Marchand left Fashoda. He returned home by the eastern route and in May 1899 reached Djibouti by way of Ethiopia. On 30 May he arrived in Toulon, whence he was taken to Paris by special train. By the Anglo-Egyptian treaty of 19 January 1899, the Sudan had been declared an Anglo-Egyptian condominium, at least on paper. In fact Britain had the whip hand. The boundaries with the French possessions were fixed by treaty on 21 March 1899, and formalized in an "Additional Declaration" to the Anglo-French Convention on West Africa of 14 June 1898, at the request of Delcassé, who was anxious to avoid any form of overt recognition of the British position in Egypt.[88] The whole issue thus ended in a striking British victory—and a cheap one at that. The total costs of the reconquest of the Sudan or, as people said, of "Gordon's revenge," came to £800,000. British history, Winston Churchill wrote, knew no other example of "so great a national satisfaction being more cheaply obtained."[89]

With the British victory at Omdurman and the French withdrawal from Fashoda, the Sudan-Nile question had been largely solved. Menelik's advance on the Nile had been halted. By his treaty with Britain on 15 May 1902 he dropped all claims to any territory bordering on the Nile. Instead the entire Ethiopian plateau was united under his rule, thus laying the foundations for the modern and independent state of Ethiopia. Ethiopian expansion now became focused on the Red Sea. In 1897 an Anglo-Ethiopian agreement enabled Ethiopia to subject part of Somaliland. By the side of France, Britain and Italy, there was now another foreign power in Somaliland, albeit an African one. Then Menelik was struck by symptoms of paralysis. In 1908 he named his grandson as his successor.

The Italians now aimed their sights at Somaliland where, like the British, they came up against a religious resistance movement, that of Mohammed Abdallah Hasan, nicknamed the "Mad Mullah." He remained a formidable opponent and made things unpleasantly difficult for the British as well as for the Italians. In March 1905 an agreement was reached whereby he was given control of part of the Italian sphere of influence in Somaliland, which Italy had taken over from the Filonardi Company that same month. Britain and Italy fixed the borders between Italian Somaliland and British East Africa by the treaty of 15 July 1911. The "Mad Mullah," incidentally, continued to make his presence felt until 1920. In December of that year he died of influenza.

# 6
# CONCLUSION

The Fashoda crisis had a touch of the tragicomical about it. Two European countries, in many respects closely allied, went to the brink of war for the sake of a region Lord Salisbury had called a "land of marsh and fever"[90] and which Hanotaux had described as a "country inhabited by apes and by blacks who are worse than apes."[91] How were things allowed to go so far? What was the underlying issue?

Economic considerations were of little consequence. No one had many illusions on that front, even though the old myth of Sudanese gold did play a minor role. More important were the strategic interests. Once Britain had blundered into Egypt in 1882 and Salisbury decided in 1899 to stay on, the Nile and everything bound up with it assumed a new significance. Cairo replaced Constantinople as the central piece on the imperial chessboard of the political leaders. This led to the Sudanese strategy Britain introduced in the 1890s: the Sudan was to become a British sphere of influence. The logical conclusion was that the British position on the Nile must be defended as far as its source. In addition there was the great British dream of the Cape-to-Cairo route. Although this was not official government policy, it nevertheless played a part. It began to live a life of its own and became the specter of French colonialists, "the evil and arrogant dream of an English cross over Africa," as Marchand called it.[92] France did not accept the British position in Africa, any more than its policy in the Sudan, and certainly not the English cross over Africa. It made a stand against it, and so the conflict flared up.

The solution to this sort of problem was simple in principle. The rules of the African partition game were plain enough: exchange and compensation. However, they presupposed a rational evaluation of interests and a balanced diplomatic approach. That approach could not prosper while there was a race for prestige and constant public pressure. For France, by and large, Africa—and everything connected with Egypt and the Nile in particular—had always been a matter of prestige. For Britain, the Nile was primarily of strategic importance, but in Britain, too, the Empire had increasingly become a matter of prestige, which rendered it difficult to make concessions even in less strategically important areas. The arrival of Joseph Chamberlain in 1895 was a turning point: prestige gradually became as important as strategy. The Niger-for-Nile policy was abandoned. For Britain it was all or nothing now. These new factors paralyzed the cool and sovereign diplomatic moves so beloved of Lord Salisbury and his colleagues. Playtime in Africa was over. The second phase of the partition therefore had a different character from the first. The clash between Britain and France at Fashoda, the Boer War soon afterwards, and the Franco-

German Morocco crisis of 1905 were no longer skirmishes in the wings of international politics, but all-out confrontations, during which the positions of the Great Powers themselves were at stake. The Nile, the Cape and Tangier were so many clashes not only of interests but also of emotions.

It is not surprising, therefore, that the confrontation at Fashoda should have occurred: it was inevitable that the Sudan should have been drawn into the partition of Africa. No matter how inaccessible the region was, its position was such that, once the mahdist state had crumbled, the European Powers had to plunge in. The European candidates were Britain, France, King Leopold and Italy. Leopold overplayed his hand. He refused to see the difference between the Congo and the Nile. The failure of his treaty with Britain, however, made this drastically clear to him. Italy was destined to face the strongest military force in Africa while being the weakest of the Europeans. As a result, it quickly dropped out of the race. That left Britain and France. Their clash seemed as inevitable as that of two trains traveling toward each other on a single track. For Britain, its Sudanese ambitions had indeed an inevitable aspect; they were the logical outcome of its role in Egypt and of Egypt's role in the Sudan. However, the concrete effects and their phases were largely dictated by chance. Had Kitchener arrived in Fashoda a year later, the course of events would have been quite different. It would have been a matter for negotiations, not ultimata. In any case, as far as Britain was concerned the main line of approach was set.

The French road to Fashoda, by contrast, was the result of choice, not of necessity. Without any doubt, French Fashoda strategy was the result of a blunder, or rather of a series of blunders. It was formed by chance initiatives and foreign intrigues, such as Leopold's involvement in the Monteil mission. The continuity of the French plans does, however, suggest that there was also something like an underlying policy. That policy was framed by the colonial and foreign ministries, the Pavillon de Flore generally taking the initiative and the Quai d'Orsay following behind, reluctantly or otherwise.

That brings us to an important aspect of French foreign policy: uncoordinated decision-making processes. Interest in foreign, and especially in overseas, policy was slight not only among the masses but also in parliament and in the cabinet. The expertise of even those who were most involved was negligible. Legend has it that Chautemps, minister for the colonies in 1895, confused Gabon with the Sudan and Gibraltar with Madagascar.[93] In the cabinet there was no such thing as collective decision-making or coordination. It was every minister for himself, and as ministers continued to come and go, there was generally very little continuity in cabinet policy. That was, however, less true of foreign policy, where Hanotaux proved a surprisingly constant factor. However, while he admittedly provided some continuity, his policy was as unsure and unstable as his personality. Moreover, his position as a minister without political party backing was weak. The colonial party gave its support to Delcassé, and that proved crucial. The raid on Fashoda was thought up during Berthelot's interim administration and cleverly sold to him by his civil servants. Delcassé was behind it all, and there was little Hanotaux could do about it.

The colonials were undoubtedly the party most responsible for the Fashoda fiasco. There was some substance in President Faure's complaint that the French had allowed themselves to be dragged into Africa like idiots by "those irresponsible people called the colonials."[94] Yet Hanotaux made this policy his own. That was due to a number of fundamental errors, first of all the assumption that other countries would support France, and second that Britain would not raise the stakes too high. The second mistake was the greatest blunder of all, because Britain considered the Nile a matter of vital importance. That was the main difference between this and most other African questions.

Ever since the early 1880s, the partition of Africa had been a game of bluff and guile, a fight not to be taken quite seriously, something like the eighteenth-century *guerres en dentelles*. In Europe there was no room left for political pinpricks without serious consequences, but in Africa there was still ample leeway. When it came to the Nile, however, things were different, as Leopold was the first to learn. For France, the Nile was a matter of prestige, and Fashoda was therefore a bluff—as far as France was concerned. For Britain, by contrast, the Nile had become an imperial centerpiece and was therefore of overriding importance. Salisbury was man of cool assessments and long-term policies. He did not let himself be carried away by jingoist sentiment, and was fully aware of the importance of good relations with France. But even he gave the French no quarter when he realized that he was holding all the cards. Thus the crisis became deeply humiliating for France and marked a new low in Anglo-French relations.

However, Fashoda was not only a low, but also a turning point. The dazzling demonstration of Britain's determination and power in Egypt cleared the air and opened the way for a new relationship. In France imperialism based on practical considerations came to prevail over imperialism based on prestige. The reopening of the Egyptian question had been a matter of honor, an attempt to expunge the humiliation of 1882. There had been no other motive. That was set to change. After Fashoda, a new consensus emerged in French Africa policy. Henceforth the main colonial ambition would no longer be to restore French influence in Egypt, but to link up French West, Central and North Africa. Egypt no longer played a great role in this approach, but Morocco did so all the more. As a result, new possibilities for bartering spheres of influence or territory were created and hence new chances for diplomatic activity. France was prepared to accept Britain's position in Egypt in exchange for a "free hand" in Morocco. Thus the Fashoda crisis ultimately produced the preconditions for the Anglo-French Entente Cordiale of 1904, and hence for an end to more than twenty years of colonial rivalry.

# VI

# BOERS AND BRITONS IN SOUTH AFRICA, 1890–1902

What is now at stake is the position of Great Britain
in South Africa. . . . The contest for supremacy is
between the Dutch and the English.

Joseph Chamberlain

**"S**outh Africa" is a political con-
cept—it is shorthand for a country, the Republic of South Africa, much as
"America" is shorthand for the United States of America. In the past
"South Africa" was a geographical concept, comprising a territory far
larger than that of the present-day republic. Today we refer to that region
as southern Africa, which consists, in addition to South Africa itself, of
Lesotho, Swaziland, Namibia, Botswana, Zimbabwe and Mozambique.
Some writers also include Angola, Zambia and Malawi, and because the
history of these latter territories is so closely linked with that of the former,
we shall do likewise.

South Africa's special distinction is that it is the only part of the continent
in which the settlement of whites occurred on a large scale. We find this

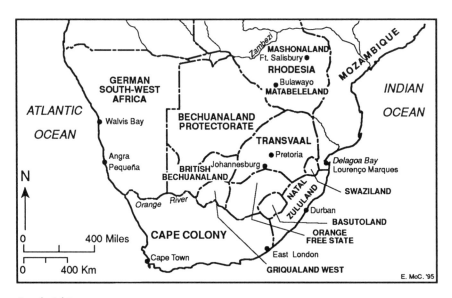

South Africa

form of colonization, the only authentic kind, in America and Australia, but it is rare in, or absent from, Asia and Africa. It has put a special stamp on the history of southern Africa. The settlement of white colonists started in the Cape, spreading from there to the rest of southern Africa. As a result, white South Africa might therefore have been much larger, and according to such imperialists as Cecil Rhodes ought to have been much larger than it actually is. That it is not is due to a long and complicated historical process. Two dates in that process are of special importance: 1652, the year the first whites settled in the Cape, and 1886, the year gold was found on the Witwatersrand. The first event marked the beginning of the white colonization of Africa; without it a white South Africa might never have emerged. The second marked the beginning of modern, industrialized South Africa; without it white South Africa would have had no future. The discovery of gold also brought a shift in the South African center of power from the Cape Colony to the Transvaal and from Cape Town to Johannesburg. This shift was to prove a crucial turning point in the history of southern Africa.

# 1
# THE HISTORICAL BACKGROUND

South Africa was not uninhabited when European ships first anchored off Table Mountain in about 1500. It was populated by various, chiefly nomadic, peoples, distinguished by the Dutch settlers into Hottentots and Bushmen, whom they considered two distinct races, in physical as well as cultural respects. Bushmen were shorter than Hottentots and spoke a different language. They were also more "primitive"—hunters and gatherers—while Hottentots had developed to the higher level of herdsmen. This traditional distinction was for a long time maintained by historiographers. Today we no longer use these terms, but refer to the Hottentots as Khoi or Khoikhoi and to Bushmen as San, the term Khoisan being used for both. The differences between them are therefore not so strongly emphasized nowadays, the less so as both peoples differ markedly from the neighboring Bantu. The latter used to be referred to as Kaffirs, from the Arabic word *kafir*, meaning infidel. That term too has been dropped. We speak now of Xhosas, Tswanas and Sothos.

We do not know precisely when these peoples settled in southern Africa, but they probably arrived between A.D. 500 and 1000. In any event the Europeans arrived later. Of these latecomers the Portuguese were, as so often, the first, Bartholomeu Diaz rounding the Cape in 1488. The Dutch followed them on the trail of the much-coveted oriental spices. In 1647 a

Dutch ship, the *Haerlem,* was wrecked in Table Bay. The crew stayed on for a year until another ship came to pick them up. During the interval they lived on what the land produced. Upon their return to Holland, their commander suggested to the directors of the Dutch East India Company that they would do well to set up a permanent revictualling station or halfway house at the Cape. It was this suggestion that led thirty-two-year-old Jan van Riebeeck to set sail from Texel in Holland with a small flotilla, consisting of the *Drommedaris,* the *Reijger* and the *Goede Hoop,* on Christmas Eve 1651. He arrived in the Cape more than three months later, on 6 April 1652. The white presence in South Africa had begun. Van Riebeeck and his men were servants of the Company, temporarily stationed at the Cape. Hence they were not true colonists, though soon afterwards permanent settlers were admitted as well. These were men not in the service of the Company but free burghers who farmed the land on their own account, and it was with them that the process of white colonization in South Africa started. At about the same time slaves were first imported from East Africa, Madagascar and India. The result was the emergence of a pluralistic society in the Cape.

The Dutch East India Company was never very sure what to do with the newly acquired possession. A purely restrictive policy might have ensured that the settlement remained what it had originally been intended to be, namely, the company's revictualling station. For economic and strategic reasons, however, it was decided to admit immigrants, the result being a colony that the company did not really want. The Cape thus remained a languishing and rather unenterprising small settlement, with Cape Town as its commercial center and Stellenbosch as its agricultural center. Yet there was no complete lack of dynamism. The impetus came from the "trekboers," or traveling farmers who left the colony and set out in search of fresh pastures. They were the South African version of the North American pioneers, men who, axe and Bible in hand, lived a hard but pious life in their far-flung log cabins. They constituted a society of individuals, united by God's Word and the common struggle against the blacks.

In 1795, when French revolutionary forces overran the Netherlands, the Cape was occupied by Britain. At first this appeared to be a temporary arrangement since by the Treaty of Amiens the colony was returned to the Batavian Republic in 1802, but soon afterwards hostilities broke out anew, and in 1806 the Cape was again occupied by British forces. This occupation was ratified by the Treaty of London in 1814, Britain having established its colonial and maritime supremacy during the Napoleonic wars. Growing stronger still in the nineteenth century, it turned the Cape into the most important link in the great imperial chain joining Britain to the Far East.

British rule opened a new phase in the history of South Africa. The white settlers in the Cape were of diverse origin; in addition to Dutchmen there were many Germans and French Huguenots. This community developed a lifestyle of its own, so much so that it became possible to speak of a national, Afrikaans, identity. The Afrikaners looked upon the British government as a foreign administration, and the resulting tension between Boer and Briton was to dominate the history of modern South Africa. This tension also underlay the emergence of a movement that was to give the history of South Africa a new twist: the Great Trek of 1835 to 1837.

### THE GREAT TREK

Trekboers, as we have said, had been known in the Cape for a long time, but the Great Trek was a novel political act, an expression of the Afrikaner colonists' longing for independence. Piet Retief, one of the trekboer leaders, wrote a manifesto explaining why they were leaving the Cape to found a free and independent community. They were making for—the text was in English and the style almost Jeffersonian—"a wild and dangerous territory," relying on themselves and on God alone: "We quit this colony under the full assurance that the English government has nothing more to require of us, and will allow us to govern ourselves without its interference in future."[1] In other words the Boers had opted for "Liberty." We might also put it differently and in less exalted terms. They were looking for land and detested the modern English ideas, especially the muddled belief in the equality of white and black.

The Great Trek took place between 1835 and 1837 and led to the settlement by whites of large parts of eastern South Africa, territories that were to become known as the Transvaal, the Orange Free State and Natal. The Trek also led to a number of wars with the Africans, and especially with the Zulus, who had built up a gigantic army under their bellicose leader Shaka. Shaka had introduced military reforms on a large scale: he had equipped his troops with new and shorter assegais, which were no longer thrown but used as hand weapons; he deployed his troops in a "horn," that is, with the main force in the center and two flanking regiments to encircle the enemy; finally, by the introduction of compulsory military service he had created a standing army. Before battle his soldiers' morale would be boosted by war dances and ritual feasts, after which the troops would take an emetic and be made to vomit into a pit six feet square; the vomiting pit, the *nkatha yesiwe*, was a sacred national shrine.[2] Within a span of ten years, from 1818 to 1828, the Zulus became the most powerful and most feared nation in the region. Large areas became depopulated as the inhabitants fled from their advancing forces. In 1828 Shaka was murdered by his two brothers, one of whom, Dingaan, followed in Shaka's footsteps.

The Great Trek led to contacts between the Boers and the Zulus. The Boers were in search of almost entirely depopulated regions in which to settle, and, led by Piet Retief, entered into negotiations for land with Dingaan. On 6 February 1838 these negotiations were brought to a successful conclusion, and to celebrate the occasion Retief and his party were invited to a feast in Dingaan's kraal. During the Zulu war dance staged for the visitors Dingaan leapt to his feet and shouted, "Death to the wizards!,"[3] whereupon the guests were massacred. Seeking retribution, the Boers went to war, and for the first few months suffered terrible losses. But before the year was out "Dingaan's treachery" had been avenged: on 16 December 1838, the Boers scored a great victory at the Battle of Blood River. One year later, Dingaan's power was broken. The Boers proclaimed his half-brother, Mpande, king and took possession of half of Zululand. They now had their own republic, Natal. The Transvaal and the Orange Free State followed.

In Natal, however, the Boers were not to have much of a future. The territory was annexed by Britain in 1843, the strategic importance of this coastland being considered too great to be left in foreign hands. The Boer republics in the interior, the Transvaal and the Orange Free State, were of lesser strategic worth and were thus let off more lightly. True, they too were the subject of disputes, but Britain recognized their independence with the signing of the Sand River (1852) and Bloemfontein (1854) conventions.

There were now four white political entities in South Africa: the Cape Colony and Natal under British rule, and the two Boer republics. The term "republic" was a rather grandiose description of what were in fact extremely small states. At the time the Transvaal numbered barely 25,000 white inhabitants and the Orange Free State roughly half that.[4] Following the Bloemfontein Convention, the Free Staters immediately started to form an independent administration. Their constitution enfranchised all white males over the age of eighteen, who elected a *Volksraad* (the legislative assembly) and a state president. The South African Republic, as the Transvaal was officially called, was run along similar lines, except that in addition to the president there was also a powerful commandant-general. The two republics, although similar in many respects, differed in a number of ways. Thus while the Free State modeled its political organization on that of the Cape Colony and constituted a more settled society, the Transvaal remained a typical frontier state.

The Cape Colony was not densely populated either. At the time, it had some 200,000 inhabitants, the majority of them nonwhite. The European population was made up of Britons and "Dutchmen," and was dominated by the former. British policy in the white colonies was based on the 1893 Durham Report and aimed at the development of "responsible government," that is, self-rule. The first step in that direction in the Cape was the election of a representative assembly in 1853, and by 1872 the Cape had become a self-governing colony with its own administration and a prime minister answerable to its own parliament.[5] The position of the British governor was more or less that of a constitutional head of state, and he therefore had little say over foreign policy. However, he was also high commissioner for South Africa, and as such responsible for relations with all other peoples and states in South Africa. That rendered his office one of the utmost importance. The governor-cum–high commissioner and the prime minister of the Cape Colony became the leading political figures there, the first representing British imperial interests above all, and the second Cape colonial interests. The two sets of interests did not always coincide, and the conflict between them in the Cape was to play an important role in relations with the Boer republics. It was also responsible for the use of a peculiar and sometimes rather confusing terminology, "colonialism" being reserved for the policy of Cape Town and "imperialism" for the policy of London.

In addition to the two Boer republics and the Cape Colony, there was another white colony in South Africa, Natal, which fell under British rule after the annexation of 1843. The road to self-government here took longer than in the Cape, and it was not until 1892 that Natal gained internal autonomy.

Though the four territories differed markedly, they had one thing in common, their expansionism. Over the years they all extended their spheres of influence and came unavoidably into contact and conflict with the black population. Competition for land between white and black thus became a permanent theme in the history of South Africa. The most vigorous expansion was that of the Cape Colony. It was directed eastward. Nine so-called Kaffir wars and the ultimate swallowing up of Kaffraria were the result. Thanks to its eastward expansion, the Cape Colony moved ever closer to Natal, with which it ultimately shared a border. Natal in its turn had continuous problems with the Zulus as it expanded toward the north. The Boer republics, too, tried more or less successfully to extend their respective spheres of influence. Very soon, however, the conflict between Boer and Briton was to become more important than the clash between white and black. In 1881 this conflict led to the First Boer War or, as the Afrikaners call it, the First War of Liberation.

### DIAMONDS AND THEIR CONSEQUENCES

The Anglo-Boer war of 1881 was in a sense a clash between two different worlds, between the old and the new. It was the culmination of a protracted process of alienation and separation. The Boer republics were founded on Calvinism, racial discrimination and territorial expansion. The Boers were accustomed to owning almost unlimited amounts of land. All Boers were entitled to their own *plaats* (farmstead) and to 7,500 acres of ground, considered more or less as their natural right. As a result their borders were continually being extended. To the British, Boer social organization seemed hopelessly old-fashioned. Britain was opposed to racial discrimination, largely on practical grounds. Moreover, it took a different view of South

Africa's future. It wanted a strong but not very large settlement in the Cape
to protect its shipping interests, and it wanted to acquire that as cheaply
as possible. Its policy made no provision for land-hungry, racist, primitive
and illiterate Boers who kept on annexing fresh territory. The British
wanted nothing to do with any of that, but they also wanted no trouble,
having already had quite enough, and having learned their lesson after the
conflicts of the 1840s. The best thing was to leave the Boers alone as far
as possible. As long as they did not try to expand toward the coast, they
posed no threat to the strategic interests of the British Empire. Peaceful
coexistence was therefore the order of the day and laissez-faire the pass-
word.

In the 1870s, however, it was not in Britain alone that voices were being
raised in favor of a more forceful imperialism and a more active colonial
policy; in the Cape Colony, too, there were Britons to whom the backward
Boers were a thorn in the side. Finally, there were new developments that
had turned South Africa into a focus of international interest. These developments had followed the chance discovery in 1867 of a diamond in a
settlement near the northern border of the Cape Colony with the highly
appropriate name of Hopetown. When the stone arrived in Cape Town, a
senior government official declared, "Gentlemen, this is the rock upon
which the future success of South Africa will be built."[6] Prophetic words
indeed. Diamonds were to transform South Africa. Within three years its
external trade had trebled, millions were invested in an economy that had
been stagnant until shortly before, and further millions eagerly lent to the
Cape government to invest in railroad construction.[7]

The first diamond finds were made along both banks of the Vaal, roughly
sixty miles above its junction with the Orange River. These finds were the
so-called dry diggings, diamonds that could be dug out of the gravel and
sand by individual prospectors using primitive equipment. The most important deposits were discovered at Colesburg Kopje, which would later
be called Kimberley after the British colonial secretary. Many more diamonds lay buried in deeper strata, but to bring these up required mining
operations, which meant investment, engineers, organization—in short,
capitalism. Thus the search for diamonds created a new industry.
Thousands of prospectors from the Transvaal and Natal, from the Orange
Free State and the Cape, made for the diamond fields, and further
thousands joined them from Europe, America and Australia. The Great
Trek had been as nothing by comparison. Within a few years, Kimberley
had grown into South Africa's second most important town, ceding pride
of place only to Cape Town. Anthony Trollope visited the area in 1877 on
one of his great journeys and called Kimberley "one of the most remarkable
spots on the face of the earth."[8] People worked there like ants in an ant
heap, thousands burrowing all at once in the great hole from which the
diamonds were extracted. The Africans were taught to work there for their

own benefit, according to Trollope, because "work is the great civilizer of the world."[9] Trollope went on to explain that by learning to work the Africans would in the long run also absorb civilization and Christianity, and he concluded that there was no other spot on earth where "the work of civilizing a Savage is being carried on with so signal a success."[10]

The inhabitants of this "diggers' republic" constituted, if not a cultured, then certainly a motley crew. Barnett Isaacs, better known as Barney Barnato, was one of the most prominent of these. He was the son of a London Jewish shopkeeper, and his skills consisted of little more than prizefighting and acting. His best known act was reciting "To be or not to be" while standing on his head. His capital ran to sixty dozen cigars, which he sold at a considerable profit before going into the diamond trade.[11] He believed in two things: his luck and the theory that the blue ground at Kimberley held diamonds. He was proved right in both respects. By 1880 Barney Barnato was earning £1,800 a week, roughly a thousand times as much as an English worker. He and his associates, among them Alfred Beit, "the shy millionaire," and Cecil Rhodes, about whom more below, were to play major roles in the history of South Africa.

The diamonds were found in a kind of no-man's-land on the frontier of three territories: the Cape, the Free State and the semi-independent Griqualand West. Which of these territories had the greatest claim to the diamond fields was never quite clear, though the Free State probably held the strongest title. However, after arbitration by the lieutenant-governor of Natal, the disputed area was assigned to Nicolaas Waterboer, the Griqua leader. Since Waterboer had asked for British protection, Griqualand West was at once incorporated into the Cape Colony. Many Boers felt that the British had stolen the diamond fields from them and were left feeling bitter. They were soon to have even more cause for resentment.

The Disraeli government came to power in Britain in 1874 and displayed an active interest in colonial and imperial affairs. In 1867 the colonial secretary, Lord Carnarvon, had successfully ushered in the federation of Canada. According to him, the same method was the answer to South Africa's problems. He accordingly proposed inviting delegates from the various parts of South Africa to a conference on federal government. He also planned to split the Cape Colony into two, the Eastern and the Western Cape. The citizens of the Colony, however, wanted no part of the federal plan. They had only just been granted self-government, and they considered these London initiatives nothing short of an abrogation of their newly won rights. Nor were they in favor of the proposed split-up.[12] The Boers were even less keen on the idea. Doomed before it began, the conference, convened in London in August 1876, achieved little. Lord Carnarvon then decided to steer a different course and to annex the Transvaal without further ado. One month later a good opportunity offered itself. The Transvaalers had once again become enmeshed in a war with several African tribes and had suffered a heavy defeat. Their government was on the verge of bankruptcy. An attack by Zulu forces seemed imminent. The Transvaalers, Carnarvon reasoned, would probably be only too happy to be taken over by Britain. He decided to act accordingly and gave orders to Theophilus Shepstone, the Natal delegate to the London Conference, to proceed with the annexation.

Shepstone (1817–1893), the son of a Transkei missionary, held an important post in the government of Natal. He was special commissioner in Natal and as such in charge of relations with the Zulus, a people he knew well and whom he had even come to resemble a little, according to some. In any case, the famous novelist Sir Henry Rider Haggard called him a "curious, silent man, who had acquired many of the characteristics of the natives amongst whom he lived."[13] Sir Bartle Frere, the governor of the Cape Colony, called him an "Africander Talleyrand, shrewd, observant, silent, self-contained, immobile."[14] Shepstone believed in good government by good people and moral uplift through Christian education. He expected little good of the white colonists, who, he believed, thought only of themselves. Since salvation for the blacks had therefore to come from London, his aim was to impose British rule on all South Africa. On 4 January 1877 he rode into the Transvaal with twenty-five mounted Natal policemen and made for Pretoria. There he held consultations with the Volksraad, beginning with sherry and champagne and ending, on 12 April 1877, with the incorporation of the Transvaal into the British Empire. The Transvaal government put up little resistance, and the annexation was quite straightforward, although Britain was soon to have serious problems, not with the Boers but with the Zulus.

Lord Carnarvon, the architect of the British South Africa policy, sat in London, but the implementation of that policy was in the hands of the man on the spot, the British governor-general of the Cape Colony and high commissioner for South Africa, Sir Bartle Frere. Frere (1815–1884) saw eye to eye with Carnarvon. He was a convinced imperialist of the enlightened school and president of the Geographical Society, with honorary doctorates from Oxford and Cambridge.[15] He was brilliant and ambitious, impulsive and impatient, and had the reputation of being so convincing a humanitarian that he was even able to persuade the sultan of Zanzibar to sign a treaty against slavery. He was one of the leading proconsuls of his day, and had previously been governor of Bombay and a member of the Indian Council. The governorship of the sleepy Cape Colony would have been far too undemanding a post for him, and so, not surprisingly, he was chosen by Carnarvon for greater work: to bring about the federation of South Africa.

Frere arrived in Cape Town shortly before 12 April 1877, the date on which Shepstone proclaimed the annexation of the Transvaal. That, according to Frere, was a step in the right direction. Frere was, however, more concerned with the power of the blacks than with that of the whites. He was convinced that South Africa would have no peace until British sovereignty was recognized by all the people who lived there, and above all by the Zulus. In his view, the latter posed a permanent threat to peace and quiet.[16] That was something of which Shepstone had convinced him. Britain was dependent on the "caprice of an ignorant and bloodthirsty tyrant," which was intolerable.[17] The answer was war, and that ran counter to the views of the British cabinet. At the time, Britain had its hands full with the Balkans. Worse still, a war was threatening in Afghanistan. The last thing London wanted was a war in South Africa. "A native war," Carnarvon informed Shepstone in January 1878, "is just now impossible and you must avoid it."[18] Yet that was precisely where Frere was heading. Taking advantage of the poor communications with London, he presented Whitehall with a series of faits accomplis that put the British cabinet on the spot.

### THE ZULUS

On 11 December 1878 Frere sent an ultimatum to King Cetshwayo of the Zulus. Since he was certain that it would be rejected, he had in fact issued a declaration of war. The result was as impressive as it was surprising: Britain suffered the greatest defeat in its colonial history. On 22 January 1879 a mighty Zulu army of 20,000 men routed the British forces at Isandhlwana. The British camp had not been properly protected or defended. Despite warnings from none other than President Kruger, no attempt had been made to set up a *laager*.[19] There had been some 800 Europeans inside the camp. After the battle only 30 of them were left alive. More British officers were killed than at the battle of Waterloo.[20] The Zulus, too, had suffered great losses. They mourned at least 2,000 dead.[21]

After Isandhlwana Britain had no alternative but to strike back; the defeat had to be avenged. The Zulu war that followed was one of the great colonial campaigns. Reinforcements, requested and sent, included the Prince Impérial of France, the son of Napoleon III. On 1 June 1879, the prince set out to inspect a spot in the area that had shortly before been named Napoleon Koppie in his honor. The patrol, somewhat casually, did not notice until the last moment that they were under threat from Zulu warriors. "Please hurry, Your Highness," cried one of the company, but it was too late; the younger Napoleon was unable to mount his horse in time. While the rest fled, he stayed behind without a horse but with his great-uncle's sword in his hand. That, however, proved of little avail against the Zulu assegais. Next day a column of more than a thousand men sent in search of him found his body, naked, run through in seventeen places and with a tuft of Zulu hair clasped in his fist. The news came as a bombshell to Britain. For the press, it was the event of the year and made an even greater impression than Isandhlwana. In France the sensation was, of course, greater still, and the prince's death was said to be the result of a plot, the guilt being placed variously on the French government, the British or the Freemasons.[22]

The man now sent to South Africa to restore order was Sir Garnet Wolseley. When he arrived in Cape Town in 1879, Wolseley (1833–1913) was just forty-six years old, but was already a military legend. The son of an impoverished army officer, he himself was commissioned at the age of eighteen, as a reward for services rendered by his father, and went out to Calcutta. He served in India, in Russia (during the Crimean War), in China and in Canada. He became known as a military reformer, and especially as the author of the *Soldier's Pocket Book*—a work that ran to 400 pages and was packed with practical advice for officers and men—and as president of the Society for the Prevention of Bad Language. His greatest hour came in the campaign against the Ashanti, which made him first, Britain's youngest, and later, its most famous general. He then returned to Britain and enriched the English language with the phrase "all Sir Garnet," a new, and at the time popular, term for "all correct."

After the Gold Coast came Natal, of which Wolseley was appointed governor in 1875, followed by a staff appointment in England and another stint in India. Wolseley had meanwhile become so famous that the British press called him "Our Only General." He was a brilliant soldier but a social misfit, notoriously selfish, a social upstart and a show-off. Queen Victoria disliked him intensely and told Disraeli that he was a self-centered "braggart." "So was Nelson, Ma'am," was Disraeli's laconic reply.[23] After Isandhlwana, "Our Only General" seemed the obvious man for the job. He left for South Africa in 1879 with every necessary authority: the rank of full general, the governorship of Natal and Transvaal, and the post of high commissioner for "native and foreign affairs." Wolseley thus held all the reins, and the campaign he waged was most successful. Zulu military power collapsed with the capture of Cetshwayo's royal kraal in Ulundi on 4 July 1879. Not long afterwards, Cetshwayo himself was captured. Wolseley was refused permission to annex Zululand, and instead divided it into thirteen small kingdoms, all at loggerheads with one another. Cetshwayo's power was broken. At the end of his tether, he applied to the British government for help against his rivals, traveling to London in 1882. He was not dressed in his famous grass skirt on this occasion but in morning coat and top hat, although his feet were bare. He was very popular with Londoners, and was received by Queen Victoria. However, his appeal for help was turned down. The great Zulu kingdom was never to be restored, and on 8 February 1884 Cetshwayo was found dead, probably poisoned, in his kraal.[24]

King Cetshwayo of the Zulus

## ANNEXATION

The power of the Zulus had been broken, but Britain now faced other grave problems in South Africa. The war had left fifteen hundred European dead and as many disabled. And what was Britain to do about the Transvaal? After the failure of his policy, Sir Bartle Frere was recalled from South Africa, and in April 1880 the Disraeli government made way for Gladstone's administration. Gladstone was not the man to favor annexations. During his famous Midlothian campaign he had rounded on his predecessors' Transvaal policy: "We have chosen most unwisely, I am tempted to say insanely, to place ourselves in the strange predicament of the free subjects of a monarch going to coerce the free subjects of a republic, and to compel them to accept a citizenship which they decline and refuse."[25] Small wonder, then, that the Transvaalers had high hopes for a new and independent future for their country. Things were not, however, to turn out that way. Following the British elections, rhetoric gave way to realism. On 15 June 1880 Gladstone informed the Transvaal government that the queen's sovereignty had to be maintained come what may. Britain had obligations toward the "natives" and toward the loyalists in the Transvaal. The new cabinet thus continued the policy of the old. "Confederation,"

Gladstone explained, "is the pole-star of the present action of our government."[26] It was his government's hope that a confederation, which in practice amounted to self-government under British sovereignty, would satisfy the Boers, but it did nothing of the kind. On the contrary, in 1880 the Boers opted for armed resistance. The leading figure behind their decision was Paul Kruger.

That someone like Paul Kruger (1825–1904) should have a leading role to play in the history of South Africa was something that irritated a great many Britons. A man with his looks, manners and ideas was patently unfit to be the head of a modern state. Yet it was because of these very qualities that Paul Kruger became the undisputed leader of his country. Kruger was avowedly not a man with modern views. He was a true-blue Afrikaner. Born the son of a trekboer, he had left the Cape on the Great Trek with his parents at the age of ten, in the party led by Andries Potgieter. He was obviously a keen soldier since he was made an assistant field cornet when he was only sixteen, and was later promoted to commandant and in 1858 to commandant-general, the second highest office in the state. But Kruger was a man not only of the gun but also of the Word: in 1859 he was one of the founders of the Dutch Reformed Church of South Africa.

Courage, obstinacy and bigotry made him a born leader. When Shepstone annexed the Transvaal in 1878, Vice-President Kruger was one of the few who refused to submit. He was not a man for collaboration or accommodation, and went straight to London to protest. When his protest fell on deaf ears he returned and formed a triumvirate with Piet Joubert and Marthinus Pretorius for the express purpose of leading the resistance to the British incursion. In 1881 Kruger took the Transvaal into the First Boer War (regarded by the Boers as the First War of Independence). In 1883 he was elected president, an office to which he would be reelected many times and that he would hold until his country was defeated in 1902.

During all these years, Kruger offended and irritated his British opponents to an exceptional degree. They found him "decidedly ugly" and his table manners "gigantically horrible."[27] Kruger greased his hair with so much rancid coconut oil that he had to use his pocket comb even at dinner. When he dressed for diplomatic functions in morning coat and top hat he looked more like a circus ringmaster than the head of state of an independent republic. Mrs. Leyds, the wife of Willem Leyds, Kruger's first minister or "state secretary," was deeply concerned for her chair covers and table linen every time "Oom Paul" (Uncle Paul) came to visit, "because out of Oom Paul's mouth came not only wise words but also the inevitable spittle."[28] Needless to say, all these idiosyncrasies gave further ammunition to Kruger's adversaries, the aristocratic officers and administrators from proud England, who thought they knew best how the world should be run. Joseph Chamberlain called him "an ignorant, dirty, cunning and obstinate man."[29] His first great antagonist, Sir Bartle Frere, knew better than that,

Paul Kruger rides out

however. "Mr. Paul Kruger," he wrote, ". . . is a very shrewd fellow, who veils under an assumed clownish manner and affectation of ignorance considerable ability."[30] Kruger's strength lay on the one hand in his marked political ability, his power to lead and to reconcile, to see through his opponents and to manipulate them, and on the other hand in the fact that the Boers recognized him as one of their own. He knew the whole box of tricks and played the political game with verve and success. General Nicolaas Smit, the hero of Majuba, reported that when Kruger could not have his way and all other means had failed, he would not hesitate to take his interlocutor's hand, burst into tears and plead for sympathy. "Who can resist a man like that?" Smit wondered.[31]

Kruger was a typical Boer, the archetypal frontiersman, pious, puritanical, dour, headstrong and individualistic, living exclusively for the greater glory of God and for his family. He had had little schooling and was not an educated man, had grown up in a highly parochial society and did not know the ways of the world. All his life long he lived in simple style. As state president he rode to work in a coach with a mounted escort, but his wife continued to milk the cows on the land that went with his official residence in Pretoria.[32] His salary was high, but he spent very little of it. His considerable savings went to his extended family (in 1900 he had 156 children, grandchildren and great-grandchildren).[33] He was a fundamentalist who took the Bible as literally as possible. Love of freedom and religion were the ideals he shared with his sixteenth-century Dutch predecessors and exemplars. That did indeed make him an anachronism, as is so often alleged, but also the Transvaal's man of destiny.

## THE FIRST BOER WAR

Toward the end of 1880, Kruger and his burghers launched an armed rebellion against British rule and proclaimed an independent republic. The Boers laid siege to the British garrisons in Pretoria, Potchefstroom and Lydenburg, and defeated the British forces brought up from Natal at Laing's Nek and Majuba. The capture of Majuba ("Hill of Doves") by the Boers on 27 February 1881 was their greatest victory in the war. As a result, Majuba assumed a special significance. While it was a reminder to the British of a humiliating defeat, it became the symbol for the Boers and their sympathizers of a victorious struggle for independence.

These sympathizers were mainly to be found among the Boers' kinsmen in Europe and South Africa. First of all, the Transvaal enjoyed the ardent support of the Orange Free State. The Boer victory also aroused great enthusiasm in the Netherlands and led to a change of attitude there toward the Afrikaner brother nation. Originally, that attitude had been less than lukewarm. Cowardly, treacherous, hypocritical, mendacious, immoral, inhospitable, lazy, dirty and ungrateful were just some of the epithets that were applied to the Boers. Their language, Afrikaans, was "the ugliest and most hybrid dialect ever known."[34] After Majuba, however, the picture changed radically. The national anthem of the Transvaal, written by the Dutch poet Catharina van Rees, illustrated the new spirit that had gripped the Low Countries:

> Know ye the people stout of heart
> And yet so long oppressed
> Who gave their blood and gave their all
> For freedom and for right.[35]

The president of the Society for Dutch Literature, the renowned historian Robert Fruin, extolled the Boer victory at the annual meeting of the society and called Majuba the beginning of a new age, even for his own country. There was renewed hope that the Netherlands might regain its place in the world, he said, in the wake of "that memorable Sunday morning when Dutch resolve and courage on Majuba hill succeeded in turning an initial setback into brilliant victory." Even the Boers' dialect would now take a turn for the better because "with the refinement of culture, even the language, however much it may have been neglected, must return to its original purity."[36] The victory at Majuba thus led not only to a new appreciation by the Dutch of their Afrikaner cousins, but also helped to strengthen national sentiment in the Netherlands.

In the Cape Colony, similarly, the national pride of the Afrikaners was

Scottish soldiers at Majuba Hill

boosted. "The annexation of the Transvaal has taught the people of South Africa that blood is thicker than water," declared Jan Hendrik Hofmeyr, one of the leading Cape politicians.[37] "Onze Jan" ("Our Jan"; 1845–1909) came from an old Cape family. At the age of sixteen he became a journalist, and at twenty-seven editor-in-chief of the most important Dutch-language paper, *De Zuid-Afrikaan*. In 1879 he was also elected member of parliament for Stellenbosch. He championed the Dutch language and organized the Hollanders in the Cape politically. To that end he first founded the *Boeren Beschermings Vereeniging* (the Farmers' Protection Union) and later became a leading member of the *Afrikaner Bond* (the Afrikaner Alliance). He was in favor of federation but bitterly opposed to annexation and therefore to British policy in the Transvaal. Much as there was a Home Rule for Ireland movement in Britain, a Home Rule for the Transvaal movement emerged in the Cape under Hofmeyr's leadership.

After Majuba, the British government was confronted by a serious dilemma. "The question," Lord Derby said in 1884, "is do you want to create another Ireland in South Africa?"[38] The answer was no, of course. But what was the alternative? The cost of avenging the humiliating defeat would be high and the long-term effects uncertain. Gladstone's government accordingly opted for consultation and reconciliation, a course of action whose upshot was the Pretoria Convention, signed on 5 April 1881. By it, Britain recognized the independence of the Transvaal within its existing boundaries, but prohibited further expansion. The republic for its part recognized British suzerainty, symbolized by the presence of a British resident in Pretoria.

The suzerainty clause had been introduced in order to keep the British cabinet in line.[39] It was a vague term with no clear significance, and was thus able to satisfy all parties. Gladstone's critics said that "suzerainty is sovereignty with the bottom knocked out."[40] Gladstone himself explained to the House of Commons that it meant the maintenance of British influence over relations between the Transvaal and other countries, the better to protect the interests of the native population. The Boers did not wholly agree with that interpretation, nor were they entirely satisfied with the situation. At the end of 1883 Kruger, who had been president of the Transvaal since April, traveled to London to negotiate. His aim was the complete independence of the Transvaal, and this he achieved at the London Convention signed on 27 February 1884. By that convention, suzerainty was scrapped and the British resident left Pretoria. In return the British government exacted a price: the annexation of Stellaland and Goshen.

### BECHUANALAND

Stellaland and Goshen were two small states set up by freebooters from the Transvaal and Bechuanaland. These two statelets had proclaimed themselves grandly as republics. Neither was of any great importance except as part of what was to become known as the "road to the north" and was to have an important bearing on the future of the Cape Colony. If that colony was to expand, it could only do so in a northerly direction, the sea lying to the south. However, the northern frontier was beset with problems. To the west stretched the Kalahari desert, and to the east the Boer republics blocked the way. Only the region between them, Bechuanaland, still lay open. It was here, therefore, that the road to the north was to be found. It carried trade to and from the interior, and was also frequented by missionaries, whence its other name, the Missionaries' Road. But no matter what it was called, it had to be kept open, which made the determination of the western borders of the Transvaal a matter of some importance. The problem was a novel one, since the drawing of borders was an exceptional event in these parts. The Pretoria Convention, as we have said, had prohibited expansion by the Transvaal beyond the existing borders, but where exactly were they? The Boers had a cavalier attitude to such matters. They grabbed what land they could. Nor had the various conventions with Britain specified border demarcations in any great detail. When it came to the westward thrust of the Transvaal, however, this matter began to be of some practical importance. That, incidentally, was not primarily a concern of the British government. Lord Derby, colonial secretary since the end of 1882, declared, "Bechuanaland is of no value to us . . . for any Imperial purposes . . . ; it is of no consequence to us whether Boers or Native *Chiefs* are in possession."[41] But it did have a bearing on the future of the Cape Colony, and hence on British imperial collaboration in South Africa. Lord Knutsford, the later colonial secretary, was quite clear on that point: Bechuanaland "was only taken . . . on the understanding that the Cape would take it."[42] That was why the London Convention fixed the western border of the Transvaal so as to leave the road to the Cape Colony open, and that was also why Britain, several months later, in May 1884, saw fit to sign protectorate treaties with chiefs in southern Bechuanaland, which was thus brought into the British sphere of influence. The Cape Colony was not, however, keen to meet the costs of administration, and so everything devolved for the time being upon the British taxpayer.

The first deputy commissioner of the region to be appointed was John Mackenzie, a missionary and a fervent imperialist of the idealistic kind. It was his firm conviction that the British Empire had to bring the Africans under its protection so as to bring them peace, progress and Christianity. London's duty was to defend them from the racist Boers and also from the exploiters in the Cape Colony. Mackenzie was thus an imperialist, but no colonialist. Sir Hercules Robinson, the British governor-general and high commissioner in South Africa, was not greatly enamored of so much idealistic fervor, and Mackenzie was not left at his post for long. He was replaced in August 1884 by a man who was both an imperialist and a colonialist, Cecil Rhodes. The consequences were not long in coming. On 30 September 1885 Bechuanaland was incorporated into the British Empire. The southern section, between the Orange and the Molopo rivers, which was a British protectorate already, became a British crown colony. The South African Suez Canal, as Rhodes called the road to the north, was now safely in British hands. What the government of the Cape Colony had left undone, the imperial government in London carried through. "Bechu-analand was saved by 'Grandmama,' " as Rhodes put it.[43]

## TAKING STOCK

The British attitude to the First Boer War was remarkable. In an age of jingoism, nationalism, imperialism and revanchism it was highly unusual to allow a defeat to go unavenged, and to restore their liberty to a people. Ideological factors were undoubtedly at play, for Gladstone's liberal idealism was not simply a rhetorical device. However, his policy was not based on purely idealistic grounds either. It also had a practical basis. For what precisely did Britain want in South Africa? Territorial expansion was not its aim. That only involved expense and caused trouble. Expansion was up to the Cape Colony, if it felt that way inclined. Britain's own imperial objectives in Africa were limited. It aimed to govern from a distance, favoring a form of control perhaps best described as "paramountcy," a vague term whose meaning, moreover, changed more than once. It was in fact a strategic concept. Its essence was that Britain must not be threatened, that no one must be allowed to damage its interests. As far as foreign threats were concerned, that was a straightforward affair: at the time no foreign Power was trying to gain a foothold in South Africa. Only the Zulus and the Boers remained to be dealt with. Britain had settled accounts with the former in 1879, and the Transvaal had been annexed in 1877. However, because of the strong national feelings it had generated among the Boers, that annexation had proved anything but an unqualified success. After the fiasco of 1880, Lord Kimberley observed in 1882 that there could be no thought of a federation for some time. British ambition must therefore be confined to "paramountcy and influence at the Cape together with coastal dominance along the flanks of southern Africa."[44] Majuba could only be avenged and imperial influence restored at a very high price, and neither Whitehall nor Westminster was prepared to pay it. Government and Parliament alike were intent upon spending as little as possible.

The combination of the Boer longing for freedom and the British desire for an "empire on the cheap" therefore paved the way for a policy of reconciliation. Time, they thought in London, would work to Britain's advantage. The Cape Colony would develop into a self-governing but loyal colony, allied to the British Empire. It would extend its sphere of influence to the interior. In the long run the Boer republics, too, would have to make common cause with the Cape in one way or another. Progress could not be held back, after all, not even by Paul Kruger, and both British imperial and financial interests would thus be safeguarded. However, these developments presupposed two things: first, that the Cape Colony would retain its supremacy in South Africa, and second, that no foreign Power would ever think of interfering in South Africa. Neither presupposition turned out to be correct. In 1884 Germany set out along the colonial path and began to show an intrusive interest in South Africa as well. Two years later gold was discovered on the Witwatersrand. With that the center of power in South Africa shifted from the Cape to the Transvaal, and British imperial strategy collapsed like a house of cards.

# 2
# FOREIGNERS AND GOLD STRIKES, 1884–1886

### GERMANY AND SOUTHERN AFRICA

Ever since Britain had acquired the Cape from the Netherlands, no other European power had interfered in South Africa. The Portuguese had laid claim to the coasts of Angola and Mozambique, but apart from the Boer republics, the whole of southern Africa had remained untouched by foreign influences. This was all to change when Germany took to colonialism.

It began in South-West Africa, where German missionaries had long been at work. Their attempts to introduce civilization and Christianity were more than somewhat frustrated by the continual clashes between two nomadic peoples, the Hereros and the Hottentots. Trade played its part in stoking this conflict with the sale of arms and strong liquor. Neither the German nor the British government could or would guarantee their missionaries effective protection; South-West Africa was considered a region not even fit for a penal colony.[45] The only commercial attraction was the presence of rich guano deposits on the offshore islands. In the 1840s there was a trading boom in this type of bird excrement. Hundreds of ships dropped anchor off the South-West African coast and rival guano collectors took to pelting one another regularly with rotten penguin eggs.[46] The fact that South-West Africa was to have a different destiny was due to the German trader Franz Lüderitz.

Franz Adolf Eduard Lüderitz (1834–1886), like so many African businessmen, was an adventurer. He had not had much of an education but had traveled a great deal, roaming through the United States and Mexico. His father was a rich tobacco merchant in Bremen, and when he died in 1878 he left his son a considerable fortune. The son then met a young compatriot called Heinrich Vogelsang who had also inherited a tobacco fortune, albeit a more modest one, and who was equally bored. The two, deciding that their future lay in Africa, bought a 260-ton brig, the *Tilly*, and loaded it with goods for barter. Before the *Tilly* sailed, Vogelsang had gone to South Africa to acquaint himself with the commercial prospects. The *Tilly* itself arrived in late March 1883, and Vogelsang then sailed in it to Angra Pequeña, having taken the precaution of giving the port authorities a false destination. He arrived in Angra Pequeña in April, put up a prefabricated hut and named it "Fort Vogelsang."[47] On 1 May he bought the "Bay Agra Peguena and the adjacent land 5 (five) miles in all directions" from the Hottentot chief Joseph Fredericks, on behalf of the Lüderitz company. The price was 200 rand (approximately £100) and 200 rifles. On 12 May he hoisted the German flag over Fort Vogelsang and wired Lüderitz: "Land acquired from chief against single payment."[48]

That was just the beginning. In 1883 a new treaty was signed in which the borders of Lüderitzland, as it was now called, were far more impressively defined as stretching from the Orange River to 26° S. The new territory extended from 100 kilometers north to 300 kilometers south of Angra Pequeña, with a depth of what Chief Fredericks called 20 miles. He meant British miles, but the Germans insisted that the treaty referred to German miles, equal to 7.5 kilometers each, thus laying claim to 150 instead of about 30 kilometers.[49] Lüderitz had now become a neighbor of the Cape colonists, and the latter protested. Their feelings were expressed unequivocally in an address to Lord Salisbury, which ended with, "My Lord, we are told that the Germans are good neighbours, but we prefer to have no neighbours at all."[50]

The problem, of course, was what the German and British governments would do with the wild plans of their subject on the one hand and the xenophobic reactions of their colonists on the other. As far as the first were concerned, the German government made it known on 18 August 1883 that Lüderitz could count on the Reich's consular assistance and protection. In September Berlin notified London of Lüderitz's land purchase. At the same time, Berlin inquired if Britain had any claims to the area and, if so, on what grounds.

It is not certain whether Bismarck had already decided to annex the territory when he took these preliminary steps. Perhaps he was simply trying to establish that there were no other claims and to leave the question of sovereignty open.[51] Britain, in any case, still believed firmly in Bismarck's indifference to colonies. That explains London's peculiar reaction. The British reply was that Britain had no claims, save to Walvis Bay and the islands off Angra Pequeña, but would consider the claims of any third parties an infringement of Britain's "legitimate rights."[52] That was not a clear reply, though certainly an arrogant one, which could only be explained by Britain's surprise at Bismarck's question. Needless to say, the British answer did not satisfy Bismarck, who asked for further elucidation. Britain promised to look into the matter, but six months later there was still no unequivocal answer. That annoyed Bismarck, and in April 1884, when Lüderitz again asked urgently for protection because he had heard that the Cape Colony wanted to annex Angra Pequeña, Bismarck decided to act. On 24 April 1884 he informed London and Cape Town that the protection of the German Reich (*Reichsschutz*) had been extended to Lüderitz. Many people have looked on that as the date of birth of the German colonial empire, but London did not share that view, at least at first. Instead, Britain considered the proclamation of the *Reichsschutz* as no more than a form of personal protection, which had been promised to Lüderitz before, and not as the establishment of a protectorate. That was precisely Bismarck's intention, for he was not yet prepared to inform London of his conversion to colonialism, but hoped to be able to establish a few more claims before anyone realized what he was up to.[53]

The British government now found itself in a quandary. The territory itself was of no interest to London, but it would never do to leave the Cape Colony in the lurch by doing nothing about the latest German steps. However, the Cape government did not really know what it wanted, or rather it did know, but what it wanted was unacceptable: annexation without responsibility. It accordingly asked London to annex the entire coastal strip as far as Walvis Bay. The British government eventually agreed, but wanted to have the territory added to the Cape Colony, in which case the Cape government would be responsible for maintaining law and order in the area. That would mean that even the German traders would enjoy adequate protection and be able to pursue their business in peace. It had still not dawned on Britain that Germany was bent on annexation. However, the Cape government demurred, largely because of local political difficulties. "They cried out like children for it," said a British official, "and now that it is offered to them they hesitate to take it."[54]

So time passed, as Bismarck approvingly watched his consul, Gustav Nachtigal, winning the treaty-signing race in West Africa with the British consul, Edward Hewett. In June 1884 Bismarck sent his son Herbert to London for a long overdue clarification of the issue. Germany did indeed want to establish a protectorate over South-West Africa. To Bismarck's surprise, Lord Granville, the foreign secretary, who was only too glad to wash his hands of the whole business, raised no objection. Thus a long period of confusion drew to an end. On 7 August 1884 came the official declaration that the German Reich was annexing Angra Pequeña. Soon afterwards the annexation was extended to the entire coastal area between the Cape Colony and Portuguese Angola. A thousand kilometers of Africa's coastland were now in German hands. The first governor of German South-West Africa was Dr. Heinrich Goering, whose son, Hermann, was later to gain greater notoriety.

It soon became obvious that Germany would not stop at South-West Africa. Toward the end of 1884 a German reconnaissance party crossed St. Lucia Bay, in southeast Africa, its leader, Dr. A. F. Schiel, clad in Prussian army uniform.[55] Had Schiel's expedition resulted in the establishment of a German colony in southeast Africa, a major strategic problem would have been created, as British South Africa would, so to speak, have been caught between German spheres of influence in the west and the east. Moreover, a German East Africa might have reached an understanding with the Transvaal and offered the republic the access to the sea Britain wanted to prevent at any cost. The British response was not slow in coming. On 18 December 1884 Britain annexed St. Lucia Bay. The scramble for South Africa had begun in earnest.

The liberal little Englanders in Gladstone's cabinet watched these developments with composure. They were neither anti-German nor expansionist. "I don't mean to be pedantic," Gladstone said, ". . . but I would welcome the Germans as our neighbours in South Africa, and even as neighbours in the Transvaal."[56] On Boxing Day 1884 Lord Granville, the foreign secretary, wrote to Lord Derby, his colleague in the Colonial Office, that there was something ludicrous about the general race for colonies and that he wished Britain could be kept out of it. "We are not jealous of Germany."[57] Lord Derby replied two days later. He, too, saw "something absurd" in the scramble for colonies but, he added, there was a difference between fresh conquests and hanging on to what was yours. The Cape as well as Natal would be endangered were the coast between the two colonies to fall into foreign hands. Though the territory had not been assigned to Britain by international law, it was British de facto and must stay that way. The entire coast of South Africa, from the Orange River in the west to the Portuguese possessions in the east, he concluded, had to remain under British influence.[58]

The British government was not imperialist, and British interests did not call for annexations in South Africa. The British attitude in this area during these years was defensive in character and strategic in design. Even the later arch-imperialist Joseph Chamberlain said in September 1884 that for imperial purposes Britain needed no more territory in South Africa than Cape Town and the bay, a second Gibraltar, in other words.[59] The problem was that Cape Town was no Gibraltar but the center of an extensive colony with a mixed population. Moreover, this colony was competing with others for influence over the interior. That was why successive British governments, be they liberal or conservative, made up of little Englanders or imperialists, became increasingly involved in the problems of South Africa. No matter how absurd it all may have looked to Granville or Derby, there was no way back. With German intervention in southern Africa, the partition of this part of Africa was truly under way. Internal developments in South Africa were soon to accelerate this process.

## GOLD

One factor was even more important for the future of South Africa than the wishes of the Iron Chancellor, and that was the discovery of gold on the Witwatersrand. It had, of course, been known well before 1884 that the Transvaal was a rich source of minerals, and of gold in particular. As early as 13 November 1879 Wolseley had written to Hicks Beach, the then colonial secretary, "The Transvaal is rich in minerals; gold has already been found in quantities, and there can be little doubt that larger and still more valuable gold-fields will sooner or later be discovered."[60] Such discoveries, Sir Garnet continued, would undoubtedly attract a large English population to the Transvaal. The Boers would in the long run become the minority, the country being thinly populated. As a result, a pro-British majority would arise in the Transvaal and the basis be laid for its incorporation in the British Empire. In the meantime, Britain would have to consolidate its position and maintain its authority.

Wolseley predicted the consequences of the gold discoveries correctly, and many of the developments would indeed follow the course he had outlined. But there was one important difference. Wolseley had written his letter in order to drive home the point that Britain would meanwhile have to stand by the annexation of the Transvaal. That was, however, something Britain was unable or unwilling to do after Majuba. Hence by the time the gold rush started the Transvaal was no longer a British colony but a Boer republic, and the basis of Wolseley's plan had been swept away. In 1884 the Struben brothers demonstrated that gold could be mined in the Witwatersrand in commercially viable quantities. Two years later the Main Reef was discovered, and the gold rush began.

Though South Africa's gold and diamonds are often mentioned in one breath, gold mining on the Rand was not comparable to diamond mining in Kimberley. In Kimberley everything had started with individual speculators, and it was not until later that mergers led to the creation of large syndicates capable of exploiting the deeper layers. On the Rand, large enterprises were needed from the outset with enough capital to buy the land, explore the ground and construct the mines. The gold was extracted from deep layers of conglomerate which the Dutch charmingly nicknamed "banket," after a traditional Christmas sweetmeat containing almonds of which they were reminded. The gold-bearing strata were sometimes more than a kilometer below the surface. Shafts had to be sunk and lifts installed. Gunpowder and dynamite were needed, as well as coal to run the steam engines and steam trains. Coal, fortunately, was found locally in large quantities; gunpowder and dynamite had to be imported. Capital and labor were the crucial factors.

Capital was readily raised. The London and New York stock exchanges were only too happy to supply the necessary funds. The expanding world economy was crying out for gold. Workers, too, appeared in large numbers, attracted to the Rand not by the thousands, but by the ten thousands. Johannesburg was the world's fastest growing city. On 17 July 1896, ten years after its founding, a census was held—opposed incidentally by President Kruger on biblical grounds—which showed that the white population numbered just over 50,000. A mere 6,000 of these were Transvaalers, the others having arrived from all over the globe. Sixteen thousand had come from Great Britain and 15,000 from the Cape. The rest included 3,000 Russian Jews, 2,000 Germans, and 800 Netherlanders. The colored, or mixed-race, population was roughly the same size. The census also listed 42,000 Natives (Bantus) and 5,000 "Asians and others," a total population, therefore, of more than 100,000.[61] In just over ten years the white population of South Africa increased from 600,000 to more than a million. Gold had created a new white South Africa.

This new Babel amazed visitors from abroad. An English lady, describing her trip to Johannesburg in 1889, wrote: "Never in the history of the universe was such an extraordinary city conceived or carried out as Johannesburg. . . . Day after day comes the news of fresh discoveries. . . . We are simply living in a sea of gold."[62] In a stable, closed, puritanical and pastoral society there had thus arisen a city replete with all the vices of modern civilization. Sir William Butler, British commander-in-chief in South Africa, called Johannesburg a "Monte Carlo superimposed on Sodom and Gomorrah."[63]

The gold strikes also had massive economic repercussions. The Transvaal had until then been an agricultural country, divorced economically from the rest of the world. Within a few years it was producing 20 percent of the world's gold, and calculations showed that it owned 25 percent of the world gold supplies. The total value of South African exports doubled between 1886 and 1896, gold accounting for more than half of the increase. Gold shares enjoyed a prodigious popularity. From 1888 to 1889 there was a real boom, and the London Stock Exchange was dominated by the "Kaffir Circus."[64] Not only was there an explosion of Transvaal exports, but imports swelled as well. A large number of commodities had to be brought in from abroad to sustain the mining industry and to supply the growing population with food and the all-important alcohol. Mining and industry stimulated trade and transport. The Transvaal had become the economic heart of South Africa. The future of the Cape Colony would from then on depend upon its relations with the Transvaal, and hence Britain's imperial future in South Africa, too, became largely dependent on the policy of the Kruger government.

Within a brief span of time the elements of the South African equation had been drastically transformed. The economic and political center had shifted from Cape Town to Johannesburg and Pretoria. Germany, Europe's strongest Power, had established itself in South-West Africa and shown interest in southeast Africa. If the Transvaal was not prepared to accept British leadership, then Britain's entire future in South Africa would be jeopardized. In view of what had gone before, Britain could not count on a great deal of sympathy from the Transvaalers. The gold discoveries, however, had also introduced a factor favorable to Britain. Wolseley's prediction had come true: by virtue of the continuous influx of foreign immigrants, the Boers were indeed becoming a minority. The replacement of recalcitrant Boers with anglophile newcomers would thus result, not from outside pressure but from inevitable developments inside the Transvaal. For the time being, "uitlanders," foreigners, admittedly did not have full citizens' rights in the Transvaal, but in the long run their political claims would prove irresistible. Now, once these foreign workers became full citizens, the political power of Kruger's Boers would be broken. In the view of many observers, time was thus working in Britain's favor and it was all just a question of being patient. However, there were also those without patience, for whom things were not moving nearly fast enough, and who, moreover, looked beyond South Africa. One of these was Cecil Rhodes.

## 3
# RHODES AND RHODESIA, 1890–1893

### CECIL RHODES

Cecil John Rhodes did not live to a ripe old age. He was born on 5 July 1853 in Bishop's Stortford, Hertfordshire, not far north of London, and died on 26 March 1902 in Muizenberg, South Africa. He thus never made his half century. Cecil was one of many children, the sixth to be precise, born to the vicar of Bishop's Stortford. His father came from a good family, and after Harrow and Trinity College, Cambridge, devoted his life to the church. He was known as "the good Mr. Rhodes." Cecil himself did not go to public school but attended the local grammar school and left for South Africa when he was not yet seventeen, not so much because his health was poor, as has often been claimed, as in order to make his fortune. He was following in the footsteps of his brother Herbert,[65] who was trying to grow cotton on a farm in the interior of Natal. Cotton-growing was also Cecil's first job before he made for the diamond fields in October 1871. Among the few books he took with him to Kimberley were Marcus Aurelius's *Meditations* and Gibbon's *Decline and Fall of the Roman Empire*, surprising reading for a fortune hunter.

The Kimberley diamond fields were to become the foundation of Rhodes's wealth, and ultimately of his political power. Here Rhodes met not only his later associate and collaborator Dr. Leander Starr Jameson, but also his fellow fortune-seeker, Charles Dunell Rudd. Rudd, who, unlike Rhodes but like the latter's father, had gone to Harrow and Trinity, had excelled there at athletics and especially at running the mile. According to his own testimony, he had gone out to South Africa to help restore his overtrained lungs to health.[66] Rudd and Rhodes were both without means.

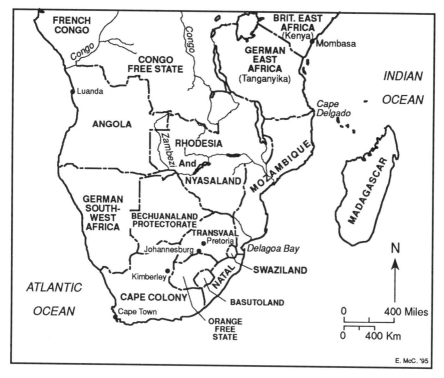

Southern Africa

What little money they had they invested in various enterprises, not all of which were connected with mining. Thus these two empire-builders to be made their first profit from the sale of ices and cold drinks, in great demand during the hot months. Another venture was pumping water from flooded mines. Pumping and ice cream, together with diamonds, thus constituted the basis of their first fortune. By the time Rhodes returned home in 1873 to go to Oxford, he was already a rich man.

He went to Oxford to improve his education, as befitted a man of his background, intellect and ambition. But Oxford had social as well as intellectual attractions. There he could meet the caliber of man he would need and with whom he liked to associate. Rhodes was unable to devote all his time to his studies, of course, since he also had his business, and commuted between beautiful Oxford and Kimberley, of which, Trollope wrote, "I know no spot more odious."[67] Still, Kimberley, too, had its advantages. With mechanization of the mines came expansion and the emergence of a game at which Rhodes proved to be a master: the game of mergers. His nickname became "the great amalgamator." His greatest suc-

Cecil Rhodes

cess was the creation of the De Beers Consolidated Mining Company, which was to become the most powerful South African diamond concern and was to control 90 percent of the world's diamond production. His chief competitor was the former conjuror and prize-fighter Barney Barnato, but even this "cunning little Jew," as Rhodes called him, could not stand up to the combination of Rhodes and Rothschild, and ultimately joined them.[68]

After diamonds came politics. In 1881 Rhodes not only took his B.A. at Oxford, but also his seat in the Cape Assembly as the member for Barkly West. Political activities did not impede his large-scale expansion projects. In 1889 his British South Africa Company was granted a royal charter, by virtue of which it was later able to subject the whole of Rhodesia. Besides his roles as diamond king and politician, Rhodes was now also a conquistador. A year later he became prime minister of the Cape Colony, in which new role, as head of government of a civilized country, he had to keep to the rules and observe the law. That was something Rhodes found difficult to do, as the Jameson Raid was to demonstrate in 1895. The Raid was in the best tradition of desperados and conquistadors, but did not befit Rhodes's new role of statesman and politician, the less so as it misfired. The failure of the Jameson Raid proved to be Rhodes's political downfall.

He resigned his premiership and from then on was to follow and influence politics from the sidelines alone. Cecil Rhodes died during the Boer War, before his great aim, the subjection of the Boer republics, had been achieved.

A man like Rhodes was bound to give rise to legend, adulation and denunciation. His was an exceptional personality, singular in all respects. His appearance was as impressive as his appetite, his drinking and his smoking. He took champagne before lunch and before dinner, and at meals would mix it with stout. Keir Hardie called him a "confirmed drunkard—a dipsomaniac."[69] He loved no woman other than his mother; Rhodes's household consisted of men alone, and all his secretaries were attractive young men. This has naturally given rise to much speculation. It seems quite certain that he was homosexual, but what followed from this fact is not known. In any case he did not allow his sexual predilections to influence his politics. Rhodes's country estate in Grote Schuur was impressive but not ostentatious. His bedroom was austere and enlivened only by a portrait of Bismarck. His bathroom was of gigantic proportions, constructed of green and white marble; the bath itself was eight feet long and hewn from massive granite. Rhodes had an obsession with bathing and shaving. No matter where he was—at home, in a tent, in the open air or on a train—his ablutions were never forgotten.

Rhodes's passion, however, was neither washing nor bathing, nor was it directed at his handsome secretaries. His greatest passion was the British Empire. "All this to be painted red; that is my dream," he once remarked, pointing at the map of Africa.[70] Yet his ambitions were not confined to Africa; he believed that the British Empire must also embrace the Holy Land, the seaboard of China and Japan, the Pacific Ocean and South America—as we see from his "Last Will and Testament," drawn up in 1877.[71] Rhodes was an enthusiastic maker of wills and left a large number behind him. In one of them, dated 1888, he left almost his entire fortune to Lord Rothschild. This was somewhat surprising, since the beneficiary was by no means short of money. Rothschild had, however, been singled out for a special mission: to use the money in order to establish a secret order, the Society of the Elect for the Good of Empire. It was to be modeled on the Society of Jesus. "Take the constitution of the Jesuits if obtainable and insert 'English Empire' for 'Roman Catholic religion,' " were Rhodes's simple instructions.[72] It seems unlikely that Rhodes himself had ever read the constitution of the Jesuit order, nor is it even clear what he knew about its objectives. Probably, like so many others, he had been impressed by the *Macht und Geheimnis der Jesuiten* (the Power and Secret of the Jesuits).

Rhodes lacked a consistent political philosophy. Hofmeyr considered him "a regular beefsteak, John Bull Englishman."[73] He was a social imperialist and considered the acquisition of new land and new markets an essential means of avoiding social tension and civil war. His ideas were shaped by

Rhodes monument in Cape Town

the classics and also by the writings of Gibbon, Darwin, Ruskin and Spencer. He was greatly impressed by Winwood Reade's *The Martyrdom of Man*, first published in 1872. Reade had previously written several unsuccessful novels, had made three great voyages to Africa without being acknowledged as an explorer, and had died in 1875 at the age of thirty-seven. The *Martyrdom of Man* was to earn him great fame, albeit posthumously. It was a sweeping cultural history of mankind, presented under the headings of war, religion, freedom and intellect. Its most striking feature was its break with the Eurocentric historiography so characteristic of the time and the stress it laid on the importance of Africa. Rhodes was deeply impressed by its message.

Rhodes's own theories were unclear, his daydreams Utopian, and his fantasies grandiose. That was nothing very unusual. A great many dreams have been spun beneath the dreaming spires of Oxford, as well as in the tents of gold and diamond prospectors, certainly during that age of imperialism when no limits to growth had yet been set. The unusual thing about Rhodes is that he translated his dreams into plans and his plans into action. The greatest of these actions was undoubtedly the expansion toward the north. It culminated in the establishment of a colony measuring not far short of 400,000 square miles, larger than Spain, France and Benelux put together.

### RHODESIA

The British annexation of Bechuanaland in 1885 had secured the road to the north. With it, a wedge had been driven between German South-West Africa and the Transvaal. The British sphere of influence now extended as far as the Zambezi, and access to the great lakes had been kept open. At the same time it had also become possible to encircle the Transvaal by further British expansion toward the north. The northern frontier of the Transvaal was the Limpopo. Above it lay a territory vaguely referred to as North and South Zambezia, the boundary between these two being the Zambezi River. The southern region lay in the temperate zone and was deemed suitable for white colonization. Above it lay tropical Africa, unsuited to white inhabitation but nevertheless of importance because it provided access to British East Africa. Southern Zambezia comprised Matabeleland and Mashonaland, so named after their most important peoples, whose subjection was of strategic importance to Britain.

The Matabele had previously lived in the Transvaal but had been driven out by the trekboers. They had then withdrawn beyond the Limpopo, and in about 1838 had made Bulawayo their capital. They controlled a large area, the frontiers of which were uncertain and moreover kept changing, but included almost the whole of what is now Zimbabwe, parts of northern Botswana and, across the Zambezi, stretched into western Zambia. Their empire had been built on conquest and was based on "brutal tyranny" over the people they had subjected.[74] That, at least, was how observers described it at the time. In fact the Matabele were not nearly as dominant as they seemed to be, their subject people continuing to pose a threat to them.[75]

These subject people included the Mashona. Their land, in the northeast of what is now Zimbabwe, was believed to be very rich in gold; a German traveler was convinced that it was the biblical Ophir, and Rider Haggard used it as the setting for *King Solomon's Mines*.[76] This, of course, rendered it highly attractive to many Europeans, and the weakness of the Matabele empire could therefore be said to have lain in its alleged wealth. The king himself, however, dismissed all the theories about the rich gold deposits of his country as nonsense. Gold is not hidden away in rivers, he told an English visitor, "gold is found in stones." "The king," the visitor concluded, "did not grasp the point of our geological arguments."[77]

This king was Lobengula, the formidable chief of the Matabele. He made a great impression on visitors. "A very fine man, only very fat," is how Rudd, Rhodes's emissary, described him, "with a beautiful skin and well-proportioned."[78] He measured six feet tall, was extremely corpulent and went about dressed in animal skins. He was in the habit of devouring huge quantities of half-cooked meat, washed down with kaffir beer. "Very much like a wild beast," Rudd went on to remark. He described the king's expression as partly apprehensive, partly happy, and partly cruel, but added that Lobengula had a "very pleasant smile."[79] An imposing figure, "every inch a king," as another observer remarked.[80]

The particulars of Rhodes's plans for Matabeleland were first presented in the *Times* on 11 November 1885.[81] Rhodes urged the British government to reach an agreement with Lobengula and to establish a British protectorate over Matabeleland. The British government, however, had other matters to consider. It did not even know who Rhodes was. "Rather a pro-Boer M.P. in South Africa, I fancy," was all Lord Salisbury had to say about him.[82] Lord Knutsford, the colonial secretary, thought he knew more. He wrote a detailed letter to Salisbury about Rhodes and his activities, but had later to confess somewhat sheepishly that he had confused Rhodes with a man by the name of Bower.[83]

Yet, while Rhodes may have been unknown in London, he had many influential friends in South Africa, among them Sir Hercules Robinson, the British governor and high commissioner, and Sir Sidney Shippard, deputy commissioner in Bechuanaland. Rhodes, moreover, had money, which for the British government was in short supply. Or rather, the government did not want to apply to Parliament for funds to go into Matabeleland. Once again the chartered company formula provided the answer. It brought together two completely different men: Salisbury, the aristocratic, cool, worldly and detached analyst of power politics, a man who considered Africa a continent made for scatterbrains, and Rhodes, the self-made upstart, the romantic and idealist in whose dreams Africa presided over the future of the British race. "Rhodes is a great Jingo," said Sir William Harcourt, "but then he is a cheap Jingo." In that second epithet lay Rhodes's greatest asset as far as Lord Salisbury was concerned.[84]

On 30 April 1889 Rhodes, Beit and Rudd informed the British government that they were prepared to collaborate with it in developing the territory north of the Cape Colony. The letter was written on paper headed "The Gold Fields of South Africa, Limited."[85] The British government responded positively and granted the British South Africa Company (BSAC) a charter on 29 October 1889. The company was authorized to sign treaties with, and to acquire land from, African native chiefs. It had to agree to combat trading in slaves and liquor and to respect native religions. Its operating territory was as good as unconfined, being described as lying "north of British Bechuanaland, north and west of the South African Republic (the Transvaal) and west of the Portuguese dominions." The German possessions and the Congo Free State were not mentioned. What was mainly involved, of course, was the territory south of the Zambezi, but no northern border was stipulated. The company would have to see to that. It had a capital of 1 million pounds sterling and was ready to set to work. In legal respects the document left much to be desired. Its flaws were to become patent later, but by then it had become politically impossible to abrogate the charter. That would have meant direct control by London, entailing great costs, "besides," Harcourt remarked, "[our] having to do all the slaughtering ourselves."[86]

### THE PIONEERS

The company did not have to start from scratch; the foundations had been laid previously. A year before the charter was granted, Charles Rudd, Rhodes's old friend and confidant, had visited Lobengula and had talked him into signing a treaty. By it, Lobengula received £100 per month, plus a thousand Martini-Henry rifles with a hundred thousand cartridges, and either a steamboat on the Zambezi or another £500. In exchange Rhodes and Rudd were granted what became known as the Rudd Concession, that is, "the complete and exclusive charge over all metals and minerals situated and contained in my Kingdom, Principalities and Dominions, together with full power to do all things that they may deem necessary to win and procure the same."[87] No other party was to be granted similar rights and concessions. The treaty ended, "This given under my hand this thirtieth day of October in the year of our Lord eighteen hundred and eighty-eight at my Royal Kraal," and was signed with Lobengula's mark.[88]

Understandably, Rhodes was very enthusiastic. "Our concession is so gigantic, it is like giving a man the whole of Australia," he wrote to Rudd.[89] For since Rudd had been given "the full power to do all things . . . necessary," no limit was set to the powers and efforts of the concessionaires. Lobengula took a different view. He claimed that all he had granted Rudd was "the right to dig in one hole."[90] Whether that was what he had really meant is open to question. Negotiations had been protracted, and the rifles he had received were of considerable value to him, but it seems quite certain that Lobengula had never intended to wind up his empire. Yet that was precisely what was about to happen.

On 1 July 1890 a large column of pioneers crossed the Shashi River into Matabeleland. Rhodes had made sure that this column included many

BSAC pioneers on the way to Mashonaland

young men from good families. If anything were to happen to them, their fate would not leave the British government unmoved.[91] On 12 September the column reached its objective, a hill in Mashonaland. The order of the day read as follows: "1) It is notified for general information that the Column, having arrived at its destination, will halt. 2) The name of this place will be Fort Salisbury." Next morning the British flag was raised on a newly cut flagpole, and after a salute and prayers the country was solemnly incorporated into the British Empire. The ceremony ended with three cheers to Her Majesty. The foundations of Rhodesia had been laid.[92]

However, Rhodes's ambitions were not confined to Matabeleland and Mashonaland. His motto could be summed up, in a variation on the American saying, as "Go north, young man." And north was where Rhodes's young men went. His agents crossed Zambezia in impetuous haste, signing treaties right and left, then rushed on over the Zambezi toward Lake Nyasa. The charter had not, after all, specified any northern boundary. In legal terms these treaties left much to be desired, but they were no less effective for that. This tempestuous expansion inevitably brought Rhodes, and with him the British government, into conflict with Portugal, Britain's oldest ally. For Rhodes's implementation of the Cape-to-Cairo dream spelled the end of the Portuguese *contra costa* dream, the vision combining Angola and Mozambique into one vast Portuguese empire in southern Africa.

### PORTUGAL AND RHODESIA

The plans for a great Portuguese empire in southern Africa had, of course, been dealt a severe blow when British authority over Bechuanaland had been established in 1885. The second blow came in 1899 when the British government granted Rhodes's company a charter, thus paving the way for British expansion across the Zambezi. With this, the possibility of joining up Angola and Mozambique had as good as vanished, but Portugal naturally still hoped to make its colonial empire as large as possible. As far as Angola was concerned, the coastal boundaries were a matter for Portugal to settle with Germany in the south and with the Congo Free State in the north. The southern borders presented no difficulties, but in the north conflicts with Leopold continually arose. In 1891, however, the parties sat around a negotiating table and agreement was reached. As for the Mozambique coast, its southern boundaries had been agreed with Britain in 1875, and its northern boundaries with Germany in 1886. The most important negotiations, however, bore on the interior boundaries, that is, on the eastern boundary of Angola and the western boundary of Mozambique.

The expansion spearheaded by Rhodes's company led to several disagreements with Portugal. First there was Barotseland, which Rhodes claimed on the basis of the so-called Lochner concession, but to which Portugal laid claim as well. The issue here was the eastern boundary of Angola. More important was the problem of the borders of Mozambique resulting from attempts to provide Northern Rhodesia with access to the Indian Ocean. The bone of contention here was the Shire Highlands in southern Nyasaland, where another British company was operating. However, Rhodes's intervention created new opportunities for the British government. The dispute over the Shire Highlands led to an Anglo-Portuguese crisis and ultimately to a major Anglo-Portuguese deal with respect to southern Africa.

The main importance of the Shire Highlands was that their possession would help Britain to keep the possibility of the Cape-to-Cairo route open. Salisbury, the British prime minister, was not at first particularly interested in their future. The Shire Highlands were not a region of any importance. The issue did, however, have a politically sensitive aspect: Scottish missionaries were active in the region, and the British public would take it amiss if these missionaries were allowed to fall under the jurisdiction of Catholic Portugal. The Portuguese appetite for expansion made this a real threat. Moreover, Salisbury considered the Portuguese claims to the Highlands to be ludicrous. "Lord Salisbury utterly rejects the archaeological arguments of the Portuguese," he wrote in a memorandum to the queen.[93] The picture changed even more, as far as Salisbury was concerned, when Cecil Rhodes seemed prepared to shoulder most of the administrative costs in the region. The British trading company operating there, the African Lakes Company, was in no position to take these on. According to Harry Johnston, it was no more than a "miserable grocery business."[94] Salisbury now dispatched the man who had uttered that phrase to the area with orders to sign treaties and to establish a British protectorate. Portugal had meanwhile drawn up a plan for an expedition of its own to the same destination, and was proud enough, but also unwise enough, to proceed with it even when Britain had made it known that it had already set up a protectorate. The British government reacted with an ultimatum: Portugal must recall the expedition without further ado. When Portugal did so, the two parties sat down to negotiate a partition treaty.

On the British side the negotiations were conducted by Salisbury, on the Portuguese side by one of the most colorful figures in the diplomatic corps at the Court of St. James, the Marquis de Soveral. Soveral had been an ambassador to London for what was even then considered a long time, during which he had made his way in London society, and in particular had formed a close friendship with the Prince of Wales. Soveral's interest in women surpassed even that of this legendary "prince of pleasure." Although his nickname, "the blue monkey," which he owed to his ever-present dark stubble, does not suggest great physical attraction, his success with women was considerable.[95] Soveral was therefore, to put it conservatively, quite a different type from Lord Salisbury, but he, too, was indisputably a shrewd diplomat. The end result of the negotiations he led turned out to be not at all bad for his country, certainly not if one remembers that Portugal held none of the trump cards. The convention signed on 20 August 1890 even preserved part of the old *contra costa* dream, Portugal being granted a link between Angola and Mozambique through a narrow corridor to be placed under joint supervision. However, this concession did not satisfy the Portuguese. In particular, there was a great patriotic outcry against the clause debarring Portugal from ceding any territory south of the Zambezi without British consent. That clause, after all, questioned the status of Portugal as a sovereign state. The Cortes accordingly refused to ratify the treaty, the government fell, and a number of months elapsed before tempers cooled. Then new negotiations were started and a new treaty was drafted, ratified in the Portuguese parliament with a big majority, and signed by the king on 11 June 1891. The new treaty was less favorable to Portugal than the old. The corridor was scrapped and with it the *contra costa* idea was buried for good. Portugal may have gained more territory north of the Zambezi than had previously been stipulated, but Rhodes was handed most of Manikaland. Moreover, Angola's eastern frontier was pushed back toward the sea, Rhodes receiving the whole of Barotseland instead of the half that had originally been allocated to him.

The treaty of 11 June 1891 was a turning point in the history of Portuguese Africa. Great territorial dreams had been dashed forever; Portugal was simply too poor and too weak to continue entertaining them. Even so, what Portugal did receive was sizable enough. After all, the treaty gave Angola and Mozambique rights to the greater part of the hinterland. In the end, Mozambique was almost one and a half times, and Angola almost two and half times, the size of France.

The British South Africa Company, too, benefited from the 1891 treaty. What Portugal had lost in comparison with the 1890 treaty now went to the company. One thing, however, Rhodes failed to obtain: the fervently desired access to the sea. Still, the company was given the right to use the Zambezi and its tributaries for transport to the coast, and Portugal undertook to build a railroad from the port of Beira to the company's territory. The borders between Northern Rhodesia and Nyasaland were fixed by an agreement between the BSAC and the British government in February 1891. The BSAC was authorized to extend its influence north of the Zambezi, but not over Nyasaland. On 14 May 1891 the Nyasaland Districts were officially declared a British protectorate. The BSAC, which had meanwhile swallowed up the Lakes Company, subsidized the new protectorate to the tune of £10,000 per annum. Rhodes's hope of bringing that territory, too, under the control of the company was not realized, for he came up against Harry Johnston, the no less ambitious British commissioner in the area. Rhodes planned to force Johnston into cooperation by cutting off the subsidy. "I am not going to create with my funds an independent King Johnston over the Zambezi," he declared.[96] Johnston, who like his colleagues received scarcely any funds from the British government, and who had to run the territory with just a handful of men, found himself cornered, but just when things were at their worst he was saved: the British government at long last produced enough money to keep the administration going. Rhodes's gamble had not come off, and Nyasaland remained a separate protectorate.

The agreements with Portugal and the creation of Nyasaland gave Rhodesia—the term that replaced Zambezia, which gradually dropped out of common usage—its final frontiers. The name "Rhodesia" was first used in 1891 to refer to what had until then been called Matabeleland. A little later, the term was used to denote all the land between the Transvaal and Tanganyika, Nyasaland excepted. In 1897 the name Rhodesia was officially recognized. "Well, you know," said Rhodes, "to have a bit of country named after one is one of the things a man might be proud of."[97] That was modestly put, because the "bit of country" was almost four times the size of Great Britain.

The Matabele had meanwhile been given short shrift. The score with them was settled on 1 November 1893, twenty miles from the capital, Bulawayo. Maxim guns had ensured that eight hundred Matabele were killed at a cost of only three white lives. On 4 November 1893 the capital fell. Lobengula fled to the north and committed suicide.[98] After the failure of the Jameson Raid, the Matabele managed to take brief advantage of the temporary power vacuum, and a rebellion broke out, but it was all no more than an epilogue. The Matabele had been defeated for good in 1893. Rhodes now came up against a more formidable adversary: Paul Kruger's Boers.

# 4
# RHODES VS. KRUGER

### HARBORS AND RAILROADS

Cecil Rhodes was no enemy of the Boers. In the Cape he collaborated closely with Jan Hofmeyr, the leader of the powerful Afrikaner Bond, the Rhodes-Hofmeyr tandem running the colony for a long time. Hofmeyr was the man who discovered in 1881 that blood was thicker than water, and he accordingly supported the cause of the two Boer republics in the Cape. Rhodes was not opposed to the republics either. His philosophy—if that is the word for it—was based on the supremacy of the Germanic race. Britons and Americans—whose rupture in 1776 he considered a tragic historical mistake—were destined to lead the world with the support of the Germans and other Teutonic peoples. In the "last will and testament" that was actually to be his last, Rhodes left most of his fortune to a fund enabling young Americans, but also Germans, to study at Oxford: "Young settlers, no bookworms," he stipulated.[99] Rhodes's political plans for South Africa did not overlook the Boers. "The Dutch are the coming race in South Africa and they must have their share in running the country," he had declared long before Majuba.[100] He meant in collaboration with the British, of course, and within the British Empire. His aim was an imperial federation. The future of the British Empire lay in the collaboration of self-governing units. The Boer republics ought to combine with the British colonies in South Africa to form a federation on the Canadian or Australian pattern, that is, as part of the British Empire. There was only one drawback to this design, but an important one, namely that the Boers wanted no part of it. They displayed a very strong hankering after independence based on powerful national sentiment. After the experiences of 1877 to 1881, moreover, they were understandably suspicious of Britain and its friends.

The hankering after independence was not, of course, enough. The question was whether the Boers could stand up to the powerful British Empire. That was something the bankrupt Transvaal republic had been unable to do in 1877, but a great deal had changed since that time. Thanks to the rise of the gold-mining industry on the Witwatersrand, the Transvaal had become the economic center of South Africa, the referee of the game played by the white South African colonies. The rules of the game, however, were yet to be defined. If the Transvaal, locked into the interior of South Africa and having to rely on others for its imports and exports, were to align itself with the Cape Colony or Natal, then the economic future of these two colonies would be assured. If, however, the Transvaal were to acquire harbors of its own or gain access to other British ports, then a truly independent and potentially very prosperous and quickly growing white state would arise in South Africa, with a national character of its own and a historically fostered anti-British bias. That state might at the same time become a springboard for Germany, Britain's great European rival in southern Africa. The Germans had already secured something like a bridgehead in the Transvaal. They had streamed in their thousands to the gold fields, and Kruger had given them important positions and monopolies. German exports had grown quickly, and German investments were considerable.[101]

Everything therefore hinged on harbors, coasts and railroads. The Transvaal itself had no access to the sea and was moreover debarred from it; British policy had always been to gain control of all the coasts of southern Africa. That policy had been pursued with much diligence and had been crowned with almost total success. From the Orange River in the west to Delagoa Bay in the east, the entire coast, with the exception of Thongaland, was safely under British control. But having advanced into Swaziland in 1894, the Transvaal now seemed poised to break through to the coast. To avert that danger, Britain annexed Thongaland in June 1895. The last gap had thus been sealed, and it looked very much as if the Transvaal would never have a seaport of its own. The only hope it had left lay in collaboration with Portugal, which owned Delagoa Bay, and with it the finest harbor in East Africa, Lourenço Marques.

Delagoa Bay could even then look back on a long history. Over the years it had been claimed by a number of countries, including Portugal, Britain and the Transvaal. The issue had been settled peacefully in 1875, following arbitration by the French president, Patrice de MacMahon, who had awarded the bay to Portugal. The distance from Johannesburg to Lourenço Marques was under 250 miles, less than to East London, the nearest harbor in the Cape Colony. A railroad to Delagoa Bay would render Kruger's republic economically independent. In 1886 the member for Barkly West, Cecil Rhodes, observed in the Cape parliament, "If the Delagoa Bay Railway is carried out, the real union of South Africa will be indefinitely deferred."[102]

In January 1887 a start was made on the Portuguese section of the Delagoa Bay line. In June 1892 a national loan enabled the Transvaal Republic to add the final section. The loan was floated in London, and Rothschild presided over its success. Rothschild was of course Rhodes's friend, but business comes first. A railroad line was also being constructed from the Cape, and in September 1892 the first train from Cape Town steamed into Johannesburg. The Cape Railway had won the race. For a time it enjoyed a monopoly, but it was clear that it would only be of short duration and that Kruger held the fate of the Cape Colony in his hands. A boycott of the Cape Railway would spell not only the loss of the millions invested, but also jeopardize the economic future of the colony. There was thus an obvious conflict of interest between the Transvaal and the Cape Colony, and the Afrikaners in the Cape Colony had no option, for all their sympathy with their kinsmen, but to rally around Rhodes. It was a simple matter of economic survival. That was the background to what at first sight seemed to be the astonishing coalition of Britons and Afrikaners, of Rhodes and Hofmeyr, in the Cape Colony. It was also the background to the conflict between Kruger and Rhodes, which began on 17 July 1890 when Rhodes became prime minister of the Cape Colony.

At the time Rhodes was just thirty-seven years old. Paul Kruger was sixty-four, and had been president of the South African Republic for seven years. Until the fiasco of the Jameson Raid put an end to his political career, Rhodes was Kruger's greatest antagonist. Thereafter that role would fall to Alfred Milner, the British governor of the Cape Colony. The first five years of Rhodes's premiership thus presented the peculiar picture of a political struggle between an elderly, uneducated and frugal trekboer and a self-made millionaire and Oxford graduate young enough to have been the old man's son. Small wonder that one of Rhodes's last biographers called it an "oedipal conflict."[103]

### THE UITLANDER QUESTION

The Transvaal showed all the signs of a booming society. The population mushroomed as emigrants poured in from all over the world, drawn by the gold mines. The social consequences were almost as marked as the economic ones. From a sleepy, traditional, pastoral community with deep religious roots, the Transvaal became a multiracial, heathen society, moving to the hectic beat of modern life. There was little affinity between the two population groups, the old and the new. The first was made up of large, traditional and pious families, the other of young adventurers. Boer society was agrarian and almost autarchic. The fate of the newcomers, called "uitlanders" (foreigners) by the Boers, was bound up with the mines and their associated industries. Freedom of trade and transport and unimpeded imports and exports were what suited them best. Kruger's policy of monopolies and concessions governing the sale of alcohol, gunpowder and dynamite was against their interests.

The main problem, however, was political: the uitlanders were "migratory workers," not citizens of the republic. Unlike the Cape Colony, where the franchise was "color-blind," and the census, not color, determined admission to the polling booth, the Boers did not grant the vote to black people. The British thought that unfair, but were even more incensed by the fact that a large group of white people, including many of their kinsmen, should also have been disenfranchised. The actual demographic ratio of the two groups is unclear, nor can it be reconstructed for lack of reliable census data. Both Rhodes and Kruger exaggerated the number of uitlanders, the former to demonstrate how scandalous it was to debar so large a group of people from political rights, the latter to show how stupid it would be to grant the franchise to so many outsiders, since by doing so the republic would place its future in the hands of foreigners. In fact there were probably more Boers than uitlanders in the Transvaal, but when it came to adult males the uitlanders outnumbered the Boers, the migrant workers preferring to leave their families behind until such time as they were well and truly settled. Since the franchise was confined to white males, this last factor was of great electoral importance.[104]

At first, uitlanders had to pay £25 annually for five years before they could become naturalized and obtain the vote. That was a fairly large sum of money at the time. Later, the franchise was limited even further: the qualification was extended from five to fourteen years' residence and the minimum age put at forty years. To sugar the pill, a Tweede Volksraad (second legislative assembly) was set up especially for foreigners, but this body had very limited powers. Similar bodies and attempts to reach a compromise, however welcome, were not enough to satisfy the uitlanders, who therefore formed a fertile breeding ground for agitation and protest. They set up a National Union for the defense and furtherance of their interests, an organization that Rhodes and his men at first viewed with some suspicion. It did not, however, take them long to realize that these malcontents could be used for a greater objective: the fight against Kruger. For the uitlanders' lack of civic rights had handed Rhodes a powerful propaganda weapon; in fact, the suffrage was to play a central role in his war of nerves against Kruger.

The uitlanders could be used in yet another way. The ideal method of toppling Kruger was to organize a "spontaneous" revolt in Pretoria or Johannesburg and then to intervene, ostensibly for the purpose of restoring law and order and protecting "our threatened kinsmen." This scenario was to be employed with success many times in the course of the twentieth century. It was also to be the scenario for the Jameson Raid, so called after the man picked to spearhead the intervention. The Jameson Raid was, however, one of the few cases in which the strategy resulted in a complete fiasco and a public scandal that led to the political downfall of its chief plotter. Had it all taken place a century later, the incident might have been referred to, in the jargon of our times, not as the Jameson Raid, but as Jamesongate.

The idea that a time might come when the Cape would have to intervene in the Transvaal on behalf of the uitlanders had not originated with Rhodes or Jameson. The British governor, Sir Henry Loch, had toyed with such a plan as early as May 1894, when the uitlanders had clashed with the Transvaal government, refusing to serve in the Transvaal army for the purpose of quelling an uprising by the natives.[105] The Imperial Police had been massing in Mafeking, not far from Johannesburg, and the uitlanders were given promises of support. The affair was, however, hushed up, and there was no British intervention. In 1895 Loch was succeeded by an old hand, Sir Hercules Robinson, who had also been governor and high commissioner from 1880 to 1889, during which time he had acquired an interest not only in the BSAC but also in the De Beers mines, and was thus doubly dependent on Rhodes. But Sir Hercules, over seventy and in poor health, was no longer able to perform the labors of Hercules. In the event, that suited Rhodes's book.

Rhodes's plan was a variant of Loch's scenario, with a number of refinements. Thus Rhodes no longer had need of the Imperial Police, for his British South Africa Company had also been granted policing powers in its charter and ran a police force of its own. That was essential, for Rhodes doubted whether the British government would be prepared to intervene by force during an uitlander revolt. "You fellows are infernally slow," he told one of their spokesmen.[106] Rhodes would clearly have to act on his own. The only problem was that Bechuanaland—the launching pad for any intervention in the Transvaal—lay outside the territory defined by the charter. However, the British government was happy to oblige. On 17 November 1895 the British crown colony of Bechuanaland was incorporated

into the Cape Colony and the Imperial Police disbanded. The border between Bechuanaland and the Transvaal was placed under the control of
the BSAC. Troops and supplies were concentrated along this border and
arms smuggled into the Transvaal, hidden in oil barrels with false bottoms
and in railroad trucks under layers of coal. Once in Johannesburg, they
were temporarily stored in the mines. The Raid was thus well prepared.
However, its outcome depended on two factors: the success of Jameson's
coup and the uitlanders' will to resist.

### THE JAMESON RAID

Leander Starr Jameson (1853–1917), the man who was to lend his name
to one of the most spectacular fiascoes in colonial history, was born in
Edinburgh, the eleventh and last child of a man who, after practicing less
than successfully as a lawyer, went on to earn his living as journalist in
London. The son, trained as a doctor, decided to turn his back on a promising medical career and, just like his later friend Rhodes, followed his elder
brother to South Africa, where he built up a successful medical practice in
Kimberley. He was in great demand, especially by the ladies, but he was
not the marrying kind and combined his medical practice with a great
passion for poker and other games of chance. In 1878, shortly after his
arrival in Kimberley, he met Rhodes and started a lifelong friendship with
him. He became a shareholder in Rhodes's enterprises and entered his service. His medical knowledge stood him in good stead when, during a del-
icate mission to King Lobengula, he used morphine to relieve the king's
gout.[107] Subsequently he administered Matabeleland on Rhodes's behalf.
In 1895 he became Rhodes's right-hand man in planning their greatest
gamble: the Jameson Raid.

The gist of the plan was that at a given signal the uitlanders would start
an uprising. Jameson would then invade the Transvaal with 1,500 men
armed with machine guns and field pieces to be held in readiness close to
the border. They would also be issued with 1,500 extra rifles for arming
the uitlanders. Three Maxim machine guns and 5,000 rifles would be smuggled into Johannesburg. Together with the 1,000 rifles already in uitlander
hands, there would be enough weapons for 9,000 men. In addition, the
Pretoria arsenal would have to be taken by storm, yielding another 10,000
rifles and a few field guns. That would be enough. The leaders of the uitlanders meanwhile provided Jameson with a letter in which they begged
him to rush to their aid to protect thousands of helpless and innocent men,
women and children from the Boers. All expenses were guaranteed, the
petition concluded. Only the date was still missing, to be filled in by Jameson himself in due course.[108] That date was provisionally set at 29 December 1895.

Jameson was an adventurer, and in themselves his plans and actions were not very important. What mattered was the political background to the affair. The plan had been concocted by the prime minister of the Cape Colony. That the British government, too, was kept abreast of the plan has always been denied, as is only to be expected. As Rhodes put it to a young officer, "You cannot expect a Prime Minister to write down that you are to seize ports etc."[109] Joseph Chamberlain, the British colonial secretary, was only too well aware how helpful it was to be ignorant of things from time to time. "I did not want to know too much," was his brief comment on the affair.[110] It is, however, difficult to imagine how he could not have been aware of the plan, and even more difficult to determine what objections he could have raised. The plan squared with Chamberlain's imperialist ideas and suited his impetuous temperament and his predilection for direct action.[111]

On Boxing Day 1895 Chamberlain wrote to Lord Salisbury, the prime minister, that all they could do now was to wait and see. "If the rising is successful it ought to turn to our advantage."[112] The leaders of the uitlanders, however, lost their nerve and insisted that the Raid must be postponed, in any case until after race week. Clearly, horse racing mattered more to them than the "polo tournament," which was the code name for the Raid.[113] In the end, they made it known that they preferred to wash their hands of the whole rising-cum-invasion plan, and promised to come up with another one that dispensed with an invasion. Every stop was now pulled out to persuade Jameson to shelve the whole idea.

However, the leaders of the uitlanders were afraid that Jameson, the born gambler, might proceed with his plan all the same and thus force their hand. To be doubly safe they sent two messengers to his headquarters in Pitsani, one on horseback and the other by train. Rhodes's office in Cape Town, too, let Jameson know that the plan was off. The telegram, in code, but not particularly difficult to interpret, read, "Public will not subscribe one penny towards it even with you as director."[114] That was on Saturday, 28 December 1895.

There now followed a weekend of terrible confusion. In Pitsani Jameson grew increasingly determined. He sent word to Cape Town that he would go into action unless he was officially and explicitly ordered not to. No such direct order ever arrived. There has been much speculation as to why not. Did Jameson's telegram reach Rhodes too late? Rhodes gave the impression that that was not the case. When the report reached him that Jameson had set out even though Johannesburg had not risen up in revolt, he said, "Old Jameson has upset my applecart. . . . Poor old Jameson. Twenty years we have been friends, and now he goes in and ruins me."[115] However, there is much to suggest that Rhodes did not wish to issue explicit instructions to Jameson to drop the whole business. Rhodes, too, was a gambler, and he may well have thought that, given luck, everything might still turn out for the best. However that may be, Jameson carried on and

Rhodes did nothing to stop him. On the night of Sunday, 29 December, Jameson crossed into the Transvaal.

The leaders of the uitlanders heard about the invasion on the afternoon of Monday, 30 December. The telegram they received read, "The Veterinary Surgeon has left for Johannesburg with some good horseflesh and backs himself for seven hundred."[116] Reactions were extremely confused. The rifles were brought out from their hiding places and armed units set up to preserve peace and order. One uitlander organization, the Reform Committee, took control of Johannesburg, but proclaimed its loyalty to the republic. Sir Hercules Robinson, the British high commissioner, left Cape Town for the Transvaal to negotiate with the Kruger government. On hearing of this, Rhodes hoped that everything might still turn out well, the more so as rumors were trickling in that Jameson and his raiders had beaten the Boers. The rumors were mistaken. At news of the invasion, the Boer commandos had quickly sprung into action. Many of them were still wearing their *kisklere*, the Sunday best that Transvaalers donned for the New Year. On 1 January 1896 they defeated Jameson near Krugersdorp and surrounded his troops near Doornkop. Next day, one of the raiders borrowed the white apron of a servant girl at the farm where they had barricaded themselves in and hung it out of the window. The raiders had surrendered. Jameson and his men were taken to Pretoria and put into prison. The Raid was over.

Repercussions following these events varied widely. Rhodes's political position in the Cape was destroyed. He had no alternative but to resign his premiership. However, there was also a great deal of enthusiastic support for Jameson's heroic action, especially in Britain. The *Times*, for instance, paid as much as £25 to the recently appointed poet laureate, Alfred Austin, for his moving poem, "Jameson's Ride," which appeared on 11 January 1896. The following lines undoubtedly affected many readers:

> There are girls in the gold-reef city,
> There are mothers and children, too!
> And they cry, "Hurry up! for pity!"
> So what can a brave man do?[117]

Madame Tussaud at once cleared a space in her waxworks museum for a tableau entitled "Dr. Jameson hoisting the British flag in Bechuanaland," and Queen Victoria called him "an excellent and able man." "The Boors" [*sic*], by contrast, struck her as being "horrid . . . , cruel and overbearing."[118]

The German Kaiser took a different view. Some witnesses declared that upon hearing the news he became hysterical, had a row with his ministers, and spoke of declaring war on Great Britain, proclaiming a German protectorate over the Transvaal, sending German troops, mobilizing the German fleet and several other options. The outcome was somewhat calmer

Jameson held prisoner by the Boers

and took the form of a telegram. That too, however, caused a sensation. It was sent to Kruger on 3 January 1896 and read as follows: "I express my sincere congratulations that without calling on the aid of friendly Powers you and your people, by your own energy against the armed bands which have broken into your country as disturbers of the peace, have succeeded in re-establishing peace, and defending the independence of the country against attack from without."[119]

This was the first of Wilhelm's many diplomatic blunders. British reactions were violent. What Britain objected to most was the phrase "the aid of friendly Powers." The implications were clear: Germany was ready to provide such aid if called upon to do so. The *Times* called the telegram "distinctly unfriendly," and the *Daily Telegraph* spoke of an insult. The *Saturday Review* pointed out that Britain was not seeking war, "not even with Germany," but that enough was enough: "Lord Salisbury should now tell Germany and her allies to mind their own business."[120] But that was not the end of the story. Dockers in London clashed with German merchant sailors, the windows of German shops were broken and German businesses boycotted.

The Kruger telegram had thus backfired. Instead of causing division and disappointment at the failure of the Raid, it united Britain in a wave of patriotism. This reaction can only be understood against the background of the gradually mounting animosity toward, and fear of, Germany. Britain had, it is true, more concrete disputes with France and Russia, but Germany was increasingly seen as the real danger, the true rival, the one who was gnawing away at Britain's industrial and commercial supremacy.[121] The upshot of it all was that Rhodes's blunder was offset by the Kaiser's, and that Chamberlain's position was strengthened rather than weakened. The political fallout of the Raid thus remained confined to Cape Town, and London was left unscathed.

Meanwhile Kruger sent Jameson and his accomplices to London for trial. The hearings turned into a major social event, with fierce competition for tickets to the public gallery. The accused in the end were found guilty, and Jameson and his second-in-command, Sir John Willoughby, were sentenced to fifteen months' imprisonment, with shorter sentences for the other main defendants. Jameson was released after ten months on health grounds.[122] Unlike Rhodes, he had not reached the end of his political career—far from it. The Raid had been a disaster, but it had gained him a heroic reputation. He was elected to the Cape parliament in 1900, became the leader of the Progressive Party in 1903, and was prime minister of the Cape Colony from 1904 to 1908.

An inquiry was also held into the involvement of Cecil Rhodes, Sir Hercules Robinson and even of Chamberlain, the colonial secretary. A parliamentary committee of inquiry, known officially as the South Africa Committee but quickly nicknamed the "Committee of No-Inquiry," was set up. It soon became clear that the case would never be fully and openly investigated, and it was so widely held that so many falsehoods were being bandied about that the proceedings came to be known as the "Lying in State at Westminster."[123] London's responsibility was thus swept under the carpet. Chamberlain's complicity in, or preliminary knowledge of, the Raid was never unequivocally established, but the affair did cast a slur on his reputation. More gravely, the real problem in South Africa had not been solved, and in 1899 there was a second, far larger, explosion.

# 5
# TOWARD THE SECOND BOER WAR

### AFTER THE RAID

The Jameson Raid, or rather its failure, had disastrous effects on Britain's standing in South Africa. Jameson himself languished in prison, if only for a short time; Rhodes was forced to resign and turned his back on politics for good; the British high commissioner, Sir Hercules Robinson, would soon leave his post, seriously compromised; Chamberlain may have been officially cleared of complicity, but no one in the Transvaal believed that, and few people elsewhere for that matter. The Boers were bitter and suspicious, the Afrikaners in the Cape appalled, and world opinion shocked at Britain's behavior. In other respects, too, Britain's international position left much to be desired. There were, as always, conflicts with France over Africa and with Russia in Asia. Germany, too, had now proved itself hostile. A furious dispute with the United States over Venezuela had only just come to an end and been submitted to a commission for arbitration. This was therefore not the time for a "forward policy" in South Africa. On the other hand, the question of the Transvaal had been left unresolved with the failure of the Raid. The uitlanders may not have risen up against the Kruger government, but their grievances had not gone away, and many of them were Her Majesty's subjects, entitled to the support of Her Majesty's government. Britain was therefore forced to maintain pressure on Kruger for internal reforms and for a solution to the uitlander problem.

By 1897 a new crisis was brewing, triggered by new Transvaal legislation on immigration and the expulsion of undesirable aliens, but this time the danger passed. All that Britain had been able to do was to exert moral pressure. Active political steps against the Transvaal were out of the question, and military intervention was only possible if Britain could at least count on the sympathy of a large number of Cape Afrikaners. If not, these men might easily turn into a fifth column in the Cape Colony, much as the uitlanders could serve as a British fifth column in the Transvaal. It was clear that just then such sympathy was as good as nonexistent. The Cape Afrikaners were highly critical of Rhodes and Chamberlain, and their sympathy was directed instead toward their kinsmen across the Vaal. British public opinion, too, would only support a war if the blame for it could be laid squarely at Kruger's door. That was inconceivable so soon after the abortive intervention of 1895.

Kruger's position, by contrast, had been considerably strengthened, not only in the Transvaal, where his leadership went unchallenged, but also beyond. In the Cape Colony Hofmeyr had broken with Rhodes, and in the Orange Free State elections held two months after the Raid had swept Steyn's pro-Kruger party to power. In the circumstances the British government could do only one thing, the most difficult for any government, namely, nothing. Hicks Beach argued that a wait-and-see policy was the only answer: "The great thing necessary is patience. Impatience has been at the root of all our difficulties in South Africa."[124] Chamberlain came to much the same conclusion, the waiting game being "the best for this country as time must be on our side."[125] Even the new governor and high commissioner for South Africa, who had taken office in Cape Town in May

1897, concurred. He outlined his policy as follows: "We must keep up our wickets and not attempt to force the game."[126] But this situation was not to continue for long, as the new governor was Alfred Milner, and patience was not really in his nature. Milner was to take the place of Rhodes as Paul Kruger's chief opponent.

### Sir Alfred Milner

Alfred Milner (1854–1925) was born on 23 March 1854 in Giessen, Germany. He had a rather complicated family history. Alfred was the grandson of an Englishman who had moved to Germany and married a German woman. Alfred's father, in his turn, had at the age of twenty-three married an English widow who, for reasons that are unclear, had taken her children to Germany and in whose household Milner senior had served as a tutor. Alfred was the only son of her second marriage. The family continued to live in Germany, but because he had two English grandfathers Alfred was able to take out British nationality under a statute of 1773, not repealed until 1914.[127] Many English people, in particular, have claimed that his German background explained much of his character. Thus the historian Robert Ensor writes, "In most of its salient virtues and defects his temperament conformed far more to a German than to an English type."[128]

Milner was educated at the Tübingen gymnasium and went on to gain a scholarship to Balliol College, which under its famous master, Dr. Benjamin Jowett, was then more than ever "the nursery for statesmen." Here Milner fell under the sway of the imperialist ideas of Seeley and Froude and of the social-reformist doctrines of Ruskin and Arnold Toynbee (senior). Social imperialism was in the air in Oxford at the time, and Milner readily absorbed it. After taking his degree, he first practiced law, then turned to journalism, finally opting for a career in politics and government. The first great step along this road was his appointment in 1889 as director-general of accounts in Cairo, a post he held for nearly three years. He then returned to England to take up the chairmanship of the Board of Inland Revenue.

Shortly after his return from Cairo, Milner published *England in Egypt*, the book that was to make him famous overnight. This paean of praise to the British administration in Egypt is one of the highlights of British imperialist writing, comparable with Kipling's *The White Man's Burden* and Seeley's *Expansion of England*. Milner's message was of particular appeal to the British public with its claim that British imperialism was good for the native population while being profitable for Britain. Milner was to play a major role in British imperial history not only by his work and writings, but also by the influence he was to exert on an entire generation of young civil servants. That, of course, was not until later, after the Boer War, when

Alfred Milner

Milner was put in charge of the rebuilding of South Africa. Much as Franklin D. Roosevelt and John F. Kennedy brought their brains trusts from Harvard to the White House, so Milner imported his young assistants from Oxford into South Africa. This group, which became known as "Milner's kindergarten," was later to play an important role in twentieth-century British politics, especially with its contribution to appeasement politics in the 1930s. By then, Milner himself was no longer there to lead them. He died in 1925.

Milner was a fervent and romantic imperialist. He himself said that his entire public life was dominated by "a single desire—that of working for the integrity and consolidation of the British Empire."[129] "Imperialism," he wrote in *The Nation and the Empire*, "has all the depth and comprehensiveness of a religious faith."[130] Much as Rhodes had wanted to found an imitation Jesuit, that is celibate, order for the express purpose of expanding the British Empire, so Milner had resolved, while still a very young man, not to marry, the better to devote himself single-mindedly to the interests of the Empire, a resolution he was not to break until he was sixty-seven years old. The root of his political philosophy was a firm belief in the superiority of the British race: "The British race . . . stands for something distinctive and priceless in the onward march of humanity," he declared.[131] More important than any material reward "is the bond of common blood, a common language, common history and traditions."[132] The "British race" thus comprised all the people of the United Kingdom and those of their descendants overseas who lived under the British flag. This view of racial unity as the mystical foundation of the British Empire was something Milner shared with other Britons involved with South Africa, Rhodes and Chamberlain among them. Small wonder then that Milner was made a trustee of the Rhodes Foundation, and that he assured Rhodes of his "complete sympathy with your broad ambitions for the race."[133] Like so many of his contemporaries, Milner believed that the age of the great empires had dawned, and that it would be reserved for just a few countries: America and Russia, of course, but also Germany and perhaps Britain, provided it retained its close ties with its colonies. Accordingly, "imperial unity" and "tariff reform" were his great imperial objectives.

For Milner, the future of South Africa was thus of vital importance. The British Empire could not dispense with South Africa. The colony would have to be expanded into a giant federation, something like Canada or Australia. However, South Africa's future looked uncertain. There were two alternatives. South Africa could either develop into a British dominion, or become a hostile power, dominated by the Boers. The key to this problem lay in the Transvaal. Kruger would have to be forced to rally to Britain's side. There were no solutions to the "political troubles of S. Africa except reform in the Transvaal or war."[134] Milner did not believe that reform would come about by itself, and thought it best "to work up to a crisis."[135] After having studied the situation, he informed Chamberlain of this conclusion in a long letter dated 23 February 1898, adding, however, that it was only the local side of the matter. Everything would of course hinge on an analysis of the world political situation. "It depends on the Imperial outlook as a whole."[136] And that was Chamberlain's province.

Chamberlain, too, had come to the conclusion that South Africa was at a crossroads: it would become either a new Canada or else a second United States. Chamberlain thought that the Canadian course seemed the more likely of the two. True, there was "a centrifugal tendency" in the white colonies, a tendency to break free from the Empire, but Australia and Canada proved that this course was not a law of nature. Centripetal forces were at work as well. In South Africa he distinguished three of these. In the first place, German interference was likely to underline the need for protection by London. Next, there was the internal conflict between the Dutch and the English. "The two races do not amalgamate," Chamberlain noted to his surprise. He could only come up with one explanation: "A lot of Celtic and Norman blood must be infused in us."[137] This conflict might force the Empire to exert a restraining influence. And third, there were the material and emotional benefits provided by the Empire.

All in all, therefore, Chamberlain considered the emergence of a new Canada the more likely outcome, but only if the four white colonies found some modus vivendi. Another outcome was possible: the English territories might become self-governing colonies within the British Empire, while the Transvaal and the Orange Free State would remain independent republics outside. In that case a United States of South Africa would inevitably emerge. The key to the future thus lay in the Transvaal, the natural heartland of South Africa, "the richest spot on earth," from which all the other territories took their lead.[138] It was essential to strengthen the British hold on the Transvaal and to thrust the latter into one form of federation with the British colonies or another. The classical instrument for exerting British influence in the Transvaal was well known, namely, pressure by the uitlanders. Kruger had to be forced to grant them political rights, whereupon Transvaal policy would automatically fall into the British mold. While Milner believed that time was working against Britain, Chamberlain took the opposite standpoint: the natural demographic trend favored a British South Africa.

This, however, was just one view of the matter. For even a British-dominated Transvaal was not the complete solution; it would still have to remain under direct control from London. The American settlers, too, had been of British origin, but that had not stopped them from seceding. Control of the uitlanders was as important as control of the Boers and perhaps just as difficult. In their game with the Transvaal the British held one trump card, and that had not changed: their hold on the coast. Here there was just one weak link, and that too was still the same: Delagoa Bay. Thus this lovely bay on the east coast of Africa remained of "vital importance" to the British Empire.[139] In 1898 Britain had one last chance of securing the bay and thus safeguarding its future.

### THE PARTITION OF THE PORTUGUESE COLONIES

In the 1890s Portugal was in an extremely awkward financial position, and no longer able to pay the interest on its state loans. Foreign creditors were naturally unhappy. They demanded their money and appealed to their own governments for support. The latter then applied pressure on Lisbon by means of protests and threats, although generally to no avail: Portugal's financial tribulations were too great and too longstanding. The solution seemed obvious and lay in Portugal's colonial possessions. It would have to divest itself of the most desirable of these, or at least pledge the revenue from them as security. The need to acquire securities is second nature to all bankers. In this case it was shared by several governments.

In its financial predicament Portugal turned first to its traditional ally, Great Britain. When Britain and Portugal began negotiations, the Germans grew edgy, put pressure on Portugal—the German ambassador called on the King of Portugal dressed in military uniform to lodge a protest—and asked Great Britain for clarification. The German government then tried to organize a joint protest by all the Great Powers against British intervention, but without success. "All this leaves me completely cold," the Russian foreign minister declared.[140] France was equally indifferent and washed its hands of the affair in the wake of a cabinet crisis. Britain nevertheless remained prepared to talk to Germany. After much deliberation and negotiation they reached an agreement on 30 August 1898, enshrined in three conventions. The first convention concerned a possible loan to Portugal. If necessary, Britain and Germany would provide it jointly and accept the customs duties of Angola, Mozambique and Portuguese Timor as collateral. The British share would consist of the duties collected in Mozambique south of the Zambezi—that is, inclusive of Delagoa Bay—and central Angola. The Germans would receive the rest. It was clear that what this all amounted to was a demarcation of spheres of influence. This was even more obvious from the second, confidential, convention, which mentions the partition of the territory of the Portuguese colonies in a similar manner should it "unfortunately" prove impossible to preserve their integrity. The third document, a Secret Note, laid down that neither party would meanwhile accept further concessions from Portugal unless the other received an equivalent recompense. To make doubly sure, not only this but all the negotiations were kept secret. The entire set of remarkable documents was signed on 30 August 1898 by Paul von Hatzfeldt, the German ambassador, and by Arthur Balfour, deputizing for Salisbury, who was recuperating from illness in the south of France.[141]

For Britain these conventions represented a considerable success. Britain's strategic objective had been attained: Germany had been eliminated as a potential ally of the Transvaal and as a rival in Delagoa Bay. The South African coast would now be under British control, come what may, for Delagoa Bay would either remain a part of the Portuguese empire controlled by Britain or else fall to Britain itself. Britain thus gained much more from the treaty than did Germany. In particular, Britain had no need to make sure that the conventions were actually implemented. Germany, however, would only benefit from the agreement if the Portuguese colonies were actually carved up. Britain, indeed, discovered that it had even so paid too high a price for giving away half of somebody else's colonial possessions. Chamberlain considered the negotiations nothing short of blackmail. But then, as he explained, "it is worthwhile to pay blackmail sometimes."[142]

The whole arrangement came to nothing in the end, for Portugal managed after all to float a state loan on the Paris stock exchange which helped to extricate Lisbon from its acute financial problems. Anglo-Portuguese relations now rapidly improved. Soveral had learned of the Anglo-German deal and made it clear to his government that it was impossible to play Germany off against Britain. This resulted in a series of Anglo-Portuguese negotiations culminating in a—yet again—secret agreement signed on 14 October 1899. It amounted to a reaffirmation of the Anglo-Portuguese friendship treaties of 1632 and 1664. The treaty of 1373 was not mentioned—Lord Salisbury felt that the fourteenth century was "going very far back."[143] However, all this had ceased to matter, for the Boer War had meanwhile broken out. The Anglo-German plan, never put into practice, had proved its usefulness to Britain. The specter of a German alliance with the Transvaal had been exorcized by the Anglo-German agreement on the future of the Portuguese colonies. Having lost Germany as a potential ally, the Transvaal had been completely isolated diplomatically as well as militarily. Milner had been given a free hand to put Kruger under further pressure.

### Capitalists and Uitlanders

Two groups in the Transvaal were almost permanently dissatisfied with the Kruger government. Both had links with the mines, and both were deeply implicated in the outbreak of the Boer War in 1899. These two groups were the mine owners and the miners, or the capitalists and the uitlanders. Gold mining in the Transvaal was not a simple, and not always a profitable, business. High costs were involved, just how high being largely determined by the Transvaal government. For it was the latter that fixed the railroad tariffs, and these had a considerable influence on the price of food and other imported products. The mine owners were loud in their complaints about the high transport charges. For the government, by contrast, the railroads were of political rather than economic importance. They did not want the Transvaal to become dependent on the Cape Colony and accordingly opted for sharing the cargo between the railroad lines from the Cape, Natal and Lourenço Marques. The Cape's reply was to cut its tariff, whereupon Pretoria hit back with higher charges on the last section of the line in the Transvaal. The Cape responded with another weapon: goods were henceforth to be transported over the last section by ox-cart. Kruger reacted by closing the drifts, the negotiable fords. That was going too far, and the resulting sharp protest from Chamberlain did not miss its mark. The ox-carts were given free passage again, but lost the unequal struggle with the railroads. This "drifts crisis" took place in 1895. It was but one of many forms of an ongoing cold war.

There were other complaints in the Transvaal, and more serious ones. One of these concerned the dynamite monopoly. Explosives were an important cost factor in the mining industry, representing 10 percent of the overall operating costs.[144] Small though it was, the Transvaal used more explosives than any other country on earth. As a result the dynamite monopoly was a kind of gold mine itself, bringing in a guaranteed £2 million a year. A part of the capital for the Nobel Prizes was thus acquired in the

Transvaal mines. The main financial beneficiaries were a few companies, but the political benefits accrued to the government: they provided the Transvaal with an important military trump, a gunpowder industry of its own.

The capitalists' greatest grievance was the government's labor policy. Labor accounted for over 50 percent of the production costs (20 percent going to white labor, and 35 percent to "native" labor).[145] The industrialists complained bitterly about lack of government collaboration in this field. In particular the common incidence of drunkenness led to high accident figures. The government, they claimed, ought to apply the laws against drunkenness at work more stringently, and—still more important—encourage the flow of workers to the mines instead of impeding it. If this were done then wages would fall. Lower wages for the black workers in particular were considered the most effective way of rendering mining more profitable. On this point, however, industry and the government were at loggerheads. The government was more interested in genuine Transvaalers than in uitlanders and looked upon all immigration, of whites as well as of blacks, as a threat to the peace and traditional character of the state.

That the "Randlords" were displeased is beyond any doubt. That they were out to settle accounts with Kruger has also been frequently alleged. The idea that the Boer War was a war fought for the sake of capitalists is as old as the Boer War itself. J. A. Hobson, the founder of the theory of modern imperialism, was one of many to hold this view. Hobson, a radical writer and politician, published his famous *Imperialism: A Study* in 1902, the year in which the Boer War ended. In it he presented imperialism as an economic phenomenon. Overproduction and underconsumption in Europe, he argued, had led to the end of the export of capital to overseas countries and to South Africa in particular. Hobson had published another book on this subject as early as 1900. It was entitled *The War in South Africa: Its Causes and Effects*, and alleged that South Africa had ceased to be British and had fallen into the hands of foreigners, Rhodes and Rudd being the exception. Power rested largely in the hands of a small group of international financiers, "chiefly German in origin and Jewish in race." Before he himself had been to South Africa, he had occasionally heard of such men as Beit, Eckstein and Barnato, but he had "no conception of their number or their power." Once on the Rand, Hobson had seen the light: "I thus discovered that not Hamburg, not Vienna, not Frankfort, but Johannesburg is the new Jerusalem." Jewish financial interests, according to him, were at the root of the conflict, so painful and tragic for Britain. Hobson, too, looked upon labor policy as the crux of the clash between the capitalists and Kruger. He concluded, "Put in concise form, it may be said that this war is being waged in order to secure for the mines a cheap and adequate supply of labour."[146] The theory of a Jewish capitalist conspiracy—which Hobson, incidentally, was later to recant—found a great deal of

support in left-wing circles. Thus the Trades Union Congress carried a resolution in 1900 in which the war was condemned because it only served
to render the South African gold fields safe for "cosmopolitan Jews, most
of whom had no patriotism and no country."[147]

Though the existence of capitalist grievances against Kruger was undeniable, the issue was less simple than Hobson made out. There was indeed
an "informal alliance" between the mine owners and Milner,[148] but it is
far from clear whether the former favored war or annexation. In particular,
the mine owners could not be sure that they would be better off under
Britain, a country full of philanthropic committees for the protection of
black people. Kruger, for that matter, was willing to make concessions. In
fact, his "Great Deal" of 1899 amounted to an offer that gave the mine
owners considerable satisfaction. Most British statesmen, by contrast,
looked down on them. Selborne, Salisbury's son-in-law, and colonial secretary under Chamberlain, found them "worthless and contemptible."[149]
Chamberlain, his chief, described them as "a lot of cowardly selfish blatant
speculators."[150] The gentlemen knew best of course, he said, whether or
not they wanted to come to terms with Kruger; that was their business,
but they ought to consider what the great British public would think of
such an agreement, namely, that "the Financiers had sold their cause and
their compatriots, and sold them cheap."[151] The South African conflict had
more than financial dimensions. Powerful though Beit, Barnato and Rhodes
may have been, a war for their sakes was not something the British public
would condone. Such a war needed simpler but deeper passions, and these
were not evoked by German Jewish financiers. The plight of the uitlanders
was a different matter.

The situation in South Africa was complicated, indeed paradoxical. The
Cape was a British colony but the majority of the white population was
Afrikaans, or "Dutch," as the British called them. The Transvaal, by contrast, was a Boer republic, but the proportion of Boers in the population
was steadily decreasing. The dominant population group was determined
to cling to power, an understandable resolve, for the very character of their
state and society was at stake. The Kruger government in the Transvaal
accordingly withheld political rights from the uitlanders. In the Orange Free
State, by contrast, all whites enjoyed political rights, but then there were
no mines and hence no uitlanders there.

The question of political rights for uitlanders was to dominate the last
phase of the struggle against Kruger, not unexpectedly since the issue was
a sensitive one, hingeing on discrimination and equality. Its impact should
not, however, be exaggerated. Many of the uitlanders were not British. Nor
were all of them interested in the franchise, let alone prepared to forfeit
their earlier nationality. It was nevertheless an issue that offered British
imperialism immense opportunities precisely because it appealed to the
emotions and patriotic sentiment. Cecil Rhodes found the slogan with

which the Transvaal government could be effectively harried: "Equal rights for all civilized men south of the Zambezi."[152] That slogan helped to mobilize British public opinion, something that was more important than the support of the mining magnates, since without it the British government would do nothing, and without the British government, Milner could do nothing.

NEGOTIATIONS

In February 1898 Kruger was elected president of the Transvaal for the fourth time. The chances of voting in a liberal government and a more conciliatory president were thus put off for at least another five years. The British hope that Kruger would be defeated at the polls had proved vain. His government was more firmly in the saddle than before. Milner informed Chamberlain that "at present the chances of reform in the Transvaal are worse than ever."[153] Since he believed that the alternatives were reform or war, the conclusion was obvious. Chamberlain was at one with him, but neither his cabinet colleagues nor British public opinion favored the remaining alternative, at least not for the time being. War could only be considered if the uitlander issue became so acute as to whip up a frenzy of protest among the British public, and that was unlikely to happen in response to so abstract a question as the conditions under which the franchise could be acquired. Something more provocative was needed. That provocation came in December 1898 with the death of Tom Edgar.

Tom Edgar was an English boilermaker who had knocked down another Englishman during a drunken brawl. The Johannesburg police, not known for their mild manners even then, had shot him in his own home while trying to arrest him. "An unfortunate incident," the Transvaal government and the judicial authorities declared. "Murder," screamed the uitlander press and various other pressure groups. Lengthy petitions were forwarded to Queen Victoria. Emotions ran high in Britain as well. The Colonial Office asked Milner to let them have his version of the affair for inclusion in a Blue Book to be published by the British government. Milner now saw his chance. The result was the notorious "Helots telegram" in which he likened the British in the Transvaal to Helots, serfs who were a class in ancient Sparta intermediate in status between slaves and citizens. That was a comparison that hit home in an age when every educated man knew his classics. "The case for intervention is overwhelming," wrote Milner. And he added, "The spectacle of thousands of British subjects kept permanently in the position of Helots . . . calling vainly to Her Majesty's Government for redress, does steadily undermine the influence and reputation of Great Britain and the respect for the British Government within its own dominions." Milner went on to speak of "a ceaseless stream of malignant lies" and of "mischievous propaganda." Telling proof of Britain's will and ability to maintain its position in South Africa was needed. That could best be obtained by demanding a "fair share" for uitlanders in the running of a country that owed everything to their exertions.[154] "This is tremendously stiff," was Chamberlain's view of Milner's text, and he was right of course.[155] The word "Helots" did not miss its mark. British public opinion was duly aroused.

Meanwhile negotiations had been started on the subject of the franchise. President Steyn of the Orange Free State had offered to mediate, and on 31 May 1899 Milner and Kruger met at the Bloemfontein Conference. This abortive meeting has often been called a clash of personalities. The confrontation between the young, brilliant British imperialist and the obstinate old Boer, one of the last survivors of the Great Trek, was, not surprisingly, both dramatic and picturesque. Milner's attitude has often been condemned. According to many critics he used quite the wrong approach. Langer's opinion was that he bombarded the old president with "dialectical artillery . . . as though he were a polished European diplomat."[156] Milner's "clear super-civilized mind lost patience with the tedious and devious obstinacy of the Arcadian president," writes Ensor.[157] The crux of the matter, in any case, was that the conference failed because Milner did not want it to succeed. His aim was not to obtain concessions and reach a compromise; he wanted a showdown. He himself summed up his role as follows: ". . . I precipitated a crisis which was inevitable before it was altogether too late."[158]

What Milner did, in fact, achieve with respect to the franchise was more than enough. "I congratulate you on great victory," Chamberlain telegraphed Milner when he heard the result. In a statement to the *Times* he declared that the crisis was over. Milner was alarmed. That had certainly not been his intention. On 4 June he informed Chamberlain that there were still many outstanding problems and that the conference would probably end in failure. Even before he received Chamberlain's conciliatory reply—keep calm, carry on: "Boers do not understand quick decisions"—he had broken off the negotiations.[159]

After the failure of the Bloemfontein Conference it was to be another four months before matters came to a head. Chamberlain and Milner saw eye to eye, but public opinion was not yet ready for an ultimatum. Tension had to be raised further. In 1899 Joseph Chamberlain used the same tactics with Kruger that Hitler was to use forty years later in Munich when dealing with Joseph's son Neville: the making of increasingly steep demands. In order to allay fears about the possible consequences, Milner for his part assured the British government that the Boers were sure to climb down: "I think one good slap in the face may dissipate them."[160] The odds on that were twenty to one, he also informed London, and if he was wrong, it was in any case better to have a fight now than it would be in five or ten years' time.[161]

Both sides played for time, albeit for different reasons: the British in order to muster their troops in South Africa, the Boers because, to make the best use of their cavalry, they had to wait for the summer season. The war eventually came in October 1899. The British had prepared an ultimatum to the Transvaal government, but that was never to be sent, for Kruger confronted them shortly before, on 9 October, with an ultimatum of his own. He demanded the immediate withdrawal of the British troops assembled on the borders of the republic, the withdrawal of all British reinforcements, and that no fresh British troops be supplied. The British government declared that these demands were unacceptable, and hostilities began on 11 October 1899 at 1700 hours. The Orange Free State made common cause with the Transvaal. The "great day of reckoning" so long awaited by Milner had dawned.[162]

# 6
# THE SECOND BOER WAR, 1899–1902

The Boer War had a predictable outcome but ran an unpredictable course. It was unthinkable that Britain might lose it, but it was unable to win it as quickly as it might have wished. In the end, the mighty British Empire did manage to defeat the small republics, but it was not the military walk-over that it had expected and that Rhodes had forecast.[163] Johannesburg fell on 31 May 1900, and the war seemed to be over. Yet that only served to signal the outbreak of a bitter guerrilla war in which both sides were to suffer losses on a grievous scale.

### OFFENSIVE AND COUNTER-OFFENSIVE

On paper the struggle looked very one-sided. Great Britain was making war on two small republics whose combined population was less than a quarter of a million. The struggle was indeed very one-sided, although less so than appeared at first sight. The British military machine was anything but impressive. Those were the years of major cuts in government expenditure. Every penny was turned over at least three times. Moreover, in Britain the navy, not the army, was the darling of the nation. The army budget in 1898 came to just £20 million. The high command was not up to its task and not prepared for modern war. British officers looked upon war as a kind of large-scale polo match, not as a matter of life and death.[164] Amateurism reigned supreme, especially among the aristocratic elite, and that caused offense to men of humbler descent such as Kitchener and Wolseley. The logistic provisions were exceptionally poor; it seemed impossible to arm the troops properly or even to clothe them adequately. Stand-by units were almost nonexistent, there being no more than a small British garrison in South Africa. The 10,000 men Milner had demanded were scraped together with difficulty and brought in from all over the world. The King's Royal Rifles came from Bombay and the Royal Marines from Alexandria. Other regiments and brigades arrived from Malta, Crete and any other part of the British Empire that could spare a man or two.

The troops were seasoned regulars, but used to colonial wars against "uncivilized people" such as Africans and Asians, "small wars," as they were called, campaigns, in short, that could be easily won. At Omdurman, in the battle against the mahdists, a few machine guns had proved capable of destroying an army of thousands of dervishes. The Boers, however, were an altogether different kettle of fish. "Civilized war is awful," complained one British officer after one of the first battles of the Boer War.[165]

At the beginning the Boers enjoyed numerical superiority. The Free State and the Transvaal together put over 50,000 men into the field, or more precisely into the saddle, for every Boer soldier had a mount as well as a gun. In other words, the Boers were, in fact, mounted infantrymen, which proved a great advantage to them. Military wisdom at the time had it that one mounted soldier on the veldt was worth three or four soldiers on foot.[166] They may not have been professional soldiers, but they were highly experienced in fighting natives and shooting wild animals. The average Boer was a good shot. Moreover, the Boer army had excellent Mauser rifles and field pieces made by Krupp and Creuzot and bought by the Kruger government from the proceeds of the monopolies and concessions. The Boers were familiar with the terrain, enjoyed the support of the population, and were highly motivated. Their organization seemed chaotic: they had no uniforms, and the officers were hard to tell from the men. Discipline was based not on subordination—the very essence of military order—but on equality. If the situation called for it, the commanding officer would sit on the ground and an older soldier in his chair. In that respect at least the Boers were modern. They were truly a nation at arms, a *nation armée* in keeping with the ideas of the French Revolution. The Boers were in the end able to muster close to a hundred thousand men, given the support of volunteers and rebels from the Cape, although no more than half that number was ever out fighting on the veldt at one and the same time because the land had to be tilled even while battle proceeded. British forces eventually outnumbered the Boers by more than five to one, deploying nearly half a million men. That was not, however, the case at the beginning of the war. The Boers then threw about 35,000 of their 60,000 or so available men into the field against roughly the same number of British troops.[167]

Not surprisingly, the Boers took the initiative. They crossed the border and invaded the British colonies, Natal in the south and the Cape Colony in the west. At first their successes were striking. They besieged the British at Ladysmith in Natal, Mafeking in Bechuanaland, and Kimberley in the Cape Colony. It has often been said—with regret—that they did not exploit these successes, made no major raid on the Cape Colony, tried no break-through to the port of Durban. Their tactics were therefore called weak and hesitant. However, they were not so much concerned with tactics as with strategy, and in strategic terms their approach was defensive. With their offensive, they were merely trying to stave off the threat of a British attack and meanwhile to occupy what towns might prove of military im-portance during the inevitable British counteroffensive. That would place them in an advantageous position and, as they hoped, help to bring about another Majuba. As at Majuba in 1881, the British would be made to see reason and be forced to restore the republics' independence—this time for good. That was the Boers' strategic plan and explains their actions during this initial phase.[168]

The Boers went on to a number of further successes, and the British suffered further setbacks, especially during the second week of December, which came to be known as "Black Week" in England. Colenso, Storm-berg, Magersfontein and later Spionkop were so many military feats of the Boers, yet none became a new Majuba. This time the political conditions were not propitious. At the time of Majuba, Britain had been run by the Gladstone government, an administration with strong moral principles and anti-imperialist inclinations. They had done something that governments rarely do if they have an alternative, namely, allow a humiliation to go unavenged. Things were quite different in Joseph Chamberlain's Britain. It was not that the British government was now out for vengeance, but they were bent on gaining supremacy in South Africa and were prepared to wage war to achieve it. Public opinion was ready. The political climate in about 1900 was more chauvinistic and jingoistic than it had been in 1880. The defeats of Black Week, far from dampening the war fever, led to even greater militancy and implacability. Queen Victoria addressed Balfour with the words that Margaret Thatcher quoted during the Falklands crisis: "We are not interested in the possibilities of defeat; they do not exist."[169] The British had been made to sit up and take notice, and now threw themselves with relish into the fray.

Later there was, of course, opposition to the war and especially to its excesses and cruelties. The critics were once again the Liberals, and they did not mince their words. Campbell-Bannerman spoke of "methods of barbarism."[170] Lloyd George achieved fame with his antiwar rhetoric. They were called "pro-Boer," though they did not in fact want the Boers to win. They simply considered the war unnecessary, since its objectives could have been attained by negotiation, yet they too were in favor of British suprem-acy in South Africa. Intellectual socialists such as the Fabians, by contrast, welcomed the war. It might not be just, but it was in the interest of civi-lization. Gold mines were too important to be left in the hands of small groups of irresponsible frontiersmen.[171] "The war is wholly unjust but wholly necessary," declared Sidney Webb. That was also the view of George Bernard Shaw, who, incidentally, was later to applaud Mussolini's conquest of Ethiopia.[172] The Boers, for their part, continued to pin their hopes on a change of government in Britain, and it was for this reason that they continued with their guerrilla tactics for so long. But their hopes were to be dashed. The Conservatives won the so-called Khaki election of 1900, and that meant a decline in internal opposition and continuation of the war.

Another factor that might have persuaded the British government to think again would have been the threat of foreign intervention, but that did not arise even though all Europe sympathized with the Boers. Propaganda committees and action groups sprang up everywhere, and pro-Boer journals were launched. These included *Der Burenfreund* in Germany, *Le Cri du Transvaal* in Belgium and *Op! voor Transvaal* and *Voor de Boeren* in the Netherlands, to mention just a few.[173] However, their effect was negligible. There was much talk of a "Continental League" consisting of France, Germany and Russia as a counter to British imperialism, but the differences between the prospective members were too great. Russia had no interest in Africa; France had been taught a humiliating lesson at Fashoda one year before; and Germany had been bought off by Britain with a plan to partition the Portuguese colonies. Moreover, the war was being fought many thousands of miles from Europe. European land forces did not come into the picture; all that mattered was naval power, and in that sphere British superiority was unassailable.

Britain could therefore settle scores with the two republics at its leisure, and that is what it did. To begin with, it put its own house in order. General Sir Redvers Buller—following the many defeats, better known as "Reverse Buller"—was replaced by Field Marshal Lord Roberts, who came back out of retirement for the purpose. "Bobs" himself may have been old, but he was assisted by a younger man who had already won his spurs in Africa, Kitchener.

The new campaign planned by Roberts and Kitchener wagered everything on a single card: an advance from Cape Town along the railroad line to Kimberley and Mafeking, in order to threaten Bloemfontein and Pretoria. First, though, General Piet Cronjé's army at Magersfontein had to be beaten and the siege of Kimberley relieved. After a major battle and heavy losses at Magersfontein, Cronjé's forces were encircled, starved and bombarded. Cronjé surrendered on 27 February 1900. On 13 March, Roberts entered Bloemfontein, the capital of the Orange Free State, which was declared annexed on 28 May and renamed "Orange River Colony." At the beginning of May, Roberts marched into the Transvaal. On 17 May Mafeking—defended for so long and so ably by Colonel Robert Baden-Powell, who discovered his scouting skills during those years—was relieved. On 31

May Johannesburg fell, followed by Pretoria on 5 June. On 3 September the South African Republic was transformed into the Transvaal Colony. Roberts was no longer needed; Kitchener would do the rest. On 28 November Roberts laid down his command and left South Africa. President Kruger had preceded him in September, sailing to Europe via Lourenço Marques on the cruiser *Gelderland*, provided by the Netherlands. His attempt to rally support for the Boer cause proved unsuccessful. The German Kaiser, who had sent him so cordial a telegram in 1895, now refused to receive him. Kruger died in 1904 in exile in Switzerland.

### GUERRILLA WARFARE

The war had been lost, yet it was to continue for another two years, no longer in the form of conventional warfare but as a guerrilla campaign. Boer commandos under Botha, Smuts and De Wet went on raids into Natal and the Cape Colony. They even advanced to within a few dozen miles of Cape Town and inflicted heavy losses on the British. "It is no longer real war out here," Kitchener, now commander-in-chief, complained. ". . . Like wild animals they have to be got into enclosures before they can be captured."[174] This became Kitchener's new strategy. He aimed at impeding the guerrillas' freedom of movement by dividing up the country into zones by means of barbed-wire entanglements and blockhouses. Inside these areas the Boer commandos could be hunted down and captured. Over the years a great many prisoners of war were rounded up as a result—in the end there were 32,000 Boers in prisoner of war camps, including some on the island of St. Helena and some in Ceylon. And yet the decisive victory continued to elude Kitchener.[175]

The mobile Boer commandos proved most difficult to pin down. Commanders such as Christiaan de Wet seemed all but uncatchable. Like so many before and after him, Kitchener turned to terror as a last resort. Farms were burned, cattle and possessions carried off. These were the very tactics C. E. Callwell had advocated for use with "uncivilized nations" in his *Small Wars*. Take their cattle and burn their villages, had been his advice, hit them wherever you can. Callwell admitted that this sort of warfare "may shock the humanitarian,"[176] and so it did.

Humanitarians were shocked above all by the camps Kitchener had set up. The Boers were a nation in arms, and Mao Ze Dong's dictum applied to them even then: guerrillas swim like fish in the water. They rely on the support of the population, in the Boers' case that of their women, children and servants. These people thus had to be removed, and that is why Kitchener interned them in concentration camps, a term that was to acquire the most grisly overtones a few decades later. Forty-four camps for whites were opened in all, into which some 120,000 women and children were herded.[177] Although the camps were not as bad as their name suggests, they were dreadful enough. Stories about the poor conditions and high mortality figures started to circulate quickly, and also reached England. Things were at their lowest point in the final months of 1901, when one in ten inmates died.[178] The British conscience was aroused and embodied in the person of Emily Hobhouse, whose impassioned campaign brought her into head-on conflict with Kitchener. He invariably called her "that bloody woman," and even had her arrested on one occasion.[179]

The conflict made Kitchener increasingly determined. He no longer saw any future for the Boers in South Africa. In his opinion the Boers were "a type of the savage produced by generations of wild lonely life."[180] Prisoners of war and camp inmates must not be allowed to remain in South Africa. Emigration was the solution. The Dutch would be only too glad to have them in the Dutch East Indies, he argued, and there was Madagascar, too, as far as Kitchener was concerned clearly an ideal place for packing away undesirable fellow-citizens.[181]

The protest movement now made itself felt. In November 1901 the camps were placed under civilian control after Milner, too, had protested against the harshness of the regime and the high mortality. Conditions in the camps were improved following the protests, although by the time the war ended in 1902 a total of 28,000 internees had died, including 20,000 children under the age of sixteen. Less attention was paid to the twenty-nine camps set up for the black population, even though the number of internees in them was nearly as high and the conditions if anything worse (the money allocated for living expenses was roughly half that spent on white internees). The official number of dead in these camps was 13,315, but the true figure was certainly higher, indeed considerably so. The Boer War was a war between whites, but not of whites alone.[182]


### PEACE

Like all wars, the Boer War too came to an end. Negotiations were started as early as the autumn of 1901, but were broken off without result. They resumed in April 1902, and began in earnest in May. The Boer delegates—thirty from each of the two states—met at Vereeniging and chose Botha, Smuts, De Wet, De la Rey and Herzog to negotiate with Milner and Kitchener. One thing Britain was determined upon: the Boers would have to renounce their independence. The rest was open to discussion. On 29 May the four Boer generals returned with that message to the delegates in Vereeniging, who after two days of discussion accepted this British demand by 54 votes to 6. On 31 May 1902 the peace treaty was signed in Pretoria. Independence had been lost, but the two former republics received the promise that they, just like the Cape Colony and Natal, would be granted "full responsible government" as soon as possible. Dutch and English were both recognized as the official languages. Britain was to provide financial support for restoration and reconstruction.

Kitchener viewed the result with satisfaction. He now took a much more favorable view of the Boers. "Judged as a whole," he said in an address in Johannesburg, "I maintain that they are a virile race, and an asset of considerable importance to the British Empire."[183] He himself was voted a £50,000 victory grant by Parliament, half as much, incidentally, as Roberts, and was created a viscount, less exalted again than Roberts, who was made an earl. Kitchener was, of course, younger than Roberts, and for him the title of Viscount Kitchener of Khartoum, and of Vaal in the Colony of the Transvaal, and of Aspall in the County of Suffolk was good enough for the time being. What is more, he brought back home with him the statues of Kruger, Steyn and other Boer leaders, which he had had removed from the squares in Pretoria and Bloemfontein with the intention of erecting them in the grounds of his home, there to taste the sweet fruits of victory after his retirement.[184] Alfred Milner, for his part, became Viscount Milner of St. James and Cape Town. "To the victors the spoils."

### SUMMARY

The Boer War was the greatest of all colonial wars fought in the modern imperialist era. It lasted over two and a half years (11 October 1899–31 May 1902). Britain contributed approximately half a million soldiers, of whom 22,000 found their grave in South Africa. The total number of British casualties—killed, wounded and missing—was more than 100,000.[185] The Boers themselves mustered almost 100,000 men. They lost more than 7,000 combatants and nearly 30,000 people in the camps. An unspecified number of Africans fought on either side. Their losses were not recorded but probably ran into the tens of thousands. The British War Office estimated further that 400,346 horses, mules and donkeys were lost during the war. In addition millions of heads of cattle owned by the Boers were slaughtered. The war cost the British taxpayers £200 million, ten times the annual army budget, and more than 14 percent of Britain's net national income in 1902. While the costs of acquiring British subjects elsewhere in Africa were fifteen pence a head on average, the subjection of the Boers cost Britain £1,000 a man.[186]

The Boer War has been called "the last of the gentlemen's wars" in a book by that title,[187] but it was far from being that. It was in fact the first modern war (the Russo-Japanese War shortly afterwards was to be the second). The Boer War was studied and analyzed by many foreign observers. The "lessons of the war"—the title of another book—were hotly debated.[188] They were, however, poorly understood and quickly forgotten. The only lesson this war taught was that defenders have the advantage over attackers. Yet that lesson appeared not to have been learned during the

First World War, when the doctrine of the offensive ruled. Even generals with South African experience, French and Haig among them, subscribed to it. The horrendous consequences became clear at Passchendaele and on the Yser.

The Boer War was a catastrophe for both sides, a catastrophe, moreover, that could easily have been avoided. That at least is how it seems on the face of it. The apparent bone of contention was not really of any importance. Kruger's last offer to the uitlanders was the franchise after a qualifying period of five years, against a number of concessions. Chamberlain, too, was in favor of five years, but without conditions. If need be, he was prepared to accept seven years, but coupled in that case to British participation in the organization of the franchise.[189] The question was so complicated and yet so trivial that it could not possibly be construed by any country as a *casus belli*. The British government was in fact adopting a most peculiar attitude; it was fighting to enable British subjects to get rid of their citizenship. Sir Henry Campbell-Bannerman, the Liberal leader, summed it up before the House of Commons in these inimitable words: "It would be very odd to go to war in order to facilitate British citizens in changing their nationality."[190]

Just one concession by Kruger would have satisfied Chamberlain, or most of the British cabinet in any case. Kruger did not, however, oblige. He had been outnegotiated and believed that any further concessions were pointless, since Britain was clearly bent on the total destruction of his republic. As far as Milner, his interlocutor in Bloemfontein, was concerned, Kruger was quite right, but not when it came to Chamberlain, and certainly not to Salisbury, Balfour and other members of the cabinet. And that was what mattered, for it was up to neither Milner nor even to Chamberlain, but to the British cabinet to declare war.

Kruger was therefore wrong in his assessment of the British attitude at that moment, but he was not mistaken about the crux of the conflict. Bloemfontein and all the other events of that year had been the culmination of a century of tension and conflict. In Kruger's eyes it had been a century of deceit, coercion, intimidation and banditry, with the Jameson Raid in 1895 as the final straw. Every new negotiation was weighed down by the past. As in so many wars, it was no longer just one issue, but the cumulative effect of a whole series of conflicts. Like most wars, that of 1899 thus had a logic of its own. It was the end of a long road, begun with the arrival of the British in the Cape a century earlier.

# 7
# CONCLUSION

The revictualling station set up by the Dutch at the Cape was not to remain a naval base on a rock, but was to grow into a white colony with a "turbulent frontier," a community of settlers who in the course of the century were to advance ever deeper into the interior. The discovery of gold and diamonds opened up a new phase of colonization and led to the emergence of a modern, dynamic society in South Africa. As a result the center of power shifted from Cape Town to Johannesburg, the future of the Cape Colony came to depend on Kruger and his men, and Britain's strategic position in the Cape came under threat. After the discovery of gold, moreover, strategic considerations ceased to be paramount. Great Britain could not remain indifferent to the fate of a region with the greatest known gold deposits on earth. That gold was mined for the most part by British companies, and the new inhabitants of the gold fields were largely of British descent. Britain thus had major and very real economic interests in the area and was determined to retain its influence over South Africa in one form or another.

And so British policy came into conflict with the Boers' love of independence and their commitment to the preservation of their own way of life. In that sense the Boer War was indeed a clash between the new and the old, between the nineteenth and the sixteenth centuries, as Theodor Mommsen asserted as early as 1900.[191] The Boers—with the Irish—became the biggest thorns in the side of the British Empire. Britain was well aware that it would not be easy to bring them to heel. However, the alternative, letting things drift, was unacceptable.

The war of 1899 was thus the culmination of a long process, outlined by the *Times* with remarkable lucidity as early as 1853: "Once embarked on the fatal policy of establishing a frontier in South Africa and defending the frontier by force, there seems to be neither rest nor peace for us till we follow our flying enemies and plant the British Standard on the walls of Timbuctoo."[192] The war was therefore logical, but not inevitable. It was the result of a choice made by Britain: the Boer republics would, in one way or another, sooner or later, willingly or otherwise, have to be incorporated into the British Empire. Joseph Chamberlain spoke not without cause of a "contest for supremacy" between Boer and Briton.[193] If that contest entailed war, so be it. War was the *ultima ratio* of British policy, not an attractive, but also not an inconceivable, solution. The paradox was that both parties considered war a genuine option—war or reform, said Milner; war or ruin, said Kruger—but that both insisted it would not come to war. "One good slap in the face" was enough, Milner claimed. The Boers for their part believed that Britain would climb down. Perhaps each side genuinely thought that the other was bluffing, but even those Britons or Boers who did not insisted that they did, to reassure the waverers and the worriers. The fact that both parties said there would be no war helped to bring the war nearer; it proved to be a self-denying, not a self-fulfilling, prophecy.

Britain was thus left with an unattractive alternative, so fittingly described by Lord Salisbury: "I see before us the necessity for considerable military effort—and all for people whom we despise and for territory which will bring no power and no profit to England."[194] That was in fact what it amounted to, for while the war did bring England victory, it was a victory that would bring it little joy. As early as 1910 South Africa became a Union dominated by the Boers. In 1961 it opted to become a republic and left the Commonwealth.

As a result of all this, the history of the partition of South Africa has a character all its own. It is dominated by a conflict not found elsewhere, the struggle between two white groups, between Boer and Briton. Subsequent developments in southern Africa all derive from this issue. The British annexation of what are today Botswana, Zambia, Zimbabwe and Malawi was a consequence of the expansionist policy of the Cape Colony, a policy directed toward keeping the road to the north open, isolating the German and Portuguese colonies and encircling the Transvaal. That policy was largely successful. German South-West Africa was hemmed in by Britain and Portugal and remained what it was: a rather unattractive stretch of desert. Portugal's dream of a link between its possessions in West and East Africa was frustrated by Rhodes's great leap forward, although it did acquire two large but isolated colonies, Angola and Mozambique. Southern Africa thus became a region dominated by Great Britain.

South Africa is—except for Algeria—the only part of the black continent that has attracted white settlers on a large scale and that has witnessed the establishment and growth of white settlements. It was also the part of the continent most suited to white colonization, a fact to which it owes its special history. That history differs markedly from those of North, East and West Africa. However, South Africa was never to become the second Canada or Australia of which Rhodes and other apostles of the British Empire had dreamt. It did not become a "new world." In North America, Australia and New Zealand the native population was almost entirely exterminated by white settlers. As a result these emerging white societies became new Europes transplanted overseas. In South Africa that did not happen. Here whites remained a small island in a black sea. The result was the unique situation in which that country finds itself to this day.

# VII

# EPILOGUE:
# THE PARTITION OF MOROCCO,
# 1905–1912

Agadir became the symbol of a decisive turning point
in Franco-German relations. The postwar period had
reached its end, the prewar period was upon them.

J. C. Cairns

The partition of Africa ended where it began, in North Africa. Thirty years after the Treaty of the Bardo had helped to establish a French protectorate over Tunisia, the Treaty of Fez put an end to Moroccan independence. The western flank of Algeria was thus also secured, and the entire Maghreb was in French hands. The problem of Morocco, now resolved, had dominated European politics for years and had played a most important role in the history of international relations. In the history of the partition of Africa, however, it was a mere epilogue, that partition having by and large been concluded ten years earlier: the major partition treaties signed in the 1890s had fixed the European spheres of influence in West, Central and East Africa. In 1898 heavy-handed intervention at Fashoda had ensured British control of the Sudan and the Nile. Britain's even more heavy-handed action during the Boer War, which broke out a year later, had cemented British supremacy in South Africa. The partition of Africa had therefore been completed twenty years after it had started. One problem only had been left unresolved, a not insignificant one: the future of the sharifian empire. Morocco was by no means the most trifling prize to be gained in the great European race for African possessions. On the contrary, the country was of political, strategic and economic importance, more so in any case than many other parts of Africa.

Morocco had been of interest to Europeans for centuries. The oldest European settlements in Africa, and also the only ones to exist to this day—namely, the Spanish *presidios* of Ceuta and Melilla—were conquered as early as the fifteenth century. And small wonder that they were; Morocco is after all the part of Africa closest to Europe, the distance between the two continents being less than nine miles across the Strait of Gibraltar at its narrowest point. Yet Morocco was the last part of Africa to be partitioned, though the actual partition had been preceded by a lengthy process of increasing European involvement in its internal affairs. This began with unofficial penetration but quickly took the form of political and diplomatic competition. The unusual feature of that process was that it was based not

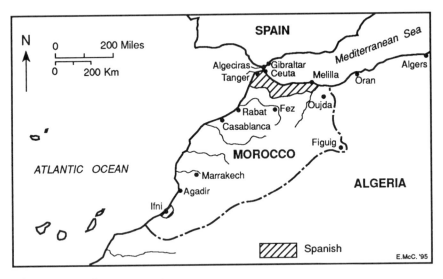

The partition of Morocco (1912)

on Anglo-French rivalry, the normal pattern in the partition of Africa, but on Franco-German dissension. Britain sided with France in the matter on that occasion and in the resulting trial of strength with Germany. In Morocco there was therefore a reversal, if not of alliances then of the old antagonisms. This development was the result of the diplomatic revolution of 1904 known as the Entente Cordiale. It ensured that the Moroccan question differed from the other conflicts surrounding the partition of Africa, and was bound up with the central conflict in Europe, that between France and Germany. It introduced a special dimension and rendered the problem highly explosive. The Moroccan question was the last chapter in the history of the partition of Africa, but more important perhaps, the first chapter in the history of the events leading up to the First World War. It is thus primarily a part of European, not of colonial, history.

# 1
# MOROCCO AND EUROPE

### THE SHARIFIAN EMPIRE

That the Moroccan problem arose so late in the day was a consequence of diplomatic relationships within Europe no less than of the peculiar position of the sharifian empire. Much of Morocco's history has been shaped by its geographical situation. The country is naturally isolated, an island, as it were. Its western border is the Atlantic Ocean, its northern frontier the Mediterranean. To the south and east it is virtually cut off by the towering Atlas Mountains. Beyond them lies the desert, which, like the sea, constitutes not only a barrier but also a link with the outside world. Since time immemorial "ships of the desert" have crossed the Sahara, joining Morocco to the east and also to its natural hinterland, black Africa, to which it was linked long before maritime contacts with Europe were established.

In the seventh century Morocco was overrun by the Arabs, who subjugated the indigenous Berbers and intermingled with them. Morocco thus became part of the Arab world and once even held pride of place in it, Fez being a noted center of Arabian culture. Morocco was never conquered by the Turks and thus never became part of the Ottoman Empire, which had extended as far as Algeria ever since the sixteenth century. The sultan of Morocco remained an independent ruler. He was a spiritual as well as a temporal lord and was revered as sharif or sherif, that is, as a descendant of Mohammed. His claims to spiritual preeminence reached out to all regions whose "inhabitants invoked the prophet's name in their prayers." According to the official view these were to be found as far as Senegal and Guinea in the south, and Egypt and the Nile in the east.[1] That was perhaps slightly exaggerated. His spiritual power was greater than his temporal power in any case, since he was recognized as a spiritual leader in even those parts of Morocco to which his political power did not extend. There were many such parts because the sharifian empire was more impressive in name than in fact. The real power varied from ruler to ruler, some reigning over no more than the environs of the four capitals—Fez, Meknes, Marrakesh and Rabat—in which the court was set up in turn. Others were able to subjugate large parts of the country. In every case, however, the area over which a sultan held sway—the *bled el Makhzen*—existed side by side with the *bled es Siba*—the territory not under his control. This state of continuous internal contention was a source of great surprise and annoyance to Europeans, especially in the nineteenth century. Without exception European travelers reporting from Morocco spoke of chaos, lawlessness and anarchy.

There were not, admittedly, many such travelers. Even in the nineteenth century Morocco was still an unknown and inaccessible country. One writer compared it to Tibet, and Walter Harris, one of the best-known authorities on Morocco, observed that although Morocco was on the Mediterranean, as far as European interest in it was concerned it might as well have been in the Pacific.[2] Harris arrived in Morocco in 1886 at the age of twenty, became the *Times* correspondent there in 1887, and stayed on until his death in 1933. He was an expert commentator on Morocco. There is also little doubt that he was a secret agent. The same was true, at least in the beginning, of another famous traveler, Charles de Foucauld. This

French cavalry officer explored Morocco from 1882 to 1884 disguised as a Russian rabbi, and in 1888 published an account of his experiences under the title of *Reconnaissance au Maroc*. Foucauld lived as colorful a life as Harris, although in a completely different fashion. He became a Trappist monk, but found that even this taciturn order was not silent enough for him and ended up as a "hermit in the Sahara"—by which epithet he became known—writing spiritual treatises as well as learned texts on the Tuareg. There were other travelers and visitors, but their number was small. Morocco sealed itself off from the outside world as best it could. It was and remained by and large *terra incognita*.

European visitors were particularly struck by the poor administration. That was something Europeans, and Englishmen above all, considered the greatest evil of "eastern countries" at the time. Sir Arthur Nicolson (the father of Harold Nicolson), who was British envoy in Tangier from 1895 to 1905, wrote that nowhere else had he met "such complete darkness as reigns here." The government was "merely a machine for raising money."[3] That was also the general view: abuses, disorder, uprisings, civil war and anarchy were typical of Morocco. Many writers put it on a par with such backward countries as China, Persia and Afghanistan. European diplomats in Morocco were of the same opinion. These men, incidentally, were ensconced in Tangier and knew little more about Morocco than what they gathered from one another; traveling in Morocco was considered a perilous and tedious business. The country had no roads to speak of.

Morocco, European observers believed, was deliberately cutting itself off from the West and hence from the forces of progress and renewal. It was therefore fated to decline. In retrospect, however, it seems that this very policy helped to preserve Moroccan independence for as long as possible. Reformers such as Khayr al-Din in Tunisia and the khedive Ismail in Egypt had enthusiastically embraced the cause of progress and development. What followed had been the same old story: debt, loans, new debts, new loans, financial tutelage and finally loss of independence. The rulers of Morocco would have no part of this, and so their country was for a long time spared such financial perils. Yet in the end Morocco, too, was drawn into debt and a policy of reforms. But that happened here later than elsewhere, and more under pressure from without than by inner conviction. Morocco's strength lay in its backwardness.

### EUROPEAN PENETRATION

In 1830 France established its rule in Algeria and thus became Morocco's immediate neighbor. Since the border between the two countries was ill-defined, the situation offered France many opportunities to penetrate Morocco, and it was quick to seize them. In addition to these purely French depredations from the east, there were incursions from the west, through harbors on the Mediterranean and on the Atlantic Ocean, involving various European countries. But whereas military expansion and political provocation were the main issues in the east, trade and economic considerations prevailed in the west.

The basis of the Moroccan economy was agriculture. Poor harvests ravaged the people no less than did diseases and epidemics. It has been estimated that from 1878 to 1884 one-third of the population died as a result of poor harvests, drought and cholera. "You see few old people in Morocco," Harry Maclean, the British military adviser,[4] observed laconically. Morocco had kept the traditional economic system or, in the words of the French historian Jean-Louis Miège, "a natural and closed economy."[5] For all that, it was, during the course of the nineteenth century, increasingly sucked into the international economic system. Maritime links were extended, post offices opened, mining concessions granted. Missions, too, stepped up their involvement, albeit their pastoral activities were confined to the care of the sick, for there were few if any potential converts. Trade also expanded but remained insignificant. The overall value of overseas trade rose during the half century from 1850 to 1900 from £2 to £3 million, Britain accounting for approximately half that figure. Yet neither for Britain nor for any other country was commerce with Morocco of any importance. Such traditional Moroccan exports as wool, skins and grain could, with the growth of world trade, increasingly be procured in other parts of the world such as Australia, India and America, and Moroccan exports continued to fall. Imports, by contrast, grew, with the result that Morocco was left with an unfavorable balance of trade.

In commercial terms Morocco was therefore of little account, but this situation was not irremediable. It has often been stressed that Morocco was once the "granary of the Roman Empire," a role, incidentally, it had had to share with many other countries, for that kind of hyperbole was in great vogue. In addition, Morocco had considerable mining potential, which held still greater appeal to the imagination, Morocco even being referred to as an Eldorado, another honor it had to share with many other parts of Africa. Far more crucial, though, was its political and strategic dimension. Morocco's location at the entrance to the Mediterranean was and is of immense importance, and Spain and Britain, the other two countries commanding this entrance, were not indifferent to this fact. Other Mediterranean countries were of course also interested, among them France and particularly Italy, which since her unification in 1870 felt destined to play a leading role in the area. Germany, finally, looked upon Morocco as one of the last regions in which it could claim a place under the sun.

Growing economic penetration accordingly went hand in hand with increased diplomatic pressure. The British, who were the most important traders in the area, took the initiative, and in 1856 succeeded in concluding a new commercial treaty with the sultan. The treaty brought many advantages to Britain, confirmed British preponderancy, and granted it a number of extraterritorial rights. British subjects henceforth fell outside the sultan's jurisdiction. This treaty was what the 1842 Treaty of Nanking had been for China: a clear violation of national sovereignty. Spain and France reacted promptly to the British challenge. Spain declared war on the Moors in 1859, occupied Tetuan, and was able to retain it at the peace it signed with Morocco in 1860. France followed suit in 1863 with a new treaty that granted it new rights as well.

These years—1856 to 1863—may be considered the prelude to a period of growing European incursion, at first in the form of what was euphemistically called "peaceful penetration." European influence expanded, and Moroccan independence shrank correspondingly. The most spectacular, and for Morocco the most infuriating, form in which that could be seen was protection. An increasing number of Moroccans—several thousands in all—placed themselves under European protection, that is, escaped from the sultan's jurisdiction and taxes. It was of course the most affluent section that took advantage of this loophole. The Madrid Conference of 19 May–3 July 1880, the culmination of diplomatic appeals by Sultan Mulay Hassan to persuade the Powers to end or curtail this system, achieved precisely the opposite result: the protection system received official recognition. This conference, in fact, spelled the end of Moroccan independence.

European penetration also led to grave financial problems. After winning the war of 1859–1860, Spain imposed a hefty war indemnity. To pay it the sultan was forced to take out a foreign loan, which placed a considerable burden on the Moroccan treasury. The loan was in foreign currency, so that "good" money poured out of the country. Mulay Hassan, sultan from 1873 to 1894, tried to prevent further European penetration by a series of reforms. He reorganized the administration, strengthened the army, and bought artillery and rifles abroad. French, British, Italian and Spanish military missions streamed into Morocco. The sultan even dreamed of having a modern fleet. In 1882 the steam gunship *Hasani*, built in Liverpool, was put into service.

The reforms failed, due mainly to the absence of a proper administrative apparatus and to resistance by the traditional elite.[6] Moreover, they proved very costly. Inflation grew apace, and attempts at monetary reform came to nothing. The choice was clear: spending less or borrowing more. The Makhzen, the central organ of the sultan's government, opted for the second alternative and hence for the path taken by Tunisia and Egypt. This did not take place under Mulay Hassan, but under his son and successor, Mulay Abdelaziz, who was just fourteen years old when he ascended the throne. Under him decline turned into crisis. In fact, he found himself in a dilemma. Resisting European influence demanded financial resources he did not possess, while bowing to European influence made him appear a plaything of the Europeans, a tool and a pawn of foreigners, in the eyes of his compatriots. The young sultan opted for the modern style and hence for the second solution. He installed electric lights in his palace in Fez and built a railroad track in the palace grounds. He introduced bicycles, cameras, cigarette lighters, lawn mowers, corsets, ostrich feathers and many other blessings of modern culture and Parisian fashion at his court. His concubines held bicycle races in the palace gardens, to the great delight of the spectators.[7] In short, he accumulated debts, and to pay them he had to farm out his customs duties, state monopolies and other revenues to foreigners. The ruling class watched all this with repugnance, and when Mulay Abdelaziz's brother, Mulay Hafid, viceroy in the south, was proclaimed rival sultan in Marrakesh in 1907, he gained widespread support. From that time onward there were therefore two rulers in Morocco, and the dissolution of the Moroccan state was complete. Europe stepped in.

### EUROPEAN POLICY AND MOROCCO

Several European countries were involved in the final act of the Moroccan drama: France, Germany, Great Britain, Italy and Spain. All of them had special interests in Morocco, but they all had more general and overriding political objectives as well. In the end every one would come away with a prize, France and Spain with part of Morocco, the rest with some form of compensation.

The country that felt it had the strongest historical and moral claim to Morocco was Spain, whose involvement with Morocco went back to the sixteenth century. Its geographical proximity provided Spain, in addition, with a ready excuse for meddling in Moroccan affairs. Moreover, Spain could claim a relatively large share of Morocco's general and shipping trade. Of Europeans resident in Morocco, Spaniards constituted by far the majority. Spain's involvement with Morocco reached its peak with the war of 1859–1860. Had Spain been a major Power, it would have made use of this war to establish a protectorate over Morocco, much as France had done in Algeria. However, Spain was not France, and when the British government let it be known that it was against such a step, Spain dropped the idea. The 1860 treaty granted it many privileges, but a protectorate over Morocco was not one of them.

The Powers, incidentally, did recognize Spain's moral right to a say in Moroccan affairs and to a share in any eventual partition. This may be deduced from the fact that the two great conferences on Morocco were held in Spain, in Madrid in 1880, and in Algeciras in 1906. Spain, for its part, played a waiting game. When France presented a partition proposal in 1894, assigning a large part of Morocco to Spain, the latter realized only too well the danger of such a proposal. The Powers were bound to address any possible protests to the weakest party, that is, to Spain. Prudently, it turned down the French proposal. Even so, after the great Spanish crisis of

1898—the war with the United States and the loss of Cuba and the Philippines—Spanish imperial ambitions became focused more than ever before on the last remnant of Spain's glorious overseas past, namely, Morocco.

Italy could be satisfied more easily. It was not greatly interested in Morocco, but after the French occupation of Tunis in 1881 it was not inclined to accept a similar French advance into Morocco. However, its defeat at the hands of the Ethiopians at Adowa in 1896 led it to rethink its African policy. Italy's last chance of continuing to play a part there lay in Libya, but French approval had to be obtained first. The most obvious answer was a straight deal: in return for French acceptance of Italian intervention in Libya, Italy would give France a free hand in Morocco. Italy did not strike at once but waited until the end of 1911 when, at the height of the second Moroccan crisis, it pounced and annexed Tripoli and Cyrenaica, the heart of the future Libya.

A similar horse-trading deal was also the basis of the Anglo-French political agreement on Morocco, but here the stakes were far greater. British consent was of crucial importance to France. Britain was the world's most important colonial and maritime power and also had the greatest economic interests in Morocco, albeit interests almost exclusively of a commercial nature. Nor did many Britons live in Morocco (in 1900 no more than about a thousand, including the Moroccan protégés), and there were no significant British investments. More important than the economic factors was the strategic importance of Morocco. Britain had no wish to see the Moroccan coast, and certainly not that part facing Gibraltar, in the hands of a rival Power. The traditional objective of British Moroccan policy had always been to avert this eventuality. The result was what was known paradoxically as an "active status-quo policy," in other words, informal imperialism. Britain, incidentally, made no attempt to interfere in Morocco directly, except for a short period under Euan Smith, the British consul, who in 1892–1893 submitted a wide-ranging contract, little short of a protectorate proposal, to the sultan. However, French agents in Fez brought strong pressure to bear on the sultan and eventually had their way: he refused to entertain Smith's proposals. So British policy remained unchanged, that is, it continued to be based on an open-door and status-quo approach until, in 1904, the Entente Cordiale transformed the picture. The British policy that ensued was not, however, so much the result of a British change of heart as of a change in French policy, and it did not remain confined to Morocco, but transformed the balance of power in Europe.

# 2
# FRANCE AND MOROCCO

### ALGERIA AND MOROCCO

In the nineteenth century French policy in Morocco was in many respects similar to that of Britain, as was, indeed, the French position. French interests in Morocco were also primarily commercial and financial. France had no large investments in Morocco, nor did large numbers of Frenchmen live there. For France, too, the Moroccan problem was mainly strategic, and, as with Britain, its concern could best be defined negatively: it wanted no European neighbor along the uncertain western frontier of Algeria.

France had tried to establish a protectorate over Morocco before 1900, once again following active steps by a consul. In 1881 Ladislas d'Ordega was appointed French consul in Tangier. He was a man with good connections in French political circles, and especially with the men around Gambetta. What Théodore Roustan had done as French consul in Tunisia, d'Ordega now tried to do in Morocco. However, Jules Ferry, the French prime minister, thought a second Tunisia too dangerous, and turned d'Ordega's plans down. When d'Ordega persisted he was transferred to Bucharest. The French, like the British, preferred to adopt a wait-and-see policy. There was, however, one important difference between them: France, unlike Britain, shared a border with Morocco. This Algerian-Moroccan border was the scene of continual incidents and problems. To cope with them, the French minister of foreign affairs, Théophile Delcassé, signed a number of border treaties with the sultan of Morocco in 1901 and 1902. As a result, Hubert Lyautey was dispatched to pacify the troubled area in 1903.

### Lyautey

Hubert Lyautey (1854–1934) would eventually become the great French proconsul and pacifier of Morocco. In 1912, after Morocco had been declared a French protectorate, he was charged as resident-general with the pacification of the country, and was to become known as "Lyautey le Marocain." Before that, in 1903, he had gone to Algeria to bring peace to the turbulent border. At the time Lyautey was nearly fifty years old. He had been born in Nancy to a distinguished family with a long military tradition, and had served in Algeria and in France, where garrison life bored him. Lyautey was a man of action but also a thinker. He was influenced by the teachings of social Catholicism rife in the aristocratic circle to which he belonged, a paternalistic social approach based on responsibility by the upper classes for the lower. He expounded this idea in a famous article entitled "Du rôle social de l'officier" (On the social role of the officer) published in 1891 in the *Revue des Deux Mondes*. The gist of his message

Hubert Lyautey

was that it behoved officers to take a personal interest in their soldiers and to treat them as fellow human beings. Such ideas and the social criticism they implied caused considerable controversy in French officers' circles, and Lyautey was advised to lie low for a while.[8] The colonies were the answer.

In 1894 he left for Tonkin, where he was attached to Gallieni, who had just begun his pacification campaign. This was the beginning of a lifelong collaboration and friendship. Lyautey later followed Gallieni to Madagascar, where they devised the "Gallieni-Lyautey method," the principles of which Lyautey explained in his pamphlet entitled *Du rôle colonial de l'armée* (On the army's colonial role).

He embarked on his Moroccan career in 1903, championing the Algerian line in France's Moroccan policy. That line was officially defensive: the pacification of the disputed Moroccan-Algerian border. In reality, however, it was offensive. As he explained in a letter to a friend, he was conducting a clandestine operation, a "discreet penetration," which should be treated as a secret but was too exciting to keep to oneself.[9] The operation, moreover, was not only exciting but also dangerous, as it might easily have international repercussions, something that alarmed the Quai d'Orsay. Not surprisingly, then, many disputes about competency arose between Lyautey and Delcassé, the minister of foreign affairs. However, thanks to the patronage of leading Parisian circles, and especially of Eugène Etienne, and thanks to the relative indifference of the political parties to these matters, Lyautey was to some extent allowed to do as he pleased.

A short time afterwards French Moroccan policy underwent a fundamental transformation. France abandoned its wait-and-see policy and made the incorporation of Morocco a declared political objective. The causes of this change of heart lay not so much in Morocco itself as in the international arena: the Moroccan question was closely linked to the official policy of the Great Powers. The changes in the Moroccan policy of Britain and France were both based on geopolitical and strategic considerations and not on a reassessment of the importance of Morocco itself. As a result, Moroccan policy became part and parcel of what Maurice Paléologue, the famous French diplomat, has rightly called "a watershed in international politics."[10]

### THE NEW COURSE AND THE ENTENTE CORDIALE

The new French policy in Morocco could be traced back to colonial circles, and particularly to the *parti colonial*. That party had been calling since 1882 for a reopening of the Egyptian question, a call that had led among other things to the Fashoda fiasco. The Fashoda incident had proved to be not only a low point but also a turning point in French colonial policy. The clear demonstration of Britain's will and ability to stay in Egypt had helped to produce a change of heart among the more realistic French colonialists; confrontation made way for a policy of compensation. Morocco was the new price France asked for putting a stop to its nuisance value in Egypt. This piece of colonial horse trading enjoyed the support of such leading colonialists as Bourde and Chailley-Bert, and of Eugène Etienne,

Théophile Delcassé

the most powerful of them all. In 1903 they founded the Comité du Maroc, the latest in a long series, with the aim of exerting pressure, by tried and tested methods, on French politicians and in particular on Théophile Delcassé, the minister of foreign affairs. That pressure was to determine French Moroccan policy.

### Delcassé

Théophile Delcassé (1852–1923) came from Pamiers in the Pyrenees, where his father was a bailiff. He read arts at Toulouse and then went on to Paris, where he earned a living as a schoolmaster. He abandoned his literary ambitions after trying without success to have one of his verse dramas performed by the Comédie Française. Next he turned to journalism and from there, like so many others, to politics. Again, like so many of his contemporaries, he fell under the spell of Gambetta, and wrote for Gambetta's two dailies, *La Petite République* and *La République Française*. In 1889 he was elected a deputy. Delcassé had a less than impressive appearance—he was so short that he wore high heels—and he was no great orator. He would probably not have gone very far in home affairs, but foreign policy was a different matter. Delcassé was one of the few who took a genuine interest in it, and that was where he made his name. In the Chamber he became known as a colonial specialist, and in 1892 he was one of the founders of the *Groupe colonial*. On 18 January 1893 he was appointed secretary of state, and on 30 May 1894 became France's first colonial minister. He was to remain at that post until 4 January 1895, and while there he helped to shape French strategy and to launch the Monteil expedition. In June 1898 he had his finest hour, becoming minister of foreign affairs with the support of the *parti colonial*. He held that post until 1905, the longest term in that office in the history of the Third Republic.

France was shaken in 1898 by two great crises, the Dreyfus affair and Fashoda. The second in particular was Delcassé's direct concern. On 2 November 1898 he ordered the evacuation of Fashoda, thus opening the way for an improvement in Anglo-French relations. Before that, however, the Franco-Russian Dual Alliance took most of his attention. That alliance was consolidated by an exchange of notes in 1897, and Delcassé was so delighted with it that he took the relevant documents out of St. Petersburg back to France hidden among his underwear.[11] During the Boer War he tried to gain German support for a joint intervention, but without success, and concluded from this that Germany was France's main rival even in the colonial field. The traditional assumption of the colonialists, namely, that colonial expansion would lead to tensions with Britain and that good relations with Germany were therefore called for, was stood on its head. These events led Delcassé to do something that many prominent members of the *parti colonial* had done before him, that is, to come to terms with the fact that France lacked the power to reopen the Egyptian question. A new course was set: Britain would merely be asked to pay a price for French acceptance of its paramount influence in Egypt. That price was Morocco.

Delcassé enjoyed the support of the colonial group and in general shared their point of view. He not only accepted their new Moroccan policy, but even went a step further than they did. He advocated more extensive collaboration with Britain, the better to strengthen France's hand in its dealings with Germany. Here lay an important difference between his approach and that of the *parti colonial*, which was always most careful not to offend Germany. The significance of that difference will become clear below. In any event, Delcassé began an active campaign to acquire Morocco.

The background to the new French Moroccan policy was thus a mixture of colonial policy and general diplomatic motives. For Britain, by contrast, the motives for abandoning its "splendid isolation" were primarily of the second kind. By the turn of the century most British political leaders had become convinced of the need to turn their back on a go-it-alone policy. The Boer War was not, of course, unconnected with that conversion, nor were the dangers in the Far East, where Russia and Japan threatened British interests. Alongside a hostile France and Russia, Germany and Japan now threatened to become serious rivals to Britain. Under Admiral von Tirpitz, German secretary of state for the Imperial Navy from 1897 to 1916, Germany was engaged on a busy program of fleet construction, the naval laws of 1898 and 1900 greatly facilitating that process. The British war office, and the admiralty in particular, did not fail to draw attention to these dangers, and though Salisbury was none too keen to abandon his traditional policy, his influence on foreign affairs diminished when he handed the foreign affairs portfolio to Lord Lansdowne in 1900. As prime minister, he of course continued to play a part in the shaping of foreign policy.[12]

The new makers of British foreign policy were now Lansdowne and the indomitable colonial secretary, Joseph Chamberlain. Both were anxious to draw closer to the new Great Powers, Germany and Japan. With Japan their efforts bore fruit very quickly: an Anglo-Japanese alliance was established in 1902. Things proved more difficult with Germany. A large part of the British diplomatic establishment considered German geopolitical ambitions a greater danger than French frustration in Africa. And many saw an even greater danger in the German navy. As a result negotiations with Germany stalled, and talks began with France on existing problems and differences. This new course also accorded with the ideas and sympathies of a man considered to exert a great influence on British policy—and who did so not least because of that widespread belief—namely, King Edward VII. In May 1903 the king made a state visit to Paris, a city with which he had become only too familiar during the many convivial visits he had made there as Prince of Wales. Parisians seemed not to have forgotten him either, despite all that had happened since. His visit turned out to be a great success. Thus while he had been greeted by the Parisian public with such militant cries as "Vive Marchand!," "Vivent les Boers!" and even "Vive Jeanne d'Arc!" on his arrival, they roared "Vive Edouard!" and "Notre Bon Edouard!" on his departure. "This must be love," was how the Paris *Punch* correspondent succinctly summed up the atmosphere in Paris.[13] It all seemed set fair for closer relations, yet many months of laborious negotiations were needed even after the king's visit.

For Anglo-French reconciliation was not simply a matter of power politics at large, but also of minor and yet concrete colonial and other concerns. Developments in Egypt and Morocco favored Anglo-French wheeling and dealing. The internal crisis in Morocco rendered the maintenance of the status quo, the old common objective of British and French Moroccan policy, untenable. A European protectorate seemed inevitable, and Britain had to be won round to France's desire that it be a French one. The bait was Egypt. Here too internal developments were undermining the status quo. France, like Bismarck, had for long been able to wave its *bâton égyptien*. The importance of this financial weapon, however, was gradually decreasing. As Egypt's financial situation improved, its dependence on the Caisse de la Dette diminished. Time was thus working against France.

All this made a reasonable case for an Anglo-French deal. The only problem was to ensure that it was even-handed and comprehensive. The main obstacle appeared to lie neither in Morocco nor in Egypt, but—somewhat surprisingly—in French fishing rights in Newfoundland. For Britain it was a *conditio sine qua non* that France must surrender its old claims in that area. The Quai d'Orsay was quite ready to cooperate, but only against territorial compensation. And where could that be found except in Africa? First the French asked for the Gambia, the British enclave in Senegal France had been trying to obtain for some time. That was too high a price for Britain. The next French demand was for Sokoto, but Britain was not in favor of that either. Then another good look was taken at the Niger. Britain made an offer, but France asked for more. Britain was willing, but only in exchange for French recognition of a British protectorate over the New Hebrides. And so it went on. In the long run everything proved too much or too difficult, and the negotiations foundered.[14]

Since the Entente Cordiale was to play so crucial a part in maintaining the European balance of power before and during the First World War, the idea that the whole affair nearly came to nothing because of a problem over fishing rights seems most odd. Luckily—so to speak—the Russo-Japanese War broke out, and European power politics resumed their normal course. The question of fishing rights was shelved during this dangerous conflict into which Britain and France, the respective allies of Japan and Russia, could so easily have been drawn. Common sense prevailed, however, and on 8 April 1904 the convention covering Newfoundland together with mutual declarations on Egypt, Morocco, Siam, Madagascar and the New Hebrides was signed. Its most important feature was the agreement on mutual diplomatic support in dealing with claims to Egypt and Morocco. These documents together formed the basis of the Entente Cordiale, or more precisely paved the way for it.[15]

Now, the Entente Cordiale is a rather vague concept. In any case, its real significance was not immediately obvious. There was no question of creating an alliance, but at most collaboration in the colonial sphere. This provision, it appears, was only incorporated into the documents at the last moment, neither government seeming to appreciate its full implications.[16] How important their collaboration and the agreements on Morocco were became clear soon afterwards, however. For there was yet another country interested in Morocco, a country that had been standing on the sidelines until then: Germany.

### THE TANGIER COUP

Germany had begun to take an interest in Morocco under Bismarck, mainly for diplomatic reasons, since in Bismarck's eyes Morocco was mainly a means of making life difficult for France. However, that policy had not met with much success. Germany, admittedly, also had economic contacts with

Morocco, but never to any great extent. As far as Germany was concerned, the Moroccan question was and remained primarily of political interest. Germany considered it its right to have a say in Moroccan affairs, and refused to allow France to brush it aside. On this Germans were agreed, but when it came to the consequences opinions differed, a fact that was reflected in German foreign policy.

No wonder, then, that this policy should have puzzled so many observers. What precisely was Germany's objective? Did it have territorial ambitions of its own, was it looking for compensation, or was it trying to strain the Entente by putting Britain and France under pressure? German diplomacy was confused and lacking in direction. Its new course, too, was anything but firm. Various elements were at work: the chancellor, the foreign minister, the German ambassador in Tangier, and last but not least the Kaiser himself. In short, Germany did not know what it wanted, but it did know that it wanted something.[17] Following the Anglo-French agreement of 1904 action of some kind was needed to halt the covert French expansion in Morocco, or at any rate to force France to consult Germany.

The Moroccan question thus assumed an importance that went far beyond concern with Morocco itself. The Moroccan crises were the only events in the entire partition of Africa to threaten world peace. The Anglo-French confrontation at Fashoda, too, had of course been extremely dangerous, but even in the well-nigh inconceivable case of its having led to a war between Britain and France, it would have been a colonial and not a European war. A war between France and Germany over Morocco, however, would inevitably have turned into a European war into which the various allies of these two Powers were bound to have been sucked, by virtue of pacts and alliances. It was for this reason that the Moroccan affair played such a special role in the partition of Africa.

Germany focused its attacks on Delcassé, whom it blamed for two things. In the first place he had signed treaties with all the European countries with an interest in Morocco—Italy, Spain and Great Britain—but had not approached Germany. Second, it appeared that he might become a leading mediator in the Russo-Japanese War. If he was successful in this, then France would take the lead in shaping international relations and might even become the leader of a Quadruple Alliance among France, Britain, Russia and Japan.[18] Germany had therefore to take action, designed to force nothing more nor less than Delcassé's resignation.

The German move came on 31 March 1905, in what was admittedly a fairly mild form. Germany had originally intended to stage a naval demonstration off the Moroccan coast, but eventually it opted for the more peaceful alternative of having the Kaiser, who was cruising in the Mediterranean, pay a visit to Tangier. The Kaiser himself did not much care for the idea of going ashore in Morocco. He felt uneasy about braving the rough seas in an open boat and was even more afraid of being assassinated

The Moroccan delegation in Algeciras

by one of the many Spanish anarchists whose presence in Tangier he suspected.[19] Yet land in Tangier he did, for the sake of the national interest. He spoke to the French chargé d'affaires and to the sultan, but made no public pronouncement. However, Richard von Kühlmann, secretary to the German legation at the time and an advocate of strong German action, put together a collection of Wilhelm's utterances and gave that out as a declaration by the Kaiser. In itself the content was relatively innocent. The Kaiser simply came out in favor of an "open door" policy and against annexations and monopolies. The implication, however, was clear enough: Germany would stand up for its interests in Morocco. The Moroccan grand vizier put it rather more picturesquely when he said that Kaiser Wilhelm had given France a tremendous kick up the backside.[20] Germany felt that it was in a strong position, because it did not believe that Britain would support France in Morocco, and because France's only true ally, Russia, was embroiled in a war in Asia.

The declaration concocted by Kühlmann had a marked effect in France. Delcassé claimed that it was nothing but bluff, that Britain stood squarely behind France, and that Germany would draw in its horns. However, the French government thought otherwise. It suddenly realized to what dangers the foreign policy of Delcassé, to whom it had given its backing until then, might lead. Prime Minister Rouvier and many of his colleagues turned against Delcassé, whose position in the cabinet was not very strong in any case, since he had cut himself off from his colleagues and had had a number of clashes with Rouvier. He had even lost the support of the *parti colonial*; his anti-German bias ran counter to the traditional policy of the "colonials," who had always considered good relations with Germany a prerequisite of an active French colonial policy. A large proportion of the *parti* refused to condone this change of course, and Delcassé thus lost the support of the Chamber when he needed it most.[21]

Rouvier was as convinced of Germany's resolve as he was of France's impotence. He had been handed a devastating analysis of the moral and material state of the French army by his military experts. On receiving it he had burst into tears, and he was never to get over the shock. On 26 April 1905 he had fresh talks with the high command. His fears were not allayed, and that very day he took a bold, if surprising, decision. He made contact with Radolin, the German ambassador, and hinted that he was ready to dismiss Delcassé. Delcassé learned within twenty-four hours of Rouvier's covert intervention from a German telegram deciphered by his code section, in which the Germans let it be known that they did indeed want Delcassé to go.[22] The French cabinet yielded, and at the cabinet meeting held on 6 June 1905 Delcassé found himself a lone voice. Rouvier's policy had carried the day, and Delcassé resigned.


# 3
# FROM TANGIER TO AGADIR

### THE ALGECIRAS CONFERENCE

Delcassé's resignation did not, of course, solve the Moroccan question, nor did the Entente dissolve. An international conference was accordingly convened to discuss Morocco and, as far as Germany was concerned, to wind up the Entente. Germany failed to attain that objective, for it was not the French but the Germans who found themselves isolated at the conference. It was held in Algeciras in southern Spain—a compromise between Madrid and Tangier—and took place from 16 January to 7 April 1906. It thus lasted for nearly three months, much to the dismay of the bored diplomats and to the delight of the Spanish delegate, who was also the owner of the leading local hotel.[23] The conference was attended by the same countries that had been present at the Madrid Conference: all the great European Powers, together with such smaller European countries as the Netherlands, Belgium, Sweden and Portugal, as well as the United States and even the sultan of Morocco, who attended in person. Two major issues were to be discussed: the establishment of an international central bank in Morocco and the organization of the police in the main ports. The question that really mattered, the Franco-German diplomatic trial of strength, was of course at the back of all the discussions.

Germany had insisted on an international conference on Morocco in the expectation that it would prove to its advantage, with France finding itself isolated by its Moroccan ambitions. That would make it difficult for Britain to side with France and hence reveal the weakness of the Entente. But Germany had miscalculated: as we saw, not France but Germany was to stand alone in Algeciras, and the Entente was to emerge strengthened, not weakened, from this trial of strength.

German isolation was the result of extremely clumsy German diplomacy. Bernhard von Bülow, chancellor since 1900, did not really know what he was after, and wavered between the firm course advocated by Friedrich von Holstein and the conciliatory policy of the Kaiser. Moreover, with the Tangier landing Germany had painted itself into a corner. Like the other Powers, it sought compensation for giving France a free hand in Morocco. However, unlike the rest, it could not easily give France license to do as it pleased there once the Kaiser had declared that the territorial integrity of the sharifian empire must be preserved. Bülow thus found himself in a quandary, and it was a long time before he made the best of a bad job by taking matters out of Holstein's hands. Holstein resigned soon afterwards. Thereupon the French government fell. This was followed again by many days of splitting hairs and procedural argument, but on 31 March agreement was finally reached. To everyone's dismay, Bülow had a heart attack while defending his policy in the Reichstag on 5 April, but to everyone's relief the final act was nevertheless signed on 7 April. The delegates were able to return home.[24]

The most important diplomatic result of Algeciras was of course the isolation of Germany and its failure to destroy the Entente. France emerged stronger from the confrontation, in terms of both actual influence over Morocco and diplomatic standing. France did not, it was true, gain a dominant hold over the central bank about to be established, but it did obtain the final say over the nominally international police force in the Moroccan ports. Even so, the situation in Morocco remained unsettled, and the Germans were still in a position to stir up enough trouble to make life hard for the French, which they proceeded to do in the next few years.

Meanwhile the Act of Algeciras provided France with adequate foreign support for a policy of military intervention. Pretexts for it abounded. The murder of a French doctor in Marrakesh led to a military incursion from Algeria. In July 1907 Oujda was occupied by French troops. A few days later new disturbances led to the bombardment of Casablanca. France and Spain then agreed on joint military action. The entire Chaouïa district was occupied. New agreements with the sultan followed. The upshot of it all was greater French (and Spanish) involvement in Morocco.

Germany did not accept the new situation, and a series of diplomatic incidents ensued. The case of the German deserters from the Foreign Legion, who escaped with the help of the German consul in Casablanca, was the most dangerous of these. However, the Franco-German agreement signed in 1909 seemed to provide a mutually satisfactory solution, though not for long—the internal situation of Morocco had deteriorated too far for that. It was the same story that had been played out in Egypt thirty years earlier: the traditional political system was on the point of collapse. The French would have liked to work through the Makhzen, but the Makhzen was no longer able to assert its authority. In fact, the Moroccan state had ceased to exist, and with it the basis of the Algeciras system had collapsed. If the French were to maintain or to extend their influence, they had to intervene directly. A ready excuse appeared in April 1911, when Mulay Hafid, besieged in Fez, asked the French for military assistance. It came in the form of a military expedition and marked the beginning of the second and last great Moroccan crisis.

### THE *PANTHER'S* LEAP

In 1909 French foreign affairs fell into the hands of the incompetent Jean Cruppi, a minister who was strongly influenced by an adventurist group of men. The culmination of his risky policy was the French march on Fez on 22 April 1911. It presented a clear break with the cautious line pursued until then—"la diplomatie de l'aventure" had begun.[25] Spain reacted immediately by occupying Larache, the Germans only after much reflection. They then sent the gunboat *Panther* to Morocco, where it dropped anchor off Agadir on 1 July 1911. At the same time Germany informed the Algeciras Powers that it had sent the *Panther* in order to protect German interests in Morocco. The second Moroccan crisis had begun.

This was the moment of truth for Joseph Caillaux, the French minister of finance, who took office as prime minister on the day of the *Panthersprung*, the panther's leap. Caillaux (1863–1944) came from a prominent and well-to-do family. By 1898, when he decided to enter politics, he could look back on a successful career in the *inspection des finances*. He had private resources and was at home in moneyed circles. Hence it was not surprising that he should have risen rapidly to the post of minister of finance. But Caillaux was satisfied with nothing less than the best, and the premiership was his next objective. He reached it in 1911 and was thus thrust into the Agadir affair without having expected such a role or being prepared for it. Caillaux's rise and personality appealed to the public's imagination. He was rich, proud and carefree, a Sunday's child in politics, a man who did not go strictly by the book. In the Agadir crisis he not only relied on the normal diplomatic channels but also used a highly personal approach.

Caillaux's main problem was how best to react to the German move, and his first objective was to establish calm and gain time. Thus he allowed the president of the republic, Armand Fallières, to go ahead with his state visit to the Netherlands as planned, and rejected military responses such as the dispatch of a French warship to Agadir. Instead he used a weapon with which he was more familiar, and applied the financial screw. The panic this caused on the Berlin stock exchange shook the German government. Caillaux meanwhile conferred with Joffre, the chief of the general staff of the army, and put a simple question to him: "Have we a 70 percent chance of winning a war with Germany?" "That we do not," Joffre replied. "Then we shall negotiate," was Caillaux's conclusion.[26] Such negotiations would normally have been conducted by the minister of foreign affairs, then Baron de Selves, but Caillaux considered him incompetent and his advisers dangerous.[27] He thus took on the job himself, and with the help of an old acquaintance, the businessman Hyacinthe Fondère, made contact with Oscar von der Lancken, a German diplomat in Paris. The intention, of course, was to open secret negotiations, but the Quai d'Orsay was still faithfully deciphering German code messages, and on 28 July a furious Selves showed him the telegrams from which he had learned that his prime minister was negotiating with Germany behind his back. These documents were to haunt Caillaux for the rest of his life.

The French ambassador in Berlin, the brilliant and renowned diplomat Jules Cambon, was now drawn into the negotiations, and quickly brought them to a satisfactory conclusion. Tensions were admittedly high, but the solution was obvious. Just like the other Powers, Germany wanted compensation for a French annexation of Morocco. The nature of the German gesture had made their intention clear enough—Germany had sent a gunboat rather than troops, and a gunboat is not what you send if you seriously mean to invade a country. Moreover, the *Panther* measured a modest 1,000 tons and had just two guns and a crew of 120.[28] It was clearly not Germany's intention to take military action in Morocco. It wanted to intimidate, not to occupy. In short, it wanted compensation.

Even the nature of that compensation was obvious. As always, it involved African territory. Alfred von Kiderlen-Wächter, the German foreign minister, knew precisely what he was after: the entire French Congo.[29] That was asking too much, but the French were anxious to please. Even so, the negotiations were not easy, the less so as the territory ceded by France would, for reasons of prestige, have to be presented as a territorial exchange. Hence Germany, too, had to cede something. After much haggling the problem was solved and a Franco-German agreement signed on 4 November 1911. Although it was received badly in both countries, it was

Establishing the French protectorate over Morocco

ratified by both parliaments. Nothing now stood in the way of a French protectorate.

### THE PROTECTORATE

On 24 March 1912 the French envoy to Tangier arrived in Fez to present a protectorate treaty to the sultan. After a few days of complicated discussions, Mulay Hafid, the former rival sultan who had in the meantime been recognized as sultan, resigned himself to the inevitable and on 30 March 1912 signed the Treaty of Fez. He then abdicated his throne in favor of his brother Mulay Yussuf and went into exile.

The Treaty of Fez opened the way for the partition of Morocco. It also stipulated that France and Spain must agree on the details. The two countries had, in fact, reached general agreement as early as 1904, but the process was complicated by a protectorate treaty that Spain concluded with the sultan on 27 November 1912. It assigned two zones to Spain: first, the coastline from Larache on the Atlantic to Melilla on the Mediterranean, but excluding Tangier, which was placed under international control; and second, a region to the south of the river Dra. Most of Morocco, however, went to France. The great dream of the *parti colonial* had been fulfilled: a territory 4,500 kilometers in length, stretching from Ceuta on the Mediterranean to Cabinda in the Congo, had been brought under French authority.

In theory the Treaty of Fez established a kind of double rule in Morocco. The sultan retained his sovereign prerogatives, but surrendered control of justice, defense, foreign affairs and finance. He could do nothing without the consent of the French resident-general. Conversely, the latter could do nothing without the sultan's consent, but that was largely a theoretical proviso. In practice, the system of double rule developed into a system of direct rule by France. The Moroccan state survived in form only. In content it became French.

The actual subjection of Morocco did not in fact proceed according to plan. Shortly after the contents of the treaty became known, the troops and inhabitants of Fez rose up and murdered every European they could find. The protectorate had therefore to be established by force, and that was to prove a protracted and expensive business. The man who would be put in charge of it, Lyautey, chose a step-by-step approach. He started with "le Maroc utile," in other words, urban and lowland Morocco, and left the Central Atlas region until later. Finally, he turned to the south. The conquest of all Morocco was not completed until 1934, twenty-two years after the Treaty of Fez was signed. In 1956, another twenty-two years later, Morocco regained its independence.

# 4
# CONCLUSION

The odd thing about the partition of Morocco was not that it should have happened at all but that it happened so late. For it came some thirty years after the partition of Africa was begun and ten years after that partition had been essentially completed. The part of Africa which lay closest to Europe, which had witnessed the first occupation by Europeans and which ever since 1830 had shared an ill-defined border with the French colony of Algeria, was nevertheless the last part of Africa to be caught up in its partition. The explanation must be sought in two main factors: Morocco's internal situation and the state of international relations. The sultans of Morocco were no Mohammed Alis. On the contrary, they seemed reconciled to their country's rather backward and old-fashioned condition. In the end, however, they, too, opted for progress and modernization and hence contracted debts and floated loans, but they did so relatively late in the day, at least when compared with their colleagues in Tunisia and Egypt. As a result international interference was for a long time kept more or less at bay.

International relations, too, ensured that Morocco was kept off the European diplomatic agenda until late in the day. Of all the European Powers, France and Spain were most closely concerned with the sharifian empire. However, Spain was in no position to adopt anything but an extremely cautious foreign policy, the fiasco of 1898 being a specter that precluded grandiose diplomatic gestures. France could do nothing in Morocco without British approval, and it could not of course count on such approval while it continued to cross Britain in Egypt. After Fashoda, when France adopted a more realistic approach, new possibilities opened up. By a series of bilateral treaties with Britain, Spain and Italy, Delcassé was able to keep the Moroccan question out of international discussions. His refusal to treat Germany in the same way was his greatest diplomatic gamble. In 1905 it proved to have been a miscalculation: Delcassé had misjudged international as well as internal French political relations. His fall was to be Germany's greatest triumph since 1870; the very same day the Kaiser made his chancellor, Bülow, a prince. Yet Germany failed to profit from this triumph, for far from being weakened the Entente was strengthened by the course of events. Admittedly Germany, like the other Powers, received compensation in the end for agreeing to a French protectorate over Morocco. In that sense it may be said to have had its way. It was being treated like the rest.

The Moroccan crisis was the most dangerous of all to have arisen during the partition of Africa. For the first time Germany and France confronted each other in Africa, and for the first time in thirty years there were fears of a Franco-German war. That war did indeed come, but not until 1914, and not because of Morocco but because of the Balkans. However, the years after 1905 were overshadowed by that coming clash of arms. In diplomatic history, the *avant-guerre* of 1914 began with the Tangier crisis of 1905. The event made a strong impression, particularly on public opinion in France. The French army, which had been thrown into moral and organizational disarray by the Dreyfus affair and its alarming sequels, now began to recover its position and authority. Nationalism and patriotism were once more held in honor. The German question was resurrected with a vengeance. War had once again become a real possibility. Six years after Tangier, the Agadir crisis brought it all back. Agadir, as the historian J. C. Cairns put it, was a symbolic turning point in Franco-German relations.[30] A year later France introduced three years' conscription, one of the clearest indications of its pursuit of military preparedness.

The Moroccan question differed in many respects from all the other questions that emerged during the partition of Africa. Its origin, course and conclusion were almost exclusively determined by developments in international, not colonial, politics. The Moroccan question was the beginning of a new period in European diplomacy, the prologue to the war of 1914. In the history of the partition of Africa, however, it was merely a tailpiece, an epilogue to a story that had been largely concluded by about 1900.

# CONCLUSION

The conquest of the earth, which mostly means
the taking it away from those who have a different
complexion or slightly flatter noses than ourselves,
is not a pretty thing when you look into it much.

Joseph Conrad, *Heart of Darkness*

$\mathbf{W}$ith the Franco-Spanish partition of Morocco from 1911 to 1912 and the almost simultaneous annexation of Libya by Italy, the partition of Africa was at an end. Except for Ethiopia, there was nothing left to share out. Soon afterwards, the First World War began, and while its main stage was Europe, fighting also took place in the wings, in Asia and Africa. Germany lost the war, and its colonies were divided among the victors. France received the lion's share of both Togo and Cameroon; the remainder went to Britain, as did German East Africa. Belgium acquired Ruanda-Urundi. South-West Africa went to South Africa, in which it was long to remain. No longer colonies, these possessions became mandated territories, administered by the colonial Powers on behalf of the League of Nations. Nor was this quite the end of the story. In 1935 Italy made a fresh attempt to gain control of Ethiopia, annexing it in 1936.

Much as the partition of Africa did not really begin in 1880, it therefore did not come to a complete end in 1914. Yet 1880 to 1914 must be looked on as the main years of partition. During that period 90 percent of Africa fell under European control. The question, of course, is why? Why did it happen, or more precisely, why did it happen then and in that way? This question has been the cause of much controversy and has exercised many minds. It is now necessary, at the end of this book, to refer to it.

### THE PARTITION OF AFRICA AS A PROBLEM

In order to establish why the partition of Africa took place when it did, one must first determine when it began. Various answers have been given by various historians, the years 1879, 1881, 1882 and 1884 all having their proponents. The precise answer does not seem particularly important. Whether the partition started a year earlier or a year later does not after all make a great deal of difference. What matters is the fact that each one of these dates denotes a particular event and hence implies a particular interpretation. Those who cite 1879 have in mind the new French expansionist policy in Senegal that began that year, and hence hold French conduct there responsible for the start of the partition. To understand that conduct, they try to explore its motivation. Again, those who cite 1881 are thinking of the Tunisia expedition and will analyze Ferry's and Gambetta's motives for launching it. The year 1882 refers to the British occupation of Egypt and raises the question of Britain's reasons for that intervention. The year 1884 refers to the arrival of Bismarck and King Leopold on the African stage, with the implication that the actions of these new players prompted the partition.

Discussion of these differences is important, and it would be as naive to argue that there is a definitive answer to this problem as to nominate some other event as the crucial trigger. There is an extensive body of writing on the subject, and various analytical expedients, such as the distinction between "partition" and "scramble," have been used to elucidate the problem.[1] We must conclude, however, that the beginning of the partition cannot be dated with certainty and that no one event can be singled out as its cause. It is not even clear what exactly we are entitled to consider a relevant "event." What is called a historical event was often a whole series of happenings consequent upon a whole chain of decisions. That chain, like all chains, was as strong as its weakest link; decisions could be taken or revoked at different levels. This is best illustrated by an example.

In 1875 Cameron "annexed" part of the Congo, but the British government backed away, and that was the end of the matter. In 1880 Brazza also "annexed" part of the Congo, but this time with French government support. Matters had thus moved one step further, but did not yet constitute an "event": the Chamber still had to ratify Brazza's treaty. Here things might have ground to a halt, for parliaments did not always do as they were asked. The Portuguese parliament, for instance, turned down the proposed treaty with Britain in 1890. The same might also have happened in the Congo, which would have brought this episode to a close. However, the French parliament did ratify the treaty, taking matters another step further, though not even that constituted an "event." After all, the Powers might have refused to recognize the treaty, as they were to do, for instance, with the Anglo-Portuguese treaty of 1884. That, too, would have been the end of the affair. However, they did not refuse, and recorded their recognition of the French claim in a series of bilateral treaties. The upshot was the creation of the French Congo, and a historical event could be added to the history books.

That historical event was therefore the culmination of a whole series of decisions, taken by different people with different motives. If we want to explain these events, we must therefore examine the various motives of the various people involved in them. We must analyze the motives of Brazza and Makoko, of the French government, the French press and French parliamentarians, and also of the political leaders of the Powers who recognized the treaty. Given that these motives differed widely, we cannot single out any one event or any one motive.

Another problem appears when we look at the consequences of given events. Thus we may read that event A led to event B or that event X was the impetus for event Y. But what exactly does that mean? If we impart an impetus to a billiard ball we set it in motion, and hence we can call the impetus the cause of the motion. But society does not run according to the rules of mechanics, and in history we do not recognize that sort of causality. Some historical actions may indeed be considered reactions to others, but not in the mechanical sense. Inasmuch as a historical action was the result of a number of decisions, so also was the reaction to it. Human beings, needless to say, are not completely free in the way they react. Actions and reactions are influenced by the dominant intellectual climate of a particular period. The belief, for instance, that the Nile must be controlled if Egypt is to be defended is not illogical, but neither is it self-evident. Yet that is what the imperialists firmly believed. It happened to be the spirit of the age, and given that spirit such a reaction was logical though not inevitable. All this does not mean that the search for the beginning or for the origins of the partition of Africa is pointless or irrelevant. All it means is that the scope of such a search is limited. In retrospect we can of course establish how one event followed upon another, and hence try to identify the event with which the whole process started, but we cannot consider that event as the prime cause from which every other event inevitably sprang.

At least as important as the question of when and why the partition began is the question of why it continued to the bitter end, until there was nothing left to divide. We can also put that question differently: what might have stopped the partition? In theory there are two possible answers: massive resistance by the Africans, or outside intervention. As far as the first is concerned, the answer is simple: that form of resistance simply did not occur. This may seem astonishing, but is understandable if we reflect on what exactly the partition of Africa entailed. It was first and foremost a paper affair, a question of treaties between European countries in which their respective spheres of influence and possessions were defined. It did not remain like that. As we have seen, effective occupation became an important objective during a later period, and that meant transforming the paper partition into a partition on the ground. No precise date can be put on that transformation, but broadly we may say that the paper partition was enacted in the 1880s and the partition on the ground during the following period.[2]

It should be borne in mind that very little happened in Africa itself during the first phase. The partition of Africa was recorded by the Europeans on their maps, but the matter rested there for the time being. These maps of Africa were therefore of a quite particular kind. Generally speaking a map is a reflection of reality, a symbolic and stylized reflection, of course, but nonetheless a representation of something that exists, either physically, such as a mountain, a river, a town, or else politically or socially, such as a state, a country, a province, a border, and so on. But what did these maps of Africa actually show? Nothing but what European diplomats had agreed in their chancelleries, namely, that they would allow one another a free run in these territories. The British historian Bernard Porter has used the analogy of child marriages in past centuries.[3] Such marriages were contracted without the partners having met, that is, they were agreed on long before the marriage was consummated. In the case of the partition of Africa, too, the partners met only after the contract was signed, and difficulties often did not arise until then. Here lies the peculiar nature of these events. At first sight they resemble what we know from European history: treaties were signed and borders laid down. But they were actually quite different. In Europe conquests preceded the drawing of maps; in Africa the map was drawn first, and then it was decided what was going to happen. These maps did not therefore reflect reality but helped to create it. Here, a familiar phrase from the 1960s applies: the medium is the message.

Naturally this practice has drawn much criticism. Thus it is often said that it has rendered the borders of Africa "unnatural." That is true but is not quite the point. The special nature of African borders is not that they are unnatural. Almost all borders are. What, after all, is natural about the borders between the Netherlands and its neighbors? Borders are not normally drawn by nature but by force, that is, by political power. The special nature of the African borders is that they did not enshrine the balance of power a posteriori but determined it a priori.

Hence it is not surprising that so little resistance should have made itself felt in the 1880s. There was simply not a great deal to resist. That was to change in the 1890s, when violence increased markedly and changed in character. The Anglo-Egyptian reconquest of the Sudan, the Italian war in Ethiopia, the Boer War in South Africa, were no longer "small wars" but major conflicts. Partition was on in earnest. Yet two marginal comments are required here. First, even during this period colonial and European wars were of a different order. The biggest war fought in Africa, the Boer War, was not between black and white, but between white and white. Yet even that war was but a pale foreshadowing of the First World War. As for the Africans, their resistance was often heroic and sometimes effective, but it was virtually never enacted on a large scale.

Second, the end of the partition did not spell the end of violence. The great German colonial war against the Herero people in South-West Africa took place in 1904, the Maji-Maji wars in Tanganyika from 1905 to 1907. The pacification of Morocco did not even begin until 1912 and was to continue into the 1930s. In a sense the conquest was never completed, because resistance increasingly turned into rebellion, uprisings and other forms of protest. It is somewhat artificial, therefore, to distinguish the conquest as a separate phase of the colonial period. We must beware of applying concepts with which we are familiar from European history to the history of Africa without further ado. In Europe we can apply a simple dichotomy: war or peace. In the colonial context, however, these twin concepts do not cover the whole of reality. Violence assumes many forms. What we call war is only that form of violence Europeans consider worthy of inclusion in the annals of history.[4] Other forms were no less frightful. Peace in the strict sense of the word never prevailed. We must remember all this when we try to assess the extent of resistance to partition, but with these reservations, we can say that the number of wars fought in Africa was relatively small, and repeat that there was no such thing as massive, collective and sustained resistance to the partition. That is why the partition was able to proceed more or less undisturbed until it came to its natural end.

The other reason why the partition continued apace was the absence of outside intervention. A comparison may help to make this clear. During the last quarter of the nineteenth century appraisals of the partition not only of Africa but also of China were widespread. China was an attractive prize for the imperialists, richer and more appealing than Africa. And China was indeed encroached upon by foreign Powers; it was put under pressure and had its coastline nibbled away, but it was never partitioned. Since historians are wont to explain what happened and not what failed to happen, there are a great many books on the partition of Africa but none on the nonpartition of China. That subject is no less interesting, however. The difference is certainly due in part to the much stronger internal structure of the Chinese empire, but in part also to international factors.

In China, the West European colonial Powers were joined by Russia, which came overland, by Japan, the only Asiatic country to become an imperial Power, and by America, which introduced its own form of imperialism, that of the "open door." That is why matters took a different course here from the one followed in Africa, where the Europeans were, so to speak, left to their own devices. In Africa they could play their familiar diplomatic game, and they played it with dedication and skill, in accordance with the rules they had devised over centuries of European politics: demands, threats, haggling, intimidation and reconciliation. So they went on partitioning until there was nothing left to partition, and did so speedily and more or less harmoniously. There was bickering and bargaining, but there were no major conflicts between the European contenders. The reason was simple: there was enough to go round. There were big prizes and small prizes, but the African lottery had no booby prizes. There was a solution to every problem: if it could not be done one way, there was always another way to do it, or, as Mack the Knife put it in Brecht's *Threepenny Opera*, "Something else might do, but this will do just as well." That is why there were few major wars between Europeans and Africans and also no major conflicts among the Europeans themselves. The period from 1870 to 1914 is known as the age of imperialism, but also as the age of armed peace.

## MOTIVES AND DECISIONS

Much as historians have brought their dedication and intellect to bear on the question of the decisive event that triggered the partition of Africa, so also have they fervently disputed its underlying motives. Their views have been many and various. Hobson, as we have already said, adopted an unequivocal stand in his classic work *Imperialism: A Study*, the first historical interpretation of the partition: imperialism was a consequence of capitalism. It was "primarily a struggle for profitable markets of investment."[5] This and other economic considerations, such as the search for raw materials and for outlets for European industry, have long dominated analyses of imperialism and of the partition. Only after the Second World War, and especially since the 1960s, has greater attention been paid to the political motives. A new chapter in the discussion was opened, to which the British historians John Gallagher and Ronald Robinson have made a leading contribution with several studies, including their *Africa and the Victorians*, published in 1961 and now considered a classic. British policy during the partition, they allege, was determined not by capitalists but by politicians, and was based not on economic but on strategic and political considerations. British policymakers were not so much concerned with Africa itself as with safeguarding British interests in Asia: "The decisive motive behind late-Victorian strategy in Africa was to protect the all-important stakes in India and the East."[6] No matter what we may think of this interpretation—and it has been challenged by many historians—what is certain is that it can only be applied to *British* policy in Africa. Countries with no Asian empire could not have been impelled by such considerations, and their policy was therefore governed by other motives. Those motives differed from country to country, from period to period, and from place to place. Economic motives such as the protection and encouragement of trade and industry did indeed play a part, but so also did such financial motives as the safeguarding of loans and investments, such political motives as strategic advantage, national ambition, electoral appeal, such ideological motives as bearing the white man's burden, and many more. Historians have examined them all and produced a substantial body of source material demonstrating that they all had a role to play, that all were taken into account and that politicians demonstrated their responsiveness to them all. That goes without saying, of course. Various pressure groups naturally urged governments to defend their particular interests. Just as naturally, governments for the most part complied. They fought for every interest they thought worth defending. The true significance of their actions, however, only became apparent when one interest had to be weighed against another, when it was essential to establish what price was worth paying and what exchange worth accepting. In politics the question is never what is wanted, but what is preferred.

This is more obvious in the case of smaller countries than it is in the case of large. Large countries are not easily forced by others into making a choice, and if they are, the result often leads to tensions. With small countries, things are different. The Netherlands, for instance, had considerable interests in the Congo, for which Dutch business naturally stood up, and which the Dutch minister of foreign affairs just as naturally instructed his diplomats to defend. However, when it came to weighing up these interests against Dutch foreign interests in general, the choice was simple: the latter prevailed.[7] Politicians like to say that the national interest comes first, but there is of course no such thing as the national interest. What does exist is a certain perception of the relative importance of the various part-interests. It all comes down to a simple truth: politicians balance these interests and base decisions on them in the way they think best. Or as Gallagher and Robinson have put it in *Africa and the Victorians*, at the level of the "official mind" interests are taken into account, and the decisions that are made are based on a particular view of these interests. Nor is there anything surprising about that. Weighing interests and taking decisions is, after all, what politics is all about.

In Africa many interests were at play, and it is generally impossible to designate any one interest as the decisive one. Which of many interests prevailed in the end can only be established in those specific cases that governments were forced to consider carefully. Various motives played their part in shaping British policy in Egypt: the Suez canal could not be put at risk, the rights of its shareholders had to be protected, the British taxpayer was not to be burdened with the costs, France was not to be alienated, and so forth. All these interests were defended, but sometimes a choice had to be made, and it is only at this point that we can establish a hierarchy of interests. Fashoda, for instance, proved that Britain considered the Sudan worth a clash with France as well as a levy on the taxpayers' purse. That tells us something about the hierarchy of interests, but does not mean that the other objectives (an "empire on the cheap" and good relations with France) were forgotten. All it means is that at the time they were considered less important than others, and that such general precepts are nothing to go by.

We can only conclude, therefore, that during the partition of Africa various motives played a part, first one and then another being paramount at any one time. This is only to be expected. There is no reason for assuming that all parties involved in the partition of Africa should have had the same motives, that Bismarck's decision to acquire colonies had the same motive as Gladstone's decision to intervene in Egypt, or that Leopold's creation of the Free State was based on the same motives as Jules Ferry's decision to send an expedition to Tunisia. The European nations had various interests and their statesmen various ideas, the different parts of Africa holding a different significance for each one. We can thus claim that Britain thought West Africa important for commercial reasons, South Africa for financial, East Africa for strategic, and other areas for yet other reasons, and that other countries had different views. Europe's interventions and undertakings in Africa involved so broad a spectrum of interests and motives that any general explanation or hypothesis inevitably founders on events that do not fit in.

### CAUSES AND EFFECTS

In this book—and in this conclusion too—we have been dwelling for the main part on decisions and the reasons for them. These are important issues but cannot be considered the end of the matter. Those interested in finding out why the partition of Africa took place when it did cannot confine themselves to men and their motives, but must also examine the objective causes and effects. To grasp what happened we must admittedly reconstruct the reasons that impelled the historical actors, and analyze their decisions, but we must do more than that. Much as, in order to understand the origins of the First World War, we cannot merely analyze the decisions taken in Vienna, Berlin, Paris, and so on, but must also analyze their background— or, if you prefer, the structural factors—so also for the partition of Africa we must examine the historical background and determine what place the partition holds in the overall picture of European imperialism in Africa. That presupposes a different level of abstraction and generalization from the one we have been applying.

At the end of *Africa and the Victorians*, Gallagher and Robinson were confronted by the same problem. They realized that although they had analyzed the political imperatives and views of British politicians, these did not lay bare the causes of the partition. The real question was the relationship between purposes and perceptions on the one hand, and objective causes on the other hand. According to them, "the subjective views which swayed the British partitioners . . . were one of the many objective causes of the partition itself."[8] That answer is not entirely satisfactory. It is not easy to pair subjective considerations with objective causes, for the subjective views are in fact reactions to objective changes. Hence it may be better to say that when we pass on from "subjective views" to "objective causes" we finish up with a different type of historical analysis, or, as the French put it, with a different historical *discours*.

The one approach, incidentally, does not preclude the other, but complements it. In the one the stress is laid on the reconstruction of reality as it was experienced at the time (the *expérience vécue*), in the other we are wise after the event. That is of course an anachronistic approach, but it is one to which we cannot really object. The historian's craft is bound to be anachronistic in a sense, inasmuch as the historian is au fait with the outcome. He knows that the steam engine marked the beginning of the industrial revolution and that Columbus's voyage to America led to the discovery of the New World. Those are things James Watt and Columbus themselves did not know and to which it is not likely that they gave much thought. Similarly, Ferry was not aware that the Tunisian expedition in 1881 marked the beginning of the second French colonial empire, nor Gladstone that British intervention in Egypt was to have so crucial an effect on the partition of Africa. Yet there is no objection to making such connections and to viewing these events retrospectively in this light. Anyone studying the causes of the industrial revolution will not, after all, simply delve into what went on in the heads of Watt, Arkwright and the rest, but also look at such general and long-term processes as capital accumulation, agrarian reform and scientific innovation. Much the same is true of the partition of Africa. Those involved took decisions based on objectives with which as a rule they were familiar, but could not have said what the outcome would be. They believed they were making history, and to some extent they were. For the rest, however, they were merely unconscious tools of what Hegel has called the "cunning of reason." The partition of Africa was the result of a series of independent and more or less "accidental" decisions. In retrospect, however, we can see that these decisions fell into a certain pattern, that they marked a new phase in Europe's relationship with Africa. This transition sprang from specific changes in Europe and Africa that took place at the time and ensured that the years from 1880 to 1914 differed from the periods both before and after.

That Africa should have been drawn into the European system of international relations was inevitable. What is far more surprising is that it should have eluded that system for so long. The explanation is actually quite simple. America was more suited to emigration and colonization than Africa, Asia more suited to commercial exploitation and trade. Africa had little to offer Europeans as a place to settle. Immigrants met an early death there, and the spoils they were after—slaves, gold, ivory—could be obtained by peaceful means. It might have been possible to establish a more powerful presence even at an earlier stage, but that would have demanded a price not worth paying. Things began to change in the course of the nineteenth century. The booty became of increasing importance once the greater part of the world had been divided up and the price of conquest was lowered to an acceptable level by Europe's growing technical supremacy. Improved medical and pharmaceutical techniques and knowledge made it possible for Europeans to live, work and fight in Africa. Better means of communication and transport facilitated the deployment of European troops. Military superiority ensured easy victories. Because the balance of power had shifted so much in Europe's favor, the expenditure was low. From 1882 to 1898, 70 million Africans were brought under British rule, the costs of this operation averaging fifteen pence per person.[9] These developments were, however, merely a necessary, but not a sufficient, condition of the partition of Africa. There was something else. A number of specific changes in Europe and in Africa not only made it possible to subject Africa politically, but also made doing so an attractive proposition.

To understand the character of the period following 1870, we must compare it with the preceding period. In the early nineteenth century, from Napoleon to Bismarck, Europe found itself in an exceptional political situation. Germany and Italy did not yet exist. Britain had eliminated France as a maritime and colonial rival. Spain, Portugal and the Netherlands, the old colonial powers, had had their day. Hence, Britain, in part thanks to its industrial lead, enjoyed de facto world supremacy, much as the United States was to do after the Second World War. All these factors were swept away in the 1870s. The second industrial revolution spread to the rest of the world and created new rivals for Britain. After its defeat in 1870 France sought compensation for its loss of continental power by adopting its traditional second option, the strengthening of its overseas role. Germany and Italy, newcomers both, fought for their place under the sun, much as King Leopold did in his own way. International relations were radically transformed in character.

Internal political factors also played a part. European governments were faced with a new phenomenon: they had to take the wishes of the electorate into account, and most of them did not relish the change. Lord Salisbury even thought it an odious development. It was no less real for that. Politics had fallen under the sway of the masses. Economic growth and social harmony became declared objectives of government policy. The Paris Commune of 1871 accentuated the danger of revolution and hence the importance of social issues all over again. The boundary between the prerogatives of the state and the realm reserved for the free play of social forces became blurred. Social and economic questions assumed increasing importance. State welfare provisions expanded. The import of tropical products at affordable prices was considered a matter of public concern. During the second phase of the partition, the protection of commercial interests abroad thus went hand in hand with the provision of cheap food for the masses at home. That called for new plantations and presupposed peace and order, in other words, effective authority.[10] Conversely, technical progress, economic growth and growing political involvement by the citizens of Europe created the conditions for a strong state. The military might of the European Powers reached unprecedented heights. In 1806 Britain took the Cape Colony with just over 6,000 men. The Dutch offered little resistance. In 1900 Britain mobilized 300,000 men against the Boers, more than four times the number Napoleon had at his disposal at the Battle of

Waterloo. African countries, by contrast, remained what they always had been: numerous and weak.

A new situation had thus been created in Europe after 1870, in home affairs as well as in foreign policy. As far as the second was concerned, the consolidation of national states led to a new power configuration characterized by strong international rivalry and constant diplomatic maneuvering. In home affairs the growing political power of the masses helped to forge closer bonds between state and society, thus blurring the traditional distinction between them. As a result attempts to assess the relative importance of political and economic factors in European imperialism are purely academic. Political and economic motives are difficult if not impossible to tell apart. We do far better to say that the politics of imperialism was a synthesis of social, economic and "purely" political factors. There was no such thing as the primacy of home affairs or foreign policy. Security abroad and the maintenance of law and order at home were inseparable objectives and of equal importance.

It is no mere chance that the new international orientation of post-1870 Europe should have roughly coincided with the second industrial revolution, but the two were nevertheless independent developments. Together they ushered in a new situation in Europe. Though these European developments have for a long time dominated discussions of imperialism, they are only one side of the picture. The other side becomes apparent when we look at developments in Africa. Robinson and Gallagher have stressed the importance of the latter, even arguing that the "crucial changes that set it all working took place in Africa itself."[11] This attention to what is now called the "peripheral," that is, the non-European, factors is merited, for the changes wrought in Africa were decisive. Egypt's financial problems led to increasing foreign interference, and this, in turn, to a "nationalistic" reaction which plunged Egypt into an internal political crisis. The mineral discoveries in South Africa led to a complete change of the balance of power in that part of the continent. The shift in demand from such "royal" products as gold, ivory and slaves to such "democratic" products as palm oil and rubber weakened the position of the traditional rulers in large parts of Africa. These and other internal developments were to some extent independent of developments in Europe. Yet there were some links between them. Both were effects of the increasing cohesion of international economic relations. In that sense we can consider them a coherent whole, and the industrial revolution as the prime cause of imperialism.

### IMPORTANCE AND RELEVANCE

What was the relevance, the importance, of this entire episode? The question has two aspects: the importance for Europe and the importance for Africa. Seen from the European perspective, neither the partition of Africa

nor the colonial phenomenon were of great relevance. As we have said, the
partition of Africa was enacted on the periphery of European politics. It
came low on the long list of preoccupations of contemporary politicians.
In economic respects, colonialism in Africa did not become important until
after the First World War. In the period between the two world wars,
however, Africa's economic importance to Europe grew appreciably. Trade
and investments expanded. Several million Europeans earned their living in
Africa temporarily or permanently.

After the Second World War the colonial period drew to a rapid close.
Paradoxically, it was only then that the colonial consciousness of Europeans began to strengthen. It was only then, for instance, that the French
started to show serious interest in their colonial empire. But by that time
the colonial age was over. In general, accepting that fact caused few problems. With some exceptions the separation proved fairly painless, and
Europe withdrew from Africa without major upheaval. A number of grandiose geopolitical plans and development schemes were admittedly drawn
up, and the French in francophone Africa kept their finger in the African
pie and sometimes on the trigger as well, but the idea that Africa was of
serious importance to Europe or indeed that it had any great future vanished fairly quickly. Grassroots opinion had it that Africa was a continent
of disasters, not of future prospects. Africa reverted to what it had been
before the partition: a continent of little importance to Europe.

Seen from a European perspective, the partition and colonialization of
Africa thus constitute no more than a strange deviation from the general
pattern of indifference. From the African perspective, the partition was
merely a prelude to a period of subjection and colonial rule. That period
was of short duration: the colonial age in Africa lasted for barely a century.
Measured against the millennia-old history of a continent where, in the
view of many scholars, the cradle of mankind once stood, that is not a
long time. During the colonial period, too, Europeans were in fact unable
to shape African economic, social and political conditions to more than a
very limited extent. To shape them at all they devised a variety of systems
with such splendid names as "association politics" and "indirect rule."
These were no more than phrases hiding an inability to govern effectively.
As they had done during the partition and the conquest of Africa, Africans
played an important role in the running of the colonial system. Without
their collaboration colonial rule would not have been possible. The Europeans were and remained dependent upon African "collaborators," and to
an important extent these men shaped the reality of colonial rule.[12] Even
under colonialism Africans thus largely remained masters of their fate. We
can go even further and observe—odd though it may sound—that their
dependence on Europe grew greater after independence. That was because
in the colonial period a number of processes had been set in motion which

did not come to fruition until years later, tying Africa more and more closely to the international economic system.

Though the colonial period was brief, it set off or speeded up a number of developments whose effects can be felt to this day. In economic or social respects, colonization brought nothing essentially new. It led only to the acceleration of a social and economic process of modernization that had been started earlier. The really new phenomenon was political: the partition of Africa stripped Africans of their sovereignty. They regained it with decolonization, but in a different form. Partition did, after all, lead to the creation of new colonial states and federations of states. Some of these were to witness certain changes to their character or borders, and some of the federations were dissolved. In the great majority of cases, however, they survived decolonization and continue to exist to this day, although not without internal or external conflicts. The modern political map of Africa has in outline been drawn in the wake of the partition of Africa. The number of political entities in pre-colonial Africa has been put conservatively at 10,000 at least.[13] These were reduced by the partition to the few dozen we know today. In that sense the division of Africa proved of great historical significance.

The colonial period is something on which most Africans look back with loathing, and about which they write with disgust. Colonial historians used to take a different view, extolling colonialism as a spur to progress and civilization. To this day we can point to assets in the balance sheet of colonialism, but it is impossible to set off the assets against the liabilities, and this we must leave to the Africans themselves. Montesquieu once called slavery a system that brought misery to large numbers of people, rendered life more comfortable for just a few, and ultimately was of no real benefit to anyone.[14] We need not be quite so negative in passing judgment on colonialism. It is, however, strange and rather sad to recall that European colonialism in Africa, which Africans nowadays consider to have been so damaging, should have been of such small importance to Europe itself.

# NOTES

The following notes are reserved for quotations and sources only. For a list of the literature consulted, the reader is referred to the Bibliography. Works not included in the Bibliography are cited fully in the notes.

INTRODUCTION

1. H.R. Trevor-Roper, *The Rise of Christian Europe* (London 1965) 9.
2. E. Sik, *The History of Black Africa* (2 vols. Budapest 1966) I, 17.
3. A. Roberts, "Introduction" in *Cambridge History of Africa*, VII, 1.
4. M. Bloch, *L'Etrange défaite* (Paris 1946) 51.

I

"THE EASTERN QUESTION": THE OCCUPATION OF TUNISIA AND EGYPT, 1881–1882

1. Robinson and Gallagher, *Africa and Victorians*, 465–466.
2. J.S. Bartstra, *Handboek tot de staatkundige geschiedenis van de landen van onze beschavingskring van 1648 tot heden* (2nd ed., 5 vols. Den Bosch 1959–1962) IV, 159.
3. Langer, *Alliances and Alignments*, 304.
4. Fieldhouse, *Economics and Empire*, 108.
5. Ganiage, *Expansion coloniale*, 29.
6. Brunschwig, *Mythes et réalités*, 24.
7. Murphy, *Ideology of French Imperialism*, 167.
8. Ibid., 169.
9. Marseille, "Investissement," 409–432.
10. Bury, *Gambetta and the Making of the Third Republic*, 68.
11. Wormser, *Gambetta*, 231.
12. Renan, *Oeuvres complètes* (10 vols. Paris 1947–1961) I, 390.
13. Bury, *Gambetta's Final Years*, 60–81 and 199–220.
14. E. and J. de Goncourt, *Journal. Mémoires de la vie littéraire* (Laffont, ed. Paris 1954) Vol. II, 819.
15. Furet, *Ferry fondateur*, 191–206.
16. Ferry, *Le Tonkin et la mère–patrie*, 37.
17. Brunschwig, *Mythes et réalités*, 77.

18. Bartstra, *Handboek*, IV, 87 (see note 2).
19. Marsden, *British Diplomacy*, 54.
20. Langer, *Alliances and Alignments*, 164.
21. Ibid., 160.
22. Ibid., 220.
23. Langer, "Tunis affair," 253 note 10.
24. J. Ganiage, "North Africa," in *Cambridge History of Africa*, VI, 174–175.
25. Van Krieken, *Khair al-Dîn*, 327.
26. Robinson and Gallagher, "Partition of Africa," 595.
27. J. Ganiage, "North Africa," in *Cambridge History of Africa*, VI, 173.
28. Broadley, *Last Punic War*, I, 164.
29. Langer, "Tunis affair," 67.
30. Marsden, *British Diplomacy*, 55.
31. Ganiage, *Origines*, 518 note 64.
32. Ibid., 548–549.
33. Langer, *Alliances and Alignments*, 221.
34. Cambon, *Histoire de la Régence de Tunis*, 128.
35. Power, *Jules Ferry*, 41.
36. Ganiage, *Origines*, 631.
37. Ibid., 633.
38. Broadley, *Last Punic War*, I, 216.
39. Power, *Ferry*, 52.
40. Brunschwig, *Mythes et réalités*, 55.
41. Rosenbaum, *Frankreich in Tunesien*, 115.
42. Gallagher and Robinson, "The imperialism of free trade," 1–15.
43. Semmel, *Rise of Free Trade Imperialism*, 2.
44. Blake, *Disraeli*, 523.
45. Cecil, *Salisbury*, IV, 300.
46. Faber, *Vision and Need*, 86–114.
47. Bergue, *Egypte*, 38.
48. Albertini, *Europäische Kolonialherrschaft*, 186.
49. Blunt, *Secret History*, 149.
50. A. Gerschenkron, "Economic backwardness in historical perspective," in D.F. Hoselitz, ed., *The Progress of Underdeveloped Areas* (Chicago 1952) 23.
51. Hallberg, *Suez Canal*, 116.
52. Ibid., 158 note 2.
53. Ganiage, *Expansion coloniale*, 87.
54. Hallberg, *Suez Canal*, 158 note 2.
55. Ibid., 83.
56. Schölch, *Ägypten*, 30.
57. Hallett, *Africa since 1875*, 83.
58. Schölch, *Ägypten*, 48.
59. Marlowe, *Anglo–Egyptian Relations*, 73.
60. Langer, *Alliances and Alignments*, 255.
61. Ganiage, *Expansion coloniale*, 88–89.
62. Hallberg, *Suez Canal*, 156.
63. Monypenny and Buckle, *Disraeli*, V, 448.
64. Cecil, *Salisbury*, II, 331.

65. Fieldhouse, *Economics and Empire*, 124.
66. Langer, *Alliances and Alignments*, 262.
67. Keddie, *Islamic Response*, 103.
68. James, *Rosebery*, 249.
69. Holstein, *Papiere*, II, 64.
70. Magnus, *Gladstone*, 105–108.
71. Bury, "Gambetta and overseas problems," 292.
72. Blunt, *Secret History*, 138–143.
73. Cromer, *Modern Egypt*, I, 235.
74. Hopkins, "Victorians and Africa," 384.
75. Collins, *Land beyond the Rivers*, 20.
76. Collins, *Southern Sudan*, 9.
77. Oliver and Atmore, *Africa*, 83.
78. Collins and Tignor, *Egyptian Sudan*, 70–71.
79. Gray, *History of Southern Sudan*, 87.
80. Ibid., 172.
81. Marlowe, *Mission to Khartoum*, 33.
82. Collins and Tignor, *Egypt and Sudan*, 75.
83. Collins, *Southern Sudan*, 17.
84. Ibid., 17–18.
85. Brown, "Sudanese Mahdiya," 146.
86. Hallett, *Africa since 1875*, 110.
87. Holt, *The Mahdist State*, 51.
88. Collins, *Southern Sudan*, 19.
89. Brown, "Sudanese Mahdiya," 153.
90. Holt, *The Mahdist State*, 50.
91. Holt and Daly, *History of Sudan*, 86.
92. Holt, *The Mahdist State*, 59.
93. Langer, *Diplomacy of Imperialism*, 103.
94. Hall, *Stanley*, 262.
95. Holt, *The Mahdist State*, 89.
96. Ibid., 90.
97. Ibid., 91.
98. Ibid., 85.
99. Maclaren, *Canadians on the Nile*, 103.
100. Hopkins, "Victorians and Africa," 79–91.
101. A. Ramm, "Great Britain and France in Egypt, 1876–1883," in Gifford and Louis, *France and Britain in Africa*, 100.
102. Taylor, *Struggle for Mastery*, 289.

II

THE CONGO AND THE CREATION OF THE FREE STATE, 1882–1885

1. Bontinck, *Autobiographie*, 164–165.
2. Clarence-Smith, *Third Portuguese Empire*, 36.
3. Ascherson, *King Incorporated*, 27.
4. Stengers, *Congo*, 10.
5. Ibid., 20.

6. J.W.B. Money, *Java, or How to Manage a Colony* (2 vols. London 1861) I, 3.

7. Stengers, *Congo*, 14.

8. Ibid., 24.

9. Ibid., 28.

10. Ibid.

11. Ibid., 23.

12. Roeykens, *Début*, 46.

13. Stengers, "Léopold II entre Orient et Afrique," 303.

14. Thomson, *Fondation*, 63 note 50.

15. Jeal, *Livingstone*, 1.

16. Hall, *Stanley*, 19.

17. Ibid., 246.

18. Hellinga, *Stanley*.

19. Brunschwig, *Avènement*, 137.

20. Nwoye, *Public Image*, 29.

21. Brunschwig, *Avènement*, 140.

22. Ibid., 141.

23. Roeykens, *Début*, 83.

24. The conference has frequently been described, *inter alia* and at length in the commemorative volume *La Conférence de Géographie de 1876*.

25. Stengers, "Introduction," in *La Conférence de Géographie*, xx.

26. Emerson, *Leopold II*, 19.

27. Wesseling, *Indië verloren*, 102.

28. Stengers, "Introduction," in *La Conférence de Géographie*, xv.

29. Ascherson, *King Incorporated*, 104.

30. Thomson, *Fondation*, 63.

31. Wesseling, *Indië verloren*, 339 note 10.

32. Thomson, *Fondation*, 66.

33. Stengers, *Congo*, 52.

34. Nwoye, *Public Image*, 58.

35. Brunschwig, *Traités Makoko*, 141.

36. Brunschwig, *Avènement*, 148.

37. Foeken, *België behoeft een kolonie*, 167.

38. Vansina, *Tio Kingdom*, 396–407.

39. C. Denuit–Somerhausen, "Les traités de Stanley et de ses collaborateurs avec les chefs africains, 1880–1885," in *Le Centenaire de l'Etat Indépendant*, 77–146.

40. Brunschwig, *Partage*, 84–85.

41. Brunschwig, *Traités Makoko*, 58.

42. Mumbanza Mwa Bawele, "Afro-European relations in the Western Congo Basin, c. 1884–1885," in Förster, Mommsen and Robinson, *Bismarck, Europe and Africa*, 469–490.

43. Alexandrowicz, "Partition," 144.

44. Bawele, "Afro-European relations," 476.

45. Ibid., 491.

46. Foeken, *België behoeft een kolonie*, 132.

47. Brunschwig, *Avènement*, 150.

48. Ibid.

49. Stengers, "Impérialisme colonial," 475.

50. Stengers, "Leopold II et la rivalité franco-anglaise," 447.

51. Ibid., 448ff.

52. Thomson, *Fondation*, 198.

53. Stengers, "Impérialisme colonial," 475.

54. Ibid., 473.

55. Ibid.

56. Clarence–Smith, *Third Portuguese Empire*, 1–19.

57. Hammond, *Portugal*, 65.

58. Axelson, *Portugal*, 38.

59. Hallett, *Africa since 1875*, 401.

60. Stengers, "Leopold II et la rivalité franco-anglaise," 436.

61. Wesseling, *Indië verloren*, 342 note 44.

62. Axelson, *Portugal*, 42.

63. Brunschwig, *Avènement*, 162.

64. Stengers, *Impérialisme colonial*, 487.

65. Stengers, "Léopold II et la rivalité franco-anglaise," 455.

66. Louis, "Sir Percy Anderson," 292–293.

67. Anstey, *Britain and Congo*, 135.

68. Ibid., 138.

69. Stanley, *The Congo*, II, 379.

70. Stengers, "Léopold II et la rivalité franco-anglaise," 453 note 1.

71. Ibid., 462.

72. Ibid., 468.

73. Bontinck, *Origines*, 202.

74. Ascherson, *King Incorporated*, 132.

75. Stengers, "Fixation des frontières," 169.

76. Eyck, *Bismarck*, III, 181.

77. Craig, *Germany*, 21.

78. Stern, *Gold and Iron*, 411 note 1.

79. Townsend, *Rise and Fall*, 79.

80. Ibid., 82.

81. Craig, *Germany*, 119.

82. Townsend, *Rise and Fall*, 60.

83. Gall, *Bismarck*, 617.

84. Holstein, *Papiere*, II, 174.

85. O. von Bismarck, *Die gesammelten Werke* (15 vols. Berlin 1924–1934) VIII, 646.

86. Ibid., XIII, 386.

87. H.A. Turner, "Bismarck's imperialist venture," in Gifford and Louis, *Britain and Germany in Africa*, 68.

88. Ibid., 66.

89. Ibid., 62; Wehler, *Bismarck und Imperialismus*, 417ff.

90. Schreuder, *Scramble for Southern Africa*, 120.

91. Langer, *Alliances and Alignments*, 313.

93. Latour da Veiga Pinto, *Portugal*, 236.

94. Axelson, *Portugal*, 69.

94. Louis, "Sir Percy Anderson," 299.

95. Latour da Veiga Pinto, *Portugal*, 212.

96. Ibid., 255.

97. Wesseling, *Indië verloren*, 125.

98. W.R. Louis, "The Berlin Congo Conference," in Gifford and Louis, *France and Britain in Africa*, 196.

99. Wesseling, *Indië verloren*, 128.

100. Wehler, *Bismarck und Imperialismus*, 325–328.

101. Brunschwig, *Partage*, 63.

102. Ibid., 65.

103. Ascherson, *King Incorporated*, 122.

104. W.R. Louis, "The Berlin Congo Conference," in Gifford and Louis, *France and Britain in Africa*, 185.

105. Ibid., 187.

106. Ibid., 191.

107. Stengers, "Introduction," in *La Conférence de Géographie*, xvi.

108. Thomson, *Fondation*, 149.

109. Ibid., 157.

110. Stengers, "Fixation des frontières," 170.

111. Ibid., 154.

112. Ibid., 172.

113. Ibid., 175–176.

114. Foeken, *België behoeft een kolonie*, 152.

115. For this and other treaties, see *Affaires du Congo et de l'Afrique occidentale. Documents diplomatiques* (Paris 1885).

116. Stengers, *Congo*, 61–63.

117. Ibid., 63.

118. Louis, "Sir Percy Anderson," 296.

119. Anstey, *Britain and Congo*, 183.

120. Emerson, *Leopold II*, 119.

121. Stengers, *Congo*, 66.

122. Ibid., 68–69.

123. K. Nkrumah, *Challenge of the Congo* (New York 1967) x.

124. Holstein, *Papiere*, II, 169.

125. H.L. Wesseling, "The Berlin Conference and the expansion of Europe: A conclusion," in Förster, Mommsen and Robinson, *Bismarck, Europe and Africa*, 532.

126. Stengers, *Congo*, 82–84.

127. Lugard, *Dual Mandate*, 12.

128. Cecil, *Salisbury*, IV, 283.

129. Louis, *Ruanda-Urundi*, 21.

130. Hargreaves, *West Africa Partitioned*, II, 222.

131. Louis, *Ruanda-Urundi*, 9.

132. Müller, *Zanzibar*, 301.

133. Lugard, *Dual Mandate*, 13.

134. Cecil, *Salisbury*, IV, 323.

135. Brunschwig, *Partage*, 85.

136. Gaillard, *Ferry*, 575.

137. Eyck, *Bismarck*, III, 422.

138. Langer, *Alliances and Alignments*, 308.

139. W.R. Louis, "Great Britain and German expansion in Africa, 1884–1919," in Gifford and Louis, *Britain and Germany*, 4.

140. Stern, *Gold and Iron*, 415.

141. Wehler, *Bismarck*, 409.

142. J. Stengers, "King Leopold's Congo, 1886–1908," in *Cambridge History of Africa*, VI, 319.

143. Ascherson, *King Incorporated*, 148.

144. Ibid.

145. Stengers, "Introduction," in *La Conférence de Géographie*, ix.

III

"COOL AND COURAGEOUS": GERMANY AND GREAT BRITAIN IN EAST AFRICA, 1885–1890

1. Coupland, *Exploitation*, 240.

2. Anstey, *Britain and Congo*, 74–75; Galbraith, *Mackinnon*, 76–82.

3. Anstey, *Britain and Congo*, 71.

4. Coupland, *Exploitation*, 377–381.

5. Ibid., 388.

6. Brunschwig, *Expansion allemande*, 79.

7. Müller, *Zanzibar*, 97.

8. Peters, *Wie Ostafrika entstand*, 10.

9. Ibid., 24.

10. Brunschwig, *Expansion allemande*, 119.

11. Peters, *Wie Ostafrika entstand*, 7.

12. Müller, *Zanzibar*, 115.

13. Ibid., 114.

14. Merritt, "German interest," 100.

15. Müller, *Zanzibar*, 121.

16. Peters, *Gesammelte Schriften*, I, 303.

17. Merritt, "German interest," 104.

18. Müller, *Zanzibar*, 138.

19. Ibid., 186. (Many an island yet lies temptingly in wait / With palmtrees and bananas: / The sea breeze blows, the breaker roars, / Onward, oh joyful Teutons!).

20. Ibid., 196.

21. Ibid., 200.

22. Coupland, *Exploitation*, 442.

23. Müller, *Zanzibar*, 301.

24. Robinson and Gallagher, *Africa and Victorians*, 191.

25. Ibid.

26. Merritt, "First partition," 596–597 note 264.

27. Text in Hertslett, *Map of Africa*, III, No. 264, pp. 882–887.

28. Müller, *Zanzibar*, 272.

29. Ibid., 362.

30. Iliffe, *Modern History*, 93.

31. Townsend, *Rise and Fall*, 118.

32. Cecil, *Salisbury*, IV, 235–237.

33. Müller, *Zanzibar*, 449.
34. Cecil, *Salisbury*, IV, 281.
35. Lewis, *Fashoda*, 41.
36. Anstey, *Britain and Congo*, 213.
37. Smith, *Emin Pasha Relief Expedition*, 54.
38. Hall, *Stanley*, 288.
39. Stanley, *In Darkest Africa*, 271.
40. Ibid., 594.
41. Townsend, *Rise and Fall*, 137.
42. Müller, *Zanzibar*, 473 and 541–542.
43. Grenville, *Salisbury*, 6.
44. James, *Rosebery*, 22.
45. B.W. Tuchman, *The Proud Tower* (Bantam ed. 1967) 7.
46. Ensor, *England*, 34 note 3.
47. A.J.P. Taylor, *Essays in English History* (Harmondsworth 1976) 125.
48. Garvin, *Chamberlain*, III, 203.
49. Cecil, *Salisbury*, IV, 323.
50. Ibid.
51. Oliver, *Johnston*, 134.
52. Collins, *King Leopold*, 10.
53. Robinson and Gallagher, *Africa and Victorians*, 283.
54. Macpherson, *Anatomy of a Conquest*, 71.
55. Perham, *Lugard*, I, 468.
56. Louis, "Sir Percy Anderson," 302.
57. Cecil, *Salisbury*, IV, 322–323.
58. Louis, *Ruanda-Urundi*, 23.
59. Robinson and Gallagher, *Africa and Victorians*, 291.
60. Stengers, "Impérialisme colonial," 484.
61. Robinson and Gallagher, *Africa and Victorians*, 293.
62. Hollingworth, *Zanzibar*, 45.
63. Text in Hertslett, *Map of Africa*, III, No. 270, pp. 899–906.
64. Townsend, *Rise and Fall*, 163.
65. Sanderson, "The origins and significance of the Anglo-French confrontation at Fashoda, 1898," in Gifford and Louis, *France and Britain in Africa*, 293; Cecil, *Salisbury*, IV, 298.
66. Galbraith, *Mackinnon*, 228.
67. Ingham, *East Africa*, 161–165.
68. C.C. Wrigley, "Apolo Kagwa: Katikkiro of Buganda," in Ikime, *Leadership*, 120.
69. James, *Rosebery*, 35.
70. Ibid., 284.
71. Ibid.
72. Ibid., 488.
73. Langer, *Diplomacy of Imperialism*, 121–122.
74. Ibid., 123.
75. Fieldhouse, *Economics and Empire*, 379.
76. Müller, *Zanzibar*, 509–510.
77. Curtin, *African History*, 414.

78. Roberts, *French Colonial Policy*, II, 379.

79. Power, *Ferry*, 125.

80. Roberts, *French Colonial Policy*, II, 380.

81. Y.-G. Paillard, "The French expedition to Madagascar in 1895: Program and results," in De Moor and Wesseling, *Imperialism and War*, 177.

82. Michel, *Gallieni*, 183.

83. R. Cornevin, "The Germans in Africa before 1918," in Gann and Duignan, *Colonialism in Africa*, I, 412.

84. Kjekshus, "Ecology control," 150–151; Iliffe, *Modern History*, 200.

85. Lonsdale, "Conquest," 858–859.

86. Lyautey, *Lettres du Tonkin et de Madagascar*, II, 112–113.

IV

SOLDIERS AND TRADERS: FRANCE AND GREAT BRITAIN IN WEST AFRICA, 1890–1898

1. Oliver and Atmore, *Africa since 1870*, 1.

2. Hopkins, *Economic History of West Africa*, 129.

3. Robinson and Gallagher, *Africa and Victorians*, 30.

4. Fieldhouse, *Economics and Empire*, 142–143.

5. A.S. Kanya-Forstner, "The French marines and the conquest of the Western Sudan, 1880–1899," in De Moor and Wesseling, *Imperialism and War*, 122.

6. Michel, *Gallieni*, 59.

7. Hargreaves, *Prelude*, 253.

8. Henrik Ibsen, *Peer Gynt*, translated by Michael Meyer (London 1963) 107f.

9. Newbury and Kanya-Forstner, "French policy," 262.

10. Michel, *Gallieni*, 83.

11. Kanya-Forstner, *Conquest*, 61.

12. Ibid., 78.

13. Kanya-Forstner, "Mali-Tukulor" in Crowder, *Resistance*, 65; Oloruntimehin, *Segu Tukulor Empire*, 241–243.

14. St. Martin, *Empire toucouleur*, 137–139.

15. Kanya-Forstner, *Conquest*, 175.

16. Crowder, *Colonial Rule*, 84.

17. Ibid., 87; Person, "Guinea-Samori," in Crowder, *Resistance*, 111.

18. Person, *Samori*, I, 273–274.

19. Hargreaves, *West Africa Partitioned*, I, 179.

20. Ibid., 180.

21. Person, "Guinea--Samori," in Crowder, *Resistance*, 129.

22. Hargreaves, *West Africa Partitioned*, I, 62–63.

23. Michel, *Gallieni*, 121.

24. C.E. Callwell, *Small Wars: Their Principles and Practice* (London 1906) 57.

25. A.S. Kanya-Forstner, "The French marines and the conquest of the Western Sudan, 1880–1899," in De Moor and Wesseling, *Imperialism and War*, 131; Newbury, "Formation," 111.

26. Dike, *Trade and Politics*, 19.

27. Robinson and Gallagher, *Africa and Victorians*, 36.

28. Ibid., 165.

29. Ibid.

30. Gramont, *Strong Brown God*, 274.

31. Perham, *Lugard*, I, 484.

32. Flint, *Goldie*, 4.

33. Ibid., 4–5.

34. Gramont, *Strong Brown God*, 275.

35. Hertslett, *Map of Africa*, I, No. 15, pp. 131–154.

36. Anene, *Southern Nigeria*, 68.

37. J. Flint, "Britain and partition," 108.

38. Rudin, *Germans*, 17 (I am a lad from Cameroon / The German colony; / Prince Bismarck had a lot to do / To win it. And he did.).

39. Flint, *Goldie*, 41.

40. Nzemeke, *Imperialism and Response*, 278–279.

41. Oliver, *Johnston*, 101.

42. Anene, *Southern Nigeria*, 66.

43. Cookey, *King Jaja*, 126.

44. Ibid., 133.

45. Crowder, *Colonial Rule*, 121.

46. Hargreaves, *West Africa Partitioned*, II, 9.

47. Hargreaves, *The Loaded Pause, 1885–1889*, subtitle of Vol. I of *West Africa Partitioned*.

48. Kanya-Forstner, "French African policy," 632.

49. Ibid., 628.

50. Cecil, *Salisbury*, IV, 323.

51. Kennedy, *Salisbury*, 225.

52. Ibid.

53. Ibid.

54. Robinson and Gallagher, *Africa and Victorians*, 390.

55. E.D. Morel, *Affairs of West Africa* (London 1902) 21, quoted in Anene, *Southern Nigeria*, 319.

56. Stengers, "Origines," 384–385.

57. Grupp, *Deutschland, Frankreich und Kolonien*, 19.

58. Andrew and Kanya-Forstner, "French colonial party, 1889–1914," 103.

59. Ibid., 127.

60. Sieberg, *Etienne*, 30.

61. Ibid., 20.

62. Ageron, *France coloniale*, 136.

63. Lehmann, *All Sir Garnet*, 163.

64. Obichere, *West African States*, 53.

65. D. Ross, "Dahomey," in Crowder, *Resistance*, 149.

66. Ganiage, *Expansion*, 179.

67. E. Chaudoin, "Trois mois de captivité au Dahomey," *L'Illustration*, No. 2471 (1890) 49, quoted in Obichere, *West African States*, 66.

68. Ganiage, *Expansion*, 180.

69. Hargreaves, *West Africa Partitioned*, II, 171.

70. Crowder, *Colonial Rule*, 103.

71. Garvin, *Chamberlain*, I, 202.

72. Jay, *Chamberlain*, 323.

73. Ibid., 321–322.
74. Garvin, *Chamberlain*, II, 349.
75. Ibid., III, 203.
76. Jay, *Chamberlain*, 216.
77. Anene, *Boundaries*, 277.
78. Perham, *Lugard*, I, 466–467.
79. James, *Rosebery*, 266.
80. Brunschwig, *Partage*, 154.
81. Gramont, *Strong Brown God*, 290.
82. Perham, *Lugard*, I, 516.
83. Hargreaves, *West Africa Partitioned*, II, 203.
84. Flint, *Goldie*, 264.
85. Gramont, *Strong Brown God*, 311.
86. Ibid., 312.
87. J.D. Hargreaves, "The European partition of West Africa," in Ajayi and Crowder, *West Africa*, 419.
88. Gramont, *Strong Brown God*, 313.
89. Ibid., 315.
90. Hirschfield, *Diplomacy of Partition*, 197.
91. Hargreaves, *West Africa Partitioned*, II, 230.
92. Perham, *Lugard*, II, 11.
93. 3 July 1899, *Parliamentary Debates*, IV, 73; 1293. Perham (*Lugard*, II, 13), from whom this reference is taken, is mistaken when he quotes the minister as saying "a million square miles."
94. Porch, *Conquest of Sahara*, 146.
95. Fuglestad, "Voulet-Chanoine," 82–83.
96. Suret-Canale, *Afrique noire*, 243.
97. Rolland, *Grand Capitaine*, 184 and 242. (Our great captain / He thinks of us; / He leads us into paradise. / Where's that, my friends? / At Zindiri, Zindiri. / Our great captain is / Wonderful, wonderful / He is our Samori.).
98. Ganiage, *Expansion*, 226.
99. Robinson and Gallagher, *Africa and Victorians*, 382.

V

THE LONG MARCH TO FASHODA, 1893–1898

1. Sanderson, *England and Upper Nile*, 1.
2. Lowe, *Salisbury*, 57.
3. Langer, *Diplomacy*, 105.
4. Hurst, *Nile*, 12–13 and 241–242.
5. Langer, *Diplomacy*, 107.
6. Cecil, *Salisbury*, IV, 330.
7. Lowe, *Reluctant Imperialists*, II, 98.
8. Ibid., I, 210.
9. Louis, "Sir Percy Anderson," 299.
10. Lewis, *Fashoda*, 37.
11. Collins, *King Leopold*, 34.
12. Iiams, *Dreyfus*, 21.

13. Andrew and Kanya-Forstner, "Hanotaux," 60.

14. Ibid., 58.

15. Grupp, *Gabriel Hanotaux*, 41.

16. Ibid., 76.

17. Andrew and Kanya-Forstner, "Hanotaux," 81.

18. Stengers, "Origines," 375.

19. Ibid., 381.

20. Tessières, "Monteil," passim.

21. Langer, *Diplomacy*, 558.

22. Sanderson, *England and Upper Nile*, 144.

23. Stengers, "Origines," 447.

24. Sanderson, *England and Upper Nile*, 145.

25. Text in Hertslett, *Map of Africa*, II, No. 163, pp. 578–583.

26. Louis, "Sir Percy Anderson," 389.

27. *La Réforme*, 26 June 1894, quoted in Stengers, "Origines," 1058.

28. James, *Rosebery*, 352.

29. Sanderson, *England and Upper Nile*, 189.

30. Andrew and Kanya-Forstner, "Hanotaux," 64.

31. Taylor, "Prelude to Fashoda," 154ff.

32. Sanderson, *England and Upper Nile*, 203.

33. Michel, *Mission Marchand*, 16.

34. Mazières, *Marche au Nil*, 75.

35. Bates, *Fashoda*, 23.

36. James, *Rosebery*, 375.

37. Langer, *Diplomacy of Imperialism*, 265.

38. Sanderson, *England and Upper Nile*, 216.

39. Stengers, "Origines," 1045.

40. James, *Rosebery*, 374.

41. Bates, *Fashoda*, 24.

42. Miège, *Impérialisme italien*, 42.

43. Smith, *Italy*, 139.

44. Miège, *Impérialisme italien*, 50.

45. Lewis, *Somalia*, 55. Text in Hertslett, *Map of Africa*, III, Nos. 288 and 289, pp. 948–950.

46. Oliver and Atmore, *Africa since 1870*, 9.

47. Miège, *Impérialisme italien*, 54.

48. Marcus, *Menelik*, 31.

49. Langer, *Diplomacy of Imperialism*, 273.

50. Sanderson, *England and Upper Nile*, 155.

51. Ibid., 302.

52. Ibid., 260.

53. Robinson and Gallagher, *Africa and Victorians*, 364 note 5.

54. Hallett, *Africa since 1875*, 126.

55. H.G. Marcus, "Imperialism and expansionism in Ethiopia from 1865 to 1900," in Gann and Duignan, *Colonialism in Africa*, I, 428–429.

56. Ibid., 435.

57. Robinson and Gallagher, *Africa and Victorians*, 305.

58. Maclaren, *Canadians*, 134.

59. Michel, *Mission Marchand*, 33.
60. Ibid., 31–35.
61. Andrew and Kanya-Forstner, "Hanotaux," 70.
62. Michel, *Mission Marchand*, 41.
63. Sanderson, *England and Upper Nile*, 274.
64. Michel, *Mission Marchand*, 51.
65. Guillen, *Expansion*, 409.
66. Andrew and Kanya-Forstner, "Hanotaux," 77.
67. Bates, *Fashoda*, 34.
68. Michel, *Mission Marchand*, 158.
69. Langer, *Diplomacy of Imperialism*, 544.
70. Michel, *Mission Marchand*, 203.
71. Bates, *Fashoda*, 118.
72. Text in Michel, *Mission Marchand*, 255–256.
73. Pakenham, *Boer War*, 319.
74. Magnus, *Kitchener*, 4.
75. Bates, *Fashoda*, 128.
76. Holt, *Mahdist State*, 221.
77. Churchill, *River War*, 300.
78. Maclaren, *Canadians*, 154.
79. Ibid., 105.
80. Sanderson, *England and Upper Nile*, 289.
81. Ibid., 281.
82. Grupp, *Hanotaux*, 132–133.
83. Sanderson, *England and Upper Nile*, 294.
84. Andrew and Kanya-Forstner, "Hanotaux," 89.
85. G.N. Sanderson, "The origins and significance of the Anglo-French confrontation at Fashoda, 1898," in Gifford and Louis, *France and Britain in Africa*, 330.
86. Sanderson, *England and Upper Nile*, 356.
87. Michel, *Mission Marchand*, 225.
88. Text in Hertslett, *Map of Africa*, II, No. 244, pp. 796–797.
89. Churchill, *River War*, 345.
90. Michel, *Mission Marchand*, 248.
91. Sanderson, *England and Upper Nile*, 311.
92. Lewis, *Fashoda*, 85.
93. Andrew and Kanya-Forstner, "Hanotaux," 94.
94. G.N. Sanderson, "The origins and significance of the Anglo-French confrontation at Fashoda, 1898," in Gifford and Louis, *France and Britain in Africa*, 322.

VI

BOERS AND BRITONS IN SOUTH AFRICA, 1890–1902

1. Marquard, *History*, 125.
2. Edgerton, *Like Lions*, 43.
3. Marquard, *History*, 137.
4. Ibid., 153.
5. Ibid., 159–162.

6. S. Marks, "Southern Africa, 1867–1886," in *Cambridge History of Africa*, VI, 359.

7. Robinson and Gallagher, *Africa and Victorians*, 58.

8. Trollope, *South Africa*, 360.

9. Ibid., 368.

10. Ibid., 369.

11. Williams, *Rhodes*, 143.

12. Marquard, *History*, 193.

13. Schreuder, *Scramble*, 44.

14. Ibid., 45.

15. De Kiewiet, *Imperial Factor*, 127.

16. Schreuder, *Scramble*, 75.

17. Morris, *Washing of the Spears*, 278.

18. Blake, *Disraeli*, 668.

19. Ibid., 670.

20. Edgerton, *Like Lions*, 4.

21. Morris, *Washing of the Spears*, 387.

22. Ibid., 518–534.

23. Ibid., 549.

24. Ibid., 607.

25. Morley, *Gladstone*, III, 27.

26. Ibid., III, 23.

27. De Kiewiet, *Imperial Factor*, 120.

28. Marais, *Fall*, 17.

29. Robinson and Gallagher, *Africa and Victorians*, 432.

30. De Kiewiet, *Imperial Factor*, 119.

31. Marais, *Fall*, 10.

32. Kruger, *Kruger*, I, 253.

33. Pakenham, *Boer War*, 259.

34. Schutte, *Nederland en Afrikaners*, 18.

35. Ibid., 17.

36. H.L. Wesseling, "Robert Fruin. De geschiedenis van een reputatie," *Jaarboek van de Maatschappij der Nederlandse Letterkunde te Leiden, 1986–1987* (Leiden 1988) 8.

37. Robinson and Gallagher, *Africa and Victorians*, 64.

38. Schreuder, *Gladstone and Kruger*, vii.

39. De Kiewiet, *Imperial Factor*, 282.

40. Fischer, *Kruger*, 118.

41. Robinson and Gallagher, *Africa and Victorians*, 203.

42. Schreuder, *Scramble*, 91.

43. Ibid., 172.

44. Schreuder, *Gladstone and Kruger*, 305.

45. H.A. Turner, "Bismarck's imperialist venture," in Gifford and Louis, *Britain and Germany in Africa*, 60.

46. Esterhuyse, *South West Africa*, 9.

47. Ibid., 39.

48. Ibid., 40.

49. Dreschler, *Let Us Die*, 23.

50. Langer, *Alliances and Alignments*, 296.

51. H.A. Turner, "Bismarck's imperialist venture," in Gifford and Louis, *Britain and Germany in Africa*, 60.

52. Ibid., 62.

53. Ibid., 76.

54. Schreuder, *Scramble*, 119.

55. Ibid., 140.

56. Magnus, *Gladstone*, 287.

57. Schreuder, *Scramble*, 152.

58. Ibid.

59. Ibid., 163.

60. Morley, *Gladstone*, III, 26.

61. Marais, *Fall*, 1.

62. S. Marks, "Southern and Central Africa, 1886–1910," in *Cambridge History of Africa*, VI, 432.

63. Marlowe, *Milner*, 60.

64. Wilson, *Imperial Experience*, 64.

65. Rotberg, *Founder*, 35.

66. Ibid., 65.

67. Ibid., 110.

68. Ibid., 200.

69. Ibid., 413.

70. Williams, *Rhodes*, 55.

71. Chamberlain, *Scramble*, 72.

72. Rotberg, *Founder*, 234.

73. Williams, *Rhodes*, 62.

74. Chamberlain, *Scramble*, 75.

75. Galbraith, *Crown and Charter*, 30–31.

76. Ibid., 29.

77. Rotberg, *Founder*, 247.

78. Samkange, *Origins*, 71.

79. Rotberg, *Founder*, 259.

80. Ibid., 247.

81. Ibid., 246.

82. Ibid., 254.

83. Robinson and Gallagher, *Africa and Victorians*, 236.

84. Butler, *Liberal Party*, 24.

85. Schreuder, *Scramble*, 247.

86. Ibid., 262.

87. Rotberg, *Founder*, 262.

88. Chamberlain, *Scramble*, 136.

89. Rotberg, *Founder*, 264.

90. Ibid., 263.

91. Galbraith, *Crown and Charter*, 147.

92. Keppel-Jones, *Rhodes*, 172.

93. Cecil, *Salisbury*, IV, 263.

94. Gann, *North Rhodesia*, 69.

95. Grenville, *Salisbury*, 184.

96. Rotberg, *Founder*, 586.
97. Ibid., 338.
98. Ibid., 442–443.
99. Ibid., 665.
100. Williams, *Rhodes*, 57.
101. Marais, *Fall*, 48.
102. Robinson and Gallagher, *Africa and Victorians*, 218.
103. Rotberg, *Founder*, 542.
104. Marais, *Fall*, 2–3.
105. Ibid., 60.
106. Van der Poel, *Jameson Raid*, 35.
107. Rotberg, *Founder*, 292.
108. Van der Poel, *Jameson Raid*, 61.
109. Ibid., 25.
110. Garvin, *Chamberlain*, III, 83.
111. Cf. Van der Poel, *Jameson Raid*, 69; and Pakenham, *Jameson Raid*; 194–199.
112. Van der Poel, *Jameson Raid*, 79.
113. Ibid., 65.
114. Ibid., 84.
115. Williams, *Rhodes*, 271.
116. Ibid., 111.
117. Ibid., 136.
118. Grenville, *Salisbury*, 102.
119. Langer, *Diplomacy of Imperialism*, 237.
120. Ibid., 241.
121. Ibid., 246.
122. Van der Poel, *Jameson Raid*, 181.
123. Butler, *Liberal Party*, 138.
124. Marlowe, *Milner*, 128.
125. Langer, *Diplomacy*, 607.
126. Milner, *Papers*, I, 227.
127. Ensor, *England*, 217 note 1.
128. Ibid.
129. Faber, *Vision and Need*, 81.
130. Ibid., 82.
131. Semmel, *Imperialism and Reform*, 172.
132. Ibid.
133. Faber, *Vision and Need*, 83.
134. Milner, *Papers*, I, 221.
135. Ibid., 222.
136. Ibid., 223.
137. Robinson and Gallagher, *Africa and Victorians*, 435.
138. Ibid., 434.
139. Ibid., 437.
140. Warhurst, *Anglo-Portuguese Relations*, 143.
141. Hammond, *Portugal and Africa*, 253.
142. Garvin, *Chamberlain*, III, 314.

143. Hammond, *Portugal and Africa*, 257.

144. Marais, *Fall*, 188.

145. Ibid.

146. J.A. Hobson, *The War in South Africa* (London 1900), quoted in Field-house, *Theory*, 64.

147. Hirschfield, "Anglo-Boer War," 627.

148. Pakenham, *Boer War*, xvi.

149. Fieldhouse, *Economics and Empire*, 357.

150. Robinson and Gallagher, *Africa and Victorians*, 432.

151. Pakenham, *Boer War*, 55.

152. Ensor, *England*, 246.

153. Milner, *Papers*, I, 221.

154. Ibid., I, 352–353.

155. Marais, *Fall*, 267.

156. Langer, *Diplomacy*, 612.

157. Ensor, *England*, 248.

158. Le May, *Supremacy*, 1.

159. Garvin, *Chamberlain*, III, 408.

160. Milner, *Papers*, I, 515.

161. Ibid., I, 385.

162. Ibid., I, 215.

163. Lockhart and Woodhouse, *Rhodes*, 488.

164. Magnus, *Kitchener*, 160.

165. Pakenham, *Boer War*, 276.

166. Magnus, *Kitchener*, 158.

167. Warwick, *South African War*, 70.

168. Pakenham, *Boer War*, 168.

169. Cecil, *Salisbury*, III, 191.

170. J.A. Spender, *The Life of the Right Hon. Sir Henry Campbell-Bannerman* (2 vols. London 1923) I, 336.

171. Porter, "South-African war," 43.

172. A.J.P. Taylor, *The Trouble Makers* (London 1957) 109.

173. Kröll, *Buren-Agitation*, 271–280.

174. Magnus, *Kitchener*, 177.

175. Marquard, *History*, 211.

176. Wesseling, *Indië verloren*, 86.

177. Cf. Marquard, *History*; 211; and S. Marks, "Southern and Central Africa, 1886–1910," in *Cambridge History of Africa*, VI, 479.

178. Farrell, *Great Anglo-Boer War*, 408.

179. Magnus, *Kitchener*, 180.

180. Ibid., 185.

181. Ibid., 186.

182. Davenport, *South Africa*, 142–146; Pakenham, *Boer War*, 572–573.

183. Magnus, *Kitchener*, 190.

184. Ibid., 191.

185. Pakenham, *Boer War*, 572.

186. J. Lonsdale, "The European scramble and conquest in African history," in *Cambridge History of Africa*, VI, 718.

187. Fuller, *Last of the Gentlemen's Wars.*
188. S. Wilkinson, *Lessons of the War* (London 1900).
189. Pakenham, *Boer War*, 100.
190. Marlowe, *Milner*, 82.
191. Marais, *Fall*, 323.
192. Schreuder, *Gladstone and Kruger*, 14.
193. Spies, *Origins*, 54.
194. Taylor, *Struggle for Mastery in Europe*, 387.


VII
EPILOGUE: THE PARTITION OF MOROCCO, 1905–1912

1. Parsons, "Foreign eyes," 2.
2. Harris, *Morocco That Was*, 3.
3. Parsons, "Origins," 7.
4. Parsons, "Foreign eyes," 2.
5. Miège, *Maroc et Europe*, II, 54 note 2.
6. Burke, *Prelude*, 213–214.
7. Landau, *Moroccan Drama*, 54; Porch, *Conquest*, 57.
8. H.L. Wesseling, *Soldaat en krijger* (Assen 1969) 135.
9. Le Révérend, *Lyautey*, 304.
10. M. Paléologue, *Un Grand Tournant de la politique mondiale, 1904–1906* (Paris 1934).
11. Andrew, *Delcassé*, 126.
12. Grenville, *Salisbury*, 324–326.
13. Rolo, *Entente Cordiale*, 165–166.
14. Ibid., 204–253.
15. Text in Hertslett, *Map of Africa*, II, Nos. 251 and 252, pp. 816–822.
16. P. Guillen, "The Entente of 1904 as a colonial settlement," in Gifford and Louis, *France and Britain in Africa*, 364.
17. Guillen, *Allemagne*, 764–777.
18. Andrew, *Delcassé*, 292–294.
19. Guillen, *Allemagne*, 847.
20. Andrew, *Delcassé*, 274.
21. Ibid., 299–301.
22. Ibid., 297.
23. Taylor, *Struggle*, 23.
24. Text of the Act of Algeciras in *Documents diplomatiques français, 2e série, Tome IX, 2e partie* (Paris 1946) 823–853.
25. Allain, *Agadir*, 279.
26. Bredin, *Caillaux*, 133.
27. Ibid., 134.
28. Allain, *Agadir*, 328.
29. Barlow, *Agadir Crisis*, 325.
30. J.C. Cairns, "International politics and the military mind, 1911–1914," *Journal of Modern History* 25 (1953) 280.

CONCLUSION

1. Brunschwig, *Partage*, 153–156.
2. Robinson and Gallagher, "Partition of Africa," 601.
3. Porter, "Imperialism and scramble," 81.
4. H.L. Wesseling, "Colonial wars: An introduction," in De Moor and Wesseling, *Imperialism and War*, 8–11.
5. Fieldhouse, *Theory of Capitalist Imperialism*, 69.
6. Robinson and Gallagher, *Africa and Victorians*, 464.
7. Wesseling, *Indië verloren*, 211.
8. Robinson and Gallagher, *Africa and Victorians*, 466.
9. J. Lonsdale, "The European scramble and conquest in African history," in *Cambridge History of Africa*, VI, 718.
10. Ibid., 699.
11. Robinson and Gallagher, "Partition of Africa," 594.
12. Robinson, "Non-European foundations," 118–140.
13. R. Oliver, "The partition of Africa: The European and the African interpretations," in *Le Centenaire de l'Etat Indépendant du Congo*, 43.
14. A. Wirz, *Sklaverei und kapitalistisches Weltsystem* (Frankfurt 1984) 214.

# BIBLIOGRAPHY

## INTRODUCTION

The subject of this book, the partition of Africa, impinges on different realms of history and has accordingly been covered in a variety of studies. These can be categorized as (1) historical studies of the European countries involved in the partition; (2) historical studies of international relations; (3) biographies of the persons concerned; (4) historical studies of European expansion and of modern imperialism; (5) studies of (the relevant parts of) African history; (6) historical studies of (aspects of) the partition. Needless to say, it is impossible to provide a full list of all these studies, nor does this bibliography pretend to be complete—at most it is intended to be useful.

With respect to the first category, it is enough to list several handbooks and surveys that have been consulted and/or are mentioned in the notes. Section 2 comprises a somewhat more detailed selection of the most recent, as well as of classical, textbooks on diplomatic history and international relations during the period under review. In addition a number of monographs dealing with the foreign policy of the Great Powers have been included. Naturally, only those countries involved in the partition are covered. A distinction has been made between the biographies of European and of African personages. Since the activities of the latter bore exclusively on specific regions, they have been listed in Section 6 under the regions concerned. European statesmen, soldiers and other imperialists, by contrast, were generally involved in more than one region. In Section 3, the most important of them are listed in alphabetical order, and a number of biographies and/or monographs devoted to them have been included. Here too, the aim has not been to provide an exhaustive list—there are more than thirty biographies of Rhodes alone, not to mention Bismarck, Disraeli and other leading figures. Emphasis has been laid on the most recent works, which generally include references to older biographies, and also on the most complete works, such as the British "official biographies."

European imperialism is closely linked to the partition of Africa, although in most cases it goes beyond it. Of the many studies on this subject, Section 4 lists those that are most relevant to the partition of Africa and to related topics. Section 5 contains a number of studies of the history of Africa and, in particular, of European involvement in it. Here, too, none but the most important sources are mentioned. For African history, the reader is especially referred to the *Cambridge History of Africa*, which contains not only excellent bibliographical essays but also complete bibliographies. For our period, Volume 6 (1870–1905) is the most relevant, its bibliographical section running to 125 pages.

The most detailed section of this bibliography is naturally that dealing with the partition of Africa (Section 6). A selection of the most important general studies will be found under "6.1 General." The bibliography is further subdivided into regional sections and thus, by and large, follows the chapters of this book. An exception has, however, been made for regions that are part of territories treated in earlier sections but the discussion of which has had to be deferred for chronological reasons. For greater convenience, all these works have been combined into a single section. Thus works on Morocco (Part VII) are to be found together with works on Tunisia and Egypt (Part I) under "6.2 North and North-East Africa." The history of the (Anglo-Egyptian) Sudan is partly covered in Parts I and IV of this book, but for obvious reasons, the bibliography has not beeen split up, all the relevant works being listed under a single heading (6.2.6).

## 1

### NATIONAL HISTORIES

#### Belgium

Kalken, F. van, *Histoire de la Belgique et de son expansion coloniale* (Brussels 1954).
Kossmann, E.H., *The Low Countries, 1780–1940.* (Oxford 1978).

#### France

Cobban, A., *A History of Modern France* (3 vols. Harmondsworth 1957–1965).
Mayeur, J.M., *Les Débuts de la Troisième République, 1871–1898* (Paris 1973).
Rébérioux, M., *La République radicale? 1898–1914* (Paris 1975).

#### Germany

Craig, G., *Germany, 1866–1945* (Oxford 1978).
Mann, G., *Deutsche Geschichte des 19. und 20. Jahrhunderts* (Frankfurt 1958).
Wehler, H.U., *Das deutsche Kaiserreich, 1871–1918* (Göttingen 1980).

#### Great Britain

Ensor, R.K.C., *England, 1870–1914* (Oxford 1969; 1st ed. 1936).
Halévy, E., *Histoire du peuple anglais au 19e siècle. Epilogue* (2 vols. Paris 1926–1930).
Thomson, D., *England in the Nineteenth Century* (Harmondsworth 1964).

#### Italy

Romano, S., *Histoire de l'Italie du Risorgimento à nos jours* (Paris 1977).
Smith, D.M., *Italy: A Modern History* (Ann Arbor 1969).

## Portugal

Livermore, H.V., *A History of Portugal* (Cambridge, England 1947).
Marques, A.H. de Oliveira, *History of Portugal* (2 vols. New York 1972).

## Spain

Carr, R., *Spain, 1808–1939* (Oxford 1966).

## 2
### INTERNATIONAL RELATIONS, 1870–1914

### 2.1 General

Kennan, G., *The Fateful Alliance: France, Russia and the Coming of the First World War* (New York 1984).
Langer, W.L., *The Diplomacy of Imperialism, 1890–1902* (New York 1951).
———, *The Franco-Russian Alliance, 1880–1894* (Cambridge, Mass. 1929).
———, *European Alliances and Alignments, 1871–1890* (New York 1950).
Lowe, C.J., and F. Marzari, ed., *Italian Foreign Policy, 1870–1940* (London 1975).
Medlicott, W.N., *Bismarck, Gladstone and the Concert of Europe* (London 1956).
Taylor, A.J.P., *The Struggle for Mastery in Europe, 1848–1918* (Oxford 1954).

### 2.2 British Foreign Policy

Howard, C., *Splendid Isolation* (London 1967).
Lowe, C.J., *The Reluctant Imperialists: British Foreign Policy, 1878–1902* (2 vols. London 1967).
———, *Salisbury and the Mediterranean, 1886–1896* (London 1965).
Monger, G., *The End of Isolation: British Foreign Policy, 1900–1907* (London 1963).

### 2.3 French Foreign Policy

Carroll, E.M., *French Public Opinion and Foreign Affairs, 1870–1914* (Washington, D.C. 1931).
Guillen, P., *L'Expansion, 1881–1898* (Paris 1985).

### 2.4 German Foreign Policy

Andrew, C.M., "German world policy and the reshaping of the dual alliance," *Journal of Contemporary History* (1966) 136–153.
Geiss, I., *German Foreign Policy, 1871–1914* (London 1976).
Hillgruber, A., *Bismarcks Aussenpolitik* (Freiburg 1972).
Holstein, F. von, *Die geheimen Papiere, Band II, Tagebuchblätter* (Göttingen 1957).

### 2.5 Anglo-French Relations

Andrew, C.M., "The Entente Cordiale from its origins to 1914," in N. Waites, ed., *Troubled Neighbours* (London 1971).

———, "France and the making of the Entente Cordiale," *Historical Journal* 10 (1967) 89–105.

Edwards, E.W., "The Japanese alliance and the Anglo-French agreement of 1904," *History* 62 (1957) 19–27.

Guillen, P., "Les accords coloniaux franco-anglais de 1904 et la naissance de l'Entente Cordiale," *Revue d'Histoire Diplomatique* 82 (1968) 315–357.

Rolo, P.J.V., *The Entente Cordiale: The Origins and Negotiation of the Anglo-French Agreements of 8 April 1904* (London 1961).

Wilson, K.M., *The Policy of the Entente: Essays on the Determinants of British Foreign Policy, 1904–1914* (Cambridge, England 1985).


### 2.6 Franco-German Relations

Guillen, P., "Les questions coloniales dans les relations franco-allemandes à la veille de la première guerre mondiale," *Revue Historique* 503 (1972) 87–107.

Poidevin, R., *Les Relations économiques et financières entre la France et l'Allemagne de 1898 à 1914* (Paris 1969).

Poidevin, R., and J. Bariéty, *Les Relations franco-allemandes, 1815–1975* (Paris 1977).

Renouvin, P., "Les relations franco-allemandes de 1871 à 1914," in A.O. Sarkissian, ed., *Studies in Diplomatic History and Historiography in Honour of G.P. Gooch* (London 1961).


## 3
### (AUTO)BIOGRAPHIES AND MEMOIRS


### Bismarck

Bismarck, O. von, *Gedanken und Erinnerungen* (Stuttgart 1898).

Eyck, E., *Bismarck. Leben und Werk* (3 vols. Zurich 1941–1944).

Gall, L., *Bismarck. Der weisse Revolutionär* (Frankfurt 1980).

Stern, F., *Gold and Iron: Bismarck, Bleichröder and the Building of the German Empire* (London 1977).

Taylor, A.J.P., *Bismarck: The Man and the Statesman* (London 1965).


### Brazza

Autin, J., *Pierre Savorgnan de Brazza* (Paris 1985).

Brunschwig, H., ed., *Brazza explorateur. Les traités Makoko, 1880–1882* (Paris 1972).

Chambrun, J. de, *Brazza* (Paris 1930).

Coquery-Vidrovitch, C., ed., *Brazza et la prise de possession du Congo, 1883–1885* (Paris 1969).

Nwoye, R.E., *The Public Image of Pierre Savorgnan de Brazza and the Establishment of French Imperialism in the Congo* (Aberdeen 1981).

West, R., *Brazza of the Congo: European Exploration and Exploitation in French Equatorial Africa* (London 1972).

## Caillaux

Allain, J.C., *Joseph Caillaux. Le défi victorieux, 1863–1914* (Paris 1978).
———, *Joseph Caillaux. L'oracle, 1914–1944* (Paris 1981).
Bredin, J.D., *Caillaux* (Paris 1980).
Caillaux, J., *Mes Mémoires* (3 vols. Paris 1942–1947).
Seager, F., "Joseph Caillaux as premier, 1911–1912: The dilemma of a liberal reformer," *French Historical Studies* 11 (1979–1980) 239–257.

## Chamberlain

Fraser, P., *Joseph Chamberlain: Radicalism and Empire, 1868–1914* (London 1966).
Garvin, J.L., *The Life of Joseph Chamberlain* (3 vols. London 1932–1935).
Hurst, M., *The Life of Joseph Chamberlain* (London 1967).
Jay, R., *Joseph Chamberlain: A Political Study* (Oxford 1981).
Judd, D., *Radical Joe: A Life of Joseph Chamberlain* (London 1977).
Kubicek, R.V., *The Administration of Imperialism: Joseph Chamberlain at the Colonial Office* (Durham, N.C., 1969).

## Delcassé

Andrew, C.M., *Théophile Delcassé and the Making of the Entente Cordiale: A Reappraisal of French Foreign Policy, 1898–1905* (London 1968).
Neton, A., *Delcassé* (Paris 1953).
Porter, C.W., *The Career of Th. Delcassé* (Philadelphia 1936).
Renouvin, P., *La Politique extérieure de Th. Delcassé, 1898–1905* (Paris 1962).

## Disraeli

Blake, R., *Disraeli* (London 1966).
Harcourt, F., "Disraeli's imperialism, 1866–1868: A question of timing," *Historical Journal* 23 (1980) 87–109.
Monypenny, W.F., and G.E. Buckle, *The Life of Benjamin Disraeli* (2 vols. London 1929).
Smith, P., *Disraelian Conservatism and Social Reform* (London 1967).

## Etienne

Sieberg, H., *Eugène Etienne und die französische Kolonialpolitik, 1887–1904* (Cologne 1968).

## Ferry

Ferry, J., *Discours et opinions* (7 vols. Paris 1893–1898).
Furet, F., ed., *Jules Ferry. Fondateur de la République* (Paris 1985).
Gaillard, J.M., *Jules Ferry* (Paris 1989).
Julien, C.-A., "Jules Ferry," in *Les Politiques d'expansion impérialiste* (Paris 1949).
Pisani-Ferry, F., *Jules Ferry et le partage du monde* (Paris 1962).

Power, T., *Jules Ferry and the Renaissance of French Imperialism* (New York 1944).

### Freycinet

Fozard, L.M., C.-L. *de Saulses de Freycinet: The Railways and the Expansion of the French Empire* (Dissertation, Boston University, 1975).
Thorson, W.B., "Charles de Freycinet: French empire-builder," *Research Studies in the State College of Washington* 12 (1944) 257–282.

### Gallieni

Gallieni, J., *Deux Campagnes au Soudan français, 1886–1888* (Paris 1891).
——, *Neuf Ans à Madagascar* (Paris 1908).
Michel, M., *Gallieni* (Paris 1989).

### Gambetta

Bury, J.P.T., "Gambetta and overseas problems," *English Historical Review* 82 (1967) 277–295.
——, *Gambetta and the National Defence* (London 1936).
——, *Gambetta and the Making of the Third Republic* (London 1973).
——, *Gambetta's Final Years: "The Era of Difficulties," 1877–1882* (London 1982).
Wormser, G., *Gambetta dans les tempêtes, 1870–1877* (Paris 1964).

### Gladstone

Magnus, P., *Gladstone: A Biography* (London 1954).
Morley, J., *The Life of W.E. Gladstone* (3 vols. London 1903).
Ramm, A., ed., *The Political Correspondence of Mr. Gladstone and Lord Granville, 1868–1876* (2 vols. London 1952).
Shannon, R., *Gladstone, 1809–1865* (London 1982).

### Goldie

Flint, J.E., *Sir George Goldie and the Making of Nigeria* (London 1960).
Muffett, D.J.M., *Empire-Builder Extraordinary: Sir George Goldie, His Philosophy of Government and Empire* (Douglas, Isle of Man, 1978).
Wellesey, D., *Sir George Goldie* (London 1934).

### Gordon

Allen, B.M., *Gordon and the Sudan* (London 1931).
Johnson, D.H., "The death of Gordon: A Victorian myth," *Journal of Imperial and Commonwealth History* 10 (1982) 285–310.
Marlowe, J., *Mission to Khartoum: The Apotheosis of General Gordon* (London 1969).
Nutting, A., *Gordon: Martyr and Misfit* (London 1966).

Strachey, L., "The end of General Gordon," in L. Strachey, *Eminent Victorians* (London 1918).


## Hanotaux

Andrew, C.M., and A.S. Kanya-Forstner, "Gabriel Hanotaux, the colonial party and the Fashoda strategy," *Journal of Imperial and Commonwealth History* 3 (1974) 55–104.
Grupp, P., *Theorie der Kolonialexpansion und Methoden der imperialistischen Aussenpolitik bei Gabriel Hanotaux* (Bern 1972).
Heggoy, A.A., *The African Policies of Gabriel Hanotaux, 1894–1898* (Athens, Ga., 1972).
Iiams, T.M., *Dreyfus, Diplomatists and the Dual Alliance: Gabriel Hanotaux at the Quai d'Orsay, 1884–1898* (Geneva 1962).


## Kitchener

Arthur, G., *Life of Lord Kitchener* (3 vols. London 1920).
Magnus, P., *Kitchener: Portrait of an Imperialist* (London 1958).


## Leopold II

Ascherson, N., *The King Incorporated: Leopold the Second in the Age of Trusts* (London 1963).
Emerson, B., *Leopold II of the Belgians: King of Colonialism* (London 1979).
Roeykens, A., *Les Débuts de l'oeuvre africaine de Léopold II, 1876–1879* (Brussels 1955).
———, *Le Dessein africain de Léopold II. Nouvelles recherches sur sa genèse et sa nature, 1875–1876* (Brussels 1956).
———, *Léopold II et la Conférence géographique de Bruxelles, 1876* (Brussels 1956).
———, *Léopold II et l'Afrique, 1855–1880* (Brussels 1958).
Stengers, J., "Leopold II et la rivalité franco-anglaise en Afrique, 1882–1884," *Revue Belge de Philologie et d'Histoire* 47 (1969) 425–479.


## Lugard

Perham, M., *Lugard* (2 vols. London 1956–1960).


## Lyautey

Lyautey, H., *Lettres du Tonkin et de Madagascar, 1894–1899* (2 vols. Paris 1920–1921).
Révérend, A. le, *Lyautey* (Paris 1983).
Rivet, D., *Lyautey et l'institution du protectorat français au Maroc, 1912–1925* (3 vols. Paris 1988).
Scham, A., *Lyautey in Morocco: Protectorate Administration, 1912–1925* (Berkeley 1970).

## Milner

Duminy, A.H., *Sir Alfred Milner and the Outbreak of the Anglo–Boer War* (Dissertation, University of Natal 1976).

Gollin, A.M., *Proconsul in Politics: A Study of Lord Milner in Opposition and in Power* (London 1964).

Halpérin, V., *Lord Milner et l'évolution de l'impérialisme britannique* (Paris 1950).

Milner, A., *The Milner Papers* (2 vols. London 1931–1935).

O'Brien, T.H., *Milner* (London 1979).

Stokes, E., "Milnerism," *Historical Journal* 5 (1962) 47–60.

Wrench, J.E., *Alfred Lord Milner: The Man of No Illusions, 1854–1925* (London 1958).


## Peters

Baer, H.M., *Carl Peters and German Colonialism: A Study in the Ideas and Actions of Imperialism* (Stanford 1968).

Baumont, M., "Carl Peters," in *Les Techniciens de la colonisation* (Paris 1947).

Krätschell, H., *Carl Peters, 1856–1918. Ein Beitrag zur Publizistik des imperialistischen Nationalismus in Deutschland* (Berlin 1959).

Peters, C., *Gesammelte Schriften* (3 vols. Munich 1943–1944).

———, *Wie Deutsch-Ostafrika entstand* (Leipzig 1912).


## Rhodes

Butler, J., "Cecil Rhodes," *International Journal of African Historical Studies* 10 (1977) 259–281.

Flint, J., *Cecil Rhodes* (London 1976).

Galbraith, J.S., "Cecil Rhodes and his 'Cosmic Dreams': A reassessment," *Journal of Imperial and Commonwealth History* 1 (1972) 173–191.

Keppel-Jones, A., *Rhodes and Rhodesia: The White Conquest of Zimbabwe, 1884–1902* (Montreal 1983).

Lockhart, J.G., and C.M. Woodhouse, *Rhodes* (London 1963).

Phimister, I.R., "Rhodes, Rhodesia and the Rand," *Journal of Southern African Studies* 1 (1974) 74–89.

Ranger, T., "The last word on Rhodes," *Past and Present* 28 (1964) 116–127.

Roberts, B., *Cecil Rhodes: Flawed Colossus* (London 1987).

Rotberg, R.I., *The Founder: Cecil Rhodes and the Pursuit of Power* (Oxford 1988).

Turrell, R., "Rhodes, De Beers and monopoly," *Journal of Imperial and Commonwealth History* 10 (1982) 311–343.

Williams, B., *Cecil Rhodes* (London 1921).


## Rosebery

Coates, F.F.P., *Lord Rosebery: His Life and Speeches* (2 vols. London 1900).

Crewe, Marquess of, *Lord Rosebery* (2 vols. London 1931).

James, R., *Rosebery* (London 1963).

Martel, G., *Imperial Diplomacy: Rosebery and the Failure of Foreign Policy* (London 1986).
Raymond, E.F., *The Man of Promise: Lord Rosebery* (London 1923).

### Salisbury

Cecil, G., *Life of Robert Marquess of Salisbury* (4 vols. London 1921–1932).
Grenville, J.A.S., *Lord Salisbury and Foreign Policy: The Close of the Nineteenth Century* (London 1964).
Kennedy, A.L., *Salisbury, 1830–1903* (London 1953).
Lowe, C.J., *Salisbury and the Mediterranean, 1866–1896* (London 1965).
Pinto-Duschinsky, M., *The Political Thought of Lord Salisbury, 1854–1868* (London 1967).

### Stanley

Anthruster, I., *I Presume: Stanley's Triumph and Disaster* (London 1956).
Hall, R., *Stanley: An Adventurer Explored* (London 1974).
Hellinga, G., *Henry Morton Stanley. Een individual-psychologische interpretatie* (Dissertation, University of Leiden 1978).
McLynn, F., *Stanley: The Making of an African Explorer* (London 1989).
Stanley, H.M., *The Congo and the Founding of Its Free State* (London 1885).
———, *In Darkest Africa* (London 1890).

### Wolseley

Lehmann, J.H. *All Sir Garnet: A Life of Field-Marshal Lord Wolseley, 1833–1913* (London 1964).
Preston, A., ed., *The South African Diaries of Sir Garnet Wolseley, 1875* (Cape Town 1971).
———, *The South African Journal of Sir Garnet Wolseley, 1879–1880* (Cape Town 1973).

## 4

#### IMPERIALISM AND EXPANSION

### 4.1 General

Baumgart, W., *Der klassische Imperialismus. Idee und Wirklichkeit der englischen und französischen Kolonialexpansion, 1880–1914* (Wiesbaden 1974).
Betts, R.F., *The False Dawn: European Imperialism in the Nineteenth Century* (Oxford 1976).
———, *Uncertain Dimensions: Western Overseas Empires in the Twentieth Century* (Oxford 1985).
Bouvier, J., "A propos des origines de l'impérialisme," *La Pensée* 100 (1961) 57–68, and 101 (1962) 115–130.
Brewer, A., *Marxist Theories of Imperialism: A Critical Survey* (London 1980).
Chamberlain, M.E., *The New Imperialism* (London 1970).
Curtin, P.D., *Imperialism* (New York 1971).

Etherington, N., *Theories of Imperialism: War, Conquest and Capital* (London 1984).

Fieldhouse, D.K., *Colonialism, 1870–1945: An Introduction* (London 1981).

Gollwitzer, H., *Europe in the Age of Imperialism, 1880–1914* (London 1969).

Hallgarten, G.W.F., *Imperialismus vor 1914* (2 vols. Munich 1963).

Headrick, D.R., *The Tools of Empire: Technology and European Imperialism in the Nineteenth Century* (Oxford 1981).

Kemp, T., *Theories of Imperialism* (London 1967).

Kiernan, V.G., *European Empires from Conquest to Collapse, 1815–1960* (London 1982).

———, *The Lords of Human Kind: European Attitudes towards the Outside World in the Imperial Age* (London 1969).

———, *Marxism and Imperialism* (London 1976).

Magdonagh, O., "The anti-imperialism of free trade," *Economic History Review* 2nd ser. 14 (1962) 489–501.

Miège, J.-L., *Expansion européenne et décolonisation de 1870 à nos jours* (Paris 1973).

Mommsen, W.J., *Imperialismustheorien* (Göttingen 1980).

———, *Der moderne Imperialismus* (Stuttgart 1971).

Moor, J.A. de, and H.L. Wesseling, eds., *Imperialism and War: Essays on Colonial Wars in Asia and Africa* (Leiden 1989).

Owen, R., and B. Sutcliffe, eds., *Studies in the Theory of Imperialism* (Harlow 1972).

Reinhard, W., *Geschichte der europäischen Expansion* (4 vols. Stuttgart 1983–1990).

Schumpeter, J.A., *Imperialism and Social Classes* (Oxford 1951).

Smith, T., *The Pattern of Imperialism: The United States, Great Britain, and the Late-Industrializing World since 1815* (Cambridge, Mass. 1981).

Stokes, E., "Late nineteenth century colonial expansion and the attack on the theory of economic imperialism: A case of mistaken identity," *Historical Journal* 12 (1969) 285–301.

Thornton, A.P., *Doctrines of Imperialism* (London 1969).

Warren, B., *Imperialism, Pioneer of Capitalism* (London 1980).

Wesseling, H.L., *Indië verloren, rampspoed geboren en andere opstellen over de geschiedenis van de Europese expansie* (Amsterdam 1988).

———, ed., *Expansion and Reaction: Essays on European Expansion and Reactions in Asia and Africa* (Leiden 1978).

Winks, R., *The Age of Imperialism* (New York 1969).

## 4.2 British Imperialism

Bodelsen, C.A., *Studies in Mid-Victorian Imperialism* (London 1960).

Bowle, J., *The Imperial Achievement: The Rise and Transformation of the British Empire* (Boston 1975).

Cain, P.J., and A.G. Hopkins, "The political economy of British expansion overseas, 1750–1914," *Economic History Review* 2nd ser. 33 (1980) 463–490.

*The Cambridge History of the British Empire. Vol. III. The Empire-Commonwealth, 1870–1919* (Cambridge, England 1967).

Christopher, A.J., *The British Empire at Its Zenith* (London 1987).

Crouzet, F., "Commerce et empire. L'expérience britannique du libre-échange à la première guerre mondiale," *Annales* 19 (1964) 281–310.

Davis, L.E., and R.A. Huttenback, *Mammon and the Pursuit of Empire. The Political Economy of British Imperialism, 1860–1912* (Cambridge, England 1986).

Edelstein, M., *Overseas Investment in the Age of High Imperialism: The United Kingdom, 1850–1914* (London 1982).

Eldridge, C.C., *England's Mission: The Imperial Idea in the Age of Gladstone and Disraeli, 1868–1880* (London 1973).

Faber, R., *The Vision and the Need: Late Victorian Imperialist Aims* (London 1966).

Galbraith, J.S., "The 'Turbulent Frontier' as a factor in British expansion," *Comparative Studies in Society and History* 2 (1960) 150–168.

Gallagher, J., and R. Robinson, "The imperialism of free trade," *Economic History Review* 2nd ser. 6 (1953) 1–15.

Halstead, J.P., *The Second British Empire: Trade, Philanthropy, and Good Government* (Westport, Conn., 1983).

Hyam, R., *Britain's Imperial Century, 1815–1914: A Study of Empire and Expansion* (London 1976).

Hyam, R., and G. Martin, eds., *Reappraisals in British Imperial History* (London 1975).

Kennedy, P.M., "Why did the British Empire last so long?," in P.M. Kennedy, *Strategy and Diplomacy, 1870–1945: Eight Studies* (London 1984).

Lloyd, T.O., *The British Empire, 1558–1983* (Oxford 1984).

Martel, G., ed., *Studies in British Imperial History. Essays in Honour of A.P. Thornton* (London 1986).

McIntyre, W.D., *The Imperial Frontier in the Tropics, 1865–1875* (London 1967).

Platt, D.C.M., "Economic factors in British policy during the 'new imperialism,'" *Past and Present* 39 (1968) 120–138.

———, *Finance, Trade and Politics in British Foreign Policy, 1815–1914* (Oxford 1968).

———, "Further objections to an 'imperialism of free trade,' 1830–1860," *Economic History Review* 2nd ser. 26 (1973) 77–91.

———, "The imperialism of free trade: Some reservations," *Economic History Review* 2nd ser. 21 (1968) 296–306.

Porter, B., *The Lion's Share: A Short History of British Imperialism, 1850–1970* (London 1984).

Semmel, B., *Imperialism and Social Reform: English Social-Imperial Thought, 1895–1914* (London 1960).

———, *The Rise of Free Trade Imperialism. Classical Political Economy, the Empire of Free Trade and Imperialism, 1750–1850* (Cambridge, England 1970).

Thornton, A.P., *The Imperial Idea and Its Enemies* (London 1959).

## 4.3 French Imperialism

Andrew, C.M., P. Grupp and A.S. Kanya-Forstner, "Le mouvement colonial français et ses principales personnalités, 1890–1914," *Revue Française d'Histoire
d'Outre-Mer* 62 (1975) 640–673.

Andrew, C.M., and A.S. Kanya-Forstner, *France Overseas: The Great War and the
Climax of French Imperial Expansion* (London 1981).

———, "French business and the French colonialists," *Historical Journal* 19 (1976)
981–1000.

———, "The French 'colonial party': Its composition, aims and influence, 1889–
1914," *Historical Journal* 14 (1971) 99–128.

———, "Gabriel Hanotaux, the colonial party and the Fashoda strategy," *Journal
of Imperial and Commonwealth History* 3 (1975) 55–104.

———, "The *groupe colonial* in the French Chamber of Deputies, 1892–1932,"
*Historical Journal* 17 (1974) 837–866.

Berge, F., *Le Sous-secrétariat et les sous-secrétaires d'Etat aux colonies* (Paris 1962).

Bouvier, J., and R. Girault, eds., *L'Impérialisme français d'avant 1914* (Paris 1976).

Bouvier, J., R. Girault and J. Thobie, *L'Impérialisme à la française, 1914–1960*
(Paris 1986).

Brunschwig, H., *Mythes et réalités de l'impérialisme colonial français, 1871–1914*
(Paris 1960).

———, "Le parti colonial français," *Revue Française d'Histoire d'Outre-Mer* 46
(1959) 49–83.

Cohen, W.B., *Rulers of Empire: The French Colonial Service in Africa* (Stanford
1971).

Comte, G., *L'Empire triomphant, 1871–1936. Tome I. Afrique occidentale et équatoriale* (Paris 1988).

Ganiage, J., *L'Expansion coloniale de la France sous la Troisième République,
1871–1914* (Paris 1968).

Grupp, P., *Deutschland, Frankreich und die Kolonien* (Tübingen 1980).

Hanotaux, G., and A. Martineau, eds., *Histoire des colonies françaises et de l'expansion de la France dans le monde* (6 vols. Paris 1930–1934).

Marseille, J., *Empire colonial et capitalisme français. Histoire d'un divorce* (Paris
1984).

———, "L'investissement français dans l'Empire colonial," *Revue Historique* 201
(1974) 409–432.

Murphy, A., *The Ideology of French Imperialism, 1871–1881* (Washington, D.C.
1948).

Persell, S.M., *The French Colonial Lobby, 1889–1938* (Stanford 1983).

Priestley, H.I., *France Overseas: A Study of Modern Imperialism* (New York 1938).

Roberts, S.H., *History of French Colonial Policy, 1870–1925* (2 vols. London
1929).

Thobie, J., *La France impériale, 1880–1914* (Paris 1982).

Yacono, X., *Histoire de la colonisation française* (Paris 1969).

Ziebura, G., "Interne Faktoren des französischen Hochimperialismus, 1871–1914,"
in W.J. Mommsen, ed., *Der moderne Imperialismus* (Stuttgart 1971).

## 4.4 German Imperialism

Bade, K.J., *Friedrich Fabri und der Imperialismus in der Bismarckzeit. Revolution, Depression, Expansion* (Freiburg 1975).

———, ed., *Imperialismus und Kolonialmission. Kaiserliches Deutschland und koloniales Imperium* (Wiesbaden 1982).

Baumgart, W., *Deutschland im Zeitalter des Imperialismus, 1890–1914. Grundkräfte, Thesen und Strukturen* (Frankfurt 1972).

Brunschwig, H., *L'Expansion allemande outre-mer du XVe siècle à nos jours* (Paris 1957).

Cornevin, R., *Histoire de la colonisation allemande* (Paris 1969).

Henderson, W.O., *Studies in German Colonial History* (London 1962).

Kuczynski, J., *Studien zur Geschichte des deutschen Imperialismus* (2 vols. Berlin 1952).

Renouvin, P., "Nationalisme et impérialisme en Allemagne de 1911 à 1914," *Revue Historique* 245 (1971) 63–72.

Schinzinger, F., *Die Kolonien und das Deutsche Reich. Die wirtschaftliche Bedeutung der deutschen Besitzungen in Übersee* (Wiesbaden 1984).

Smith, W.D., *The German Colonial Empire* (Chapel Hill, N.C., 1978).

———, "The ideology of German colonialism, 1840–1906," *Journal of Modern History* 46 (1974) 641–663.

Strandmann, M. Pogge von, "Domestic origins of Germany's colonial expansion under Bismarck," *Past and Present* 42 (1969) 140–159.

Taylor, A.J.P., *Germany's First Bid for Colonies* (London 1938).

Townsend, M.E., *The Rise and Fall of Germany's Colonial Empire* (New York 1930).

Wehler, H.U., *Bismarck und der Imperialismus* (Cologne 1969).


## 4.5 Portuguese Imperialism

Clarence-Smith, G., *The Third Portuguese Empire, 1825–1975: A Study in Economic Imperialism* (Manchester 1985).


# 5
## AFRICA


## 5.1 General

Brownlie, I., *African Boundaries: A Legal and Diplomatic Encyclopaedia* (London 1979).

Brunschwig, H., *L'Avènement de l'Afrique noire* (Paris 1963).

———, "De la résistance africaine à l'impérialisme européen," *Journal of African History* 15 (1974) 47–64.

*The Cambridge History of Africa* (8 vols. Cambridge, England 1982–1986).

Coquery-Vidrovitch, C., and H. Moniot, *L'Afrique noire de 1800 à nos jours* (Paris 1974).

Cornevin, R., and M. Cornevin, *L'Afrique noire de 1919 à nos jours* (Paris 1973).

Curtin, P., et. al. *African History* (Boston 1978).

Davis, R.H., "Interpreting the colonial period in African History," *African Affairs* 27 (1973) 383–400.

Deschamps, H., *Histoire de la traite des noirs de l'antiquité à nos jours* (Paris 1971).

——, ed., *Histoire générale de l'Afrique noire, de Madagascar et des Archipels* (2 vols. Paris 1970).

Fage, J.D., *An Atlas of African History* (London 1963).

Freeman-Grenville, G.S.P., *Chronology of African History* (Oxford 1973).

Ganiage, J., et al., *L'Afrique au XXe siècle* (Paris 1966).

Gray, R., and D. Birmingham, eds., *Precolonial African Trade: Essays on Trade in Central and Eastern Africa before 1900* (Oxford 1970).

Hallett, R., *Africa to 1875: A Modern History* (Ann Arbor 1974).

Hallett, R., *Africa since 1875: A Modern History* (Ann Arbor 1974).

Ki-Zerbo, J., *Histoire de l'Afrique noire. D'hier à demain* (Paris 1972).

Munro, J.F., *Africa and the International Economy, 1800–1960: An Introduction to the Modern Economic History of Africa South of the Sahara* (London 1976).

Oliver, R., and A. Atmore, *Africa since 1800* (Cambridge, England 1967).

Oliver, R., and J.D. Fage, *A Short History of Africa* (London 1962).

Ranger, T.O., ed., *Emerging Themes of African History* (London 1968).

## 5.2 Exploration

Brent, P., *"Black Nile": Mungo Park and the Search for the Niger* (London 1973).

Hibbert, C., *Africa Explored: Europeans in the Dark Continent, 1769–1889* (Harmondsworth 1984).

Jeal, T., *Livingstone* (London 1973).

Moorehead, A., *The Blue Nile* (London 1962).

——, *The White Nile* (London 1960).

Rotberg, R.I., *Africa and Its Explorers: Motives, Methods and Impact* (Cambridge, Mass., 1970).

Severin, T., *The African Adventure* (London 1973).

Shepperson, G., *The Exploration of Africa in the Eighteenth and Nineteenth Centuries* (Edinburgh 1971).

Simmons, J., *Livingstone and Africa* (London 1955).

## 5.3 Colonialism in Africa

Collins, R.O., ed., *Problems in the History of Colonial Africa, 1860–1960* (Englewood Cliffs, N.J., 1970).

Crowder, M., "Indirect Rule—French and British Style," *Africa* 34 (1964) 197–205.

Gann, L.H., and P. Duignan, *Burden of Empire: An Appraisal of Western Colonialism in Africa South of the Sahara* (London 1968).

——, eds., *Colonialism in Africa, 1870–1960* (5 vols. Cambridge, England 1969–1975).

Gifford, P., and W.R. Louis, eds., *Britain and Germany in Africa: Imperial Rivalry and Colonial Rule* (New Haven, Conn., 1967).

—————, eds., *France and Britain in Africa: Imperial Rivalry and Colonial Rule* (New Haven, Conn., 1971).

Johnston, H., *A History of the Colonization of Africa by Alien Races* (London 1899).

Rotberg, R.I., and A.A. Mazrui, eds., *Protest and Power in Black Africa* (New York 1970).

Wilson, H.S., *The Imperial Experience in Sub-Saharan Africa since 1870* (Oxford 1977).

### 5.4 Britain in Africa

Cairns, H.A.C., *Prelude to Imperialism: British Reactions to Central African Society, 1840–1890* (London 1965).

Gann, L.H., and P. Duignan, *The Rulers of British Africa, 1870–1914* (London 1978).

Hynes, W.G., *The Economics of Empire: Britain, Africa and New Imperialism, 1870–1895* (London 1979).

James, L., *The Savage Wars: British Campaigns in Africa, 1870–1920* (London 1985).

Louis, W.R., "Sir Percy Anderson's grand African strategy, 1883–1896," *English Historical Review* 81 (1966) 292–314.

Lugard, F.D., *The Dual Mandate in British Tropical Africa* (Edinburgh 1926).

Miers, S., *Britain, the Slave Trade and the Scramble: International Agreements and Disagreements* (London 1974).

Newbury, C.W., ed., *British Policy towards Africa: Select Documents, 1875–1914* (Oxford 1971).

Oliver, R., *Sir Harry Johnston and The Scramble for Africa* (London 1957).

Raphael, L.A.C., *The Cape to Cairo Dream: A Study in British Imperialism* (New York 1936).

Robinson, R., and J. Gallagher, *Africa and the Victorians: The Official Mind of Imperialism* (London 1961).

Uzoigwe, G.N., *Britain and the Conquest of Africa: The Age of Salisbury* (Ann Arbor 1974).

Weinthal, V.L., ed., *The Story of the Cape to Cairo Railway and River Route from 1887 to 1922* (4 vols. London 1922–1923).

### 5.5 France in Africa

Brunschwig, H., "Note sur les technocrates de l'impérialisme français en Afrique noire," *Revue Française d'Histoire d'Outre-Mer* 54 (1967) 171–187.

—————, "Politique et économie dans l'empire français d'Afrique noire, 1870–1914," *Journal of African History* 11 (1970) 401–417.

Cohen, W.B., *The French Encounter with Africans: White Response to Blacks, 1550–1880* (Bloomington, Ind., 1980).

Rouard de Card, E., *Traités de délimitation concernant l'Afrique française* (Paris 1908).

### 5.6 Germany in Africa

Gann, L.H., and P. Duignan, eds., *The Rulers of German Africa, 1884–1914* (Stanford 1977).

### 5.7 Italy in Africa

Barclay, G.S.J., *The Rise and Fall of the New Roman Empire: Italy's Bid for World Power, 1890–1943* (London 1973).
Battaglia, R., *La prima guerra d'Africa* (Turin 1958).
Boca, A. del, *Gli Italiani in Africa orientale* (2 vols. Bari 1976–1984).
Miège, J.-L., *L'Impérialisme colonial italien de 1870 à nos jours* (Paris 1968).
Schieder, W., "Aspekte des italienischen Imperialismus vor 1914," in W. Mommsen, ed., *Der moderne Imperialismus* (Stuttgart 1971).
Ségré, C.G., *Fourth Shore: The Italian Colonization of Libya* (Chicago 1976).

### 5.8 Portugal in Africa

Axelson, E., *Portugal and The Scramble for Africa, 1875–1891* (Johannesburg 1967).
Chilcote, R.H., *Portuguese Africa* (Englewood Cliffs, N.J., 1967).
Duffy, J., *Portugal in Africa* (Harmondsworth 1962).
———, *Portuguese Africa* (London 1959).
Hammond, R.J., *Portugal and Africa, 1815–1910. A Study in Uneconomic Imperialism* (Stanford 1966).
Newitt, M., *Portugal in Africa: The Last Hundred Years* (London 1981).
Warhurst, P.R., *Anglo-Portuguese Relations in South-Central Africa, 1890–1900* (London 1968).

## 6
### THE PARTITION OF AFRICA

### 6.1 General

Alexandrowicz, C.H., "The partition of Africa by treaty," in K. Ingham, ed., *Foreign Relations of African States* (London 1974) 129–157.
Asiwaju, A.I., ed., *Partitioned Africans: Ethnic Relations across Africa's International Boundaries, 1884–1984* (Lagos 1985).
Brunschwig, H., *Le Partage de l'Afrique noire* (Paris 1971).
———, "Scramble et 'Course au Clocher,' " *Journal of African History* 12 (1971) 139–143.
Chamberlain, M.E., *The Scramble for Africa* (London 1974).
Collins, R.O., *The Partition of Africa. Illusion or Necessity?* (New York 1969).
Darmstaedter, P., *Geschichte der Aufteilung und Kolonisation Afrikas* (Berlin 1920).
Hargreaves, J.D., "Towards a history of the partition of Africa," *Journal of African History* 1 (1960) 97–109.
Hertslet, E., *The Map of Africa by Treaty* (3 vols. London 1909).

Hyam, R., "The partition of Africa," *Historical Journal* 7 (1964) 154–169.

Keltie, J.S., *The Partition of Africa* (London 1893).

Lucas, C., *The Partition and Colonization of Africa* (London 1922).

Mackenzie, J.M., *The Partition of Africa, 1880–1900, and European Imperialism in the Nineteenth Century* (London 1983).

Penrose, E.F., ed., *European Imperialism and the Partition of Africa* (London 1975).

Porter, B., "Imperialism and the scramble," *Journal of Imperial and Commonwealth History* 9 (1980) 76–81.

Robinson, R,. and J. Gallagher, "The partition of Africa," in *The New Cambridge Modern History* XI, 593–640 (Cambridge, England 1962).

Sanderson, G.N., "The European partition of Africa: Coincidence or conjuncture?" *Journal of Imperial and Commonwealth History* 3 (1974) 1–54.

Shepperson G., "Africa, the Victorians and imperialism," *Revue Belge de Philologie et d'Histoire* 40 (1962) 1228–1238.

Stengers, J., "L'impérialisme colonial de la fin du XIXe siècle. Mythe ou réalité?" *Journal of African History* 3 (1962) 469–491.

*The Theory of Imperialism and the European Partition of Africa. Proceedings of a Seminar* (Edinburgh 1967).

Touval, G., "Treaties, borders and the partition of Africa," *Journal of African History* 7 (1966) 279–292.

Vignes, K., "Etude sur la rivalité d'influence entre les puissances européennes en Afrique équatoriale et occidentale depuis l'acte général de Berlin jusqu'au seuil du XXe siècle," *Revue Française d'Histoire d'Outre-Mer* 48 (1961) 5–95.

## 6.2 North and North-East Africa (Chapters 1, 5 and 7)

### 6.2.1 *General*

Ageron, Ch.-R., *Politiques coloniales au Maghreb* (Paris 1972).

*Armées, guerre et politique en Afrique du Nord, XIX–XXe siècles* (Paris 1977).

Issawi, C., *An Economic History of the Middle East and North Africa* (London 1982).

Ling, D.L., *Morocco and Tunisia: A Comparative History* (Washington, D.C. 1979).

Valensi, L., *Le Maghreb avant la prise d'Alger, 1799–1830* (Paris 1969).

### 6.2.2 *Morocco*

Allain, J.C., *Agadir 1911. Une crise impérialiste en Europe pour la conquête du Maroc* (Paris 1976).

Anderson, E.N., *The First Moroccan Crisis, 1904–1906* (Chicago 1930).

Ayache, A., *Le Maroc. Bilan d'une colonisation* (Paris 1956).

Ayache, G., *Etudes d'histoire marocaine* (Rabat 1979).

Barlow, I.C., *The Agadir Crisis* (Chapel Hill, N.C., 1940).

Brignon, J., et al., *Histoire du Maroc* (Paris 1968).

Burke, E., "Pan-Islam and Moroccan resistance to French colonial penetration, 1910–1912," *Journal of African History* 13 (1972) 97–118.

————, *Prelude to Protectorate in Morocco: Precolonial Protest and Resistance, 1860–1912* (Chicago 1976).

Cambon, H., *Histoire du Maroc* (Paris 1952).

Chandler, J.A., "Spain and her Moroccan protectorate, 1898–1927," *Journal of Contemporary History* 10 (1975) 301–322.

Dockrill, M.C., "British policy during the Agadir crisis of 1911," in F.H. Hinsley, ed., *British Policy under Sir Edward Grey* (Cambridge, England 1977).

Edwards, E.W., "The Franco-German agreement on Morocco, 1909," *English Historical Review* (1963) 483–513.

Guenane, D., *Les Relations franco-allemandes et les affaires marocaines de 1901 à 1911* (Algiers 1975).

Guillen, P., *L'Allemagne et le Maroc de 1870 à 1905* (Paris 1967).

————, "L'implantation du Schneider au Maroc. Le début de la Compagnie Marocaine," *Revue d'Histoire Diplomatique* 79 (1965) 113–168.

————, "Les milieux d'affaires français et le Maroc à l'aube du XXe siècle. La fondation de la Compagnie Marocaine," *Revue Historique* (1963) 397–422.

Harris, W., *Morocco that Was* (London 1921).

Julien, Ch.-A., *Le Maroc face aux impérialismes, 1415–1956* (Paris 1978).

Landau, R., *Moroccan Drama, 1900–1955* (London 1956).

Miège, J.-L., *Le Maroc et l'Europe, 1830–1894* (4 vols. Paris 1961–1963).

Oncken, E., *Panthersprung nach Agadir. Die deutsche Politik während der zweiten Marokkokrise, 1911* (Düsseldorf 1981).

Parsons, F.V., "Late nineteenth-century Morocco through foreign eyes," *Maghreb Review* 3 (1978) 1–5.

————, *The Origins of the Morocco Question, 1880–1900* (London 1976).

Porch, D., *The Conquest of Morocco* (New York 1983).

Rivet, D., *Lyautey et l'institution du protectorat français au Maroc, 1912–1925* (3 vols. Paris 1988).

Terrasse, H., *Histoire du Maroc. Des origines à l'établissement du protectorat français* (2 vols. Casablanca 1949–1950).

Trout, F.E., *Morocco's Saharan Frontiers* (Geneva 1969).

### 6.2.3 Algeria

Ageron, C.R., *Histoire de l'Algérie contemporaine* (Vol. II, 1871–1954; Paris 1979).

Julien, C.A., *Histoire de l'Algérie contemporaine* (Vol. I, 1827–1871; Paris 1979).

Martin, C., *Histoire de l'Algérie française, 1830–1962* (Paris 1963).

### 6.2.4 Tunisia

Bardin, P., "Les débuts difficiles du protectorat tunisien (mai 1881–avril 1882)," *Revue d'Histoire Diplomatique* 85 (1971) 17–64.

Broadley, A.M., *The Last Punic War: Tunis: Past and Present* (2 vols. London 1881).

Brown, L.C., *The Tunisia of Ahmad Bey, 1837–1855* (Princeton, N.J., 1974).

Cambon, H., *Histoire de la Régence de Tunis* (Paris 1948).

Ganiage, J., *Les Origines du protectorat français en Tunisie, 1861–1881* (Paris 1959).

Julien, C.A., *L'Affaire tunisienne, 1878–1881* (Tunis 1981).

Karouin, H., and A. Mahjoubi, *Quand le Soleil s'est levé à l'Ouest. Tunisie 1881.*
  *Impérialisme et résistance* (Tunis 1983).
Kraiem, M., *La Tunisie précoloniale* (Tunis 1973).
Krieken, G. van, *Khayr al-Dîn et la Tunisie, 1850–1881* (Leiden 1976).
Langer, W., "The European powers and the French occupation of Tunis, 1878–
  1881," *American Historical Review* 31 (1925–1926) 55–79 and 251–265.
Mahjoubi, A., *L'Etablissement du protectorat français en Tunisie, 1881–1886* (Tu-
  nis 1977).
Marsden, A., *British Diplomacy and Tunis, 1875–1902* (London 1972).
Mzali, M.S., and J. Pignon, *Khérédine. Homme d'État. Documents historiques an-
  notés* (Tunis 1971).
Rosenbaum, J., *Frankreich in Tunesien. Die Anfänge des Protektorates, 1881–1886*
  (Zurich 1971).
Smida, M., *Khérédine, ministre réformateur, 1873–1877* (Tunis 1970).
Valensi, L., *Fellahs tunisiens. L'économie rurale et la vie des campagnes aux XVIIIe
  et XIXe siècles* (Paris 1977).

### 6.2.5 Egypt

Berger, M., *Military Elite and Social Change: Egypt since Napoleon* (Princeton,
  N.J., 1969).
Berque, J., *L'Égypte. Impérialisme et révolution* (Paris 1967).
Blunt, W.S., *Secret History of the English Occupation of Egypt* (New York 1967;
  1st ed. 1922).
Bouvier, J., "Les intérêts financiers et la question d'Égypte, 1875–1876," in J. Bou-
  vier, *Histoire économique et histoire sociale. Recherches sur le capitalisme
  contemporain* (Geneva 1968).
Cromer, E., *Modern Egypt* (2 vols. London 1908).
Douin, G., *Histoire du règne du khédive Ismail* (3 vols. Cairo 1932–1941).
Farnie, D.A., *East and West of Suez: The Suez Canal in History, 1854–1956* (Ox-
  ford 1969).
Freycinet, C. de, *La Question d'Égypte* (Paris 1905).
Hallberg, C.W., *The Suez Canal: Its History and Diplomatic Importance* (New
  York 1931).
Holt, P.M., *Egypt and the Fertile Crescent, 1516–1922. A Political History* (Lon-
  don 1966).
———, ed., *Political and Social Change in Modern Egypt* (London 1968).
Hopkins, A.G., "The Victorians and Africa: A reconsideration of the occupation
  of Egypt, 1882," *Journal of African History* 27 (1986) 363–391.
Hourani, A., *The Ottoman Background of the Modern Middle East* (London 1970).
Issawi, C., "Egypt since 1800: A study in lop-sided development," *Journal of
  Economic History* 2nd ser. 21 (1961) 1–25.
Keddie, N.R., *An Islamic Response to Imperialism: Political and Religious Writings
  of Sayyid Jamal ad-Din al-Afghani* (Berkeley 1968).
Landes, D.S., *Bankers and Pashas: International Finance and Economic Imperial-
  ism in Egypt* (London 1958).
Little, T., *Egypt* (London 1958).
Mansfield, P., *The British in Egypt* (New York 1909).

Marlowe, J., *Anglo-Egyptian Relations, 1800–1956* (London 1965).
——, *Cromer in Egypt* (New York 1970).
——, *The Making of the Suez Canal* (New York 1964).
——, *Spoiling the Egyptians* (London 1974).
Mommsen, W.J., *Imperialismus in Ägypten. Der Aufstieg der ägyptischen nationalen Bewegung, 1805–1956* (Munich 1961).
Schölch, A., *Ägypten den Ägyptern! Die politische und gesellschaftliche Krise der Jahre 1878–1882 in Ägypten* (Zurich n.d.).
——, "The 'Man on the Spot' and the English occupation of Egypt in 1882," *Historical Journal* 19 (1976) 773–785.
Taboulet, G., "Aux origines du canal de Suez. Le conflit entre F. de Lesseps et les Saint-Simoniens," *Revue Historique* 240 (1968) 89–114, and 240 (1968) 361–392.
——, "Ferdinand de Lesseps et l'Egypte avant le canal, 1803–1854," *Revue Française d'Histoire d'Outre-Mer* 60 (1973) 143–171 and 364–407.
Tignor, R.L., *Modernization and British Colonial Rule in Egypt, 1882–1914* (Princeton, N.J., 1966).
Vatikiotis, P.J., *The History of Egypt from Muhammad Ali to Sadat* (London 1980).
Wilson, A., *The Suez Canal* (New York 1939).

### 6.2.6 The Nile and the Sudan

Bates, D., *The Fashoda Incident of 1898: Encounter on the Nile* (Oxford 1984).
Brown, C., "The Sudanese Mahdiya," in R.I. Rotberg and A. Mazrui, eds., *Protest and Power in Black Africa* (New York 1970).
Brown, R.G., *Fashoda Reconsidered: The Impact of Domestic Politics on French Policy in Africa, 1893–1898* (Baltimore 1970).
Churchill, W., *The River War: The Reconquest of the Sudan* (London 1960; 1st ed. 1899).
Cockfield, J., "Germany and the Fashoda crisis, 1898–1899," *Central European History* 16 (1983) 256–275.
Collins, R.O., *King Leopold, England and the Upper Nile, 1899–1909* (New Haven, Conn., 1968).
——, *Land beyond the Rivers: The Southern Sudan, 1898–1918* (New Haven, Conn., 1971).
——, *The Southern Sudan, 1883–98: A Struggle for Control* (New Haven, Conn., 1962).
——, *The Southern Sudan in Historical Perspective* (Tel Aviv 1975).
Collins, R.O., and R.L. Tignor, *Egypt and the Sudan* (Englewood Cliffs, N.J., 1967).
David, P., "Le Soudan et l'État mahdiste sous le khalifa Abdullahi, 1885–1899," *Revue Française d'Histoire d'Outre-Mer* 75 (1988) 273–307.
Delebecque, J., *Vie du général Marchand* (Paris 1941).
Eubank, K., "The Fashoda crisis reexamined," *The Historian* 12 (1960) 256–270.
Gray, R., *A History of the Southern Sudan, 1839–1889* (Oxford 1961).
Hill, R.L., *A Biographical Dictionary of the Sudan* (London 1967).
——, *Egypt in the Sudan, 1820–1881* (Oxford 1959).

Holt, P.M., *The Mahdist State in the Sudan, 1881–1898: A Study of Its Origins, Development and Overthrow* (London 1970).

Holt, P.M., and M.W. Daly, *History of the Sudan from the Coming of Islam to the Present Day* (London 1979).

Hornik, M.P., "The Anglo-Belgian agreement of 12 May 1894," *English Historical Review* 57 (1942) 227–243.

Hurst, H.E., *The Nile* (London 1952).

Keown-Boyd, H., *A Good Dusting: The Sudan Campaigns, 1883–1899* (London 1986).

Lewis, D.L., *The Race to Fashoda: European Colonialism and African Resistance in the Scramble for Africa* (London 1988).

Mazières, A.-C. de, *La Marche au Nil de Victor Liotard* (Aix-en-Provence 1982).

Michel, C., *Vers Fachoda* (Paris 1901).

Michel, M., *La Mission Marchand, 1895–1899* (Paris 1972).

Muddathir, A.R., *Imperialism and Nationalism in the Sudan: A Study in Constitutional and Political Developments, 1899–1956* (Oxford 1969).

Pascha, E., *Die Tagebücher von Dr. Emin Pascha herausgegeben von Dr. Franz Stuhlmann* (5 vols. Brunswick 1917–1927).

Sanderson, G.N., *England, Europe and the Upper Nile, 1882–1899* (Edinburgh 1965).

Shaked, H., *The Life of the Sudanese Mahdi* (New Brunswick, N.J., 1978).

Stengers, J., "Aux origines de Fachoda. L'expédition Monteil," *Revue Belge de Philologie et d'Histoire* 36 (1958) 436–450; 38 (1960) 366–404 and 1040–1085.

———, "Une facette de la question du Haut Nil. Le mirage soudanais," *Journal of African History* 10 (1969) 599–623.

Taylor, A.J.P., "Prelude to Fashoda: The question of the Upper Nile, 1894–1895," *English Historical Review* 65 (1950) 52–80.

Tessières, Y. de, "Un épisode du partage de l'Afrique noire. La mission Monteil de 1890–1892," *Revue Française d'Histoire d'Outre-Mer* 59 (1972) 346–410.

Theobald, A.B., *The Mahdiya: A History of the Anglo-Egyptian Sudan, 1881–1899* (London 1951).

Warburg, G.R., "British rule in the Nile Valley, 1882–1956, and Robinson's theory of collaboration," *Asian and African Studies* 15 (1981) 287–322.

Wright, P., *Conflict on the Nile: The Fashoda Incident of 1898* (London 1972).

### 6.2.7 Ethiopia and Somaliland

Caulk, R.A., *The Origins and Development of the Foreign Policy of Menelik II, 1865–1896* (Dissertation, London University 1966).

———, "Yohannes IV, the mahdists and the colonial partition of North-East Africa," *Transafrican Journal of History* 1 (1971) 25–42.

Darkwah, R.H.K., *Shewa, Menelik and the Ethiopian Empire, 1813–1889* (London 1975).

Erlich, H., *Ethiopia and Eritrea during the Scramble for Africa: A Political Biography of Ras Alula, 1875–1897* (East Lansing, Mich., 1982).

Gabre-Sellassie, Z., *Yohannes IV of Ethiopia: A Political Biography* (Oxford 1975).

Hess, R.L., *Italian Colonialism in Somalia* (Chicago 1966).

————, "The 'Mad Mullah' and Northern Somalia," *Journal of African History* 5 (1964) 415–433.

Jardine, D., *The Mad Mullah of Somaliland* (London 1923).

Jesman, C., *The Russians in Ethiopia: An Essay in Futility* (London 1958).

Keller, C., *Alfred Ilg. Sein Leben und seine Werke* (Leipzig 1918).

Lewis, I.M., *A Modern History of Somalia: Nation and State in the Horn of Africa* (London 1980).

Marcus, H.G., *The Life and Times of Menelik II: Ethiopia, 1844–1913* (Oxford 1975).

Roux, H. le, *Ménélik et nous* (Paris 1905).

Rubenson, S., *The Survival of Ethiopian Independence* (London 1976).

————, *Wichalé XVII: The Attempt to Establish a Protectorate over Ethiopia* (Addis Ababa 1964).

Sanderson, G.N., "The foreign policy of the Negus Menelik, 1896–1898," *Journal of African History* 5 (1964) 87–97.

### 6.3 The Congo and Central Africa (Chapter 2)

*L'Afrique noire depuis la Conférence de Berlin, 1885–1985* (Paris 1985).

Anstey, R., *Britain and the Congo in the Nineteenth Century* (Oxford 1962).

————, *King Leopold's Legacy: The Congo under Belgian Rule, 1908–1960* (Oxford 1966).

Banning, E., *Mémoires politiques et diplomatiques* (Brussels 1927).

Bently, W.H., *Pioneering in the Congo* (London 1900).

Birmingham, D., and P.M. Martin, eds., *History of Central Africa* (2 vols. London 1983).

Bontinck, F., *Aux Origines de l'État indépendant du Congo* (Louvain 1966).

————, ed., *Autobiographie de Hamed ben Mohammed el-Murjebi Tippo Tip, ca. 1840–1905* (Brussels 1974).

Brode, H., *Tippu Tip. Ein Lebensbild eines Zentralafrikanische Despoten nach seinen eigenen Angeben* (Berlin 1905).

Bruhet, J., "E. Banning," in *Les Techniciens de la colonisation* (Paris 1947).

Brunschwig, H., "La négociation du traité Makoko," *Cahiers d'Études Africaines* 17 (1965) 5–57.

Cairns, H.A.C., *Prelude to Imperialism: British Reactions to Central African Society, 1840–1890* (London 1965).

*Le Centenaire de l'État Indépendant du Congo* (Brussels 1988).

*La Conférence de géographie de 1876* (Brussels 1976).

Cookey, S.J.S., *Britain and the Congo Question, 1885–1913* (London 1968).

————, "Tippu Tip and the decline of the Congo Arabs," *Tarick* 1 (1966) 58–69.

Coquery-Vidrovitch, C., *Le Congo au temps des grandes compagnies concessionnaires, 1898–1930* (Paris 1972).

Courcel, G. de, *L'Influence de la Conférence de Berlin de 1885 sur le droit international* (Paris 1935).

Crowe, S.E., *The Berlin West African Conference, 1884–1885* (London 1942).

Farrant, L., *Tippu Tip and the East African Slave Trade* (London 1975).

Foeken, D., *België behoeft een kolonie. De ontstaansgeschiedenis van de Kongo Vrijstaat* (Antwerp 1985).

Förster, S., W.J. Mommsen and R. Robinson, eds., *Bismarck, Europe and Africa:*

*The Berlin African Conference, 1884–1885 and the Onset of Partition* (Oxford 1988).

Gavin, R.J., and J.A. Betley, eds., *The Scramble for Africa: Documents on the Berlin West African Conference and Related Subjects, 1884–1885* (Ibadan 1973).

Gray, J.M., "Stanley versus Tippoo Tib," *Tanganyika: Notes and Records* 18 (1944) 11–26.

Harms, R.W., *River of Wealth, River of Sorrow: The Central Zaïre Basin in the Era of the Slave and Ivory Trade, 1500–1891* (New Haven, Conn., 1981).

Hilton, A., *The Kingdom of the Congo* (Oxford 1985).

*Il y a cent ans . . . La Conférence de Berlin, 1884–1885* (Abidjan 1985).

Keith, A.B., *The Belgian Congo and the Berlin Act* (Oxford 1919).

Latour da Veiga Pinto, F. de, *Le Portugal et le Congo au XIXe siècle* (Paris 1972).

Lederer, A., *Histoire de la navigation au Congo* (Tervuren 1965).

Luwel, M., *H.H. Johnston et H.M. Stanley sur le Congo* (Brussels 1978).

Mazenot, G., *La Likouala-Mossaka. Histoire de la pénétration du Haut-Congo, 1878–1920* (Paris 1970).

M'Bokolo, E., *Noirs et blancs en Afrique Équatoriale. Les sociétés côtières et la pénétration française vers 1820–1974* (Paris 1981).

Mutamba-Makongo, *Makoko, roi des Bateke* (Kinshasa 1987).

Randles, W.G.L., *L'Ancien Royaume du Congo des origines à la fin du XIXe siècle* (Paris 1968).

Renault, F., *Tippo Tip. Un potentat arabe en Afrique Centrale au XIXe siècle* (Paris 1987).

Slade, R., *King Leopold's Congo: Aspects of the Development of Race Relations in the Congo Independent State* (Oxford 1962).

Stengers, J., "A propos de l'Acte de Berlin, ou comment naît une légende," *Zaïre* 8 (1953) 839–844.

———, *Combien le Congo a-t-il coûté à la Belgique?* (Brussels 1957).

———, *Congo, mythes et réalités. 100 ans d'histoire* (Paris/Louvain 1989).

———, "Le Katanga et le mirage de l'or," in *Études africaines offertes à Henri Brunschwig* (Paris 1982).

———, "Léopold II et Brazza en 1882," *Revue Française d'Histoire d'Outre-Mer* 63 (1976) 105–136.

———, "Léopold II et la fixation des frontières du Congo," *Le Flambeau* (1963) 153–197.

Stenmans, A., *La Reprise du Congo par la Belgique* (Brussels 1949).

Thomson, R.S., *Fondation de l'État Indépendant du Congo. Un chapitre de l'histoire du partage de l'Afrique* (Brussels 1933).

Vansina, J., *The Children of Woot: A History of the Kuba Peoples* (Madison, Wis., 1978).

———, *Kingdoms of the Savanna* (Madison, Wis., 1966).

———, *The Tio Kingdom of the Middle Congo, 1880–1892* (London 1973).

Willequet, J., *Le Congo belge et la Weltpolitik, 1894–1914* (Brussels 1962).

Zuylen, P. van, *L'Échiquier congolais ou le secret du roi* (Brussels 1959).

## 6.4 East Africa (Chapter 3)

Austen, R.A., *North-West Tanzania under German and British Rule: Colonial Policy and Tribal Politics, 1889–1939* (New Haven, Conn., 1968).

Bennett, N.R., *Arab versus European: Diplomacy and War in Nineteenth Century East Africa* (London 1986).
———, *A History of the Arab State of Zanzibar* (London 1978).
Coupland, R., *East Africa and Its Invaders: From the Earliest Times to the Death of Seyyid Said in 1850* (London 1938).
———, *The Exploitation of East Africa, 1856–1890: Slave Trade and the Scramble* (London 1939).
Deschamps, H., *Histoire de Madagascar* (Paris 1951).
Elliss, G., *The Rising of the Red Shawls* (Cambridge, England 1985).
Galbraith, J.S., *Mackinnon and East Africa, 1878–1895: A Study in the "New Imperialism"* (Cambridge, England 1972).
Gregory, J.W., *The Foundation of British East Africa* (New York 1979; 1st ed. 1901).
Hanotaux, G., *L'Affaire de Madagascar* (Paris 1896).
Harkema, R.C., *De stad Zanzibar in de tweede helft van de 19e eeuw en enkele andere Oost-Afrikaanse kuststeden* (Groningen 1967).
Hollingsworth, L.W., *Zanzibar under the Foreign Office, 1890–1913* (London 1953).
Iliffe, J., *A Modern History of Tanganyika* (Cambridge, England 1979).
———, "The organization of the Maji-Maji rebellion," *Journal of African History* 8 (1967) 495–512.
———, *Tanganyika under German Colonial Rule, 1905–1912* (Cambridge, England 1969).
Ingham, K., *A History of East Africa* (London 1962).
———, *The Making of Uganda* (London 1958).
Lonsdale, J.M., "The politics of conquest: The British in Western Kenya, 1894–1908," *Historical Journal* 20 (1977) 841–870.
Louis, W.R., *Ruanda-Urundi, 1884–1919* (Oxford 1963).
Low, D.A., *Buganda in Modern History* (Berkeley 1971).
Low, D.A., and R.C. Pratt, *Buganda and British Overrule: Two Studies* (Oxford 1960).
Martel, G., "Cabinet politics and African partition: The Uganda debate reconsidered," *Journal of Imperial and Commonwealth History* 13 (1984) 5–24.
McEwen, A.C., *International Boundaries of East Africa* (Oxford 1971).
Merritt, H.P., "Bismarck and the first partition of East Africa," *English Historical Review* 91 (1976) 585–597.
———, "Bismarck and the German interest in East Africa, 1884–1885," *Historical Journal* 21 (1978) 97–116.
Müller, F.F., *Deutschland, Zanzibar, Ost-Afrika. Geschichte einer deutschen Kolonialeroberung, 1884–1890* (Berlin 1959).
Mungeam, G.H., *British Rule in Kenya, 1895–1912* (Oxford 1966).
Munro, J.F., "Shipping subsidies and railway guarantees: William Mackinnon, Eastern Africa, and the Indian Ocean, 1860–1893," *Journal of African History* 28 (1987) 209–230.
Mutibwa, P.M., *The Malagasy and the Europeans, 1861–1895* (Ibadan 1973).
Nicholls, C.S., *The Swahili Coast: Politics, Diplomacy and Trade on the East African Littoral, 1798–1856* (London 1971).
Ogot, B.A., ed., *Kenya before 1900* (London 1976).

Ogot, B.A., and J.A. Kieran, eds., *Zamani: A Survey of East African History* (Nairobi 1974).

Oliver, R., *The Missionary Factor in East Africa* (London 1952).

Oliver, R., and G. Mathew, eds., *History of East Africa* (Vol. 1; Oxford 1963).

Ralaimihoatra, E., *Histoire de Madagascar* (Tananarive 1966).

Randrianarisoa, P., *La Diplomatie malgache face à la politique des grandes puissances, 1882–1895* (Paris 1970).

Roberts, A.D., *Tanzania before 1900* (Nairobi 1968).

Schmidt, M.E., "Prelude to intervention: Madagascar and the failure of Anglo-French diplomacy, 1890–1895," *Historical Journal* 15 (1972) 715–730.

Schweitzer, G., *Emin Pascha* (Berlin 1898).

Sheriff, A., *Slaves, Spices and Ivory in Zanzibar: Integration of an East African Commercial Empire into the World Economy, 1770–1873* (Nairobi 1987).

Smith, I.R., *The Emin Pasha Relief Expedition, 1886–1890* (Oxford 1972).

Stühlmann, F., *Die Tagebücher von Dr. Emin Pascha* (6 vols. Berlin 1917–1927).

White, S., *Lost Empires on the Nile: H.M. Stanley, Emin Pasha and the Imperialists* (New York 1969).

Wolff, R.D., *The Economics of Colonialism: Britain and Kenya, 1870–1930* (New Haven, Conn., 1974).

## 6.5 West Africa (Chapter 4)

Adeleye, R.A., *Power and Diplomacy in Northern Nigeria, 1804–1906: The Sokoto Caliphate and Its Enemies* (London 1971).

Agbodeka, F., *African Politics and British Policy in the Gold Coast, 1868–1900: A Study in the Forms and Force of Protest* (Evanston, Ill., 1971).

Ajayi, J.F.A., and M. Crowder, eds., *History of West Africa* (2 vols. London 1974–1976).

Ajayi, J.F.A., and R. Smith, *Yoruba Warfare in the Nineteenth Century* (Cambridge, England 1964).

Akintoye, S.A., *Revolution and Power Politics in Yorubaland, 1840–1893: Ibadan Expansion and the Rise of Ekitiparapo* (London 1971).

Anene, J.C., *The International Boundaries of Nigeria, 1885–1960: The Framework of an Emergent African Nation* (London 1970).

———, *Southern Nigeria in Transition, 1885–1906: Theory and Practice in a Colonial Protectorate* (Cambridge, England 1966).

Asiwaju, A.I., *Western Yorubaland under European Rule, 1889–1945: A Comparative Analysis of French and British Colonialism* (London 1976).

Balesi, C.J., *From Adversaries to Comrades-in-Arms: West Africans and the French Military, 1885–1918* (Waltham, Mass., 1979).

Barrows, L.C., *General Faidherbe, the Maurel and Prom Company, and French Expansion in Senegal* (Dissertation, University of California at Los Angeles 1974).

Boahen, A.A., *Britain, the Sahara and the Western Sudan, 1788–1861* (Oxford 1964).

———, *Ghana: Evolution and Change in the Nineteenth and Twentieth Centuries* (London 1975).

Brunschwig, H., "Les origines du partage de l'Afrique occidentale," *Journal of African History* 5 (1964) 121–125.

Chailley, M., *Les Grandes Missions françaises en Afrique occidentale, 1794–1900* (Paris 1967).

———, *Histoire de l'Afrique occidentale française, 1638–1959* (Paris 1968).

Cookey, S., *King Jaja of the Niger Delta: His Life and Times* (New York 1974).

Coombs, D., *The Gold Coast, Britain and the Netherlands* (London 1963).

Cornevin, R., "Les divers épisodes de la lutte contre le royaume d'Abomey, 1887–1894," *Revue Française d'Histoire d'Outre-Mer* (1960) 161–212.

Crowder, M., *Colonial West Africa: Collected Essays* (London 1978).

———, *The Story of Nigeria* (London 1962).

———, *West Africa under Colonial Rule* (London 1968).

———, ed., *West African Resistance: The Military Response to Colonial Occupation* (New York 1971).

Crowder, M., and O. Ikime, eds., *West African Chiefs: Their Changing Status under Colonial Rule and Independence* (New York 1970).

Dike, K.O., *Trade and Politics in the Niger Delta, 1830–1885* (Oxford 1965).

Ekundare, R.O., *An Economic History of Nigeria, 1860–1960* (London 1973).

Fage, J.D., *Ghana: A Historical Interpretation* (Madison, Wis., 1955).

———, *A History of West Africa: An Introductory Survey* (Cambridge, England 1969).

Flint, J.E., "Britain and the partition of West Africa," in J.E. Flint and G. Williams, eds., *Perspectives of Empire* (London 1973).

Fuglestad, F., "A propos de travaux récents sur la mission Voulet-Chanoine," *Revue Française d'Histoire d'Outre-Mer* 68 (1980), 73–87.

———, *A History of Niger, 1850–1960* (Cambridge, England 1983).

Fyfe, C., *A History of Sierra Leone* (London 1962).

———, *A Short History of Sierra Leone* (London 1979).

Gailey, H.A., *A History of the Gambia* (London 1964).

Ganiage, J., "Un épisode du partage de l'Afrique. Les affaires du bas Niger, 1894–1898," *Revue Historique* 254 (1975) 149–188.

Gramont, S. de, *The Strong Brown God: The Story of the Niger River* (Boston 1976).

Gray, J.M., *A History of the Gambia* (Cambridge, England 1940).

Griffeth, L., "Samori Toure," in O. Ikime, ed., *Leadership in Nineteenth Century Africa. Essays from Tarikh* (London 1974) 43–61.

Hargreaves, J.D., *Prelude to the Partition of West Africa* (London 1963).

———, *West Africa Partitioned. Vol. I: The Loaded Pause, 1885–1889* (London 1974).

———, *West Africa Partitioned. Vol. II: The Elephants and the Grass* (London 1985).

Hirschfield, C., *The Diplomacy of Partition: Britain, France and the Creation of Nigeria, 1890–1898* (The Hague 1979).

Hopkins, A.G., *An Economic History of West Africa* (London 1973).

———, "Economic imperialism in West Africa: Lagos, 1890–1892," *Economic History Review* 2nd ser. 21 (1968) 580–606.

Ikime, O., *Niger Delta Rivalry: Itsekiri-Urhobo Relations and the European Presence, 1884–1936* (London 1969).

Isichei, E., *A History of Nigeria* (London 1983).

———, *History of West Africa since 1800* (New York 1977).

Jones, G.I., *The Trading States of the Oil Rivers: A Study of Political Development in Eastern Nigeria* (London 1963).

Kanya-Forstner, A.S., *The Conquest of the Western Sudan: A Study in French Military Imperialism* (Cambridge, England 1969).

———, "French African policy and the Anglo-French agreement of 5 August 1890," *Historical Journal* 12 (1969) 628–650.

Kimba, I., *Guerres et sociétés. Les populations du "Niger" occidental au XIXe siècle et leurs réactions face à la colonisation, 1896–1906* (Niamey 1981).

Kimble, D., *A Political History of Ghana: The Rise of Gold Coast Nationalism, 1850–1928* (Oxford 1963).

Knoll, A.J., *Togo under Imperial Germany, 1884–1914* (Stanford 1978).

Körner, H., *Kolonialpolitik und Wirtschaftsentwicklung. Das Beispiel Französisch Westafrikas* (Stuttgart 1965).

Legassick, M., "Firearms, horses and Samorian army organisation, 1870–1898," *Journal of African History* 7 (1966) 95–115.

Lynn, M., "The 'Imperialism of free trade' and the case of West Africa, c. 1830–c. 1870," *Journal of Imperial and Commonwealth History* 15 (1986) 22–40.

Manning, P., *Slavery, Colonialism and Economic Growth in Dahomey, 1640–1960* (Cambridge, England 1982).

Newbury, C.W., *British Policy towards West Africa: Select Documents, 1875–1914, with Statistical Appendices, 1800–1914* (Oxford 1971).

———, "The development of French policy on the Lower and Upper Niger, 1880–1898," *Journal of Modern History* 31 (1959) 16–26.

———, "The formation of the government general of French West Africa," *Journal of African History* 1 (1960) 111–128.

———, "The protectionist revival in French colonial trade: The case of Senegal," *Economic History Review* 2nd ser. 21 (1968) 337–348.

———, "Victorians, republicans, and the partition of West Africa," *Journal of African History* 3 (1962) 492–501.

———, *The Western Slave Coast and Its Rulers: European Trade and Administration among the Yoruba and Adja Speaking Peoples of South-Western Nigeria, Southern Dahomey and Togo* (Oxford 1961).

Newbury, C.W., and A.S. Kanya-Forstner, "French policy and the origins of the scramble for West Africa," *Journal of African History* 10 (1969) 253–276.

Niane, D.T., and J. Suret-Canale, *Histoire de l'Afrique occidentale* (Paris 1961).

Nzemeke, A.D., *British Imperialism and African Response: The Niger Valley, 1851–1905, a Case-Study of Afro-British Contacts in West Africa* (Paderborn 1982).

Obichere, B.D., *West African States and European Expansion. The Dahomey-Niger Hinterland, 1885–1898* (New Haven, Conn., 1971).

Oloruntimehin, B.O., "Franco-Samori relations, 1886–1889: Diplomacy and war," *Journal of the Historical Society of Nigeria* 6 (1971) 67–92.

———, *The Segu Tukulor Empire* (London 1972).

———, "Theories and realities in the administration of colonial West Africa from 1890 to the First World War," *Journal of the Historical Society of Nigeria* 6 (1972) 289–312.

Osae, T., S.N. Nwabara and A.T.O. Odunsi, *A Short History of West Africa* (New York 1968).

Padmore, G., *The Gold Coast Revolution: The Struggle of an African People from Slavery to Freedom* (London 1953).

Person, Y., *Samori. Une révolution dyula* (3 vols. Dakar 1968–1975).

Phillips, A., *The Enigma of Colonialism: British Policy in West Africa* (London 1989).

Porch, D., *The Conquest of the Sahara* (Oxford 1986).

Quinn, C.A., *Mandigro Kingdoms of the Senegambia: Traditionalism, Islam and European Expansion* (London 1972).

Rolland, J.F., *Le Grand Capitaine* (Paris 1977).

Rudin, H., *Germans in the Cameroons, 1884–1914: A Case Study in Modern Imperialism* (London 1938).

Ryder, A.F.C., *Benin and the Europeans, 1485–1897* (London 1969).

Saint-Martin, Y.-J., *L'Empire toucouleur, 1843–1897* (Paris 1970).

———, *Le Sénégal sous le Second Empire. Naissance d'un empire colonial* (Paris 1989).

Schnapper, B., *La Politique et le commerce français dans le golfe de Guinée, 1838–1871* (Paris 1961).

Séré de Rivières, E., *Histoire du Niger* (Paris 1965).

Smaldone, J.P., *Warfare in the Sokoto Caliphate: Historical and Sociological Perspectives* (Cambridge, England 1977).

Smith, R., "Peace and palaver: International relations in pre-colonial West Africa," *Journal of African History* 14, no. 4 (1973) 599–621.

Suret-Canale, J., *Afrique noire, occidentale et centrale* (Paris 1958).

Weiskal, T.C., *French Colonial Rule and the Bayule Peoples: Resistance and Collaboration, 1899–1911* (Oxford 1980).

Wilks, I., *Asante in the Nineteenth Century: The Structure and Evolution of a Political Order* (Cambridge, England 1975).

## 6.6 Southern Africa (Chapter 6)

Atmore, A., and S. Marks, "The imperial factor in South Africa in the nineteenth century: Towards a reassessment," *Journal of Imperial and Commonwealth History* 3 (1974) 106–139.

Axelson, E., "Portugal's attitude to Nyasaland during the period of the partition of Africa," in B. Pachai, ed., *The Early History of Malawi* (London 1972) 252–263.

Aydelotte, W.O., *Bismarck and British Colonial Policy: The Problem of South-West Africa, 1883–1885* (Philadelphia 1937).

Benyon, J., *Proconsul and Paramountcy in South Africa: The High Commission, British Supremacy and the Sub-Continent, 1806–1910* (Pietermaritzburg 1980).

Binks, C.T., *The Last Zulu King: Life and Death of Cethswayo* (London 1963).

Birmingham, D., *The Portuguese Conquest of Angola* (Oxford 1965).

Blainey, G., "Lost causes of the Jameson raid," *Economic History Review* 2nd ser. 18 (1965) 350–366.

Blake, R., *A History of Rhodesia* (London 1977).

Bley, H., *Kolonialherrschaft und Sozialstruktur in Deutsch-Südwestafrika, 1894–1914* (Hamburg 1968).

Butler, J., *The Liberal Party and the Jameson Raid* (Oxford 1968).

Cartwright, A.P., *The Corner House: The Early History of Johannesburg* (Cape Town 1965).

———, *The Gold Miners* (Cape Town 1962).

———, *Valley of Gold* (Cape Town 1984).

Clarence-Smith, G., "The myth of uneconomic imperialism: The Portuguese in Angola, 1836–1926," *Journal of Southern African Studies* 5 (1979) 165–181.

Cobbing, J.R.D., "Lobengula, Jameson and the occupation of Mashonaland," *Rhodesian History* 4 (1973) 39–56.

Colvin, I., *The Life of Jameson* (2 vols. London 1922).

Davenport, T.R.H., *The Afrikaner Bond: The History of a South African Political Party, 1880–1911* (London 1966).

———, *South Africa: A Modern History* (London 1978).

Delius, P., *The Land Belongs to Us* (Berkeley 1983).

Drechsler, H., *"Let Us Die Fighting": The Struggle of the Herero and Nama against German Imperialism, 1884–1915* (London 1980).

Duminy, A., and C. Ballard, *The Anglo-Zulu War: New Perspectives* (Pietermaritzburg 1981).

Edgerton, R.B., *Like Lions They Fought: The Zulu War and the Last Black Empire in South Africa* (London 1988).

Endfield, C., *Zulu Dawn* (London 1979).

Esterhuyse, J.H., *South-West Africa, 1880–1894: The Establishment of German Authority in South-West Africa* (Cape Town 1968).

Farwell, B., *The Great Anglo-Boer War* (New York 1976).

Fischer, J., *Paul Kruger: His Life and Times* (London 1974).

Fuller, J.F.C., *The Last of the Gentlemen's Wars* (London 1937).

Galbraith, J.S., *Crown and Charter: The Early Years of the British South Africa Company* (Berkeley 1974).

Gann, L.H., *The Birth of a Plural Society: The Development of Northern Rhodesia under the British South Africa Company, 1894–1914* (Manchester 1958).

———, *A History of Northern Rhodesia: Early Days to 1953* (London 1964).

———, *A History of Southern Rhodesia: Early Days to 1934* (London 1965).

Goodfellow, C.F., *Great Britain and South African Confederation, 1870–1881* (Cape Town 1966).

Guy, J., *The Destruction of the Zulu Kingdom: The Civil War in Zululand, 1879–1884* (London 1979).

Hall, K.O., *Imperial Proconsul: Sir Hercules Robinson and South Africa, 1881–1889* (Kingston, Ont., 1980).

Hall, R., *Zambia* (London 1965).

Hanna, A.J., *The Beginnings of Nyasaland and North-Eastern Rhodesia, 1859–1895* (Oxford 1956).

———, *The Story of the Rhodesias and Nyasaland* (London 1960).

Helten, J.J. van, "German capital, the Netherlands Railway Company and the political economy of the Transvaal, 1886–1900," *Journal of African History* 19 (1978) 369–390.

Henderson, I., "Lobengula: Achievement and tragedy," in O. Ikime, ed., *Leadership in Nineteenth Century Africa: Essays from Tarikh* (London 1974) 138–153.

Hirschfield, C., "The Anglo-Boer War and the issue of Jewish culpability," *Journal of Contemporary History* 15 (1980) 619–632.

Hofmeyr, J.H., *Het leven van Jan Hendrik Hofmeyr (Onze Jan)* (Cape Town 1913).

Isaacman, A.F., *The Tradition of Resistance in Mozambique: Anti-colonial Activity in the Zambesi Valley, 1850–1921* (London 1976).

Jaarsveld, F.A. van, *The Awakening of Africander Nationalism, 1868–1881* (Cape Town 1961).

Jaarsveld, F.A. van, A.P.J. van Rensburg and W.A. Stals, eds., *Die eerste Vrijheidsoorlog* (Pretoria 1980).

Judd, D., *The Boer War* (London 1977).

Katzenellenbogen, S.E., *South Africa and Southern Mozambique: Labour, Railways and Trade in the Making of a Relationship* (Manchester 1982).

Kiewiet, C.W. de, *British Colonial Policy and the South African Republics, 1848–1872* (London 1929).

———, *The Imperial Factor in South Africa* (Cambridge, England 1937).

Kröll, U., *Die internationale Buren-Agitation, 1899–1902* (Münster 1973).

Kruger, D.W., *Paul Kruger* (2 vols. Johannesburg 1961–1963).

Kruger, R., *Good-bye Dolly Gray: The Story of the Boer War* (London 1959).

Kubicek, R.V., *Economic Imperialism in Theory and Practice: The Case of South-African Gold-Mining Finance, 1886–1914* (Durham, N.C., 1979).

Lee, E.,*To the Bitter End: A Photographic History of the Boer War, 1899–1902* (Harmondsworth 1985).

Lehmann, J., *The First Boer War* (London 1972).

Loney, M., *Rhodesia: White Racism and Imperial Response* (Harmondsworth 1975).

Lovell, R.I., *The Struggle for South Africa, 1875–1899: A Study in Economic Imperialism* (New York 1934).

Macmillan, W.M., *Bantu, Boer and Briton: The Making of the South African Native Problem* (2nd ed. Oxford 1963).

Macpherson, F., *Anatomy of a Conquest: The British Occupation of Zambia, 1884–1924* (London 1981).

Marais, J.S., *The Fall of Kruger's Republic* (Oxford 1961).

Marks, S., "Scrambling for South Africa," *Journal of African History* 23 (1982) 97–113.

Marks, S., and A. Atmore, eds., *Economy and Society in Pre-Industrial South Africa* (London 1980).

Marks, S., and S. Trapido, "Lord Milner and the South African state," *History Workshop* 8 (1979) 50–80.

Marquard, L., *The Story of South Africa* (London 1966).

Mason, P., *The Birth of a Dilemma: The Conquest and Settlement of Rhodesia* (Oxford 1958).

May, G.H.L. Le, *British Supremacy in South-Africa, 1899–1907* (Oxford 1965).

Maylan, P.R., "The making of the Kimberley-Bulawayo railway: A study in the operations of the British South Africa Company," *Rhodesian History* 8 (1977) 13–33.

————, *Rhodes, the Tswana and British Colonialism: Collaboration and Conflict in the Bechuanaland Protectorate, 1885–1899* (Westport, Conn., 1980).

Mutswairo, S.M., *Mapondera: Soldier of Zimbabwe* (Washington, D.C., 1978).

Mutunhu, I., "Lobengula and the Matabele nation: His monarchical rise and relations with missionaries, Boers and the British," *Journal of Southern African Affairs* 5, no. 1 (1980) 5–22.

Nutting, A., *Scramble for Africa: The Great Trek to the Boer War* (London 1970).

Onselen, C. van, *Studies in the Social and Economic History of Witwatersrand, 1886–1914* (2 vols. New York 1982).

Pakenham, E., *Jameson's Raid* (London 1960).

Pakenham, T., *The Boer War* (London 1979).

Pélissier, R., *Les Guerres grises. Résistance et révoltes en Angola, 1845–1941* (Orgeval 1977).

Poel, J. van der, *The Jameson Raid* (London 1951).

————, *Railways and Customs Policies in South Africa, 1885–1910* (London 1933).

Porter, A., "British imperial policy and South Africa, 1895–99," in P. Warwick, ed., *The South African War: The Anglo-Boer War, 1899–1902* (Harlow 1980) 37–56.

————, "Lord Salisbury, Mr. Chamberlain and South Africa," *Journal of Imperial and Commonwealth History* 1 (1972) 3–26.

————, *The Origins of the South African War: Joseph Chamberlain and the Diplomacy of Imperialism, 1895–1899* (Manchester 1980).

————, "The South-African War, 1899–1902: Context and motive reconsidered," *Journal of African History* 31 (1990) 43–57.

Price, R., *An Imperial War and the British Working Class: Working Class Attitudes and Reactions to the Boer War, 1899–1902* (London 1972).

Ranger, T.O., *Revolt in Southern Rhodesia 1896–1897: A Study in African Resistance* (London 1967).

————, ed., *Aspects of Central African History* (London 1968).

Ritter, E.A., *Shaka Zulu: The Rise of the Zulu Empire* (London 1955).

Roberts, A., *A History of the Bemba: Political Growth and Change in North-Eastern Zambia before 1900* (London 1973).

————, *A History of Zambia* (London 1976).

Rosenthal, E., *Gold! Gold! Gold! The Johannesburg Gold Rush* (London 1970).

Rothberg, R.I., *The Rise of Nationalism in Central Africa. The Making of Malawi and Zimbabwe, 1873–1964* (Cambridge, Mass. 1966).

Samkange, S., *Origins of Rhodesia* (London 1968).

Schreuder, D.M., *Gladstone and Kruger: Liberal Government and Colonial "Home Rule," 1880–1885* (London 1969).

————, *The Scramble for Southern Africa, 1877–1895. The Politics of Partition Reappraised* (Cambridge, England 1980).

Schutte, G.J., *Nederland en de Afrikaners. Adhesie en aversie* (Franeker 1986).

Shillington, K., *The Colonisation of the Southern Tswana, 1870–1900* (Braamfontein 1985).

Sillery, A., *The Bechuanaland Protectorate* (Oxford 1952).

————, *John Mackenzie of Bechuanaland, 1835–1899* (Cape Town 1971).

Spies, S.B., *Methods of Barbarism? Roberts, Kitchener and Civilians in the Boer Republics, January 1900–May 1902* (Cape Town 1977).

———, *The Origins of the Anglo-Boer War* (London 1972).

Stevenson, S.B., "A difference of opinion in the Colonial Office, 1893," *Rhodesian History* 9 (1978) 99–114.

Stokes, E., and R. Brown, *The Zambesian Past: Studies in Central African History* (Manchester 1966).

Trollope, A., *South Africa* (Cape Town 1973; 1st ed. London 1878).

Vail, L., and L. White, *Capitalism and Colonialism in Mozambique: A Study of the Quelimane District* (London 1980).

Warhurst, P.R., *Anglo-Portuguese Relations in South-Central Africa, 1890–1900* (London 1962).

Warwick, P., *Black People and the South African War, 1859–1902* (Cambridge, England 1983).

———, ed., *The South African War: The Anglo-Boer War, 1899–1902* (Harlow 1980).

Wilson, M., and L. Thompson, eds., *The Oxford History of South Africa* (2 vols. Oxford 1969–1971).

Winter, P.J. van, *Onder Krugers Hollanders* (2 vols. Amsterdam 1937–1938).

Zijl, M.C. van, *Die protesbeweging van die Transvaalse Afrikaners, 1877–1880* (Pretoria 1979).

# APPENDIX 1: IMPORTANT TREATIES AND AGREEMENTS

| NAME | DATE | SUBJECT |
|------|------|---------|
| Brazza-Makoko treaty | 10 September 1880 (ratified by French Chamber on 22 November 1882) | France gains sovereignty over the Congo region |
| Treaty of Pretoria | 5 April 1881 | Transvaal declared independent but under British suzerainty |
| Treaty of the Bardo | 12 May 1881 | French protectorate over Tunisia (de facto) |
| Treaty of La Marsa | 8 June 1883 | French protectorate over Tunisia (de jure) |
| Anglo-Portuguese treaty | 26 February 1884 (never ratified) | Britain recognizes Portuguese claims to the mouth of the Congo |
| London Convention | 27 February 1884 | Transvaal declared independent |
| Act of Berlin | 26 February 1885 | Agreements on the Congo and the Niger; general agreements |
| Anglo-German agreement | 1 November 1886 | Anglo-German share-out of spheres of influence in East Africa |
| Treaty of Uccialli | 2 May 1889 | Italy claims protectorate over Ethiopia |
| Leopold-Mackinnon treaty | 24 May 1890 (not recognized by British government) | Treaty between King Leopold and Mackinnon's IBEAC: Leopold gains access to the Upper Nile; Britain keeps the Cape-to-Cairo route open |

| NAME | DATE | SUBJECT |
|------|------|---------|
| Zanzibar-Heligoland treaty | 1 July 1890 | Britain cedes Heligoland; Anglo-German spheres of influence in East Africa staked out |
| Anglo-French exchange of letters | 5 August 1890 | Mutual recognition of British protectorate over Zanzibar and of French protectorate over Madagascar; Say-Barruwa line in West Africa defined |
| Anglo-Portuguese treaty | 20 August 1890 | Delimitation of borders of Angola and Mozambique with South Africa and Rhodesia |
| Anglo-Italian treaty | 24 March 1891 | Italy is kept out of the Nile region |
| Anglo-Portuguese agreement | 11 June 1891 | Delimitation of Anglo-Portuguese spheres of influence in East Africa |
| Anglo-Congolese agreement | 12 May 1894 | Leopold obtains Equatoria and part of Bahr el-Ghazal and a lease of part of the western bank of the Nile; Britain secures Cape-to-Cairo corridor |
| Franco-Congolese agreement | 14 August 1894 | Leopold surrenders part of the leased territory but retains the Lado enclave; France gains access to the Nile |
| Treaty of Addis Ababa | 26 October 1896 | Italy recognizes sovereignty of Ethiopia |
| Anglo-French Niger convention | 14 June 1898 | Anglo-French partition of spheres of influence on the Niger (France obtains Nikki, Britain obtains Sokoto) |
| Anglo-German agreements | 30 August 1898 | Plan for the partition of Portuguese colonies |
| Anglo-Egyptian convention | 19 January 1899 | Anglo-Egyptian condominium in the Sudan |
| Anglo-French declaration (additional article to Niger convention of 14 June 1898) | 21 March 1899 | France is kept out of the Nile valley; Fashoda question settled |

| NAME | DATE | SUBJECT |
|---|---|---|
| Franco-Italian agreement | 14 December 1900 | France obtains a "free hand" in Morocco; Italy in Libya |
| Peace of Vereeniging | 31 May 1902 | End of Boer War; Britain annexes the Transvaal and the Orange Free State |
| Anglo-French convention ("Entente Cordiale") | 8 April 1904 | Recognition of respective spheres of influence in Morocco and Egypt |
| Act of Algeciras | 7 April 1906 | French and Spanish interests in Morocco recognized |
| Agreement between Britain and Leopold II | 9 May 1906 | Leopold cedes Bahr el-Ghazal but retains the Lado enclave for the remainder of his life |
| Franco-German agreement | 9 February 1909 | Germany accepts France's special claims to Morocco |
| Franco-German treaty | 4 November 1911 | German recognition of French sphere of influence in Morocco; Germany receives compensation in the Congo |
| Treaty of Fez | 30 March 1912 | French protectorate over Morocco |

# APPENDIX 2: SYNCHRONIC SURVEY

|  | GENERAL/EUROPE | NORTH AFRICA |
|---|---|---|
| 1880 | 1st Ferry cab. (to 1881) | Madrid Conference (on Morocco) |
| 1881 | 2nd Gladstone cab. (to 1885) | French occupation of Tunisia |
| 1882 | Triple Alliance (Germany-Austria-Italy) | British occupation of Egypt |
| 1883 |  |  |
| 1884 | 2nd Ferry cab. (to 1885) | London Conference on Egyptian finances |
| 1885 |  |  |
| 1886 | British Liberals split; 2nd Salisbury cab. (to 1892) |  |
| 1887 |  |  |
| 1888 |  |  |
| 1889 | End of Boulanger crisis |  |

| WEST AND CENTRAL AFRICA | SOUTHERN AFRICA | EAST AFRICA AND THE NILE | |
|---|---|---|---|
| Brazza-Makoko treaty | | | 1880 |
| | 1st Boer War | | 1881 |
| Ratification of Makoko treaty; Association Internationale du Congo founded | | | 1882 |
| | Lüderitz establishes trading station in S.-W. Africa; Kruger president of the Transvaal | | 1883 |
| Berlin conference (to Feb. 1885); German protectorate over Togo and Cameroon | German protectorate over S.-W. Africa | Carl Peters in East Africa | 1884 |
| | | German protectorate over East Africa; fall of Khartoum | 1885 |
| Royal Niger Company granted charter | Start of gold rush to the Witwatersrand | Anglo-German agreement on East Africa | 1886 |
| | | Emin Pasha Relief Expedition (to 1890) | 1887 |
| | | | 1888 |
| Behanzin king of Dahomey | BSAC granted charter | Treaty of Uccialli; Menelik emperor of Ethiopia | 1889 |

| | GENERAL/EUROPE | NORTH AFRICA |
|---|---|---|
| 1890 | Bismarck steps down; Comité de l'Afrique Française founded | |
| 1891 | | |
| 1892 | 4th Gladstone cab. (to 1894) | |
| 1893 | Union Coloniale Française founded | |
| 1894 | Hanotaux at Quai d'Orsay; Rosebery cab. (to 1895); Franco-Russian Alliance | Mulay Abdelaziz becomes sultan of Morocco |
| 1895 | 3rd Salisbury cab. (to 1902) | |
| 1896 | | |
| 1897 | | |
| 1898 | Delcassé at Quai d'Orsay; Dreyfus affair; 1st German naval bill | |
| 1899 | | Anglo-Egyptian condominium over Sudan |
| 1900 | Bülow German chancellor (to 1909) | |
| 1901 | Death of Queen Victoria; Edward VII succeeds | |
| 1902 | Anglo-Japanese alliance | |
| 1903 | | |
| 1904 | "Entente Cordiale" | |
| 1905 | Fall of Delcassé | First Moroccan crisis (Tangier) |
| 1906 | | Algeciras Conference |
| 1907 | "Triple Entente" | Mulay Hafid counter-sultan in Morocco |
| 1908 | | |

| WEST AND CENTRAL AFRICA | SOUTHERN AFRICA | EAST AFRICA AND THE NILE | |
|---|---|---|---|
| Anglo-French agreement (Say-Barruwa line) | Rhodes prime minister of Cape Colony | Zanzibar-Heligoland treaty; Leopold-Mackinnon treaty | 1890 |
| | | | 1891 |
| | | | 1892 |
| 3rd Ashanti war (to 1894) | Anglo-Congolese treaty; Franco-Congolese treaty | | 1893 |
| French annexation of Dahomey | Delagoa Bay railroad opened | British protectorate over Uganda | 1894 |
| 4th Ashanti war (to 1896) | Jameson Raid | Grey declaration (on the Nile) | 1895 |
| | Kruger telegram | Battle of Adowa; Marchand mission sets out; Gallieni in Madagascar | 1896 |
| | | | 1897 |
| Anglo-French Niger agreement; Samori captured | | Battle of Omdurman; Fashoda crisis | 1898 |
| Voulet-Chanoine expedition | Beginning of Boer War | | 1899 |
| | | | 1900 |
| | | | 1901 |
| | End of Boer War | | 1902 |
| Kano and Sokoto (northern Nigeria) invaded | | | 1903 |
| | Herero rebellion (to 1908) | | 1904 |
| | | | 1905 |
| Lagos and southern Nigeria united | | | 1906 |
| | | | 1907 |
| | | | 1908 |

| | GENERAL/EUROPE | NORTH AFRICA |
|---|---|---|
| 1909 | | Franco-German agreement on Morocco |
| 1910 | Death of King Edward VII; George V succeeds | |
| 1911 | | Italian annexation of Libya; 2nd Moroccan crisis (Agadir) |
| 1912 | | Franco-Spanish protectorate over Morocco |
| 1913 | | |
| 1914 | Beginning of First World War | |

| WEST AND CENTRAL AFRICA | SOUTHERN AFRICA | EAST AFRICA AND THE NILE | |
|---|---|---|---|
| | | | 1909 |
| | Union of South Africa | | 1910 |
| | | Death of Menelik | 1911 |
| | | | 1912 |
| | | | 1913 |
| Northern and Southern Nigeria united | | | 1914 |

# INDEX

**About the Author**

H. L. WESSELING is Professor of General History at the University of Leiden, Holland, and Director of the Netherlands Institute for Advanced Study (NIAS).

ISBN 0-275-95137-5

90000>

EAN

HARDCOVER BAR CODE

# AFRICA IN 1914

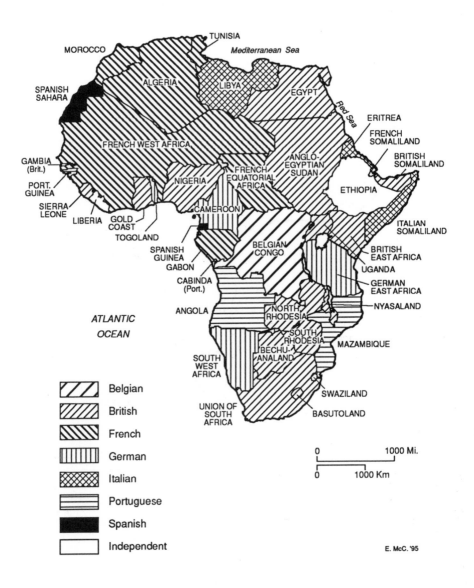

TUNISIA
MOROCCO
Mediterranean Sea
ALGERIA
LIBYA
SPANISH SAHARA
EGYPT
Red Sea
ERITREA
FRENCH SOMALILAND
FRENCH WEST AFRICA
BRITISH SOMALILAND
GAMBIA (Brit.)
ANGLO-EGYPTIAN SUDAN
PORT. GUIGNEA
NIGERIA
FRENCH EQUATORIAL AFRICA
SIERRA LEONE
ETHIOPIA
LIBERIA
GOLD COAST
CAMEROON
ITALIAN SOMALILAND
TOGOLAND
SPANISH GUINEA
BELGIAN CONGO
BRITISH EAST AFRICA
GABON
UGANDA
CABINDA (Port.)
GERMAN EAST AFRICA
ATLANTIC OCEAN
ANGOLA
NORTH RHODESIA
NYASALAND
SOUTH RHODESIA
MAZAMBIQUE
BECHU- ANALAND
SOUTH WEST AFRICA
SWAZILAND
UNION OF SOUTH AFRICA
BASUTOLAND

| | |
|---|---|
| Belgian | |
| British | |
| French | |
| German | |
| Italian | |
| Portuguese | |
| Spanish | |
| Independent | |

0          1000 Mi.

0          1000 Km

E. McC. '95